Fatal Self-Deception
Slaveholding Paternalism in the Old South

Slaveholders were preoccupied with presenting slavery as a benign, paternalistic institution in which the planter took care of his family, and slaves were content with their fate. In this book, Eugene D. Genovese and Elizabeth Fox-Genovese discuss how slaveholders perpetuated and rationalized this romanticized version of life on the plantation. Slaveholders' paternalism had little to do with ostensible benevolence, kindness, and good cheer. It grew out of the necessity to discipline and morally justify a system of exploitation. At the same time, this book also examines masters' relations with white plantation laborers and servants – a largely unstudied subject. Southerners drew on the work of British and European socialists to conclude that all labor, white and black, suffered de facto slavery, and they championed the South's "Christian slavery" as the most humane and compassionate of social systems, ancient and modern.

Eugene D. Genovese is a retired professor of history. He served as chair of the Department of History at the University of Rochester and taught at other institutions. He also served as president of the Organization of American Historians and of The Historical Society, and he was a member of the Executive Council of the American Historical Society. He is the author of nine other books, most recently *Miss Betsey: A Memoir of Marriage*.

Elizabeth Fox-Genovese (1941–2007) was Eleonore Raoul Professor of Humanities at Emory University, where she was founding director of Women's Studies. She served on the Governing Council of the National Endowment for the Humanities (2002–07). In 2003, President George W. Bush awarded her a National Humanities Medal; the Georgia State Senate honored her with a special resolution for her contributions as a scholar, teacher, and citizen of Georgia; and the fellowship of Catholic Scholars bestowed on her its Cardinal Wright Award. Among her books and published lectures are *The Origins of Physiocracy: Economic Revolution and Social Order in Eighteenth-Century France*; *Within the Plantation Household: Black and White Women of the Old South*; *Feminism without Illusions: A Critique of Individualism*; and *Marriage: The Dream That Refuses to Die*.

MAY   2012

Advance Praise for *Fatal Self-Deception*

"In this remarkable culmination of four decades of intense study, Eugene Genovese and the late Elizabeth Fox-Genovese marshal their impressive knowledge of slaveholding Southerners. With no holds barred, they examine the disparate emotions and self-justifications of slaveholders' ideas, including a true picture of the complex and even contradictory ideas of paternalism. Their analysis deepens our understanding of the social relationships that shaped the history of the American South, relationships with vast implications even today. Steeped in comprehensive research, *Fatal Deception* is cultural, social, legal, and philosophical history at its best – simply brilliant."

– Orville Vernon Burton, Clemson University, author of *Age of Lincoln* and *In My Father's House Are Many Mansions: Family and Community in Edgefield County, South Carolina*

"This thoughtful treatise lets slave owners speak for themselves, showing how they struggled to square paternalism with the need for profit. Readers get a fresh look at the Southern master's relationships with a host of household members. By drawing on an immense number of original sources, the Genoveses persuasively argue that slave owners practiced self-deception, not hypocrisy, by viewing their way of life as the best possible for all concerned."

–Jenny Wahl, Carleton College

Fatal Self-Deception

Slaveholding Paternalism in the Old South

EUGENE D. GENOVESE

ELIZABETH FOX-GENOVESE

CAMBRIDGE
UNIVERSITY PRESS

CAMBRIDGE UNIVERSITY PRESS
Cambridge, New York, Melbourne, Madrid, Cape Town,
Singapore, São Paulo, Delhi, Tokyo, Mexico City

Cambridge University Press
32 Avenue of the Americas, New York, NY 10013-2473, USA

www.cambridge.org
Information on this title: www.cambridge.org/9781107605022

© Eugene D. Genovese 2011

First published 2011

Printed in the United States of America

A catalog record for this publication is available from the British Library.

Library of Congress Cataloging in Publication data

Genovese, Eugene D., 1930–
Fatal self-deception : slaveholding paternalism in the Old South / Eugene D. Genovese,
Elizabeth Fox-Genovese.
    p. cm.
Includes bibliographical references and index.
ISBN 978-1-107-01164-9 (hardback) – ISBN 978-1-107-60502-2 (paperback)
1. Slavery – Southern States – History – 19th century.   2. Plantation owners – Southern States –
History – 19th century.   3. Paternalism – Southern States – History – 19th century.   4. Slaves –
Southern States – Social conditions – 19th century.   5. Plantation workers – Southern States –
History – 19th century.   6. Whites – Southern States – Social conditions – 19th century.
I. Fox-Genovese, Elizabeth, 1941–2007   II. Title.
E441.G39   2011
306.3′620975 – dc22   2011006212

ISBN 978-1-107-01164-9 Hardback
ISBN 978-1-107-60502-2 Paperback

For Deborah Ann Symonds
Gifted Scholar and Wonderful Friend
and
For her partner, Melissa Cano, and their children, Sarah and Sam

The despot can never feel sure that he is loved. . . . The services of the indifferent seemed to us not acts of grace, and favours extorted appeared to give no pleasure. And so it is with the services proffered by men in fear: they are not honours. For how can we say that men who are forced to rise from their seat to honour their superiors desire to honour their oppressors? . . . These acts, I suppose, may not unfairly be taken for acts of servility.

– Xenophon*

* Xenophon, "Hiero," *Scripta Minora*, tr. E. C. Marchant (LCL), 1§37. Greek philosophers and artists promoted the image of the tyrant as isolated, friendless, and in constant fear for his life.

Contents

Preface

In previously coauthored books by Elizabeth Fox-Genovese (1941–2007) and Eugene D. Genovese, her name came first, on the principle of Ladies First or, if you prefer, "F" before "G." This book, too, is a product of decades of professional collaboration in research, in the editing of each other's drafts, and in countless discussions. Here, I place my own name first because, although Betsey contributed considerably to *Fatal Self-Deception*, her declining health prevented her criticizing, reviewing, and fine-tuning the drafts. Had she lived, she might well have made substantial changes in style and content. Hence, I assume full responsibility for errors and infelicities.

"The War" refers to the war of 1861–65. We use *sic* only when it seems indispensable. Words in italics are from quoted texts. The names of identified authors of anonymous publications appear in brackets. A question mark indicates that the author in brackets is probable. We use "Southerners" to mean the whites who constitute our principal subject. We identify blacks discretely, although well aware that they were no less Southerners. If we had to qualify "Southerners" every time we referred to whites, the text would become well-nigh unreadable.

The manuscript received expert criticism from Douglas Ambrose, Stanley Engerman, Robert L. Paquette, Fay Yarbrough, and two anonymous critics recruited by Cambridge University Press. Karen E. Fields's painstaking and often biting criticism reinforced her reputation as one not to trifle with. David Moltke-Hansen devoted an extraordinary amount of time and energy to helping us get the book in shape. Our thanks to Christopher Luse and Scott Gavorsky for collecting materials, checking references and quotations, and criticizing style and content. We owe a large and continuing debt to the Watson-Brown Foundation for its generous support.

Abbreviations

ACP	*American Cotton Planter and Soil of the South*
AR	*African Repository*
AS	*The American Slave: A Composite Autobiography,* ed. George Rawick, 19 vols. (Westport, Conn., 1972)
BDC	*Biographical Dictionary of the Confederacy*, ed. Jon L. Wakelyn (Westport, Conn., 1977)
DBR	*De Bow's Review*
DGB	*Dictionary of Georgia Biography*, ed. Kenneth Coleman and Stephen Gurr, 2 vols. (Athens, Ga., 1983)
DHE	*A Documentary History of Education in the South before 1860,* ed. Edgar W. Knight, 5 vols. (Chapel Hill, N.C., 1949–53)
DNCB	*Dictionary of North Carolina Biography*, ed. William S. Powell, 6 vols. (Chapel Hill, N.C. 1979–94)
EC	*Encyclopedia of the Confederacy*, ed. Richard N. Current, 4 vols. (New York, 1993)
EE	Electronic Edition: Chapel Hill, N.C.
ERD	*The Diary of Edmund Ruffin*, ed. William Kaufman Scarborough, 3 vols. (Baton Rouge, La., 1972–89)
HLW	*Writings of Hugh Swinton Legaré* [ed. Mary S. Legaré], 2 vols. (Charleston, S.C., 1846)
JCCP	*The Papers of John C. Calhoun*, ed. successively Robert Lee Meriwether, Edwin Hemphill, and Clyde N. Wilson, 26 vols. (Columbia, S.C., 1959–2003)
JDP	*The Papers of Jefferson Davis*, ed. Haskell M. Monroe, Jr., James T. McIntosh, et al., 11 vols. (Baton Rouge, La., and Houston, Tex., 1971–2004)
JHTW	*The Collected Writings of James Henley Thornwell*, ed. John Adger and B. M. Palmer, 4 vols. (Carlisle, Pa., 1986)
JSH	*Journal of Southern History*
LCL	Loeb Classical Library (Cambridge, Mass.)

LSU   Louisiana State University
NCHR   *North Carolina Historical Review*
RM   *Russell's Magazine*
SA   *Southern Agriculturalist, Horticulturalist, and Register of Rural*
           Affairs
SBN   *The South in the Building of the Nation*, ed. J. A. Chandler,
           12 vols. (Richmond, Va., 1909)
SC   *Southern Cultivator*
SCHS   *South Carolina Historical Magazine*
SCTA   *South Carolina Temperance Advocate and Register of*
           Agricultural and General Literature
SLM   *Southern Literary Messenger*
SPR   *Southern Presbyterian Review*
SQR   *Southern Quarterly Review*
TCWVQ   *The Tennessee Civil War Veterans Questionnaires*, ed. Coleen
           Morse Elliott and Louise Armstrong Moxley, 5 vols. (Easley, S.C.,
           1985)
TRP   *The Papers of Thomas Ruffin*, ed. J. G. deRoulhac Hamilton,
           4 vols. (Raleigh, N.C., 1918)
UNC   The University of North Carolina at Chapel Hill
USC   University of South Carolina at Columbia

Manuscript Collections

Acklen Family Papers*
Samuel A. Agnew Journal*
David Wyatt Aiken Autobiography (ms.)*
Elisha Allen Collection, at Georgia Department of Archives and History (Atlanta)
Harrod C. Anderson Papers, at LSU
Anderson-Thornwell Papers*
Garnett Andrews Papers*
Arrington Papers*
Ashmore Plantation Journal*
Aylett Family Papers, at Virginia Historical Society (Richmond)
Eleanor J. W. Baker Diary, at Duke University
Everard Green Baker Diaries*
[Barbour Papers]: Plantation and Farm Instruction, Regulation, Record, Inventory and Account Book of Philip St. George Cocke, at University of Virginia
Barnsley Papers*
R. R. Barrow Residence Journal*
Mary Eliza Battle Letters, at North Carolina State Archives (Raleigh)
Thomas L. Bayne Autobiographical Sketch*
Mary Bethell Diary*
John Houston Bills Diary*
Priscilla Bond Diary, at LSU
Esther G. Wright Boyd Notes and Recollections, at Tennessee State Library and Archives (Nashville)
Gustave A. Breaux Diaries, at Tulane University
Rosella Kenner Brent Recollections, 1862*
Keziah Brevard Diary, at USC

* at the Southern Historical Collection, UNC.

William Brisbane Receipt Book, at Duke University
Britton Family Papers, at LSU
Iveson Brookes Papers, at Duke University
Bruce Family of Berry Hill, at University of Virginia
Lucy Wood Butler Diary*
Cabell-Ellet Papers, at University of Virginia
David Campbell Private Diary, at Mississippi Department of History and
    Archives (Jackson)
Campbell Family Papers, at Duke University
Franc M. Carmack Diary*
Mary Eliza Carmichael*
Kate Carney Diary*
Carson Family Papers, in Small Collections: Tennessee State Library and
    Archives (Nashville)
Ϲ. C. Carter Collection, at Southeastern Louisiana University (Hammond)
Mary Jane Chester Papers*
Langston Cheves Collection, at South Carolina Historical Society
    (Charleston)
Eliza Clitherall Autobiography*
Cole-Taylor Papers*
Comer Farm Journal*
Juliana Margaret Conner Diary*
Cooper Papers, at Tennessee State Library and Archives (Nashville)
John Hamilton Cornish Diary *
J. B. Cottrel Diary*
Henry Craft Diary*
Curry Papers, Library of Congress
J. M. W. Davidson Diary*
William R. Davie Papers*
Anne Tuberville (Beale) Davis Diary and Meditations*
Thomas Roderick Dew Papers, at College of William and Mary
Dromgoole and Robinson Papers, at Duke University
Durnford Letters, at Tulane University
Belle Edmondson Diary*
Elliott-Gonzales Papers*
William Ethelbert Ervin Journal*
Holden Garthur Evans Diary, at Mississippi Department of Archives and
    History (Jackson)
Susan Fisher Papers*
Ingersoll Meredith Flournoy, comp., "Excerpts from the History of the
    Flournoy Family," typescript at Louisiana State University
[Flournoy]: M. F. Ingersoll, ed., "Excerpts from *History of the Flournoy
    Family*," at LSU

---

* at the Southern Historical Collection, UNC.

J. B. Fort Papers, at Tennessee State Library and Archives (Nashville)
David Gavin Papers*
Sarah Gayle Diary*
William Proctor Gould Diary*
Iveson L. Graves Papers*
James H. Greenlee Diary *
John Berkeley Grimball Papers*
Meta Morris Grimball Journal*
William Hooper Haigh Diary and Letters*
Rev. Francis Hanson Diary*
Gustavus A. Henry Papers*
William P. Hill Diary*
Mrs. Isaac Hilliard's Diary*
William H. Holcombe Papers*
Caroline Mallett Hooper Papers*
Franklin A. Hudson Diaries*
Hughes Family Papers*
Fannie Page Hume Diary*
Susan Nye Hutchinson Journal*
Andrew Hynes Papers, at Historic New Orleans Collection
Jackson–Prince Papers*
Joseph Jones Collection, at Tulane University
Kimberly Papers*
M. P. King Plantation Record*
Mitchell King Papers*
Thomas Butler King Papers*
Francis Terry Leak Diary*
George M. Lester Collection, at LSU
Liddell Papers, at LSU
John Berrien Lindsley Papers, at Tennessee State Library and Archives (Nashville)
Eliza L Magruder Diary, at LSU
Louis Manigault Diary, at Duke University
Basil Manly Papers*
Basil Manly, Jr., Papers*
Eliza Ann Marsh Diary*
Massenburg Farm Journal*
James E. and Samuel Matthews Letters, at Mississippi Department of Archives and History (Jackson)
Mayes-Dimitri-Stuart Papers, at Mississippi Department of Archives and History (Jackson)
Lucilla Agnes (Gamble) McCorkle Diary*
John McDonogh Papers at Tulane University

* at the Southern Historical Collection, UNC.

Dr. McGuire Diary, at Tulane University
William N. Mercer Papers, at LSU
William Porcher Miles Papers*
Minis Collection*
Pattie Mordecai Collection, at North Carolina State Archives (Raleigh)
Columbus Morrison Journal*
John Nevitt Plantation Papers*
Newstead Plantation Diary*
H. C. Nixon Collection, at Alabama Department of Archives and History
 (Montgomery)
Haller Nutt Papers, at Duke University
Orange Grove Plantation Diaries, at Tulane University
Orange Grove Plantation Papers, at Tulane University
David Outlaw Papers*
Palfrey Papers, at LSU
Benjamin F. Perry Papers, at USC
Ebenezer Pettigrew Papers, at North Carolina State Department of Archives
 and History (Raleigh)
Louise Taylor Pharr Book*
Ulrich Bonnell Phillips Papers, at Yale University
Physician's Account Book, 1830–31, at Library of Congress
Physician's Fee Book, 1847–50*
Physician's Record Book, 1855–62*
Pinckney Family Papers, at USC
Philip Henry Pitts Diary and Account Book*
Mary Junkin Preston Papers, at Washington and Lee University
John A. Quitman Papers*
David A. and Malinda Ray Papers*
Reid Papers*
Renwick Papers, at Duke University
David Rice Plantation Journal, at LSU
Alfred Landon Rives Papers, at Duke University
Roach-Eggleston Papers*
Nancy McDougall Robinson Collection, at Mississippi Department of
 Archives and History (Jackson)
Edmund Ruffin, Jr., Plantation Journal*
Henri de St. Geme Papers, at Historic New Orleans Collection
George Washington Sargent Books*
H. M. Seale Diary, Jan. 10, 1857, at LSU
Sheppard Papers, at Duke University
Henry E. Simmons Letters*
Singleton Family Papers*
"Slave Papers," at Library of Congress

* at the Southern Historical Collection, UNC.

Josiah Smith Lettercopy Book*
Mrs. Smith Journal, at Duke University
William Ruffin Smith Papers*
Alonzo Snyder Papers, at LSU
Southall and Bowen Papers*
Richard H. Stewart Account Books, 1841–60, at LSU
Oscar Stuart and Family Papers, at Mississippi Department of Archives and
    History (Jackson)
Sturdivant Plantation Records*
Tayloe Papers, at University of Virginia
Francis Taylor Diary*
Ella Gertrude Clanton Thomas Diary, at Duke University
Ruffin Thompson Papers*
Waddy Thompson Papers, at USC
Thornwell Papers, at USC
Clarissa E. (Leavitt) Town Diary, at LSU
Trousdale Papers, at Tennessee State Library and Archives (Nashville)
William F. Tucker Papers*
Dr. H. M. Turner Account Book*
Isaac Barton Ulmer Papers*
William D. Valentine Diaries*
Wade Family Papers, at Library of Congress
Sarah Lois Wadley Private Journal*
John Walker Diary*
T. Watts, "A Summer on a Louisiana Cotton Plantation in 1832" (ms.), in
    Pharr Book*
Henry Young Webb Diary*
Weeks Papers, at LSU
James William White Papers*
Maunsel White Papers*
Calvin H. Wiley Papers*
W. H. Wills Papers*
Anita Dwyer Withers Diary*
Witherspoon-McDowall Papers*
Robert and Newton Woody Papers, at Duke University
Wyche-Otey Papers*
Benjamin C. Yancey Papers*
Edward C. Yellowsley Papers*

* at the Southern Historical Collection, UNC.

Introduction

It is natural that the oppressed should hate the oppressor. It is still more natural that the oppressor should hate his victim. Convince the master that he is doing injustice to his slave, and he at once begins to regard him with distrust and malignity.

– Chancellor William Harper of South Carolina[1]

Decades of study have led us to a conclusion that some readers will find unpalatable: In most respects, southern slaveholders said what they meant and meant what they said. Notwithstanding self-serving rhetoric, the slaveholders did believe themselves to be defending the ramparts of Christianity, constitutional republicanism, and social order against northern and European apostasy, secularism, and social and political radicalism. Just what did slaveholders say and mean? Southerners, having measured their "domestic slavery" against other ancient and modern social systems, declared their own social system superior to alternatives and a joy to blacks as well as whites. Viewing the free states, they saw vicious Negrophobia and racial discrimination and a cruelly exploited white working class. Concluding that all labor, white and black, suffered de facto slavery or something akin to it, they proudly identified "Christian slavery" as the most humane, compassionate, and generous of social systems.[2]

The westward movement of planter households significantly altered economic development, national politics, and southern culture. More specifically, the difficulties and hardships of emigration strengthened relations between masters and slaves and a sense of the interdependence of plantation households. In 1853, a planter with the nom de plume "Foby" decreed: "All living on the plantation, whether colored or not, are members of the same family and to be treated as such. . . . The servants are distinctly informed that they have to work and obey my laws, or suffer the penalty." The master "possessed all judicial, legislative, and executive power and arrogates the settlement of disputes to himself." With these few sentences, "Foby" depicted the master-slave relation in a paternalistic household that entailed duties, responsibilities, and privileges without denying despotism and violence. Kindness, love, and benevolence did not define paternalism, which depended on the constant threat and actuality of violence. The household, as celebrated by apologists, may often have softened attitudes and behavior, but countervailing pressures remained and often prevailed. Above all, commodity production required profit maximization, which more often than not entailed severity. Mary R. Jackman observes in *The Velvet Glove*, her arresting sociological study of paternalism: "The presumption of moral superiority over a group with whom one has an expropriative relationship is thus flatly incompatible with the spirit of altruistic benevolence, no matter how much affection and breast-beating accompanies it. In the analysis of unequal relations between social groups, paternalism must be distinguished from benevolence." Jackman adds that the dominant group's characterization of subordinates as having distinct personal attributes frees superordinates to claim that the needs of the subordinates are also distinct from those of the dominant group.[3]

From the long-settled Southeast to the newly settled Southwest, self-serving slaveholders equated paternalism with benevolence. "The government of our slaves," Governor George McDuffie of South Carolina declared, "is strictly patriarchal, and produces those mutual feelings of kindness which result from a constant interchange of good offices." "Omo," a planter in Mississippi, advocated plantation hospitals and improved medical attention for slaves, explaining that whether a slave lived or died, "We have the satisfaction of knowing that *we have done what we could – we have discharged our duty*." Even candid masters who recognized grave faults in slavery judged it necessary for the preservation of a humane social order. Representative Waddy Thompson of South Carolina raised the specter of all-out race war in the wake of emancipation. He berated "that very worthy band of gentlemen, the fanatics of the North, a most notable set of Philanthropists, who seek to place the black race in a worse condition than they now are." The Presbyterian Reverend Robert L. Dabney of Virginia, an imposing theologian, deftly related the southern vision of the family to rejection of the free labor system. All civilized societies, he wrote, depressed labor, but free labor societies spawned impoverishment and Malthusian population crises. Masters' households, he insisted, absorbed laborers and created a floor beneath which the living standards could not sink.[4]

The expression "our family, white and black" – easily dismissed as romantic flourish – bared essential characteristics of a worldview. Although it contained ideological posturing, gaping contradictions, and a dose of hypocrisy, it contained as well a wider vision that lay at the core of the slaveholders' sense of themselves as men and women. That vision had as its inspiration a mixture of beliefs and needs. As Christians increasingly committed to walking in the ways of the Lord during the second Great Awakening and its aftermath, planters felt it their responsibility to care for their slaves spiritually as well as physically. In the wake of slavery's progressive domestication in the eighteenth-century Chesapeake and nineteenth-century lower South, planters needed to think about and communicate their expectations of both their slaves and themselves in relation to their slaves. Those expectations reflected as well planters' needs to think well of themselves as slaveholders and slaves' needs to foster and manipulate planters' feelings in order to encourage care and limit abuse.

These reciprocal if unequal relations, expectations, and motives informed slaveholders' embrace and deployment of the age-old idea of the family as the basic unit of society. Forging that idea into a neo-Aristotelian doctrine of human interdependence, they launched a counterrevolution against secular rationalism, radical egalitarianism, and majoritarian democracy. They ended with one or another version of "slavery in the abstract" – personal servitude as the proper condition of all labor regardless of race. We have explored the growing attraction of "slavery in the abstract" in Elizabeth Fox-Genovese and Eugene D. Genovese, *Slavery in White and Black: Class and Race in the Southern Slaveholders' New World Order* (New York, 2008). In *Fatal Self-Deception*, we begin with a sketch of the slaveholding household. Planters came to include slaves in their understanding of their households, but not white servitors or free blacks. Chapter 3 explores this difference. Even when a governess joined the family at table, the planter understood her to be a stranger and a hireling – unless and until, that is, he or his son married her. Slaves often judged white servitors as of inferior class to the planter family. At the same time, slaves often associated with lower-class whites in the neighborhood – on hunts, at grog shops, and in gaming. Whites and blacks frequently mingled in worship as well – often to listen to black preachers.[5]

Countless Southerners, slaveholding and nonslaveholding, congratulated themselves on their Christian virtue, but not without considerable querulousness and troublesome opposition. Chapter 1 starts with a contrary judgment – Jefferson's indictment of slavery in his *Notes on the State of Virginia*. On balance, the majority of slaveholders in the South increasingly came to reject this indictment, judging mastery a discipline and a responsibility that at once benefited the slave owner and the slave, morally and materially.

Although unconvinced, J. S. Buckingham of England reported around 1840 that well-traveled Southerners believed that blacks faced extinction if deprived of their masters' protection. In the 1850s, George P. R. James, the novelist and British consul in Virginia, grumbled in *The Knickerbocker Magazine* that planters, with their "tenderness and affection," failed to notice that blacks worked poorly and lacked the capacity to achieve civilization. When Anderson, a slave in St. Mary's Parish, Louisiana, ran away, John Palfrey, his master, remarked, "I am not otherwise uneasy about him but that he may eat green corn, melon, or whatever he may find there, which will be sure to make him sick & if not taken in time may operate fatally." During the War, Northerners and Europeans met Southerners who saw themselves as protectors of blacks against an emancipation that they expected to prove fatal.[6]

Slaveholders saw themselves as the best, the sincerest, indeed, the only friends that American blacks had. John C. Calhoun and Nathaniel Beverley Tucker recoiled from the suggestion that their slaves would be better off as free men. The antislavery Thomas Colley Grattan, the British consul at Boston, asked Calhoun about the reaction of the last slave he had liberated. Astonished, Calhoun replied, "I liberate a slave! God forbid that I should ever be guilty of such a crime. Ah, you know little of my character, if you believe me capable of doing so much wrong to a fellow-creature." At the Nashville Convention of 1850, Tucker, scolding Ohio for its hostility to blacks, asked God to forbid that he would ever want to introduce paternalistic southern slavery into a black-hating Ohio that would abuse the privileges of masters and behave inhumanely toward its slaves: "No, sir – I would not so wrong the Negro." For the slaveholders, the Bible did not call for equality in this world, but it did firmly uphold the unity of the human race. Thus, the pseudoscientific racism prevalent in the North represented gross apostasy.[7]

The editors of *Southern Quarterly Review* might be suspected of disingenuousness for their declaration in 1847, "Manumit them, place them in collision with the white race, and you ensure their destruction." But in 1844 the Methodist Bishop James O. Andrew wrote privately to Leonore, his wife, that he could not free their slaves, "How could I free them? Where would they go, and how support themselves?" Thomas G. Clemson wrote to Calhoun, his father-in-law, that although slavery hurt whites economically and was "very bad for the State," it did protect blacks. The Massachusetts-born Episcopal Reverend George W. Freeman of North Carolina, later bishop of Arkansas, wrote a proslavery tract while ministering to slaves. He concluded that emancipation would end badly. Antislavery Cumberland Presbyterians had trouble convincing church brethren that the slaves could survive emancipation. Even the radical antislavery German press in Missouri acknowledged that many pious slaveholders hesitated to free slaves, fearing that freedom would ruin them. For all the sincerity and piety that went into the making of this common southern attitude, it contained a grim implication, spelled out by Representative James Garland of Virginia in 1835 and reiterated in 1841 by the Reverend T. C. Thornton, the president of Centenary College in Mississippi. Garland warned abolitionists against inciting slaves to rebel and murder women and children: "We should revenge to the utmost their blood upon the heads of those who shed it." Thornton charged that abolitionists were flirting with racial extermination, warned that Southerners, honor-bound to defend their rights, would exterminate blacks rather than capitulate to northern aggression. More softly, the antislavery Henry St. George Tucker of Virginia justified slavery as a "stern necessity." Immediate emancipation invited a war of racial extermination, for the blacks could not be assimilated to political life. Yet, as a judge, he bent the law to facilitate emancipation by will.[8]

When the War ended, no few white Southerners asserted that emancipation lifted a burden from them. Blacks now had to sink or swim on their own. Whites, dispirited by the collapse of their national revolution, faced social chaos and the loss of political and economic power. They had long insisted that blacks could not survive without white masters. Now, determined to survive one way or the other, they inadvertently worked to transform dire prediction into self-fulfilling prophecy.

This abrupt and wrenching end to the world of the slaveholding paternalist did not end paternalism, which continued to shape memories of slave owning and of some features of interracial, interpersonal relations. Yet the model of the household as the center of "our family, white and black," no longer held. We initially developed our understanding of the dynamics and consequences for slaves of this worldview in *Roll, Jordan, Roll* (EDG, 1974), then explored its Atlantic origins in *Fruits of Merchant Capital* (EF-G and EDG, 1983). Four years later, *Within the Plantation Household* (EF-G, 1988) analyzed the operation of the plantation household as the center and model of social, economic, and cultural production and reproduction. *The Mind of the Master Class* (EF-G and EDG, 2005) explored the evolving religious and historical dimensions of this worldview, while our *Slavery in White and Black* (2008) examined its logical implications and articulations. In *Fatal Self-Deception* we consider the underlying emotional drives and the end of the world shaped by paternalism, concluding an investigation that has taken more than four decades.

In the interval, paternalism has gained critics but also currency. For example, since the publication of *Roll, Jordan, Roll*, it has been argued that paternalism was a myth simply because slaveholders betrayed their organic conceit of "my family, black and white," when they sold their slaves. Here, we explain how slaveholders managed to square that circle and still understand themselves as paternalists. Because the ground beneath their feet was unstable does not mean that they were insincere. Indeed, their desperate need to deceive themselves propelled Americans, black and white, into our greatest national tragedy.

I

"Boisterous Passions"

> The Devil was to be overcome, not by the power of God, but by His righteousness.... But since the devil, by the fault of his own perversity, was made a lover of power and a forsaker and assailant of righteousness – for thus also men imitate him so much the more in proportion as they set their hearts on power, to the neglect or even hatred of righteousness, and as they either rejoice in the attainment of power, or are inflamed by the lust of it. Not that power is to be shunned as though it were something evil; but the order must be preserved, whereby righteousness is before it. For how great can be the power of mortals? Therefore let mortals cleave to righteousness; power will be given to immortals.
>
> – St. Augustine[1]

In *Notes on the State of Virginia,* a distressed Thomas Jefferson penned an indictment of slavery that reverberated for decades, causing Southerners no end of pain, anger, and soul searching:

> There must doubtless be an unhappy influence on the manners of our people produced by the existence of slavery among us. The whole commerce between master and slave is a perpetual exercise of the most boisterous passions, the most unremitting despotism on the one part, and degrading submissions on the other. Our children see this, and learn to imitate it.... The parent storms, the child looks on, catches the lineaments of wrath, puts on the same airs in the circle of smaller slaves, gives a loose to his worst passions, and thus nursed, educated, and daily exercised in tyranny, cannot but be stamped by it with odious peculiarities. The man must be a prodigy who can retain his manners and morals undepraved by such circumstances.[2]

Jefferson had predecessors for his anxiety over slavery's effects on masters. Educated Southerners knew Locke's psychological portrait of children as natural seekers of dominion. And they knew Montesquieu's critique of the master's unlimited authority, which Jefferson, in effect, paraphrased. The slaveholder, Montesquieu wrote, "insensibly accustoms himself to the want of all moral virtues, and thence becomes fierce, hasty, severe, choleric, voluptuous, and cruel." The Reverend David Rice, father of western Presbyterianism, and other late eighteenth-century emancipationists assailed slavery for undermining the moral and political virtue of the white community, especially of its young men. In the 1760s, George Mason of Virginia denounced slavery for impairing the morals of whites, much as it had impaired the morals of the Romans and led to the decay of ancient civilization. Mason returned to the theme at the federal Constitutional Convention: "Every master of slaves is born a petty tyrant." Oliver Ellsworth of Connecticut taunted him: If so, Mason and other Virginians should free their slaves. Ebenezer Hazard of Philadelphia described southern gentlemen in 1778: "Accustomed to tyrannize from their infancy, they carry with them a disposition to treat all mankind in the same manner they have been used to treat their Negroes."[3]

St. George Tucker in his edition of *Blackstone's Commentaries* (1803) denied that Virginians had a sanguinary disposition, but, quoting Jefferson's *Notes on the State of Virginia* at length, he held that slavery unfitted blacks for freedom and unfitted whites for equality. David Ramsay of South Carolina sounded an alarm, although, in his *History of the Revolution*, he praised the masters' humanity and kindness. In the 1830s, Ezekiel Birdseye of East Tennessee, an abolitionist, picked up the theme without mention of Jefferson. In letters to the *New York Emancipator and Republican* and to Gerrit Smith, he spoke of planters' sons as violent men who pursued "fashionable sports." Growing up amid scenes of violence against slaves and lacking proper parental supervision, they learned to indulge their passions. In 1832, community leaders and students at the University of North Carolina heard a version of Jefferson's moral indictment from William Gaston, a distinguished jurist, whose published lecture went through five editions by 1858. The proslavery J. A. Ingraham of Natchez lamented that too many girls had "negresses" to wait on them hand and foot and bring them their first glass of water in the morning.[4]

Black and white abolitionists summoned Jefferson's spirit in their crusade against slavery, notwithstanding their condemnation of his putative "hypocrisy" in remaining a slaveholder. Antislavery moderates, too, appealed to Jefferson to condemn slavery as a nursery for tyrants. The Baptist Reverend Francis Wayland, president of Brown University, remarked, "Those who enslave the bodies of others, become in turn the slaves of their own passions." Ralph Waldo Emerson spent little time in the South, but he lacerated Southerners for their "love of power, the voluptuousness of holding a human being in [their] absolute control." Southerners wanted slaves primarily for the "immunities and the luxuries" they made possible. In an address in 1845 on the anniversary of West Indian emancipation, Emerson spoke of South Carolina, Georgia, and Alabama as "semi-barbarous" and "debauched." Angelina Grimké contended that hundreds of thousands of Southerners "do not hold their slaves, by any means, as much 'for purposes of gain,' as they do for the lust of power." She added that the power lodged in a slaveholder made any man a tyrant – that no human being could be trusted with such authority over another. In 1856, Josiah Quincy of Massachusetts extended Jefferson's warning of "boisterous passions": The slaveholders' rule at home, made them feel entitled to rule everywhere. Adam Gurowski, a Pole who fought for the Union, depicted "the slavery gentleman" as a "scarcely varnished savage" ruled by "reckless passion and will."[5]

Foreign and northern travelers generally endorsed *Notes on the State of Virginia*. Charles Wesley protested that white children had slaves of their own age "to tyrannize over, to beat and abuse out of sport," and George Whitefield, notwithstanding his accommodation to slavery, said much the same. In later years, Horace Fulkerson, touring the lower Mississippi Valley, remarked that slavery had deeply affected the character of masters: "Accustomed to implicit and unquestioning obedience, they could illy brook contradiction and opposition from their equals." In the 1850s Frederick Law Olmsted, an architect and newspaper correspondent, stopped at a dirty house in northeastern Tennessee. The "disgusting" bed offended him less than a white boy's shocking language to a slave girl who showed up a bit late to attend to him. Visiting a successful planter in eastern Texas, Olmsted found two sons: "One was an idle young man. The other was already, at eight years old, a swearing, tobacco-chewing young bully and ruffian." The planter ordered his son to stop cursing, only to be met with, "Why? You do it." The Reverend Robert Everest of England spoke harshly: "As in ancient Europe, so in modern Asia, the young lord, or slave-owner, is brought up from his cradle to know no control of his will, and he consequently becomes a tyrant. The young American slave-owner is, in this respect, on a par with the young Asiatic." An historian's caveat from Daniel Blake Smith: If Jefferson were right about boisterous passions, we should find planter families highly charged, but personal correspondence and diaries show little evidence.[6]

Europeans especially picked up on Jefferson's remarks about child rearing. David Macrae, speaking for some British travelers, thought southern children generally better disciplined than northern, who defied and denigrated parents. Yet Frances Trollope justly railed at "the infant tyranny of white children towards their slaves." She indignantly reported the "puny bullying and well-taught ingenious insult of almost baby children towards stalwart slaves, who raised their heads toward heaven like men, but seemed to have lost the right of being so classed." Matilda Charlotte Houstoun, the English novelist, was appalled to hear of a plantation mistress who slapped an adult male slave in the presence of children. Catherine Cooper Hopley, an English governess in Virginia, disciplined the children in her care, warmly thanked by their mother, who admitted that she herself had no such success. Hopley admired Southerners but regretted that parents "are too indulgent, too much accustomed to control an inferior class, and to allow their children to control that class, to reconcile to themselves the idea of compelling obedience in their own children when once past infancy, which would perhaps be placing them too much on a par with the negroes."[7]

Two famous women – Harriet Martineau of England and Fredrika Bremer of Sweden – reflected for posterity. Martineau asked, "What is to be expected of little girls who boast of having got a negro flogged for being impertinent to them, and yet are surprised at the 'ungentlemanly' conduct of a master who maims his slave?" Yet she also wrote of "strong and strongly disciplined" women who ruled over "barbarous" communities, enforced rules, and provided for people incapable of taking care of themselves. She considered women who shrank from their duty "perhaps the weakest women I have anywhere seen." Bremer, visiting a plantation in Georgia, admired southern ladies as wives and mothers but thought young girls largely inactive and of little help to their mothers. She sadly noted, "Parents, from mistaken kindness, seem not to wish their daughters to do anything except amuse themselves and enjoy liberty and life as much as possible." Bremer, who thought they would be happier if they made themselves more useful, recounted the judgment of a "noble lady of New Orleans": Surrounded by slaves from the cradle, the white child commanded them, expected satisfaction of any caprice, and demanded stern punishment for a slave who thwarted his will.[8]

In 1836, ten prominent Presbyterians in Kent denounced slavery as an encouragement to the moral depravity of masters and slaves and, echoing Jefferson, singled out masters as under constant temptation to indulge passions and appetites. Henry Clay, by reputation a kind master, hired the young Amos Kendall to tutor his children. Kendall commented on Clay's preteen boys, Thomas and Theodore: "Yesterday Mrs. Clay being absent, Thomas got into a mighty rage with some of the negroes, and threatened and exerted all his little power to kill them." A few months later: "Hearing a great noise in the kitchen, I went in and found Theodore swearing in a great rage with a knife drawn in attitude to stab one of the big negroes." Mary Jane Chester, a student at Columbia Female Institute in Tennessee, exemplified another white attitude when she sent her love to servants. "I wish that Nancy was here to do up my clothes & to help me Dress." John Evans, overseer to George Noble Jones, wrote to his employer, "I informed the People that they had another young Master by the Name of Noble Wimberley." James Sanders Guignard of the low country began life like many of his class: On his eighth birthday, his grandmother gave him a present – a black girl. No wonder, then, that William David Beard, a nonslaveholding renter, lashed out at the lazy sons of slaveholders who made slaves fetch them a glass of water.[9]

Black children as well as adults had to call white children "little massa" or "little missie," sometimes without the "little." Anna Matilda King of Georgia, worried sick over debts, wrote to her husband, Thomas Butler King, "I wish we could get rid of ALL at THEIR VALUE and leave this wretched country. I am more and more convinced it is no place to rear a family of children. . . . To bring up boys on a plantation makes them TIRANICAL as well as lazy and girls too." That was 1844. In 1858, she wrote to her husband, "We have not done well by our noble sons. Each one should have been made to go to work for themselves as soon as their education was completed." Richard Taylor of Louisiana, son of President Zachary Taylor, thought the moral effect of slavery on his sons deplorable. Elisha Hammond of South Carolina lectured his son,

James Henry Hammond, the future governor and senator: "More than half the young men raised in the Southern States are sooner or later ruined by disapation [*sic*] but this I trust will not apply to you." During the War, Lucy Breckenridge of Virginia wrote,

> I feel that I am a true abolitionist in heart – here I have been crying like a foolish child for the last half hour because I saw Jimmy chasing poor, little Preston all over the yard beating him with a great stick, and Sister not making him stop but actually encouraging him. . . . I shall never forget Viola's expression of suppressed rage – how I felt for her. My blood boiled with indignation. I never saw such a cruel-tempered and wicked child as Jimmy. I guess *my* sons had better not beat a little servant where I am! I am so thankful that all of us have been properly raised and never allowed, when we were children, to scold or strike a servant.[10]

Slaves described the warm and wonderful relations they had as children with the white boys, some of whom remained friends for life, but more often, they underscored Jefferson's charges. They told of three-year-old white boys whom black children had to call "master" or get whipped; of boys who grew up with black playmates to polish their boots, put away their toys, clean up after them, carry their schoolbooks, and do their bidding; of boys who thought nothing of hitting or kicking an old slave who displeased them. And then, there were white boys who, without malice or nastiness, simply took for granted privileges and prerogatives of every kind. Solomon Northup, whose slave narrative breathes authenticity, told of a slaveholder's ten- or twelve-year-old son who took special delight in whipping slaves, even the venerable Uncle Abram. Northup conceded the young monster some noble qualities, but wrote: "Mounted on his pony, he often rides into the field with his whip, playing the overseer, greatly to his father's delight."[11]

Indeed, overseers' sons, with their fathers' approval, often lorded over adult slaves as well as children, brandishing whips and playing little tyrant. "Come on, nigger," the son of an overseer called to the slave boy his father had bought. "I'm no nigger." "Yes, you is, my pa paid $200 for you. He bought you to play with me." James W. C. Pennington, Maryland's "fugitive blacksmith," described how white children imitated their father and the overseer, demanding obedience from the slave boys whom they "tortured." Here and there hints appeared of sibling rivalries between the white and black boys. Gus Feaster told of a slave who taught himself to read and won his master's approval for his pluck and brains. The master's two sons beat him badly one day but probably never again, for their father "wo[re] Bill and Jule out" for it. Henry Gladney of South Carolina recalled, "Little Marse John treat me good sometime, and kick me 'round sometime. I see now dat I was just a little dog or monkey, in his heart and mind, dat 'mused him to pet or kick me as it pleased him." The eight-year-old Rebecca Jane Grant was whipped for refusing to call a slaveholder's son half her size "massa." Privileged whites told of teasing black playmates – or adult slaves – unmercifully, playing pranks and tormenting them without necessarily wishing them harm. Their victims could curse or stomp their feet but could not complain or find a protector.[12]

Value judgments aside, did the depictions offered by antislavery and proslavery observers differ in essentials? In 1856 the intellectually formidable David Flavel Jamison, a fine historian who a few years later chaired South Carolina's secession convention, delivered the annual address to the South Carolina Agricultural Society. The staunchly proslavery Jamison defined the planter as a "ruler," adding, "The slaveowner is more – he is, to a certain extent, necessarily a despot."[13]

Edmund Burke's Cautionary Tale

Jefferson's exposé of slavery's deleterious effects on white character met wide approbation and reinforcement but also powerful counterattacks. In particular, Southerners proudly recalled Edmund Burke's great speech on conciliation with America:

> In Virginia and the Carolinas they have a vast multitude of slaves. Where this is the case in any part of the world, those who are free are by far the most proud and jealous of their freedom. Freedom is to them not only an enjoyment, but a kind of rank and privilege. Not seeing there, that freedom as in countries where it is a common blessing and as broad and general as the air, may be united with much abject toil, with great misery, with all the exterior of servitude; liberty looks, amongst them, like something that is more noble and liberal. I do not mean, Sir, to commend the superior morality of this sentiment, which has at least as much pride as virtue in it; but I cannot alter the nature of man. The fact is so; and these people of the Southern Colonies are much more strongly, and with a higher and more stubborn spirit, attached to liberty than those to the northward. Such were all the ancient commonwealths; such were our Gothic ancestors; such in our days were the Poles; and such will be all masters of slaves, who are not slaves themselves. In such a people the haughtiness of domination combines with the spirit of freedom, fortifies it, and renders it invincible.[14]

Burke had countless admirers throughout the South, nowhere more than Virginia. John Randolph of Roanoke proclaimed Burke "an intellectual banquet," "a treasure," and "a mine of eloquence, sagacity, and political wisdom!" William Wirt advised aspiring lawyers, "You will find a rich mine of instruction in the splendid language of Burke." Daniel K. Whitaker, the editor of *The Southern Literary Messenger* and then *Southern Field and Fireside*, attributed to Burke "amazing genius." To Professor Nathaniel Beverley Tucker of the College of William and Mary, Burke was "the most profound of political philosophers." James P. Holcombe, Edmund Ruffin, and George Fitzhugh invoked Burke.[15]

Decade after decade, Southerners recalled Burke's warning against attempts to trample them. Henry W. Miller, addressing students at the University of North Carolina, called him "that great man," as did Hugh Legaré of South

Carolina and the northern-born President Jasper Adams of the College of Charleston. Robert Y. Hayne, reminding Daniel Webster of it during their famous senatorial debate, referred to George Washington as an illustration of slavery's fine influence on personal and national character. Representative William Drayton of Charleston followed suit in a vigorous tribute to the great slaveholding Virginians of the Revolutionary era. Twenty years later in Boston, Senator Robert Toombs of Georgia hurled Burke's message in the face of the abolitionists. As the sectional struggle waxed hotter in the 1840s and 1850s, college students repeatedly heard their professors recall Burke's tribute. The Baptist Reverend Basil Manly, president of the University of Alabama, and Representative John Perkins, Jr., of Louisiana recalled Burke's words to rally support for slavery, as did David J. McCord of South Carolina. The slaveholders' spirit of liberty, Manly remarked, removed the dangers of the "adventurous and levelling spirit of agrarianism" that agitated the masses. After the War, students at the University of Georgia continued to hear such luminaries as Senator Benjamin Hill and J. L. M. Curry of Alabama echo Burke's words.[16]

John Taylor of Caroline, Jefferson's friend, detested Burke, but on this matter he sounded like him. Taylor, who rarely took issue with Jefferson in public, condescendingly noted that *Notes on the State of Virginia* had been written "in the heat of a war for liberty" and the promise of the French Revolution. Referring to the great men of Greece and Rome, Taylor twisted the knife: Was not Thomas Jefferson himself a living refutation? "Slaves are too far below, and too much in the power of the master, to inspire furious passions." Slaveholders did not rage at slaves any more than at horses; the great majority viewed slaves as objects of benevolence. White children, "from their nature were inclined to soothe, and hardly ever to tyrannize over them." Southerners despised submission and flattery, "which cause us rather to hate servility than to imbibe a dictatorial arrogance."[17]

Jefferson described colonial Virginians as improvident and without a proper work ethic. He traced the roots of these infirmities to monarchical government and the prevalence of slavery. After Jefferson returned from France in 1789 and fell silent on slavery, a young relative asked him to explain the extraordinary politeness of Virginia gentlemen. He replied that Virginians had been trained in "the finest school of manners and morals that ever existed in America." By 1815 at the latest, Southerners, including Virginians, were following the proslavery Taylor, not Jefferson. Echoing Taylor during the Missouri debates, Representative William Smith of South Carolina described *Notes on the State of Virginia* as a product of a youth spent under the influence of speculative philosophy. Smith dismissed the notion of "boisterous passions" as a nonsensical misunderstanding of the patriarchal nature of the master-slave relation.[18]

George Tucker, Jefferson's political follower and able biographer, strove for a balanced estimate of the moral effects of slavery. His remarks compel particular attention because he considered slavery doomed to economic extinction. Tucker described Virginians as "open-handed and open hearted; fond of society, indulging in all its pleasures, and practising all its courtesies." But with Virginia's well-earned reputation for hospitality came "the kindred vices of love of show, haughtiness, sensuality." Many among the wealthy added to "the allowable pleasures of the chase and the turf . . . the debasing ones of cock-fighting, gaming, and drinking." Tucker acknowledged that slavery tended to make masters "indolent, proud, luxurious and improvident," and convinced of their own natural superiority. Simultaneously, slaves all too easily convinced themselves of their own inferiority. Unusual for his day, he rejected racism. Only emancipation could dispel racial prejudices, but those very prejudices blocked emancipation. Tucker nonetheless cautioned against exaggerating the vices of slavery: "Domestic slavery in fact places the master in a state of moral discipline, and according to the use he makes of it, he is only made better or worse." Slavery elevated a basically good man and transformed a bad man into a horror with "evil propensities." Tucker extolled those who, when taught "to curb these sallies of passion or freaks of caprice" or embrace "a course of salutary restraint," strengthened their "virtues of self-denial, forbearance, and moderation." He found proof in the great Virginians – Washington, Jefferson, Madison, and Monroe – who had graced the American presidency. In 1854, a contributor to *Southern Literary Messenger* cited Tucker's *Jefferson* for slavery's positive moral effects on whites, and in 1861, John Randolph Tucker echoed his kinsman in a paean to slavery's strengthening of white character by the imposition of self-discipline.[19]

From M. R. H. Garnett in Virginia to Samuel A. Cartwright in Mississippi, some important Southerners hyperbolically asserted that the slave states had produced all of America's greatest and morally exemplary statesmen and generals. Senator Stephen Mallory of Florida boasted that when Americans turned to great men to fill the presidency, they had chosen slaveholders seven times, from Washington to Zachary Taylor. Representative Edward Stanly of North Carolina supported slavery only because he knew of no safe way to dispose of it, but he too defended the slaveholders' rectitude. In 1845, Jefferson Davis cited John Adams, James Otis, Elbridge Gerry, and John Hancock as eminent Northerners who "had all sprung from a State which tolerated slavery." Governor John A. Winston of Alabama – still at it in 1856 – stressed the contribution made by an inferior race to the formation of the southern gentleman and a more "enlightened manhood." The refrain continued long after the War. Speaking for many, Wharton Jackson Green, writing at the beginning of the twentieth century, ridiculed the notion that slavery undermined white character, offering Jefferson, Andrew Jackson, John C. Calhoun, Jefferson Davis, and others in refutation.[20]

The scholarly and generally sober President Thomas Roderick Dew of the College of William and Mary told his students that, unquestionably, Virginia had produced the greatest number of profound American statesmen. Virginians, the historian Henry Howe wrote, did not permit their children to tyrannize over slave children, who – in any case – returned all blows. Others affirmed that slavery strengthened southern character – that the master's need to feel the love and respect of his slave generated patience, magnanimity, and noble affections. Nathaniel Beverley Tucker of Virginia declared that white enslavement of blacks encouraged moral improvement in both races. Chancellor William Harper of South Carolina wrote that God would brand slavery intolerable if masters treated slaves dishonestly or meanly.[21]

Morals

Did these politicians and men of letters believe their own rhetoric? Their personal papers leave little doubt. Governor Robert F. W. Allston of South Carolina privately lauded J. H. Hammond on the publication of his reply to the British abolitionist Thomas Clarkson:

> I beg leave to congratulate you on the taste for which you have given your preference i.e. the life & pursuits of a Planter which if view'd aright, regulated by the principles of Religion, that highest philosophy, enlighten'd and aid'd by Science, affords both the means & opportunity to do as much good, and contributes to the true dignity of man, the elevation and just influence of his character, quite as much as any other avocation whatever.[22]

In defending the slaveholders' character and honor, men who usually spoke with reserve fell into self-adulation. For E. A. Pollard of Virginia, slavery "inspires us with independence, refines the soul, and nourishes a graceful pride." William H. Trescot of South Carolina, an intellectually superior diplomat and historian, pointed to John Rutledge, Charles Pinckney, William Lowndes, John C. Calhoun, and Langdon Cheves to maintain that slavery "has made us a grave, earnest, resolute, just people." Thomas Cobb of Georgia, an impressive legal scholar and devout Presbyterian layman, considered blacks congenitally incapable of understanding causation and mentally capable of progressing only so far. But then Cobb portrayed Russian serfs as no better. Accordingly, he suggested that Jefferson had exaggerated: The young Southerner "*is accustomed to rule*" and displays a spirit of independence that brooks no opposition. "Within a proper limit this is not an evil. Indulgence makes it a sin." A. B. Meek, a leading light among Alabama's men of letters, traced much of the South's intellectual and moral character to the beneficent effects of slavery. For Daniel Hundley of Alabama, who spent many years as a businessman in Chicago, slavery's effect on the young accounted for "the natural dignity of manner peculiar to the Southern Gentlemen." Only occasionally did a voice rise from the slave states to support Jefferson. William L. Breckenridge of St. Louis scoffed at the idea that slavery encouraged good qualities in masters. Local newspapers in the lower South reprinted his article.[23]

Intellectuals, then as now, loved to contradict one another even when they were on the same side. Francis Pickens turned the tables on critics of slavery by arguing that planters worked steadily to manage their slaves, whereas northern capitalists, free of daily responsibility for their workers, had time to indulge their fancies. Dr. E. H. Barton, the president of the New Orleans Academy of Science, nonetheless upheld the more common proslavery view. Slavery, he maintained, "elevates the tone of the superior, adds to its refinement, allows more time to cultivate the mind, exalts the standard in morals, manners, and intellectual endowments."[24]

In proclaiming the wonderful effects of slavery on white character, Southerners received reinforcement from both sympathetic and hostile Europeans and Northerners who, happily or grudgingly, paid tribute to the slaveholders' graciousness, propriety, courtesy, hospitality, and assorted aristocratic virtues. Books, articles, and newspapers, read abroad as well as in the South, bolstered southern contentions. In the 1850s, D. W. Mitchell, an Englishman who spent years in Virginia, doubted that any people in the world matched Southerners as judges of human character. He described southern gentlemen as more European than American in habits, appearance, and character, largely because slavery compelled them to study human nature and learn the self-control necessary to govern. For once agreeing with an Englishman, John Mitchel, the Irish radical, maintained that great power bred self-restraint and a sense of responsibility. Southerners, he wrote in the *Southern Citizen* (Knoxville), expected a gentleman to control his passions and speak softly to servants. Turning to Jefferson's critique, Mitchel wrote, "It is a favorite saying of the Northern people, and the English, that the evil of Slavery is to make the boys impious and cruel. The opposite is true. Christianity has conditioned mores, and if a boy has a young negro or two of his own to govern, he does it under the eyes of parents and neighbors."[25]

Southern clergymen rose to the defense of the slaveholders' character and morals. The Episcopal Reverend Jasper Adams, in his textbook, *Elements of Moral Philosophy*, credited southern education for instilling in young Southerners "familiarity with the forms of social intercourse, an address uniting dignity with ease, confidence without arrogance, simplicity and naturalness without rudeness, and refined cultivation without affectation." Bishop William Meade praised the Christian character of education in Virginia, crediting it as "the fruitful nursery of patriots and orators and statesmen." Despite misgivings, "I rejoice to believe, and I acknowledge that the institution of slavery, by affording more leisure and opportunity to some for the attainment of the most thorough education, has contributed to this." With a glance at Jefferson, he referred to the slave's dependence on his master as "a continual and effective appeal to his justice and humanity." Meade admitted that evil passions sometimes ruled but insisted, "The milder virtues are much more frequently called forth."[26]

In the 1850s, the Presbyterian Reverend A. A. Porter of South Carolina boasted, "We are well content to remain as we are – a slaveholding people – and invite the world to compare us with our neighbors." Porter spoke for proslavery theorists in implicitly challenging opponents to deny that most of the world embraced some form of unfree labor in 1860. The Baptist Reverend Iveson Brookes of Georgia appealed to Scripture and history to show that slavery produced exceptionally good character in Southerners. The Baptist Reverend Thornton Stringfellow of Virginia, the author of significant pamphlets in defense of slavery and slaveholders, urged careful reading of 1 Peter to find "much to secure civil subordination to the State, and hearty and cheerful obedience to the masters, on the part of servants." Peter says nothing about masters here but implicitly identifies the danger to Christianity as arising "on the side of *insubordination among the servants*, and a *want of humility with inferiors*, rather than *haughtiness among superiors* in the church." Stringfellow, who owned some thirty slaves, concluded that slavery "deserves to expand."[27]

In North Carolina, the Reverend Mr. Deems raised William Haigh's eyebrows: "His sermon Sunday closed strangely.... 'Jesus Christ as a Gentleman.'" The Methodist Reverend R. H. Rivers, a moral philosopher at Wesleyan University in Alabama, stated flatly in his popular textbook on moral philosophy, "Slavery exerts no evil effects upon the master." Rivers went too far for the proslavery Methodist Reverend H. N. McTyeire, who warned that the master "is tempted continually to the exercise of injustice and oppression." When secession and war loomed, the Reverend George Howe, a pillar of southern Presbyterianism, looked back on Jefferson's "often quoted" critique of slavery as "in many respects so unjust." Shortly after the War, Thomas M. Hanckel, in a memoir on the death of Bishop Stephen Elliott of Georgia – "a Southern slaveholder and a representative of Southern society" – cited his character as a sufficient answer to those who believed that slavery corrupted masters.[28]

Apprehensive Parents

Self-congratulation notwithstanding, slaveholders feared that their children, particularly their sons, lived under dangerous temptations. Parents raised boys to be slave masters but also to be ready to assume responsibility for the household, white and black, if their fathers died suddenly. Yet they knew that slaveholding threatened to make boys irresponsible and willful rather than strong and judicious. Guided by their preachers, they struggled for balance. Fathers impressed on sons the awful burden that awaited them. Sterling Ruffin of North Carolina looked forward to bringing his daughter home from school, having her "under our immediate care and direction." He explained to Thomas, his sixteen-year-old son:

> A Girl of her age should not be left to the care of a boarding Mistress, as there is nothing so easily injur'd as the reputation of a Virgin; they are tender flowers that cannot bear the Wintery blasts, or Summers heats. I therefore now call upon you, should it please the Eternal and allwise Creator to deprive them of my aid, to be the protector of my familys rights and Earthly happiness.[29]

To the charge that slavery induced pride, anger, cruelty, selfishness, and licentiousness in young masters, John Fletcher of New Orleans, the author of a learned proslavery tract, replied that all power, including that of a husband over a wife, invites abuses and puffs up the pride of the weak-willed. Neither Fletcher nor anyone else gainsaid what they dared not discuss openly.

Mores forbade references to sexual relations among children, but white boys at tender ages could command black girls – and, more easily, black boys. The more well-to-do slaveholders sent their sons to distant academies and colleges in part to get them away from the sexual temptations of plantation life. The Methodist Bishop James O. Andrew of Georgia criticized parents for sending their children away to school as protection against the influence of slaves, only to plunge them into other destructive circumstances. Better, he said, to have a small farmstead so they can live at home and reduce the danger.[30]

One parental fear, enmeshed in silence, cut more deeply than any other. Oral tradition suggests more incidences of homosexuality, especially in elite circles, than reported. Thus, southern sources – correspondence, diaries, public documents – drop only a rare hint about white boys' sexual relations with black playmates. Yet Southerners knew from Greek and Roman legal and literary sources that homosexuality had flourished under ancient slavery and helotry. For one among many, Thomas R. R. Cobb, Georgia's foremost legal scholar, drew on Aeschines' "Against Timarchus" to expound the Greek law of slavery and to pay tribute to Solon, Draco, and other bygone lawgivers who had upheld moral standards. Aeschines, not yet ready to attack Demosthenes, the real object of his wrath, said of Demosthenes' friend and supporter Timarchus, "You will find that the life he has lived has been contrary to all laws." He cited laws intended to protect boys against the lust of pedophile teachers and other authority figures. Aeschines thereupon invoked laws against male prostitution, violation of which would alone bar the perpetrator from participation in public debates. Notoriously, Timarchus, "a kept man," had sold his body to one rich man after another to pay off debts for gambling, drunkenness, and assorted debaucheries. Southerners doubtless took the measure of the casual attitude. For example, they learned from Suetonius of Julius Caesar's bisexuality – his "evil reputation for both sodomy and adultery" – and of Curio's calling Caesar "every woman's man and every man's woman."[31]

Closer in time and place, Southerners appear to have known little about sexual practices in slaveholding Brazil; at any rate, they did not discuss them openly. We would do well to proceed with extreme caution in extrapolating from the experience of Brazil, in which white boys' sexual exploitation of black slave boys provoked levity. The account given by Gilberto Freyre, the great Brazilian historical sociologist, of relations in Brazil cannot readily be transferred to the American slave states but nonetheless remains suggestive, especially in view of the passive function that slave boys often served in the houses of the great Roman aristocrats:

> The furious passions of the Portuguese must have been vented upon victims who did not always share his sexual tastes, although we know of cases where the sadism of the white conqueror was offset by the masochism of his native or Negro partner. So much for the sadistic impulses of the man toward women – which not infrequently derived from the relations of the master toward the Negro slave boy who had been his playmate in youth. Through the submission of the black boy in the games they played together, and the one known as *leva*

pancadas ("take a drubbing"), the white was often initiated into the mysteries of physical love.[32]

To counteract dangerous tendencies at home, a good many parents chose to send their sons to military schools. By 1860 the slave states had eleven of the twelve private or state-supported military schools in the United States, with The Virginia Military Institute of Lexington, Virginia (VMI), and the Citadel of Charleston, South Carolina, the most prestigious. Only in part did they aim to train young men for military service. Leading clergymen, including the prestigious Reverend James Henley Thornwell, a champion of high scholastic standards, praised the Citadel for the thoroughness of its academic work and for developing the talents of young men of the lower classes. Most graduates did not go on to military careers, nor did most parents want them to. They expected military schools to shape character, not to make military officers. William Browne sent his son to VMI in 1841 with an introduction: "He is our only son, who was sorely afflicted by illness in his early youth, & may therefore have been more indulged than was proper.... I submit him to your guidance with the utmost confidence." Southern military schools had a special responsibility: They provided opportunities for the sons of yeomen, middling folk, and professionals, as well as of planters.[33]

In 1825, Captain Alden Partridge, promoting military schools, argued that they kept students away from the dissipation and irresponsibility common to colleges. Robert Allston's mother sent him to West Point to learn the discipline necessary to command slaves. In 1857, J. Hardeman Stuart, a student at the University of Mississippi, supported his father's decision to send a younger brother to a military school: "As you know he is constitutionally inert, and the rigid discipline of a Military Academy will probably alter this." Stonewall Jackson, teaching at VMI, had his hands full with hard-drinking, unruly cadets who raised hell in town and had to be taught – in a common expression of the day – to "walk orderly." Bishop J. H. Otey of Tennessee, having troublesome sons, recommended VMI to a Dr. Cook, who was looking for the right place for his boys. In 1893, John Peyre Thomas, in his history of the Citadel, frankly admitted: "Reared from infancy to manhood with servants at his command to bring his water, brush his shoes, saddle his horse, and, in fine, to minister to his personal wants, the average Southern boy grew up in some points of character dependent, and lazy and inefficient." Thomas thought that the Citadel's discipline helped to correct those deficiencies. In the midst of student unrest at the Citadel, Richard Yeadon quoted Xenophon on the need for social discipline and did not forget to mention the special need for discipline in a slaveholding society.[34]

Jefferson's testimony stung generations of slaveholding parents, who displayed apprehension for their children, especially the boys. Philip Fithian wrote that Robert Carter and his wife had "a manner of instructing and dealing with children far superior, I may say it with confidence, to any I have ever seen, in any place, or in any family." They keep their children "in perfect subjection to themselves, and never pass over an occasion of reproof; and I blush for many of my acquaintances when I say that the children are more kind and complaisant to their servants who constantly attend them than we are to our superiors in age and condition." Conscientious and upright students complained that college officials went too easy on student troublemakers and slackers. J. Allen Hill, a student at the University of Georgia in 1828, thought President Joseph Meigs too lenient and prone to believe that he could tame students by moral suasion. Those brats, he fumed, "generally sons of the rich, had been accustomed to every indulgence and were consequently impatient of restraint." Much vicious behavior ensued, and, alas, the bad company had a serious effect on Hill's own morals.[35]

Sending boys off to school to protect them from plantation temptations entailed risks. The Presbyterian Reverend Dr. Smyth of Charleston noted that boys away at school were "surrounded by new and trying temptations." The University of Nashville legislated against students' having servants, carriages, or dogs in an effort to discourage ostentation. Yet even the denominational colleges, with less affluent students, provided slaves to haul wood and water and clean up rooms. Wake Forest College, however, rejected student demands that slaves clean their boots. Some planters feared that boys who associated with scions of much wealthier families would fall prey to self-indulgence and financial irresponsibility, thereby negating some of the reasons for sending them away in the first place. And mothers had a special worry. Medical journals reported venereal diseases uncommon on plantations, but physicians' account books hint at more cases of gonorrhea than the journals suggested.[36]

Young Gentlemen in Fields and Stores

Contrary to Jefferson's hyperbolic generalization, an untold number of planters, ministers, and proslavery intellectuals spent their youth as farm boys, learning the place of hard work in character formation. Langdon Cheves of South Carolina, the yeoman's son who became president of the Bank of the United States, did field work before the age of ten. Even in the low country, white boys joined black in grinding corn, viewing it as something of a sport. In the Southwest, Zachary Taylor tamed his wild, Yale-educated son Richard by making him manage a plantation. When Jefferson Davis quit school in rebellion against the discipline, his father sent him to the fields to work with the slaves. The two-day experience sent him scurrying back to school. Other teenagers took over a small farm to provide for their families when their fathers died. The vigorous campaign to establish manual labor schools arose to combat the tendencies that Jefferson saw. The clergy, preaching the nobility of labor, supported manual labor schools largely as character-building institutions. Still, matters did not always end well. Admonitions notwithstanding, John J. Crittenden of Kentucky exemplified slaveholders who pushed their sons to maintain a strong work ethic without much success.[37]

In the 1890s, Leonidas Lafayette Polk of North Carolina, the Populist leader, recalled a common southern boyhood. He was born and raised on a plantation of thirty slaves or so, "by one of those plain old farmers" who in some respects qualified as "an old fogy." His father believed in honest, hard work and taught his sons that even a millionaire's son must be taught to work. His father had another "old fogy idea": It took twenty-one years to make a man, and he would have "no fourteen year old young gentlemen about his premises." The young John Albert Feaster Coleman of South Carolina, who directed and worked with his father's field hands, made harsh comments on "uppertons" for whom such work was "a perfect disgrace." Governor Joseph Brown of Georgia and his wife, small slaveholding devout Baptists, taught their children to work for themselves, lest their morals be corrupted. As a rule, from age eight to ten the sons of small slaveholders did farm work; afterward they usually worked with the slaves at critical moments in the production schedule: Senator Benjamin Hill and his brothers worked in the fields with slaves, keeping the same hours and doing the same work. In later years, Hill returned to Jefferson's words, concluding, "No people ever exhibited a more hospitable and refined society, nor one in which the standard of morals was higher, than did the Southern people under slavery."[38]

Sons of planters and the well-to-do, as well as farm boys, worked in stores. Even in the more aristocratic districts, some planters and prominent politicians began their careers as storekeepers. Patrick Henry and Mirabeau Buonaparte Lamar, the president of the Republic of Texas, were among those who failed as store owners. Well-educated, ambitious young men sought clerkships in the more substantial stores, which paid higher wages than the average wages of a plantation overseer. Clerking offered apprenticeship that led into the large and respected merchant class. Langdon Cheves and Henry Watkins Allen, the Confederate governor of Louisiana and a rich sugar planter, began their careers as store clerks. Senators Judah P. Benjamin of Louisiana and Willie P. Mangum of North Carolina were sons of storekeepers. In North Carolina, the list included Allen Turner Davidson, a Confederate congressman; Osborne Giles Foard, a planter and state legislator; and Robert C. Pearson, a merchant and bank president. In Georgia: the Presbyterian Reverend Samuel J. Cassels and Clifford Anderson, a state legislator who had worked as a hotel clerk. Francis Richard Lubbock clerked in a hardware store in Charleston on his way to the governorship of Texas. Federal judge John Baxter of Tennessee had worked as a storekeeper in South Carolina. Robert L. Carruthers, a farm boy who became a justice of the Supreme Court of Tennessee, worked as a clerk in a mercantile house, rising to become a partner. Catherine Cooper Hopley, an English governess in Virginia, remarked that even store clerks were too well bred to hurry their customers.[39]

General stores and bookstores became community centers, attracting the local intellectual and social elite. Citizens read newspapers and sermons aloud as part of discussions on political and social affairs, providing an informal educational experience for browsers and store employees. In the 1850s bookstores sold Bibles, Shakespeare, Scott, biographies of Washington and Franklin, dictionaries, sheet music and instruments as well as pictures, frames, artwork, cutlery, and sometimes liquor. Russell's Bookstore in Charleston, with gaslight ceiling fixtures and a coke fire, served as a gathering place for evening conversations and discussions for such eminent intellectuals and men of affairs as Dr. Samuel Henry Dickson, Mitchell King, Alfred Huger, J. L. Petigru, the Catholic Bishop Lynch, the Episcopal theologian James W. Miles, the classicists Hugh Legaré and Basil Gildersleeve, Charles Tabor (the editor of *The Charleston Mercury*), and the poets William J. Grayson and Henry Timrod. Outside of Charleston, southern-rights men thought that the more successful storekeepers had close connections with northern merchants, which often led to strong friendships and intermarriage. Mobile, for example, had many Northerners and merchants, most of whom were politically much more moderate than most Alabamans.[40]

Dr. William H. Holcombe of Natchez told of life with a father who took the measure of slavery in Virginia, freed his slaves, and departed for the Midwest. Holcombe's father taught his ten-year-old son "an object lesson in the dignity of labor which has never been forgotten." One day his grandmother sent William to the store to get a jug of molasses. He refused: "It cut a pretty figure lugging molasses through the Street like a little darkie." His father commanded him to do as he was told: "I will teach you that all honest labor is respectable and to be respected, whether it be done by a bootblack or a President." He instructed Willie's grandmother to make sure that he served as molasses boy for the family thereafter. William became ardently proslavery, but he took that lesson to heart.[41]

Some Southerners, stung by Jefferson's charge that slavery produced spoiled brats, recommended a vigorous sporting life as a supplement to or acceptable equivalent for ordinary labor. Chief Justice John Belton O'Neall of South Carolina praised Robert Y. Hayne as a representative South Carolinian shaped by "rural labors and rural sports" to become physically and mentally strong, energetic, and patient, with a sense of responsibility and an unconquerable purpose. Representative Reuben Davis of Mississippi protested the injustice of supposing that Southerners "were given up to enfeebling self-indulgence and luxury." The sons of the gentry were "brought up in habits of a free and fearless activity." Hundley argued that the outdoor life produced healthy men immune to the mental disorders that infected a less vigorous northern society. As for spoiled children, the English-born Amelia Barr, who settled in Texas, offered a grim thought: Because many southern babies died during their first year or so, mothers doted on and spoiled them.[42]

Early twentieth-century recollections of Tennessee Confederate war veterans from all classes provide a window on slaveholders' attempts to raise their sons in a manner designed to prove Jefferson wrong. A minority of planters' sons admitted to having done little or no work but explained that they were in school most of the year. So did a good many sons of small slaveholders, and professionals, who said that their fathers expected them to plow and do hard work when home on vacation. Having to work with slaves brought out competitive instincts. The father of John Russell Dance owned between fifty and a hundred slaves but worked his son hard. Dance remarked, "I plowed and worked with the hoe. Some of my hardest work as a boy was trying to beat the fastest negro cotton picker." Edwin Maximilian Gardner proudly reported that he and his brother picked as much cotton as the best slaves.[43]

Such testimony might be dismissed as self-serving were it not that small slaveholders and nonslaveholders attested to its truth, suggesting that only a minority of the wealthiest planters encouraged idleness in their sons. Then too, small slaveholders and nonslaveholders expressed respect for the hard work that planters put into the management of plantations. The overwhelming majority of slaveholders had fewer than twenty slaves and did not qualify as planters; circumstances demanded that their sons work in the fields. They tried to arrange to have their sons work alongside and as hard as the slaves. A typical case: Although William Sidney Hartsfield's parents owned twelve slaves, he worked in the fields "from very early morning until late at night." Did the sons of planters and slaveholding yeomen work as hard as the field slaves? Some, like Robert P. Adair, appear to have enjoyed doing so. His father, a Tennessee planter, sent him to school, but he preferred to plow and work on the farm. Doubtless, most thought that they worked as hard as slaves; most slaves probably thought differently. But farmers do, after all, work hard.[44]

A planter who wanted a son to succeed him – what planter did not? – often put one or more to work as a fledgling overseer, which meant that they were expected to do every kind of work they would later supervise. A big planter might easily have spoken as did the father of Ireneaus F. Fisher, the owner of only four slaves. Young Ireneaus complained that his father worked him harder than he worked his slaves. Father's reply: "I want you to learn to work and if you ever take up business and fail, you will have an experience that dont fail." By the time Abram David Reynolds entered his teens, his father, who owned 147 slaves in 1861, worked him in a tobacco factory as well as on the farm.[45]

John Triplett Thomas and other wealthy slaveholders in the Virginia Piedmont required their sons to learn an assortment of plantation tasks and trades so that, when they became planters, they could train their slaves properly. Even lowcountry planters, despite or because of enormous wealth, took measures to engage their sons in physical labor as necessary to their character and sense of responsibility. Robert F. W. Allston believed that a planter's sons should work as overseers in order to learn the rice business properly. Charles Manigault put his sons to work: "Any property I may have Created, or Inherited, I would rather, see *it sink in the ocean* than go to an idle, loafer of a Son." The Manigaults, nonetheless, had their share of loafers. So Henry considered his spendthrift brother.[46]

Weighed in the Balances

Slaveholders hoped to scotch their sons "boisterous passions" by making them do manual labor or sending them away to school, but they remained doubtful of the outcome. "In taking from the negro all power of resistance," wrote Edward J. Pringle of South Carolina, "we leave the master a prey to unbridled passions that may sometimes betray him into excess." Pringle vaguely suggested that absolute power must reside "within the bounds of what humanity permits," and he favored legalization of slave marriages and restraints on separation of families. Much depended on criteria and, above all, the balance of effects. The Reverend J. A. Lyon's "Report to the General Assembly of the Presbyterian Church," signed by distinguished ministers and laymen, ominously noted that slavery humanized the character of the master only to the extent that it rose to biblical standards. Master and slave, the report declared, rise or fall together. Countless slaveholders made every effort to train their boys to be responsible, humane adults, not petty tyrants, and we may marvel at how many succeeded under the worst of temptations. For all that, nothing emerges so clearly as the core of truth in Jefferson's indictment, however overwrought and questionable its specifics. And that core of truth by itself condemned slavery as a system.[47]

When the War came, Southerners took up the long-gestating cry of being a people apart from Northerners. Contrary to postwar apologetics, the leading voices of the Old South frankly acknowledged the centrality of slavery to the formation of a distinct southern people. They, in effect, stood with Anthony Trollope: "The South is seceding from the North because the two are not homogeneous. They have different instincts, different appetites, different morals, and a different culture." But Southerners would have added: "rooted in different social relations." Thomas Caute Reynolds, the Virginia-born lieutenant governor of Missouri, challenged the state Senate to affirm that the North and the South were "two distinct nations" and "different peoples." The Reverend H. A. Tupper of Washington, Georgia, spoke to his flock in 1862 of an "unnatural" Union: "That difference in pursuits, and interests, and institutions, and education, and manners, and political and social views, has made us virtually two people – as much two as any people could be of the same language and color." Addressing the Franklin Society of Mobile in 1854, John Forsyth – Jacksonian Unionist, governor of Georgia, U.S. secretary of state – spoke of North and South as different peoples and cultures.[48]

More pointedly, to the applause of J. D. B. De Bow, the South's most influential magazine editor on the eve of the War, David McCord extravagantly asserted that slavery raised the level of southern civilization. The greatness of the revolutionary generation in Virginia and South Carolina, McCord argued, demonstrated as much: "All the greatest and freest people of antiquity were slaveholders." W. R. Aylett of King William County, Virginia, a prominent planter and grandson of Patrick Henry, contrasted the "noble, generous and patriotic" sons of the South, whose character had been shaped by slavery, with the "cold, money-minded, calculating" Yankees. In a ploy unusual for a Virginian, he ended by appealing to the spirit of South Carolina to call for a scorched-earth resistance to any attempt to uproot slavery from southern soil. Frederick A. Porcher of South Carolina allowed that climate alone accounted for substantial differences, but he singled out slavery and the presence of blacks as critical. Slavery constituted "an essential element in Southern civilization." Professor Albert Taylor Bledsoe of the University of Virginia, who spent years in the Northwest, condemned northern society: "Mammon is its god, and nowhere has he more devout and abject worshippers, or has set up a more polluted civilization than in the North."[49]

Well after the War, Stanton Elmore of Alabama described the life of masters as "powerful and yet much alone": "When a hundred slaves did the bidding of one master, and every great plantation was a principality, a little despotism, there were Americans subject to influences now little known of in America or elsewhere." Writing in 1916, Harvey Toliver Cook, a professor of Greek at Furman University and a staunch supporter of the old regime, reflected on the lessons of ancient history: "Slaveholding was imperialism in small change and it placed in the will of the master a power which few men and fewer governments have been found sane and wise enough not to abuse."[50]

Notwithstanding the gulf that separated slaveholders' self-celebrations from the negative judgments of adversaries, the similarity of the appraisals of character and personality compels consideration of the experience of William Ellery Channing, who had tutored for eighteen months in Richmond. Praising Virginians' warmth, hospitality, and graciousness, he commented: "Here I find great vices, but greater virtues than I left behind me." Virginians "*love money less* than we do." But in the end the vices outweighed the great virtues: "Could I only take from the Virginians their *sensuality* and their *slaves*, I should think them the greatest people in the world."[51]

A question that few contemporary partisans wanted to hear and even the most good-spirited citizens could not resolve has plagued every people in every age: To what extent can a people's virtues be separated from its vices? Specifically, to what extent did command of slaves produce masters whose finest virtues were inextricably intertwined with poisonous vices? And to what extent – if at all – can the virtues be recaptured on more just social foundations?

2

The Complete Household

A complete household or community is one composed of freemen and slaves.
– William J. Grayson

Fredrika Bremer of Sweden encountered two slaves about to fight because one had slighted the other's master. Edward Bourne of Tennessee talked about his father's only slave, "who nearly killed another negro, because he reflected upon my father." It was an old story. Quintilian pleaded that slaves had justification for killing free men who offended their masters. He quoted Cicero's "Defence of Milo," a work assigned in southern schools: "Milo's slaves did what everyone would have wished his own slaves to do under similar circumstances." An ideological imperative embedded itself in the southern slaveholder's psyche. Slaves became quasi-kin: Whites referred to "our family, white and black," and blacks referred to "my white folks." Indeed, throughout the world, masters, to preserve self-esteem, needed to credit every such story. They called slaves "my children," and slaves called them "father."[1]

Although gentlemen in seventeenth-century Virginia considered white indentured servants household members and considered black slaves chattel, a reversal occurred in the eighteenth century. George Washington typified eighteenth-century Virginians, much as Patrick Calhoun typified nineteenth-century South Carolinians. Referring to their slaves as "my people," they tried to know something about each. Slowly, the reality of the plantation as household induced a sensibility expressed in the language of "family." In 1774, John Harrower, an indentured Scots tutor, wrote to his wife: "Our Family consists of the Coll., his Lady & four Children, a housekeeper, an overseer and myself all white. But how many blacks young and old only the Lord knows for I believe there is about thirty that work every day in the fields besides the servants about the house." Anna McKnight, a poor woman in Berkeley County, Virginia, pleaded with President Thomas Jefferson, "My slaves are as My Children & if I could Procure 5 hundred dollars I can secure all I have."[2]

John Randolph of Roanoke, who emancipated hundreds of slaves by will, long wondered about the course to pursue. In 1814 he lost three-quarters of an exceptionally fine crop and lamented, "With a family of more than two hundred mouths looking up to me for food, I feel an awful charge on my hands." He could not shut his heart to "the cry of humanity and the voice of duty." Rather than abandon his "best and most faithful friends" to cruelties sustained at law, he preferred to suffer with them. Randolph, toward the end of his life, asked antislavery gentlemen to consider the strong and lasting friendships of masters and slaves. "The slave knows that he is bound indissolubly to his master, and must from necessity remain always under his control. The master knows that he is to maintain and provide for his slave so long as he retains him in his possession. And each party accommodates himself to the situation." Decades later, the Presbyterian Reverend Robert Lewis Dabney, who managed his mother's twenty or thirty slaves in Virginia, said, "Whatever may be the influence of slavery on the happiness of the negroes, it would most effectually destroy that of the master, if they were all [indulgent] like me." Even the hard-headed, proslavery Louisa McCord of South Carolina replied to a comment about her modest jewelry that people with two hundred children could not afford diamonds.³

An instructive event occurred at the University of Mississippi. In 1860, the fire-eating Governor Pettus hauled F. A. P. Barnard, the widely respected, soon-to-be-famous, northern-born chancellor of the university, before the board of trustees on charges of being unsound on slavery. The board and Barnard agreed that, if true, the charges would render him unsuitable to preside over a south-ern University. After a fair inquiry, the board acquitted him. He had expelled a student for beating a woman servant and, apparently, had accepted her evidence against a white man. The incident stoked the fears of some Missis-sippians that Barnard harbored antislavery tendencies. He defended himself on high ground: "I was but doing my duty as a Christian master, to protect my servant from outrage; and...I am sustained in this view by the highest authorities."⁴

Southerners chose not to dwell on the dark side of slaveholding. Henry A. Murray of England froze when he learned that they could lawfully kill runaways. Yet slaveholders' private diaries, family letters, and conversations revealed that special sense of family to their view of themselves as individuals and as a people; to their sense of moral worth; to their honor and self-esteem. And they could turn to freedmen as well as slaves who frequently referred to "our white folks." In *Eros and Freedom in Southern Life and Thought*, Earle Thorpe has captured an essential aspect of the transition in southern mores: "The process which wrought a change from the Old South's aristocratic and paternalistic family – which included slaves – to the New South's white family – which largely excluded Negroes (except possibly the maid or chauffeur who lived in) – is part of the process which throughout the Occidental world brought the modern family into being."⁵

The slaveholding concept of household challenged reigning transatlantic the-ories of property, government, and social order, projecting alternative theories with wide political implications. Presbyterians led the southern clergy in maintaining that since families, like societies, required menial services, servitude inhered in the human condition. In Augusta, Georgia, the Reverend Joseph R. Wilson explained that God included slavery as an organizing element in the family order that supports church and state: "No household is perfect under the gospel which does not contain all the grades of authority and obedience, from that of husband and wife, down through that of father and son, to that of master and servant." The Reverend Frederick A. Ross in Alabama, the Reverend William A. Hall of Louisiana, and the Reverend J. C. Coit of South Carolina, among many, preached that God first established the family, giving man only rights compatible with the good of the family and the government derived from it. The Reverend George D. Armstrong of Virginia added, "Of all the unreal visions which 'the foolish heart darkened' has conjured up, none is more unreal than the vision of man standing by and for himself. Of all the foolish imaginations which man has dignified with the name of philosophy, none is more foolish than that such independence is necessary to a righteous responsibility." Armstrong walked a straight line between his *The Theology of Christian Experience* and *The Doctrine of Baptism: Scriptural Examinations* and his *The Christian Doctrine of Slavery*, which projected family-based Christian slavery as the solution to class war in free labor countries. The Apostles, he said, censured the abuses of ordained institutions, not the institutions. No sensible man repudiated the marriage relation because of evils everyone knew existed. And so for slavery.[6]

Proslavery social theory sought to understand the resistance of the South to a historic shift in the North and in Western Europe. Early industrialization in the Northeast drew the family's surplus labor from the home, separated family members, and steadily created a class of free laborers. Much of the Northwest as well as the South slowed the process. Family farms retained their household character and rendered northern farmers and nonslaveholding southern farmers – as well as planters – similar in some respects. But the shared features had radically different implications in North and South. In the North, the shortage of landless agricultural laborers constrained the expansion of commodity production, encouraging self-sufficiency and mechanization. Farmers generally strove to enter the market. Those who sought substantial wealth had to rely primarily on land speculation and investment in nonagricultural pursuits. Wealthy landowners and landless agricultural workers were separated from household production. Southern farmers who entered the market to a significant extent assumed high risks. In order to raise staples they expanded the household's slave labor force, which enhanced production and consumption. Accordingly, the household ideology grew naturally from the political economy of slavery. The expression "my family, white and black," projected an authentic reality with multiple meanings. Samuel Galloway of Georgia, a northern-born political economist, pictured a God-given economic system: "Each family is a unit in the mart. The family is a reservoir into which commodities flow, and from which each member receives continuous supplies. The patriarch gathers around him a circle of dependents."[7]

Both proslavery and antislavery thought grounded authority in the male head of household, only slowly conceding rights to women, children, and other dependents. Slaveholders upheld the principle of legitimate authority in the household and polity. They recoiled from a transatlantic marketplace ideology that propelled thought and action toward radical egalitarianism and threatened the family itself. Upon receiving condolences from Waddy Thompson of upcountry South Carolina, Senator Andrew P. Butler wrote, "I am much gratified by your expression. . . . Out of one's own family there is not much real fixedness." Any capitalist, any free worker, any peasant might have uttered those words, but by "family" a slaveholder meant "household" with slaves or "servants."[8]

In 1836 the Episcopalian Bishop Levi Silliman Ives, a transplanted Northerner, praised the Reverend George W. Freeman of Raleigh, North Carolina, for his published sermon, *The Rights and Duties of Slaveholders.* Freeman dated slavery from God's curse on Adam and Eve and their progeny, with the command that mankind labor for sustenance. Outside of Eden, inequality reigned. The father as head of the family commanded his children's labor. Much as God declared Adam executive head of the household, responsible for the fate of the human race, so Christian Southerners declared the male head responsible for household behavior and honor. As the household increased in size and its operations grew more complex, the father spent more time in planning and superintendence, and the idle, improvident, weak, and incapable became dependent on the intelligent and strong. Community safety, indeed survival, required repression of the lawless and vicious.

Paternal Authority

Slavery "increases the tendency to dignify the family," C. G. Memminger told the Young Men's Library Association of Augusta, Georgia, in 1851. With each planter a patriarch, society "assumes the Hebrew form," restricts the state to external functions, and leaves private life to domestic regulation. To Southerners, the North stood in a deepening contrast. In 1860 the Episcopalian Reverend William O. Prentiss, in a Fast-day sermon in Charleston, arraigned the North for undermining the family and parental discipline:

> Children are urged to obedience on the sole ground of the parent's superior wisdom, not because the parent exercises an authority divinely delegated – When the wisdom of parental rule is no longer appreciated and acknowledged by the child, he assumes to himself the government of his own actions, or listens to the moral suasion of another more competent than his natural adviser.

The Yankee wife obeys her husband not because she accepts a divinely commanded duty but because he persuades her. No wonder, Prentiss thundered, marriage and the family in the North were unraveling. The Methodist Bishop James O. Andrew of Georgia emphasized gentleness in the rearing of children, but he too demanded firm discipline. Parents must govern their children, not vice versa.[9]

Proslavery spokesmen disagreed with Plato's admonition to masters to issue orders without explanation. They preferred Aristotle's view that the slaves' moral capacity required explanation and instruction. They also agreed with Isocrates that a man who mismanages his domestic affairs will probably mismanage matters of state. The Presbyterian Reverend James Henley Thornwell of South Carolina, the South's most formidable theologian, preached more specifically that a man must sustain his household in order to qualify as a philanthropist. Thornwell, like other educated Southerners, knew *The Satyricon*, in which Trimalchio declares, "I don't practice in the courts, but I've educated myself to run the household." Xenophon taught a special lesson: He compared the household to a disciplined army of well-fed troops who respected and deferred to their commander. And Xenophon's Socrates considered landowners' wives essential to well-ordered estates and called on husbands to train them to assume outdoor and indoor responsibilities, which required intelligence and strong character.[10]

Parents and educators counseled young ladies to be model slave mistresses, who encouraged their men to be good masters. *Russell's Magazine* applauded the Methodist Reverend C. W. Howard's address to the young ladies of Cassville Female College, in which he placed slavery at the heart of southern country life and appealed to mistresses to protect slaves from oppression. Unfortunately, men whom slaves agreed were good masters did not always control brutal wives. The Reverend Israel Campbell had been a slave in Kentucky and had a kind master, whose wife swore, screamed, and ranted. She had thought that she married a rich man, but he proved a hard-working man who made a modest living. Embittered, she took her frustrations out on their slaves. Lewis Charlton of Maryland had a master with "a kind heart and many noble qualities," whose "harsh, cruel, hard-hearted" wife hated blacks.[11]

Democratization of the northern family did not proceed as fast as Southerners charged, but it did proceed fast enough to justify alarm. Southerners, filing indictments large and small, could hardly believe that northern states accepted nude bathing, albeit with restrictions. Southerners especially worried about the erosion of paternal authority, which remained central to their ideal of a Christian family. Louisa McCord, scorning Harriett Beecher Stowe's notion of guilt-stricken kind masters, replied that guilt-free masters acted from patriarchal responsibilities, and Calvin H. Wiley, North Carolina's educational reformer, added that the father's place in the family established his authority over his slaves. Edward B. Bryan of South Carolina reshaped the argument: Expulsion from the Garden of Eden meant that each child had to be taught to labor under direction; therefore, parents had supreme authority over children. For Representative Lawrence Keitt, slavery flowed from the absolute authority of the father. For the moderately antislavery Henry St. George Tucker of Virginia, the mother owed obedience to the father. The father's commands were to be obeyed.[12]

Property in Man?

A deceptively simple question: Did masters own their slaves, body and soul? Did they hold property in man? Or did they merely hold property in the slaves' labor and service? Despite the apparent simplicity of the question, its implications and ramifications weighed heavily on proslavery ideology and the slaveholder's conscience.

Thomas Ruffin, North Carolina's great jurist, shook the image of the slave-holding household as a set of mutually advantageous family relations. In *State v. Mann*, he rebuffed parent-child and master-apprentice analogies. The slave sur-rendered his will, "doomed in his own person and his posterity to live without knowledge and without capacity to make anything his own, and to toil that another may reap the fruits." In *State v. Will*, the Supreme Court of North Carolina upheld the right of a slave to kill a white man who threatened his life. Bartholomew Figures Moore, attorney for the defense, argued, "Absolute power is irresponsible power, circumscribed by no limits, save its own imbe-cility." Moore supported the masters' wide discretionary powers but stressed the need for civilized limitations. He characterized southern slavery as owner-ship of services, not men, contrasting it with his understanding of slavery in ancient Rome, and rejected the argument that slavery reduced man to a thing. As Mark V. Tushnet demonstrates, Ruffin distinguished slavery as a business – as market relations – from slavery as human relations left to the master's juris-diction. Ruffin added a pregnant qualification to the "Rough Draft" of his decision. Could a master be charged with battery against a slave? "This Court disclaims the power to lay down such a rule, or to enforce it, without it be first prescribed by the legislature." And in the "Second Draft": "While therefore Slavery exists among us or until it shall seem fit to the Legislature to interpose express enactments to the contrary, it will be the imperative duty of the Judges to refrain from laying down any rule, which can diminish that dominion of the Master." The usually logical Ruffin did not explain how the legislature dared do so if the master's power must be rendered absolute in order to secure the slave's submission. He left the qualification out of his final version.[13]

James P. Holcombe of Virginia maintained that the "harsh and unnatural" claim of absolute power over human chattel deformed Roman slavery. "In the United States the double character of the slave, as a moral person and as a subject of property, has been universally acknowledged, and to a greater or lesser degree protected, both by public sentiment and by the law of the land." State courts, confronting the same problem, handed down decisions and opinions that interpreted legislative intent as specifying attributes of slaves-as-property without denying the slaves' human rights.[14]

Thomas Ruffin's behavior as a master revealed a strong sense of paternalistic responsibility. An active Episcopalian, he wrote to the Baptist Reverend John Holt about a twelve-year-old consumptive slave girl near death. She wanted to be baptized, and Ruffin considered it his duty to arrange for her to have the sacrament. Holt agreed on condition of immersion in proper Baptist fashion. A year later, Ruffin delivered an address before the State Agricultural Society of North Carolina in which he affirmed that more than the master's interest dictated humane treatment of slaves: "There is a stronger tie between them. Often born on the same plantation, and bred together, they have a perfect knowledge of each other, and a mutual attachment." The master provided protection, sustenance, and religious guidance in return for the slave's obedience and faithful service. Ruffin insisted that masters knew and loved their slaves. Conflict arose only when slaves disputed a master's authority, which he saw as unnatural and usually provoked by outsiders. He asked a commonly asked question: "Why should this propitious state of things be changed?" The *Charleston Mercury* asserted that the British aristocracy did not know its servants, whereas "the natural aristocracy of the southern States" did. Ruffin defended authority in "domestic life" as generally considerate and mild, tending toward "an elevation in sentiment in the superior, which generates a humane tenderness for those in his power." Despite impressive dialectical reasoning, Ruffin could not sustain the hard doctrine of *State v. Mann*. In any case, although the ideological as well as technical implications of *State v. Mann* extend widely, we here focus on their bearing on the problem of ownership in human beings or their labor.[15]

Slaveholders struggled to extricate themselves from the conundrum. In an exchange of letters with David Ross of Richmond on Gabriel's Rebellion (1800), William Dunbar of Mississippi praised the humanity of Spanish slave laws and advocated kind treatment. He simultaneously wanted strict laws and enforcement of the master's quasi-absolute power. Moses Liddell of Louisiana instructed his son St. John in 1841 never to require too much of slaves and to treat them with kindness. He must nonetheless chastise them for disobedience and obstinate behavior. On balance: "Keep a clear conscience in these matters." Hugh Davis of Alabama declared plantation management the province of the master, who must govern by a patriarchal "code of love."[16]

Explicitly and implicitly, if ambiguously, southern courts and public opinion distinguished between property in man and property in services. The *Southern Literary Messenger* accepted the term "property in man" but denied that it was absolute. John C. Calhoun, opposing congressional reception of abolitionist petitions, denounced as slander the charge that Southerners dealt in human flesh and claimed ownership of bodies. R. R. Collier of Petersburg carried the message to the Virginia legislature. Godfrey Barnsley, the owner of a hundred or so slaves, cited Edward B. Bryan's *Letters to the Southern People*, to assert, "No man owns another, because all men belong to the supreme ruler of all things." Led by the prestigious *Southern Presbyterian Review*, church publications upheld slavery as property only in service. The divines believed that labor yielded an economic surplus necessary to sustain a ruling class and civilization itself and that domestic slavery provided the most humane and moral form. Most held open the possibility of slaves' elevation to higher status as serfs or formally free but socially dependent laborers. They embraced slaves' human rights and advocated laws to protect their families, promote literacy, and punish cruel masters. They thus denied or substantively redefined property in man.[17]

Proslavery divines invited formidable abolitionist attack by assimilating slaves to household and assimilating household and family to state governance. The doctrine of property in man, even disguised as property in services, directly contradicted the doctrine of property in self and in labor power. Rejecting proslavery theory, northern employers of free labor made a moral virtue of the exclusion of hired laborers from their households. In Massachusetts, Thomas T. Stone told the Salem Female Anti-Slavery Society that slavery converted man into a commodity: "Man – Property! The two conceptions are irreconcilable. If man, then not property; if property, then not man." The proslavery divines demanded humane treatment of slaves, but their dogma of property only in services gave short shrift to the letter of the law, to much evidence, and to common sense. The Baptist Reverend Richard Fuller, debating the antislavery Baptist Reverend Francis Wayland, dismissed the notion that property in man reduced slaves to chattel. Property in furniture differs from property in a horse, and property in a horse differs from property in man. To treat horses like furniture would be "barbarous." Wayland retorted that the master's right to compel service required severe slave laws. Slavery thereby stood condemned, for the master had to curb the slave's moral and intellectual development, lest he encourage rebellion. Fuller charged that Wayland begged the question. Capitalists held free laborers to service, if by different means. Power, not right, remained at issue, and Wayland's doctrine undermined all authority and legitimate power.[18]

The notion of property in services undergirded the theory of "warranteeism" advanced by Henry Hughes of Mississippi and its corollary, that the southern social system did not constitute slavery at all. In support of Hughes's formulation, William Gilmore Simms of South Carolina, E. A. Pollard of Virginia, and Alexander Stephens of Georgia called slavery "a misnomer." T. R. R. Cobb of Georgia and George Sawyer of Louisiana – substantial legal scholars – reviewed court records to demonstrate that "chattel" applied to slaves only for specific purposes and that slaves had rights to their own bodies. In 1848, Jefferson Davis called slavery "property held to service" and "a common-law right to property in the services of man." In 1861, a contributor to the *Southern Literary Messenger* cited the Confederate Constitution to maintain that, strictly speaking, slavery did not exist in the United States.[19]

Strong voices nevertheless arose to defend property in man. Chancellor William Harper of South Carolina called it a legally sanctioned social relation; Alexander McCaine of Maryland called it a moral imperative. When, in 1840, Governor William H. Seward of New York refused comity in fugitive slave cases, Conway Robinson of Virginia angrily replied that property in man inhered in the concept of private property and that the North's demurral created an insurmountable obstacle to sectional reconciliation. In 1841, the *Raleigh Register* and the *Charleston Mercury* protested the timidity of Southerners who shrank from defense of property in man. Twenty years later, the *Georgia Weekly Telegraph* defended property in man by citing biblical references to slaves as "money." Representative Sampson W. Harris of Alabama appealed to the authority of the Founding Fathers to sustain the slaveholder's right to recapture a fugitive slave, over whom he exercised claim to his person, not merely to his service. George P. Elliott defiantly declared: "If there exists in the whole revelation of biblical theology and morals, anything second only to the declared advent of the Messiah, it is the establishment of the right of man in man as property." The Reverend Joseph R. Wilson characterized a slave as in permanent bondage to a master, having full legal power over him. In 1861, Robert H. Smith of Alabama proclaimed that the Confederacy disdained euphemisms and called its blacks "slaves." The influential John Fletcher of New Orleans strove for nuance: "Qualifiedly, we are the property of the great family of man, and are under obligations of duty to all; more pressingly, to the national community of which we compose a part, and so on down to the distinct family of which we are a member." Men hold all property as a trust; slaves cannot be treated as mere brutes. Fletcher concluded that if a man had absolute property in his own person – as antislavery men asserted – then he had the right to alienate it.[20]

Proslavery divines respected Fletcher but balked at his reasoning. Thornwell denied that masters owned slaves' bodies and heatedly upheld the principle of control of services. In reply to William Ellery Channing, he echoed Hegel (without attribution) and invoked the English theologian John Taylor on Ignatius Loyola to describe property in a man as "a palpable impossibility." Thornwell labeled a "flagrant contradiction" an attempt to appropriate the conscience, will, and understanding of another human being. The Methodist Bishop Henry Bascom and the Catholic Bishop John England agreed that property in man belonged to Jesus Christ. They declared unlawful a slavery that reduced the slave to a commodity held by a master with full dominion over him.[21]

Southern Presbyterians – S. J. Cassells, R. L. Dabney, John Adger, William Pope Harrison, Charles Colcock Jones, Ferdinand Jacobs – stood with Thornwell, as did spokesmen for other Protestant denominations in the South and such prominent clerical and lay Northerners as John Henry Hopkins, Samuel Seabury, Solon Robinson, and John Richter Jones. "J. F. S.," a southern Methodist, ridiculed Henry Wadsworth Longfellow for thinking that masters owned slaves' bodies. The Baptist Reverend Thornton Stringfellow of Virginia condemned Roman law for reducing the slave to the status of a thing and praised southern law for recognizing his human rights. He recalled that God forbade the coveting of a neighbor's house, wife, man or maidservant, ox, or horse: "Here is a patriarchal catalogue of property, having God for its author, the wife among the rest."[22]

The argument for property solely in services buckled under antislavery criticism. In 1836 a committee of the Presbyterian Synod of Kentucky supported gradual emancipation: "[The slave's] very body, his muscles, his bones, his flesh, are all the property of another." The committee condemned heartrending family separation and other atrocities. Wayland and others dismissed proslavery philosophical and legal dialectics as worthless abstractions, arguing simply and sensibly that enforcement of property rights in slaves' services required command of the body. The Reverend R. T. Stanton of Connecticut asked: If slaves are not chattel, why do not the laws protect their marriages and family relations? Thornwell and other usually well-tempered southern divines responded furiously, betraying a sense that they found this abolitionist argument unanswerable.[23]

A rational kernel of the slaveholders' denial of property in man may be gleaned from Orlando Patterson's wry comment that the law granted husbands and wives firm property rights in each other's persons:

> If we do not accept the Roman and civil law conception of absolute ownership, then ownership, stripped of its social and emotional rhetoric, is simply another name for property; it can only mean claims and powers vis-à-vis other persons with respect to a given thing, person, or action. This is what a master possesses with respect to his slave; it is also exactly what a person possesses with respect to his or her spouse, child, employee, or land.[24]

Calvin H. Wiley, defending the extended slaveholding household, inadvertently cast in a new light the thesis that slavery unified labor and capital. He stressed that even a non-Christian master could not avoid sympathy for his slaves: "He sees, hears, feels all the troubles of his servants." Appealing to the principles espoused in Adam Smith's *Theory of Moral Sentiments*, Wiley wrote: "The owner of the African slave is his absolute master; & he has but one plain interest which can only be subserved by the obedience, industry & honesty of his slave." But if that is the case, what happens to Wiley's notion that the "absolute master" holds property in his slave's labor, not in his body?[25]

Despite embarrassments, the slaveholders pressed on. In 1829, William Branch Giles and James Madison echoed the Virginians of the federal Constitutional Convention, refusing to base representation for slaves in property rights. They defined slaves as persons whose masters had a duty to represent them and protect their rights. The Methodist Reverend William A. Smith of Virginia, a professor of moral philosophy, described "domestic slavery" as "part of the family relation" in which the master controls the time and labor of family members, including slaves. Southern slavery constituted "one of the forms of the general system of slavery," which includes English villeinage, Russian serfdom, and Mexican peonage. The Arminian Smith and the Calvinist Thornwell led southern divines in projecting a Christian household that included laborers. They moved from a defense of slavery as one possible social system to espousal of slavery as a model for the future. Yet Southerners had inadvertently abandoned their own principle. By agreeing to the constitutional compromise that counted three-fifths rather than all slaves for electoral purposes, they retreated from the concept of a hierarchical household in which the master represented all members.[26]

The Congregationalist Reverend George Cheever countered for the abolitionists: "The right of representation includes and necessitates the right of suffrage." Wendell Phillips cited the British Chartists to warn that employers could coerce workers into voting their way, although he thought American workers not easily coerced. In reply, Dabney declared laborers justly disfranchised under slavery, since "[t]hey were at the same time made parts of the families of the ruling class." Accepting hierarchy as a fact of life, Dabney located its origins not in church or state but in the family, defined to include slaves. A delicious irony: In 1850, opponents of constitutional reform in Louisiana complained that the counting of slaves for legislative apportionment in effect gave them the vote.[27]

Defense of ownership of the body grew slowly but steadily in the eighteenth century. A doctrine based on a right to service passed into a doctrine of personal estate, with laborers as property. As property in the body emerged as practice, the theoretical distinction faded. Yet, from the beginning, all except the most obtuse or cynical slaveholders recognized that property in man's body could not morally or practically be rendered absolute and that, therefore, the theoretical and legal problem remained.[28]

In South Carolina during the War, the contradictions in the attempt to transform ownership of human beings into the ownership of services inspired a wicked satire in a "Memorial to the Convention of the Episcopal Church." Deadpan, it called for denial of the Book of Common Prayer to slaves, since it was designed for "congregations of responsible beings capable of form- ing domestic ties and enjoying personal rights." Obviously, slaves had to be excluded: "It is, therefore, as a whole unfit for congregations, where the front pews *own* the free sittings – assemblages composed, in varying proportions, of two classes of Christians, one of which bought the other yesterday and may sell it to-morrow."[29]

Household Problems

The household might have been perfectly idyllic, but in whom could the master and mistress place confidence? Elizabeth Thom of piedmont Virginia trusted her mammy to exercise a healthy influence over the children, but she trusted no one else's mammy to do as well. The antislavery Harriet Martineau thought that black nurses taught white children to lie and be slovenly. Mary Howard School- craft of Beaufort, South Carolina, wrote, "Nothing is more potent in a child's mind than the prejudice its black nurse instills against a step-mother." "A Former Resident of Slaves States" held mammies responsible for the spoiled- brat character of slaveholding boys. Charles William Holbrook of Mas- sachusetts, a tutor on a plantation in North Carolina, reported with disgust that his pupil had lice combed from her hair: "Horror! she gets them from the little niggars." Governor Henry A. Wise of Virginia did not appreciate every- thing taught by his black nurse, for he hired a white nurse for his own children. He did not want them pampered as he had been.[30]

Whites nonetheless acknowledged that they learned a great deal from slaves. Some illiterate slaves had wide practical experience and marvelous memories for detail, from which white children profited. J. G. Clinkscales said of Unc' Essick (uncle Essex): "He knew so much and could do so many things. His uniform kindness to us and his unfailing patience with us very greatly endeared him to us." Dembo, the carriage driver, taught the children of Caleb and Hannah Coker about wild animals. "Uncle Jim" taught Atticus Greene Haygood of Georgia to hunt and fish. Here and there, slaveholders hired out slave women to care for white children.[31]

Agricultural reformers, notably John Taylor of Caroline in *Arator* (1818), railed against planter absenteeism, firing their heaviest salvos at the dangerous practice of entrusting plantations to overseers. Unlike the big planters of Virginia, those of the Carolina/Georgia low country preferred to live in port cities – Charleston, Beaufort, Savannah. Absenteeism grew with expansion into the upcountry. Lowcountry planters left their plantations up to six months at a time; some went to their plantations perhaps only twice a year. Residents of middle and northern Georgia, for example, owned plantations in southwestern Early County. Jesse Sanford of Milledgeville, Georgia, died in 1827 with hundreds of slaves distributed among six plantations. J. H. Hammond, in a spirited defense of slavery, admitted the presence of the evil in the South Carolina low country. In response, some planters refused to divide their plantations even when they proved economically unwieldy. Ashbel Smith of Texas – "much attached" to his slaves – would not risk their being mistreated out of his sight. Maunsel White of Louisiana, an absentee, learned of trouble among the slaves on his son's plantation: "No man nowadays should own a plantation without living on it all the time." Managerial efficiency nonetheless compelled the division of plantations once the slave force reached eighty or so. Ideally, a father ran one plantation and his sons the others.[32]

Although most absenteeism remained "local," a good many slaveholders visited their out-of-state plantations. Wade Hampton II, one of the largest, lived in Columbia, South Carolina, but spent much of the fall and winter at his plantations in Mississippi. He managed his nine hundred slaves competently despite time spent in hunting and at racetracks. Gustavus Henry of Tennessee, who devoted most of his time to politics, visited his Mississippi plantation regularly to see that the overseer managed efficiently and humanely. Francis Terry Leak of Mississippi took his family for a six-week visit to his second plantation in Arkansas. Although some planters owned plantations in another state or at a great distance within the same state, even most of the bigger planters did not. Rather, like William L. Yancey, they lived in towns and, in the words of the Baptist Reverend Iveson Brookes, "performed the (to me irksome) task of riding over to my Plantation in the forenoon." Others set up a second plantation nearby under a son or overseer. In the Mississippi River cotton parishes of Louisiana in 1860, local absenteeism ran from about 35 percent in Tensas to 81 percent in Concordia, with other parishes at about 40 percent. Away from the Mississippi River, absenteeism ran about 15 percent. Sugar planters were more likely to live on their plantations in order to provide close management. In black-belt counties across the South, local absenteeism often ran above 50 percent, with most planters living in the nearby towns from which they rode out to their plantations twice a week. Few planters in Texas lived in town. Another decade might have produced greater absenteeism, but

Texas resembled the North Carolina low country, which did not have many absentees.[33]

Presumably, plantation management suffered even from local absenteeism. Catherine Edmondston of North Carolina worried that her constant absences made her slaves "awkward, inefficient, and even lazy." The Methodist Reverend H. N. McTyeire, supported by other denominational leaders, warned Christian planters against blaming overseers for mistreatment of slaves. Bishop Andrew dwelt on the "thousands" of absentee planters, especially in the rice and sugar districts. "A Planter" observed that the instruction of slaves in Christian doctrine and ethics required overseers who were committed Christians.[34]

The abolitionist Angelina Grimké overshot her mark when she criticized South Carolina planters for spending less than half the year on their plantations, occupying much of their time with politics, sports, and parties and taking the condition of their slaves on trust from the overseers' reports. She did not explain her reason for thinking that slaves would fare better under the watchful eyes of the masters she tirelessly berated as power-drunk, selfish, irresponsible, and even sadistic. The biggest planters had too many slaves to know them personally, but some large absentee planters like Zachary Taylor ranked among those with good reputations as solicitous masters who knew their people. Nathaniel Heyward, the largest rice planter of his day, managed between 2,000 and 2,500 slaves on 17 plantations clustered around the Combahee River. He certainly did not know most of them, yet he remained in residence and reputedly never sold a slave. Charles Heywood, Nathaniel's son, did know his 500 slaves. Account books, diaries, and correspondence reveal that planters with as many as a hundred slaves knew them, albeit some a great deal better than others. A grotesque telltale sign of the direct contact: Almost invariably, masters gave personal attention to runaways. Frequently, masters protested that slaves ran away without provocation and had suffered no ill treatment – a judgment the slaves doubtless did not share. In such cases, even usually mild masters had all the self-justification they needed for whipping with extreme severity.[35]

Slave Sales

"Our family, white and black," had its reality, but a grimly qualified reality it was. The burning contradiction in the ideology of the southern household lay in slave sales. Slaveholders argued that throughout the world, notably in Africa, poor people sold their children into slavery. The slaveholders knew, however, that the practice had largely disappeared from the parts of Europe they considered the most civilized.[36]

Proslavery replies might easily be dismissed as dishonest, did not so many come from people deservedly known for probity. Incredibly, Armstrong defied overwhelming evidence to rebuff vehemently accusations of family breakups. Why, he had never seen such a thing. But then, Louisa and David McCord had never seen a slave trader welcomed into a gentleman's home. Edmund Ruffin had never heard of bloodhounds used to chase runaways. A big planter assured a British traveler that he had never heard of a grown slave's being whipped.

Yet those who counted themselves among "The Chivalry" did not hesitate to separate spouses by sale if one proved recalcitrant. John Brown, a fugitive slave from Georgia, replied tartly to Julia Tyler: "It is all very well for Mrs. Tyler to say that families are not often separated. I know better than that, and so does she."[37]

The crudest proslavery spokesmen argued that blacks invested little affection in each other and quickly got over a sense of loss. Private papers and public testimonials show that few slaveholders swallowed that cant. Usually, Southerners admitted the evil and replied *tu quoque*, feebly arguing that economic pressures drove poor northern families westward and compelled as many involuntary separations as occurred among southern slaves. A contributor to the *Southern Presbyterian Review* maintained that slave families suffered fewer forced separations than families of laborers anywhere in the world. Ostensibly, masters separated husbands from wives and parents from children only for "fault" – for making trouble. Joseph Jones of Savannah regretted that his parents had sold a troublesome slave family since it included Lafayette, his favorite slave. Lafayette, weeping bitterly, chose to remain with the Joneses rather than go with his unfeeling and often cruel father.[38]

The primary argument rested on economic exigency. Creditors pressed masters. Almost no one defended the separation of husbands and wives, although many may have been indifferent. But it seemed more humane to sell a young slave or two rather than risk foreclosure and the breakup of the plantation household. Henry Hughes, protesting the breakup of slave families, allowed a small exception – unless necessary for family subsistence. Unfortunately, in a debt-ridden, cash-poor economy, that necessity plagued more slaveholders than Southerners cared to count. The argument proved worse than none at all, for it damned slavery by forgiving the sinner while testifying to the sin.[39]

McTyeire consoled distressed whites by interpreting sales from economic necessity as protection against impoverishment, since it transferred slaves from impecunious owners to those capable of caring for them. Marianne Palmer Gaillard and Elizabeth Randolph were not easily consoled. Gaillard prayed for the Christian forbearance to face her family's economic difficulties. She grieved over the "unavoidable" sale of slaves: "I cannot part with them with as little concern as though they were cattle." Randolph wrote to her daughter Mary when her father had to sell some slaves. "I never saw people more distressed than one & all, and yr. Papa not the least, he says he never was so much distressed in life & determined never to part with any more." The English-born Amelia Barr found Memphis "charming" but never forgot the hopelessness on the faces of the black women at slave auctions. A much-distressed Rachel O'Connor of Louisiana had to sell slaves to cover debts. Plaintively, she asked her half-brother not to disrupt slave families and, in particular, to take good care of Patience, who had served loyally for twenty-two years.[40]

Sandie Pendleton appealed to his uncle John Page for financial help to get through college. The financially shaky Page promised to help "even if I had to sell a Negro." The northern-born Corinna Brown, who married into a planter family in Florida, said – perhaps facetiously – that she was anxious to visit Rome and was willing "to sell a couple of 'niggers' & start off." A different kind of story: Keziah Brevard sold five impudent slaves rather than impose "such servants on any of my heirs."[41]

The abolitionist Charles Elliott admitted that "thousands" of slaveholders tried not to split families but that economic pressures left them little choice. Just so. Jefferson, for example, insisted that he would never willingly sell a slave to pay debts and would remain governed by their happiness. Even the enormously wealthy Manigaults saw their rice plantation swept by five epidemics between 1848 and 1854, with a net loss of ninety-two slaves. The Manigaults had the resources to weather the financial storm, but they had to replace those slaves. A slave bought meant a slave sold, often with separations. Richard Yeager of Kentucky long treated his slave mistress and their children well until one day he saw a chance for a financial killing. He sold his mistress and three boys – separately. Years later, Isaac Johnson, one of the sons, cried out: "He had sold his own flesh and blood. That is what made American slavery possible. That is the 'Divine institution' we have heard so much about, the cornerstone of the proposed Confederacy." Slave sales turned the stomachs of those who witnessed them. Joseph B. Cobb, Mississippi's popular writer, portrayed the horrors of the domestic slave trade and the separation of families for all to see. After the War, J. S. Wise penned a fond portrait of life in old Virginia but concluded that the mere sight of a slave auction should have told Southerners that slavery was wrong.[42]

Slaveholders oscillated between self-confidence and folly, between special pleading and whining, between self-congratulation and exasperation. In Boston, the black Baptist Reverend J. Sella Martin eschewed satire in an address to a mass meeting called to protest the hanging of John Brown: "Cruelty is part and parcel of the system. If slavery is right at all, then its terrors and horrors – the whip, the manacle, the thumbscrew, the paddle, the stake, the gibbet – are right also."[43]

Proslavery apologetics sometimes descended to the ludicrous. In 1856, Edwin Heriot of Charleston charged – without pretense of evidence – that "low" nonslaveholders committed nine-tenths of the cruelties against slaves. The antislavery Josiah Quincy of Massachusetts inadvertently offered support for Heriot's position. He charged slavery with reduction of the mass of southern nonslaveholders to degradation in some respects worse than that suffered by the blacks. Yet after the War, planters promulgated Black Codes based on the assumption that control of labor required control of the laborers' bodies. Neither the slaveholders nor their successors could reply adequately to the abolitionist challenge. Without de facto if not indeed de jure ownership, just how were they supposed to secure control of plantation labor?[44]

3

Strangers within the Gates

> And the Lord said unto Moses and Aaron, This is the ordnance of the Passover: There shall no stranger eat thereof: But every man's servant that is bought for money, when thou has circumcised him, then shall he eat thereof. A foreigner and a hired servant shall not eat thereof.
>
> – Exodus 12:43–45

When southern slaveholders dared, they proclaimed themselves masters of all they surveyed despite the ambiguous status of hired whites. Yet, "plantation" and "household" were by no means identical terms. Able plantation employees, white and free black – even most tutors and governesses – won respect but, with few exceptions, did not qualify as members of the "family, white and black." David Brown, a northern missionary, observed that Southerners used "household" in the "Scripture sense, including slaves, but not *hirelings*." Hugh Legaré of South Carolina, among others, traced the southern distinction between slaves and free workers to ancient Jewish law and to Roman law and tradition, which reduced employees to servile status.[1]

Sundry White Servants

Transatlantic public opinion stigmatized white servants as dishonest, lazy, and untrustworthy. Hence, when Paul Trapier of South Carolina entered Harvard in 1822, he was astonished to find himself waited on by white servants. By the 1850s, however, some elite families in port cities – Charleston, Mobile, Savannah – had white servants. The hiring of a good white nurse occasioned self-congratulation in Charleston since, as a contributor to the *Southern Presbyterian Review* complained, native whites, no matter how poor, shunned servants' work. Clara Solomon of New Orleans hated to lose Mary, her Irish maid, who left to take care of her own relatives: "These Irish girls, their most fault is in having such a quantity of relations." Rosalie Roos of Sweden reported that Charlestonians considered black servants much more reliable than "lazy" and "insolent" whites, who, if dissatisfied, left at will. Grace Brown Elmore of Columbia expressed a common thought – black servants were much more loyal than white.[2]

Many Southerners, especially elite women, had difficulty in seeing Irish servants as white. Northerners did no better. Employers took vast liberties with their supposedly dependent creatures, who resented the condescension. Since Northerners stigmatized Irish servants much as Southerners stigmatized blacks, they often put up with incompetence if accompanied by cheerful deference. Letitia A. Burwell of Virginia found that New Yorkers worked white servants harder than Virginians worked black slaves and showed them less consideration. Eliza Middleton Fisher wrote to her mother in the Carolina low country that everyone in Philadelphia judged black servants "more respectful & manageable" than white. Thomas Low Nichols, who admired the South, thought that southern blacks had impeccable manners and carried themselves with grace and dignity, in stark contrast to northern free blacks. Wealthy Americans, like the wealthy everywhere, demanded deference, punctuality, efficiency, good cheer, and obedience. But those sterling qualities rarely appeared among northern servants, who – if we may credit the whining of their betters – grew worse over time. Matilda Charlotte Houstoun, an English novelist, described the few American-born servants in New York as well-paid and cheeky rather than deferential, and she found both Irish and black servants held in contempt.[3]

Complaints about white servants abounded. Embarrassed foreigners objected to being seated in inns at table with their own or other people's servants. In private homes, employers complained that the "help" acted as if they were doing a favor by showing up for work. Note: "help," not "servants"; "employers," not "masters" or even "bosses." However much immigrants needed jobs, they carried high heads, provoking complaints of sauciness. In the 1840s and 1850s, Irish immigrants in northeastern cities pushed free blacks out of jobs as domestics, waiters, and hotel servants. Some Northerners, speaking of servants, tried to promote the illusion of "family," especially as the prestige of domestic labor declined. Southerners snorted. The *Mississippi Free Trader and Natchez Gazette* reprinted a piece from Boston's *Daily Mail* that blistered Northerners who treated domestics as little more than "white slaves" and "mere machines." Few white women in the South, no matter how poor, worked as domestics before or after the war.[4]

Benjamin Silliman and other well-traveled Yankees concluded that the fixed order of social classes rendered British servants content with their lot. Southerners who traveled north or to England judged those white servants more harshly. Generally, they decided that their own irritating house slaves were not so bad after all. Thomas Jefferson allowed that, when in Washington, he preferred white servants, "who when they misbehave, can be exchanged." Maria Bryan Harford of Georgia, visiting the North, expressed surprise at meeting a kind, obliging white servant, for such were rare. In the 1830s, Lucien Minor of Virginia reported that genteel New Englanders raged over the poor quality and insolence of white servants and the high wages they commanded. He seemed bemused by servants who accepted only specific tasks, whereas southern slaves had to do as they were told. The conservative Sarah Mytton Maury of England defended American servants against her countrywomen's fault finding. American servants, she wrote in the 1840s, were better paid, more respectful, and less disposed to steal. She praised white and black, free and slave, but expressed special admiration for the house slaves of New Orleans. Southerners, she added, spoke more respectfully to their house slaves than Northerners did to their servants. Amelia Murray reinforced the characterization of northern servants as more trouble than they were worth. Yet she said that southern black servants – notwithstanding cheerfulness, deference, and formal obedience – knew how to get away with murder and do everything except the essential tasks. Sara Pryor of Virginia concurred but with a difference. She said of Mammy Grace of the Gilmer household that when she curtseyed and said, "Your servant, master," she displayed not so much deference as "dignified self-respect."[5]

During the War, New Englanders cried out for black domestic servants, whom they expected to prove superior to the whites they had long put up with. Alas, few blacks were willing to leave the South for the proffered brave new world. After the War, David Macrae of Scotland remarked that, at best, northern mistresses lived with white maids in a state of "armed neutrality." Southern women who moved to the North gnashed their teeth over the well-nigh unbearable independence and impertinence of white servants.[6]

During the 1850s, white domestics appeared with increasing frequency on plantations and in wealthy townhouses. Indeed, they became something of a fad in chic circles in and around Natchez and Mobile. Despite a reputation for sexual promiscuity, deceit, thievery, and insubordination, Irish and German girls began to replace black maids. Here and there, French cooks and nurses pushed out black mammies. A few communities – Jews in Mobile, Moravians in central North Carolina, some colleges and public institutions – preferred white servants to black, whether from distaste for slavery or for blacks or for some other reason.[7]

In the early 1850s, the Methodist *Southern Lady's Companion* of Nashville endorsed an appeal by Sarah J. Hale for the training of women physicians. Speaking in Philadelphia and Boston, she denounced the growing practice of admitting northern men to midwifery and complimented New England for beginning to sanction women physicians, who assured "delicacy" in the treatment of patients and spurred necessary research in sexual disorders. During the War, James Norman, C.S.A., informed his wife that white ladies faced hostility from the soldiers they volunteered to serve. "Several ladies of the highest character & respectability have angel like driven down from Mobile," only to become the object of base and shameful remarks. In the South, poorer white women as well as doctors' wives set themselves up as professionals, and plantation mistresses often turned to white neighbors for themselves and their slaves. Amelia Henry of Charleston, the mother of a respected Jewish politician, practiced for many years, but physicians, coveting the business, railed against allegedly incompetent midwives.[8]

The ladies of Richmond charged Varina Davis with disloyalty for hiring a white nurse, although the well-to-do of Washington had long hired Irish "Biddies" for their children. Frederick Law Olmsted reported from Natchez that more and more of the richest planters were turning to Frenchwomen to care for their children. Newspaper advertisements suggest that white and free black wet nurses found steady employment. Still, many available white women did not look appealing. The Reverend James Henley Thornwell's wife wanted a white wet nurse, but the Reverend James Adger, after scouring advertisements in Charleston, told him: "One of them only was white, and she had a child a year old and was such a dirty looking creature that I am sure Mrs. Thornwell would not let her touch her child. I fear there is no chance of getting such a nurse as you want here." C. C. Jones, Jr., of Georgia, having fired a nurse, offered to pay well for a replacement. He moaned, "Very little satisfaction is to be experienced with hired servants."[9]

Mary Howard Schoolcraft of Beaufort, South Carolina, turned aside French chefs: "The blacks are proverbially cleaner in scouring the cooking-pots, and securing fresh water from the spring to put them to boil, than any *white* French cook, of much greater pretension." R. Q. Mallard of Georgia considered French cooks inferior to black cooks in the preparation of wholesome and tasty food: "The African female intellect has natural genius . . . for cooking."[10]

Southern travelers to Europe returned with stories about the eternal "servant problem." They found white menials an execrable lot, unfit for the confidence of ladies and gentlemen; conversely, they considered black slaves, despite faults, a blessing. Floride Calhoun preferred white servants. Her spirited daughter did not. From Belgium in 1846, Anna Maria Clemson wrote to her father John C. Calhoun: "I wish Mother could have six months trial of the meanness, debased condition, & utter want of truth, & honesty, among the servants of this country." A trial would make her mother "sick of white servants for life." She added, "I don't know what I should do without Basil, who tho' careless & negro like, is faithful, & honest, & really a treasure to me." Observation of northern white servants led Southerners to appreciate their often-maligned black house servants. Dr. Richard D. Arnold of Savannah wrote to his daughter Ellen of Philadelphia, "I do not believe anybody, North or South, has better servants than we have. God knows I should be very unwilling to exchange them for mere hirelings." The northern-born Margaret Junkin Preston allowed that Virginians sometimes spoiled their servants, but added, "Is not this better than the utter and entire want of interest and sympathy that exists between Northern mistresses and their domestics?"[11]

Some Northerners who moved to the South resisted prevalent southern mores and ideology, and some combined attitudes. During the War, the Union General Benjamin Butler denounced transplanted Northerners for carrying southern views in their hearts and for being the worst of rebels. Henry E. Handerson successfully tutored in plantation families in Louisiana, went on to a fine career in medicine, and won recognition for his translation of Johann Hermann Baas's *Outlines of the History of Medicine and the Medical*

Profession. Handerson loved the Union, disliked slavery, and opposed secession; he nonetheless imbibed southern racial attitudes and served in the Confederate army. Some Northerners with no apparent sympathy for secession or southern political principles declined to leave. The friends of Cathie Morrill urged her to return to Maine in 1861, but she remained in Virginia for another two years. Tutoring for a family in Charlottesville, she received "only great kindness and courtesy." Caroline Seabury of Massachusetts, who taught French at Columbus Female Institute in Mississippi, moved north during the War only after much soul searching, for she had developed a fond attachment to her community. She was fired from the Institute simply for being northern-born and despite recognition as a local heroine for her selfless efforts during the smallpox epidemic of 1857. Instead of leaving, she became a tutor in the family of Col. George Hampton Young, a large planter.[12]

Some nurses and governesses found themselves assimilated to the white household. Others, although not considered family members, held special places. John Berkeley Grimball managed his white servant's financial affairs. The widowed John P. Kelly, a mill owner in Culpeper County, Virginia, left his home and children to Frances Thornhill, his competent white housekeeper. During and after confinement not every lady trusted her slave nurse. Eliza Clinch's excellent Sarah was expecting herself, and the smart and efficient Fanny did not want to be troubled with children. Clinch found that the demand for good nurses, white or free black, outran the supply.[13]

Governesses and Tutors

"The drawing room is the nursery," Mary Hering Middleton of South Carolina wrote in 1841, after being driven crazy by quarreling children. Hired white women assumed considerable responsibility in planter families. When they did well, they often won the family's lasting affection. An English governess taught Mary Bayard Devereaux Clarke of North Carolina and her sisters at home, while their brother John went to Yale. The family believed that the young women received as good an education at home as John did at Yale. Mary Clarke's subsequent careers as an author and editor bore them out. Mrs. Burnley, a slaveholding widow, did various chores for the family of Francis Taylor, who included her in family dinners and social functions. Julia Tyler of New York, the wife of President John Tyler, preferred Irish servants and formed a particularly strong attachment to Catherine Wing, who managed the black servants for her. The Belgian-born Rosalie Stier Calvert, uncomfortable with blacks, hired a white servant for herself and her children. Eugenia Levy Phillips of Mobile, a fervent secessionist and the wife of a prominent Jewish politician, hired as a "confidential maid" Phoebe Dunlap, an Irishwoman who became her fast friend and lived with her for fifteen years. On John Houston Bills's large plantation in Tennessee, Mrs. McNeal excelled in care of his children for six years: "A most excellent lady – possessing a superior mind & was truly a mother to the writer."[14]

Anne Royall of Maryland, a stormy petrel of political journalism, growled that the well-to-do in Alabama had slaves and illiterate whites care for their children and then paid tutors to "unlearn" their children's bad English. Yet the ladies in long-established communities found "excellent" white nurses. The lowcountry Allstons had a fine Irish nurse, Mary O'Shea, and Miss Ayme, a governess and tutor, whom they applauded despite her gossip about family affairs. Others hired white women who doubled as seamstresses or performed other functions. Some poor whites lived on the periphery of the household. In South Carolina, Aleck Woodward's master gave Sallie Carlisle, a poor woman, a house and garden on his plantation, where she wove, sewed, and taught trades to young slaves.[15]

Not all white servants behaved well. A widowed planter in North Carolina married the family's New England servant, only to find her dreadful and a cruel mistress. Why had he acted so hastily? "My people needed a mistress, my children a mother." It was bad enough when old Mrs. Speights got caught stealing from the Wallace household in Norfolk; it got worse when she spread false stories about Elizabeth Curtis Wallace and her neighbors, bringing the occupying Yankees down on their heads. Some turned out too well to suit public opinion. Henry Middleton of South Carolina brought a German woman to Washington as governess for his daughters. To the consternation of high society, she married the Prussian ambassador.[16]

In eighteenth-century Virginia and the Carolinas, tutors, like governesses, entered the family circle more easily than other hired whites. They included indentured servants, freemen in search of gainful employment, and ministers who supplemented their income. Female tutors ranged from indentured servants to respectable but financially strapped widows. Tutors then and long afterward expected to be received into the family circle. William J. Welles wrote to Ebenezer Pettigrew upon accepting appointment as family tutor in 1827, "It is now in my power with pleasure (to myself) to comply with your obliging engagement of me, as making one of your family – and it is hoped, that by a steady and punctual attendance on my part, to the tuition and morals & manners of your children, I shall merit the approbation of madam Pettigrew & yourself." John Davis, a tutor on Thomas Drayton's plantation in South Carolina, was entranced:

> The affability and tenderness of this charming family in the bosom of the woods will be ever cherished in my breast, and long recorded, I hope, in this page. My wants were always anticipated. The family Library was transported without entreaty into my chamber; paper and the apparatus for writing were placed on my table; and once, having lamented that my stock of segars was nearly exhausted, a negro was dispatched seventy miles to *Charleston* for a supply of the best *Spanish*.[17]

Planters welcomed as good friends, but not as members of the household, the children of neighboring planters who tutored in their families. More commonly, presentable middle-class young men went on to fine careers after having tutored children of wealthy planters. No few college professors, lawyers, and ministers began as tutors, among them Henry W. Allen, the Confederate governor of Louisiana. Henry Timrod, who loved poetry and hated the study of law, tutored for the Lowndes family. Alexander Glennie, the rector of All Saints Episcopal Church, arrived in South Carolina from England to tutor Francis Marion Weston's son. William Henry Foote, the historian, taught Stuart Robinson, an Old School Presbyterian leader in Kentucky. R. R. Howison of Virginia, an historian, taught Marion Harland and her sister, whose father demanded that they be taught as rigorously as boys. Margaret Junkin regretted that home schooling deprived her of school discipline and the companionship of classmates.[18]

Francis Terry Leak of Mississippi hired David Laughton to tutor his children and then secured for him a professorship of ancient languages and belles lettres at Franklin Female College in Holly Springs. The politically charged but personally amicable relations of Jefferson Davis and John A. Quitman began sweetly enough: When Davis was a lad, Quitman tutored him in Spanish. In the Delta, a Mr. Herbert read *Paradise Lost* with the seventeen-year-old Harry St. John Dixon but proved incapable of teaching him algebra. When Charles Dabney studied at William and Mary in 1849, he warned his father to prepare his younger sibling more carefully. His able tutor had not prepared him in mathematics as well as in Greek and Latin. And learning at home had cut him off from the rough-and-tumble relations with peers he now faced in college. He urged that his siblings be sent to a local school for at least a year before they entered college.[19]

Tutors often became local schoolteachers. A planter who let his children's tutor a neighbor's child risked being deluged with requests from other neighbors. Before long, the "private tutor" became the local schoolmaster. The northern-born S. S. Prentiss began his flamboyant career in Mississippi politics as a plantation tutor and metamorphosed into the local schoolmaster. So did professional tutors like Catherine Cooper Hopley of England. Virginia's highest social circles welcomed and respected these tutors, who participated, if marginally, in family circles.[20]

Good tutors did not come cheap. As late as the 1840s and 1850s, some plantation districts lacked schools, and the children of the well-to-do relied on tutors. Salaries varied widely, depending on range of subjects and extent of duties as governesses and disciplinarians. Amos Kendall earned every penny of the $300 a year Henry Clay paid him to tutor his ungovernable brats. In much of the South, $300 annually (a common overseer's salary) was considered about right. As the need for tutors outran the supply, salaries rose. In South Carolina by the late 1840s, salaries for the best had risen to $400–500, and William Gilmore Simms heard that William Gregg, the wealthy industrialist, paid $1,000. He also reported that Samuel Burns, an exceptional tutor in Charleston, had retired with a fortune. In the late 1850s the Allstons paid Miss Ayme $500 a year, but in Mississippi, Leak paid half as much. What did these salaries mean to tutors? In 1852, Tryphena Blanche Holder of Massachusetts moved to Mississippi as a plantation tutor. Paid a few hundred dollars plus room and board, she made enough money to help her widowed mother in Massachusetts. She married Dr. David Raymond Fox, a small slaveholder and physician in Plaquemines Parish, Louisiana.[21]

Joseph Holt Ingraham thought that a "very great" number of plantation tutors in the Southwest were not worth the money. In 1833, David Rice, a Pennsylvania-born sugar and cotton planter in St. Martin's Parish, Louisiana, drafted a reply to a request for information on local education. He crossed out the following outburst: "I have known more than one young man in this country whose Fathers had employed private tutors in their families for several years who were incapable of making the most simple calculations." In South Carolina, Simms, frustrated by unsatisfactory tutors and the lack of a good school, saw the best tutors lured elsewhere by large salaries. Charles Dabney of Mississippi complained that his generally able tutor did not prepare him well enough to enter William and Mary. A disgusted Edmund Ruffin reported that Virginians had to send to New England for competent tutors. The well-recommended woman he hired to tutor his daughter proved deficient in scholarship and manners. A different problem: Lucy Rebecca Buck of Virginia, tutoring her younger siblings, cried, "I'm convinced my forte is not the management of juvenile masculinity."[22]

Occasionally, a tutor married his pupil. After graduating from the College of Charleston, John Girardeau, the Presbyterian theologian, tutored for Thomas Hamilton and married his daughter Penelope. Enoch Hanford of Connecticut, a Yale graduate, who became a professor of languages at South Carolina College and a prominent lawyer, married one of the children he had tutored for William DeWitt of Society Hill. Mary McLean Bryant of Ithaca, New York, tutored for Duncan Cameron, remained single, and settled in as a permanent member of the family. The Bavarian Charles Dolkert, "professor of music," in Oakbowery, Alabama, taught school and tutored for Edward S. McCurdy, who welcomed him and his wife into the family circle. Some Yankee women went south to marry a rich planter, arousing no special resentment unless they proved indifferent teachers.[23]

The closer a tutor drew to the family circle, the more control he or she had over the children's discipline. And that sometimes led to unpleasantness. Tutors in eighteenth-century Virginia had considerable latitude to punish lazy pupils, although trouble might ensue when one parent proved softer than the other. An overseer who rose to become a planter asked a prospective tutor, "Can you *drive* well, Sir." But some parents who wanted children "driven" turned against a tutor who drove. In 1837, W. A. Graham defended a "tutoress" who had whipped her pupil. He lost the case. Although Anna Matilda King thought her children's tutor first-rate, she did not brook his excessive scolding of and quarreling with the children. A frustrated Charles William Holbrook of Massachusetts taught three boys and a girl on a North Carolina plantation: "Find it still requires a 'heap of' patience to get along with my pupils." Tom whispered during a session, and Holbrook "corrected him." Tom protested that other teachers allowed whispering. "I told him that it was not allowed in the schools of N. York & Boston; he then said 'G! there is where they teach them to become 'Abolitionists.' This shows how early the young are prejudiced against the institutions and people of the North!" Holbrook exploded that Mr. Lee, an adult in residence, "wipes his mouth and hands on the *table cloth!* What would people of the North think of such conduct at the table?!"[24]

The well-to-do carefully recruited tutors certified as ladies or gentlemen worthy of admittance to family intimacy. All went well for a competent and pious tutor. Yet, although tutors and governesses might feel accepted into the family circle, they soon learned that if the host family squabbled internally or with neighbors, one side or the other ostracized them. Sarah Morgan of Baton Rouge, caught in the maelstrom of the War, wondered if she would have to become a teacher or governess. The thought chilled her: "I never see a governess that my heart does not ache for her. I think of the nameless, numberless insults and trials she is forced to submit to; of the hopeless, thankless task that is imposed on her, to which she is expected to submit with out a murmur; of all the griefs and agony shut up in her heart – and I cry Heaven help a governess!"[25]

Hired Laborers

Statistics remain elusive, but records of planters and farmers reveal the frequent hiring of free laborers, white and black. At certain times, agricultural labor became scarce; at other times labor redundancy exposed disguised unemployment. Planters diversified production in part to keep slaves busy and out of mischief. Seasonal variations in cash crops sometimes compelled the hiring of free labor, generally white. Financially embarrassed women slaveholders rented out slaves at a return above that projected if they labored at home. Louisiana sugar plantations hired white and black day laborers, and local contractors recruited skilled laborers in New Orleans and nearby towns. The Presbyterian Reverend Robert J. Breckenridge, denouncing the movement to expel free blacks from Maryland, maintained that nonslaveholders faced ruin without access to free black laborers. By the War, wheat growers in Maryland, especially on the Eastern Shore, depended heavily on free black labor at harvest time. Attempts to expel free blacks met stiff resistance from whites in the countryside who needed their labor. Yet 1850s proslavery radicals invoked an unusual argument in their unsuccessful campaign for expulsion or re-enslavement: They declared that "emancipation" had not changed the status of blacks from slave to free; it had merely deprived them of a single master and made them slaves of society.[26]

Some big plantations in Virginia had about as many white tenants, craftsmen, and clerks as they had slaves. Jefferson hired a good many laborers. Although most did field work, skilled workmen taught slaves trades. Into the nineteenth century, hired white laborers built homes. "We have quite a Colony here," Eliza Davis wrote from Joseph E. Davis's plantation in Mississippi in 1834, "seven Carpenters, two brick layers & one *physician*." Planters hired landless whites, as coopers, sawyers, boat wrights, and machinists. One year Charles L. Pettigrew of North Carolina hired nearly a hundred men. His neighbor Josiah Collins III, who hired large numbers of white laborers, insisted on treating poor men with the same respect as rich. He lifted his hat when he met both, explaining that he intended "to enforce the idea that *colour* alone makes caste here."[27]

When, during the 1850s, complaints of labor shortage emerged, advocates of reopening the African slave trade warned about reliance on supplementary white labor. "To hire white men to do it," cried "Panola" of Mississippi, "will be to bring about an association between my negroes, and a set of drinking, vagabond, foreigners; for native white laborers are never to be seen for hire in this country." From Virginia to Louisiana, planters hired more tractable free blacks rather than slaves for short periods. Benton Miller of Washington County, Georgia, having to supplement the labor of his three slaves, hired a white worker who performed less well than the slaves. The northern-born Corinna and Ellen Brown of Florida had a special complaint: "White negroes are out of the question."[28]

John Randolph of Roanoke told the House of Representatives that Southerners did not have to curry favor with those who cleaned their boots and drove their carriages. Calhoun told the U.S. Senate that southern whites lived as equals, except for those who worked as menials or body servants: "No southern man – not the poorest or the lowest – will, under any circumstance, submit to perform either of them." Yet neither Randolph nor Calhoun would have disagreed with William W. Holden of North Carolina when he expressed a stereotyped southern attitude: "Let no one be ashamed of labor. Let no man be ashamed of a hard hand or a sunburnt face."[29]

"Panola" notwithstanding, native Southerners worked everywhere. Often, sons of small farmers did odd jobs to supplement family income, but native agricultural workers had as bad a reputation as foreigners did for dissolute behavior, unsteady work habits, and troublemaking. Dr. Samuel Cartwright sneered at native-born and foreign workers who "make negroes of themselves by doing drudgery work" in cotton and sugar fields. Yet planters and even farmers who needed hired hands to set up a place or during a harvest, often turned to native whites for field work. Irish immigrants worked on public projects and did plantation ditch digging and other work deemed too dangerous for slaves. An exchange in the Mississippi Delta between a planter's son and an "amusing" Irish ditch digger sheds light on the sadistic side of elite snobbishness and working-class *faux pas* in pursuit of dignity and respect. Harry St. John Dixon described the Irish worker whom he did not bother to identify by name: "He imagines he is splendidly educated, says he has studied Geometry, Trigonometry, Astronomy, &c. . . . I asked him if Syria was not one of the Apostles; he after meditating a moment very knowingly said yes." Dixon fired a number of such questions, which the Irishman tried to bluff through: "It was rich. I enjoy a good laugh, and he kept my sides literally shaking the whole time." Yet Dixon took umbrage at the tendency to treat yeomen as inferiors.[30]

White carpenters built slave cabins, coffins, furniture, door frames, roofs, and chimneys; blacksmiths repaired cotton gins and farm tools; cobblers made shoes for slaves. Some were jacks-of-all-trades. The Massenburg plantation of thirty to forty slaves in North Carolina hired whites for a few days at a time to make a roof for the barn, shoes for slaves, and chimneys for slave cabins. Richard Greenlee of North Carolina did business with three local brothers who harvested the potato crop, sold him apples, and rented land. Although planters increasingly bought northern shoes and clothing for slaves, many still found it easier or cheaper to hire a local shoemaker, seamstress, or weaver. Not everyone appreciated the workers' efforts. Cornelia Greene of Cumberland Island complained about the frightful disorder occasioned by workers hired to build a plantation home: "I thought my mother would scarcely keep her reason, particularly as we had all the time either some friend or some stranger to visit us." During the 1850s, Franklin Hudson, a sugar planter in Iberville Parish, Louisiana, hired white carpenters and sawyers at two or two and a half dollars a day and men to fix machinery at three and a half dollars a day, but he complained that the painters worked irregularly and that on any day one or more did not show up. Probably none of the workers had ever heard of Caesilius, but they exhibited something of his spirit: "Although your wages hired me to come here, do not suppose that puts me at your mercy."[31]

Slaveholders' relations with white workers ranged from correct to cool, flavored by noblesse oblige. Thus, slaveholders sometimes hired men of questionable talent, primarily to support struggling neighbors. Here and there, planters followed the example set by Charles Pettigrew of North Carolina at the turn of the nineteenth century or by his son, Ebenezer, fifty years later. Charles Pettigrew seems to have earned the gratitude of laborers and artisans for his conscientious efforts to provide as much work as possible and to treat them decently. "Seems" is all we can say, since they left no direct records. Confronted by noblesse oblige, workers do not always think what others assume they think. We may imagine, for example, how they reacted to a black driver's authority to hire them. Neither Pettigrew encouraged social intimacy or feelings of equality in workers. Occasionally, small slaveholders hired hands for long periods and made them feel part of the household. Then too, churchgoing brought masters and hired hands closer. Slaveholders, big and small, engaged in banter with white workmen or rebuked them sharply but expected blunt retorts.[32]

Countless thousands of westward-moving transients, as well as local folks, worked on plantations. The reception accorded them varied with the extent to which poor whites were kin to the rich. John Walker of Virginia hired white workers from neighboring families, paying in cash, bacon, and grain. In the central Piedmont of North Carolina landless whites accounted for 30 to 40 percent of free white households. Some were well-off artisans, but most were poor. By 1850 tenancy had become a way of life for thousands, some of whom owned livestock and were not poor by local standards. In Arkansas and Louisiana, a large if underdetermined number of landless farmers worked as tenants, sharecroppers, and day laborers, who did not always do worse than struggling small farmers. Tenancy embraced at least 20 percent of a rural white population that lived under the threat of proletarianization. By 1850, social critics in South Carolina declared the landless widespread and growing. Tenancy offered a way station to property ownership, but the reverse was also the case. Relations between planters and well-off tenants remain beclouded. A hint: Lucius Polk of Tennessee, having rented out land, decided that tenants were "a curse."[33]

Farm laborers left mixed reports. On Louisiana sugar plantations a number boarded with the overseer and an occasional skilled worker with the planter. Generally, they did not feel put-upon by aristocratic airs. John H. Lusk, who worked with slaves on a plantation in Tennessee, spoke for many who felt "respected" and "treated nice." Being "respected" meant different things to different men but did not imply access to their employer's parlor or table. Caroline Couper Lovell of Georgia visited the cabins of tenants, who received her graciously but never returned visits. Proud people did not presume on others of higher status, and they asked for aid only in extreme circumstances.[34]

Some tenant, sharecropping, and small farm women worked in planters' homes. Calhoun told John Quincy Adams that families in South Carolina hired white farm laborers but not women domestics, at least not if the family valued its reputation. A twentieth-century survey of Tennessee Confederate war veterans suggests that no more than 5 percent of wives of poor men worked for planters and well-off yeomen. Some poor farm women, working in their own homes, spun regularly or did other work for planters. In rare circumstances, white women lived with employers, but not as household members.[35]

Overseers and Their Families

"A great ruler," wrote Xenophon, "should delegate to others the task of punishing those who require to be coerced, and should reserve to himself the privilege of awarding the prizes." From colonial times to emancipation, southern planters behaved accordingly, blaming overseers for cruelty to slaves and projecting themselves as caring father figures. In 1825, James Barbour, in his presidential address to the Agricultural Society of Albemarle, Virginia, deplored the prejudice against overseers and boasted of paying well for the best possible management of slaves and crops. A decade later he complained that dependence on overseers took a heavy toll on Virginia's agriculture. Without recanting his earlier view, he chided planters for engaging ignorant "hirelings" at low wages. T. Pollok Burguyn of Ravenswood, North Carolina, dismissed the portrait of poorly paid overseers, arguing that, fed and housed by planters, they could save most of their wages. Still, J. J. Flournoy of Georgia invoked Xenophon to stress the need to have overseers as devoted to the estate as the owner himself. The *Southern Planter* of Richmond thought no men more knowledgeable about plantation management than overseers. Despite repeated attempts at reform, the overseer system and the status of overseers changed little.[36]

Planters generally allowed slaves to complain about overseers, notwithstanding pleas from men like Lewis Livingston of Virginia to trust overseers, not slaves, in disputes. Joseph Acklen of Louisiana forbade overseers from punishing a slave for complaining to his master, considering it "an insult to me" and cause for dismissal. Slaves seized the opportunity. They undermined countless overseers by appealing over their heads, implicitly asserting their prescribed status as householders, in contradistinction to strangers. Conversely, drivers (enslaved black foremen) recommended overseers, as when Isaac Stephens reported on a "fine" overseer to his master. Masters listened to slaves against overseers and against planters to whom they hired their slaves out.[37]

Both kindly masters and stern ones fired overseers for cruelty. Among the stern, Bennet Barrow cried, "They are a perfect nuisance, – cause dissatisfaction among the negroes." Planters from east to west joined Barrow in pouring out wrath in letters and diaries. William Massie of Virginia privately described his overseer as a brute, as inhuman, yet recommended him as first-rate. A. L. Brent of Virginia and Calvin H. Wiley of North Carolina preached that only good Christians could oversee slaves properly and tend to the masters' interests. Daniel Coleman, an overseer in Alabama, maintained that overseers carried an especially heavy responsibility for the slaves' moral instruction. Confronting "shrewd and cunning" slaves, overseers had to exemplify competence as well as morality. John Archibald Campbell of Alabama doubtless agreed, but, as a veteran jurist, he fell back on the advice of the ancient Romans to keep overseers in full view lest they abuse slaves.[38]

Even the most arrogant of faux aristocrats had to soothe the feelings of the touchy middling and lower classes. Class attitudes had an impact on legal as well as social relations. Justice varied according to local circumstances, notably, the relations of planters to the less affluent in time and place. John Randolph dismissed his overseer for scandalous behavior but did not take him to court. Two gentlemen warned that no matter the evidence, juries sided with the poorer men. The *Daily Alabama Journal* of Montgomery reported on a white riot in Richmond, Virginia, provoked by the governor's pardon of a black slave who had killed his overseer in a brawl. The governor explained that the murder occurred without intent in a chance incident. In North Carolina, an overseer killed a master who treated lower-class whites with contempt; he expected acquittal on grounds of self-defense. But in South Carolina the courts ruled in favor of planters' claims on the crops of tenant farmers who had failed to make rent payments.[39]

Planters who respected the expertise and character of overseers permitted personal and family intimacy within narrow limits. The principal exception consisted of sons of prosperous small slaveholders who worked as overseers in order to learn plantation management. As scions of slaveholding families, they became intimates of the master and might marry into his family. Here and there, planters certified overseers as model citizens, even as "gentlemen."

Planters prayed to find such overseers. John Berrien Lindsley remarked that the managers of British landed estates had business talents, attainments, and respectable social positions: "In our slaveholding states the large plantations ought to be managed by similar persons. The whole, low, thieving tribe of overseers should be done away, and a competent set of factors put in their place." In some cases relations between middling slaveholders and overseers were closer. Some gentlemen, with indecipherable attitudes, joined in card games at the overseer's house.[40]

Whether treated with respect, kindness, or condescension, overseers did not pass muster as household members. Thomas Jefferson recalled that Patrick Henry took special delight in camping out on overnight hunting trips with "overseers and such like people." In later years, planters and overseers hunted together, primarily for rabbits and other small game for their tables, and overseers from neighboring plantations hunted together. Union troops did not separate the threads of these complex relations. Susan R. Jervey of Middle St. John's Berkeley, South Carolina, thought they intentionally treated overseers and their families roughly. She told of an overseer's wife – "one poor woman, a Mrs. Weatherford" – whose home Union troops burned down. They distributed her property to the freedmen, leaving her nothing except some clothes.[41]

Everard Green Baker of Panola, Mississippi, sometimes invited a destitute stranger into his home, but he railed at overseers – "as a class a worthless set of vagabonds, to treat them as gentlemen turns their heads completely." Snubs enraged some overseers, but perhaps not as many as might be imagined. Those invited to table often felt like the slave in Mississippi who would not be cured of running away by the whip but was cured by having to sit at his master's dinner table. Hugh Davis of Alabama had his overseers to table, if bachelors, but they may not have enjoyed it. An overseer: "Miss Marshall is a nice young lady. Was at the table with her today twice & in the Parlor tonight & received no introduction to her." Kate Stone of Louisiana observed: "Neither they nor their families were ever invited to any of the entertainments given by the planters except some large function such as a wedding given at the home of the employer.... They did not expect to be introduced to the guests but were expected to amuse themselves watching the crowd." Slaves, too, recalled the discomfiture of overseers when invited to an employer's table.[42]

In a widely read essay, Thomas Roderick Dew urged gentlemen not to elevate men beyond their appropriate station: "If a Virginia or South-Carolina farmer wished to make his *overseer* perfectly miserable, he could not better do it, than by persuading him that he was not only a freeman, but a polished gentleman likewise, and, consequently, induce him to enter his drawing room. He would soon sigh for the fields, and less polished but more suitable companions." The birthday of E. A. Knowlton, the overseer-in-chief on a large sugar plantation in Louisiana, fell on Christmas day: "Poor folks always has poor ways and I am unfortunately one of that class. I dined with Mr. Barrow last year on Christmas we then had a magnificent dinner and in candor I think I enjoyed my dinner today Much Better than last Christmas." Knowlton thought he would decline in the future, although he hoped he would not be asked, notwithstanding his having appreciated the gesture. "Mr B & Mrs B was very kind in inviting myself & Family." In April of the following year he commented: "I would rather live with Mr Barrow for my Board and cloth than $3,000 per year if he always would treat me as kind as he has today."[43]

Southerners had a principle: A gentleman acted from pride and self-respect, which compelled him to treat everyone courteously. He acted according to his own judgment and did not submit to another's will. He judged anyone who bullied inferiors and fawned over superiors as arrogant, tyrannical, and servile. For Robert E. Lee, a gentleman did not abuse power over the weak and did not remind inferiors of their every fault and error: "He cannot only forgive, he can forget. A true man of honor feels humbled himself when he cannot help humbling others." John G. Guignard of South Carolina mentioned his overseer: "Hare says he is a poor man and we must not be hard with him – asked what fault I found with him. I told him that he drank too much and swore too much." Hare promised to reform. John Evans assured his employer, George Noble Jones, "I would not think of getting a wife without your Consent." Within a year he added, "I have always looked on you as being one of my best friends so I Shall have to beg you to assist Me a little about getting My house finished." Although overseers risked dismissal by offensive behavior, the aristocratic Grimball laughed it off, refusing to take seriously the posturing of a man who was doing a good job for him.[44]

Condescension reigned, extending well beyond the ordinary call of duty, whether out of fondness for a particular overseer or concern for a stricken human being. Grimball heard that his overseer was stealing from him but decided he was not: "The poor man is wasted to a shadow – and says he is in constant misery of Rheumatism – His coming down [to Charleston] under such dreadful bodily pains, showed a sensibility to character, which went far to convince me that he was not capable of what he was accused." Linton Stephens nursed poor Dickenson, his overseer, in the big house but could not save him. David Rogers Williams sent John Ross, his longtime Irish overseer, to Sulphur Springs to recuperate. When Jesse Bellflower, R. F. W. Allston's overseer, fell sick, Allston sat and read the Bible to him for a half hour or more every night: "It is now, if ever, an impression is to be made on poor Bellflower's untutor'd soul." When Allston was dying, Bellflower sat with and comforted him. Allston remembered Bellflower and another overseer in his will despite having always maintained social distance from these piney woods men. But then, a distressed Archibald Arrington learned that his overseer was dying from pneumonia "and am now obliged to discharge him."[45]

The overseers' livelihood depended on the perpetuation of slavery, and only the rarest of souls doubted its legitimacy. Overseers may have resented planters but hoped to own slaves. Their typical salaries of three to four hundred dollars per year made the ascent difficult but not impossible. Yet they carried heavy managerial responsibilities, worked a longer although physically less strenuous day than the slaves, and hardly ever had a day off. Saving to buy land and slaves took self-discipline and luck. A minority of overseers owned one or two slaves whom they hired out or kept as house servants. Archeological evidence from the low country and Sea Islands reinforces literary sources: Overseers usually subsisted on a diet not much different from that of the better-treated slaves. Like slaves, they ate raccoon and opossum. Like favored slaves, they had chipped china handed down by planters. Edward Blunt, an overseer, bought Lucretia Heyward and her mother. She recalled: "Does I hate Mr. Blunt? No I ain't hate him. He poor white trash but he daid now. He hab heself to look out for, enty? He wuk, he sabe he money for buy slabe and land."[46]

A few overseers entered the planter class by marrying the boss's daughter. From colonial times, a woman who married an overseer put her reputation at risk. In 1732, William Byrd denounced such a match as a gross breach of class etiquette and virtually an act of prostitution. Then and later, although planter families tried to prevent such marriages, quarrels broke out between horrified relatives and relatives moved by the pleas of a young woman in love. Phineas Miller, an educated young man from Connecticut, settled in Petersburg, Georgia, as a tutor for the widow Greene's children, took over management of her plantation, and served as overseer. He married her and then became Eli Whitney's partner in the cotton gin business. Lucy Wheeler of Mississippi shocked friends by ending her "old maid" status through marriage to her brother's overseer, a man ten to twelve years her junior. Shocked or not, Kate Carney and Sarah Carruthers "accepted the honor of putting the bride to bed." Usually an overseer risked a bullet for impregnating a planter's daughter. Aaron Anthony, a clever chap, graciously made a planter's pregnant daughter an honest woman; he wound up as her father's overseer and a slaveholder himself. Occasionally, an overseer successfully wooed a planter's daughter, forcing himself on her reluctant family. After Mary Walker, a planter's daughter, married Elijah Cook, the overseer, her parents refused to associate with her for some seven years. They finally relented, acknowledged him as a good husband, and provided for them in their will. Once married, a bride faced a lifetime of difficulty. Kate Stone paid a visit to an overseer's wife only to be jolted: "She seems entirely too nice a woman, for her fashion is evidently from the planter class. I wonder why she married him. She does not look like a contented woman."[47]

We know little about overseers' wives, children, or family life. In the 1770s, John Harrower, a Scots tutor in Virginia, noticed that some overseers hesitated to marry, lest a wife and children bind them to an unsatisfactory position. Some advertisements insisted that an overseer be a bachelor. Garland D. Harmon, probably the most renowned overseer in the South, married Emily Edge in 1845, but we know little about her or their children. Relations of overseers' wives and children with slaves remain obscure. Young slaves "tended" overseer's children and spent the night with an overseer's wife when he was away. Plantation mistresses recognized overseers' wives as individuals rather than as extensions of their husbands. William Ruffin Smith's wife, in personal letters with Mrs. Howell Adams, the overseer's wife, exchanged information on the health and condition of the family. Augustus Benner of Alabama, a planter, wrote, "She was a pious faithful industrious woman." Alice DeLancey Izard described the overseer's wife as "the civilest, most obliging Woman that can be," praising her for taking "pleasure in giving the black Women all the instruction in her power."[48]

Overseers' wives joined mistresses in providing medical attention to slaves. But planters fled to the up country or elsewhere to avoid expected epidemics, whereas overseers and their families had to brave the climate with the slaves. The Reverend Mr. Cornish, arriving on the rice coast in 1839, thought the exposure accounted for their "cadaverous" appearance. Only occasionally did a planter provide overseers with a home in a more hospitable locale in easy ride of the plantation.[49]

A good many masters and mistresses did not think much of overseers' wives, often blaming them for their husband's inadequacies. William Byrd described his overseer as henpecked. Ella Tazewell thought well of her overseer but condemned his wife as unprincipled and disloyal to the Confederacy. Planters and slaves complained of overseers under the influence of wives – "a pain," in the words of M. W. Philips of Mississippi. Lucy Skipwith wrote to her master, John H. Cocke of Virginia, that the people liked William Lawrence, the overseer, but despised Mrs. Lawrence, who took snuff and laudanum and turned her children into little ogres, alternating whippings with excessive forbearance. Cocke himself called Mrs. Lawrence a "Mississippi tobacco dipper and opium eater" and sneered at her Methodist churchgoing. Skipwith urged Cocke to fire Lawrence despite his personal popularity. He did. In 1846, John Houston Bills had a flare-up with his overseer's wife ("a fool") and fired him ("a good natured good for nothing hen pecked husband"). Some years later Bills paid tribute to Martha Cross, the deceased wife of another overseer: "an Excellent Lady – she had been ever kind to my servants & scrupulously honest in her dealings with me." Bills nonetheless fired Mr. Cross for pretending to have been taking care of his sick wife when the slaves got out of control. Bills hired Edward Myrick, whose wife was "to attend to the making of cloth & clothes, as Mrs. Cross did." In return Bills provided a black woman to cook and work for the Myricks. Planters described some overseers' wives as ringleaders in plantation thefts. Charles Manigault of North Carolina considered himself lucky: He had never heard a single complaint against his overseer's wife. "An Overseer's wife, if kind to the sick & to the Children, and considerate in all other respects, she can do much good. But if not as she ought to be, she will soon set everything wrong." With or without specifics, planters echoed the outburst of M. D. Cooper of Tennessee: "My house on the plantation can be left in charge of Old Charity under the supervision of the overseer, but I do not want the overseer's wife to be again on the plantation under any circumstances."[50]

Masters and mistresses held their breath, braced for the worst, and thanked God for a kind, honest, efficient overseer's wife who contributed to good order and harmony. The Reverend M. L. Banks of South Carolina described Abram Thomas, reputedly a top-flight manager, as a "Christian gentleman . . . courteous, refined, intelligent, and pious," adding, "His wife was his equal in every respect." The Boineaus raised orderly, obedient children: "A better regulated household I have seldom if ever visited." Carter Hill of Virginia described a mischievous black girl as controlled by an overseer's wife. The girl turned out well under the direction of the subsequent overseer's wife, who treated her kindly.[51]

Catherine Carson of Mississippi judged Suckey, an overseer's wife who kept house for her, as "honest," "managing," and attentive to the children. Episcopal Bishop William H. Otey, pleased with his overseer's work and popularity with the slaves, thought his wife "very industrious." Leak did not think his overseer efficient but praised his wife as "a quiet, discreet lady" who never caused the least trouble. Some wives won admiration as pious women who led their husbands to Christ. Huger Smith remembered the wife of Mr. Groce, a first-rate overseer in the South Carolina low country, as "a dear motherly old woman" who made the finest sausages he ever ate. She and her husband spoiled their employers' children "frightfully." He described Anna, the overseer's niece, as attractive and said that their son became an overseer. Another overseer's beautiful daughter married a Dr. Rivers. These reports indicate the wide range of duties that a wife performed in accordance with her husband's contract or her own inclinations.[52]

The sons of overseers learned something of their father's work and often followed his calling. Some served in plantation hospitals or did odd jobs. A few expressed appreciation to planters who helped them get an education and recalled mixing easily with planters' sons. Here and there, planters took an interest in the overseer's children and expressed pleasure in seeing them turn out well. Occasionally, a planter family took in an overseer's gifted son – most famously, the orphaned James Henley Thornwell – and provided for his education.[53]

Plantation mistresses visited the wives and children of overseers, much as they visited the families of local poor whites. Both parties understood kindness and generosity as the condescension appropriate to a matron–client relation. Let the overseer or his wife or children get sick, and a good plantation mistress responded as quickly as she did for her slaves. Martha Ogle Forman of Maryland stayed up all night with a dying overseer, comforting his wife and four small children. She thanked God that she had the "power to administer comfort and relief to the distressed." Mistresses looked after overseers' families in illness, arranged proper Christian funerals, and provided for them for a time. The visits paid by young masters and mistresses to the families of overseers were especially patronizing. When Mary Moragné and her party went down to the quarters to cheer up an old slave nurse, they stopped by to see the overseer's wife. Moragné supplied a tantalizing tidbit: "Elizabeth Butler, our overseer's daughter, had come in. I took my knitting & forced myself to be pleasing – this effort is sometimes good for us." She reacted typically to Mrs. M., an overseer's wife: "as much a child as any."[54]

James Rowe of Alabama wrote to his brother-in-law, "I repeat to you, don't you send out an overseer with a wife, I must know the woman (or you must know her be well acquainted with her) for me to commit to her another woman on the plantation." David Gavin of South Carolina exploded at an overseer's wife who brutally beat a slave: "I do not wish the She Devil to strike one of my people again, large or small . . . and do not believe that I shall bear one other kick up like that of Tuesday last." Mississippi's vaunted Married Woman's Property Act of 1839 did not protect the overseer's wife whose husband mortgaged her slave as collateral for his own debt, for the law did not protect property earned during coverture. In a few instances, slaves killed an overseer's wife along with her husband.[55]

Mistresses and overseers' wives shared some suffering and humiliation, notably from their husbands' philandering in the slave quarters. John Randolph of Roanoke, returning to his plantation, fired an overseer who had sired two mulatto children. The overseer died shortly thereafter, and Randolph offered condolences to his wife, expressing compassion for her long suffering. To reduce the incidence of sexual relations between overseers and slaves, some masters preferred to hire married men. The tactic seems to have worked on balance but did not prevent sexual misbehavior by married overseers. Although rarely confirmed by hard evidence, overseers' wives apparently directed their rage primarily at the black women.[56]

For an overseer's wife, as for a planter's, a husband's dalliance stung less than a romantic attachment. Evidence of liaisons, usually with single overseers, appeared from time to time. John Scott's overseer in Montgomery County, Alabama, stole his light-skinned slave girl, whom he had impregnated, and took off for parts unknown, traveling with her as man and wife. Single men could afford to be less discreet than married. James Williams, a former driver in Alabama, reported an unmarried alcoholic overseer whose colored mistress bore him three children. Planters tried – with mixed results – to prevent overseers from sexually abusing slave women. Planters and their sons fell silent about their own sexual abuses but fumed when overseers raped, coerced, or seduced slave women. The wonder is that many planters looked the other way when overseers strayed, for they constantly warned each other that sexual transgressions threatened big trouble in the quarters. Planters had frequent reminders in the reports of slave men who killed their wives' tormentors and of women who fought back, shedding or drawing blood and creating uproar. Overseers who beat slave women into submission risked indignation and dismissal but not prosecution.[57]

Usually, planters told a new overseer bluntly, in writing or orally, to stay away from slave women under penalty of discharge. Charles Tait of Alabama admonished his children, "Never employ an overseer who will equalize himself with a negro woman. Besides the immorality of it there are evils too numerous to be mentioned." Joseph Acklen of Louisiana warned, "Having any connection with any of my female servants *will most certainly* be visited with a dismissal from my employment, *and no excuse can or will be tolerated*." In Mississippi, Haller Nutt pontificated in rules for his overseer:

> Above all things avoid all intercourse with negro women. It breeds more trouble, more neglect, more idleness, more rascality, more stealing & more

lieing up in the quarters & more everything that is wrong on a plantation than all else put together.... Instead of studying or thinking about women in bed or out of bed, a man should think about what he has to do tomorrow – or for a week ahead, or for a month or year. How to take advantage of this piece of work, or that little job – In fact such intercourse is out of the question – it must not be tolerated.

Such intercourse "must not be tolerated," yet tolerated it often was, especially if an overseer proceeded discreetly with a willing or docile unmarried slave. An efficient overseer was hard to find, and planters tried not to notice violations that caused no trouble in the quarters. When mulatto children turned up on plantations, overseers rivaled local poor whites as prime suspects. Former slaves provided much testimony against them in later years.[58]

Overseers' wives, like others in the plantation web, expected and depended on a degree of paternalistic care. When an overseer died, his wife looked to generous planters to help her and the children. Yet their pleas usually suggested unpaid – and unproven – bills due their husbands, rather than a demand for charity. Planters responded in the spirit of alms for the deserving poor rather than as a duty toward a poor household member. In 1839, J. T. Leigh wrote James Knox Polk of Tennessee on behalf of Mrs. Bratton, the widow of the overseer on Polk's plantation in Mississippi. She had to leave to make room for the new overseer: "She has removed some 8 or 10 miles off in the neighborhood of Coffeeville, is poor and in want of money to procure necessaries to live on, is anxious to know whether you will come down to your plantation this fall and at what time." She wished to see Polk in order to settle her husband's accounts. In North Carolina in 1856, Charles Manigault took pity on the wife of his deceased overseer and tried to tide her over. To his chagrin, she complained bitterly about money supposedly owed her husband. After marrying another overseer who wanted to work for Manigault, she tried to get back into his good graces. Manigault, having no place for her husband, found him a job elsewhere.[59]

The plantation household had little room for free workers ("hirelings"). Despite a paternalistic gloss, the strained social relations of slaveholders and employees did not much resemble the basic relation of master and slave. It is difficult to envision a slaveholding society, in contradistinction to a society that permitted slavery, in which formally free workers escaped the condescension and contempt usually associated with personal dependence.

4

Loyal and Loving Slaves

> My husband's influence over the slaves is very great, while they never question his authority, and are ever ready to obey him implicitly, they love him!
> — Frances Fearn of Louisiana

> [My mistress] didn't never do anything to make us love her.
> — Annie Hawkins of Texas[1]

Southern masters – at least a great many – needed to feel loved by their slaves. Some of the clearest expressions came from Virginia. Nathaniel Beverley Tucker, a political and constitutional scholar, maintained that slaves naturally learned to love their masters through everyday intimacy. John Coalter, a lawyer and planter who had difficulty controlling his slaves, wrote to his wife, "To all who love me and shew it by doing their duty give my love and assurances of best services in return." The theme continued well into the twentieth century. Lily Logan Morrill described her mother, Kate Virginia Cox Logan, as confident that "the poor darkies adored her." She effected that "affectionate tone so unconsciously used by southern aristocrats to engender devotion and yet retain respect among colored retainers." Morrill's illusions did not stop there. The slaves' "pathetic devotion" deflected attention "from their own race" and turned them "whole-heartedly toward their masters' families."[2]

Travelers and sojourners reinforced the slaveholders' perceptions and self-image. Sarah Hicks Williams of New York, having married a North Carolinian, told her parents that masters and slaves, unlike northern employers and servants, had loving relations: "They are in the parlor, in your room and all over." Doors were unlocked. Mary J. Windle of Delaware easily assumed that slaves loved and idolized their mistresses, much as Sarah Mytton Maury of England – a high church Anglican who esteemed John C. Calhoun – celebrated the slave's "*affection*" for his master and the bond between them. Without denying brutality, Bishop Levi Silliman Ives of North Carolina, a New Englander, and

James Stuart of Britain spoke of the deep attachment that many slaves had to their masters.[3]

These comments recapitulated an old story. The Egyptian elite – slaveholders, landowners, and officials – answered to Pharaoh if they oppressed dependents. They defended themselves by claiming that they cared for their people, who loved them for it. Southerners drew comfort from Cicero's approval of Appius: "His slaves feared him, his children revered him, all loved him." Southerners, aware of the cruelties of Roman masters, searched for evidence of love and affection. Thomas R. R. Cobb of Georgia recalled Plutarch's story of Octavius' faithful slave who had his eyes torn out while defending his master against an enraged mob: "Many such instances of fidelity and affection are recorded." Cobb knew Appian's story of Hasdrubal, the Carthaginian general killed in Spain by the slave of a man he had had executed. U.S. Supreme Court Justice John Archibald Campbell of Alabama denounced the brutality of Roman masters but maintained, "The Roman annals contain numerous instances of the most sacred devotion of slaves to the persons of their masters." During political convulsions, numerous slaves stood by masters with "rare fidelity and affection." Kindness and goodwill prevailed as "the natural condition."[4]

An unpleasant reality: the slaveholders' anguish when their slaves seized opportunities to evince hatred, hostility, and – perhaps even worse – indifference toward those they were supposed to love. For in various ways the slaves mocked their masters' and mistresses' simultaneously heroic and despicable claims to preside over not merely a household but one great loving family. To untangle the threads of charged master-slave relations requires a far-ranging evaluation of its discrete elements, beginning with an appraisal of the masters' willingness to tolerate and even chuckle over behavior that would have driven employers of free labor mad.

Masterful Forbearance

A high-spirited people, Southerners astonished Yankees and foreigners by their forbearance. In 1784, the Abbé Robin found slaves much better treated in Virginia than in the West Indies: "The American, not at all industrious by nature, is considerate enough not to expect too much from his slave." In later years, Charles Gayarré of Louisiana, a prominent historian and quintessential southern gentleman, "got into a very sinful fit of passion, and summoning up my servant George to my august presence, I said to him, 'George, you are a great rascal, are you not?'" George, scratching his head, replied that he did not know. "Well, I do know it, George, and I am pleased to give you that wholesome information. But no matter, I forgive you."[5]

In 1820, the Supreme Court of Louisiana decided that the sale of a slave could not be voided simply because he was a thief. It explained that a slave should be expected to engage in small-scale pilfering. A decade later, the Methodist Reverend James O. Andrew of Georgia invoked the authority of

C. C. Pinckney of South Carolina to insist that rice planters, despite feeding their slaves well, lost a quarter of their crop to theft. Eliza Ann Marsh of Louisiana said matter-of-factly that she had spent the morning baking cakes, most of which the slaves promptly stole. Masters whipped slaves for stealing substantial amounts or if they caught perpetrators red-handed and had to uphold their authority. Masters expected slaves to steal, whether well-fed or not, and they knew better than to whip for every little thing. They wrote off most thefts as part of the overhead cost of maintaining order. When slaves, in a clever gambit, distinguished between morally sanctioned "taking" from master and morally offensive "stealing" from each other, they confirmed whites in their belief in the moral deficiency of blacks. Alexander Stephens endured his body servant's thievery. Victoria Welby-Gregory, a twelve-year-old English aristocrat, twisted the knife: She was surprised to find that northern hotels told guests to lock their doors and place valuables in the hotel safe, lest they be robbed by blacks. Welby-Gregory noticed no blacks in those northern hotels, and amused southern ladies reported that at home they trusted their slaves with everything.[6]

In Louisiana at the end of the century, Caroline E. Merrick, recalling her course from plantation mistress to women's rights activist, portrayed her father as calm and self-possessed, and judicious: "Even his slaves loved him." At fifteen, she married a slaveholder and carried "heavy and exacting responsibilities" on annual visits to the plantation. Merrick had no uninterrupted rest, saw any slave who called on her, and cared for the sick. When emancipation came, she cried, "Thank heaven! I too shall be free at last." In Louisiana, Julia LeGrand had trouble with a servant not easily punished since she had been in the family since infancy. Issey tried to burn down Calhoun's home. Floride Calhoun wanted her sold, but John sent her to his son's plantation instead. All agreed to keep quiet, lest she be hanged. Some planters, reluctant to sell a rebellious spirit, lived to regret their decision. Senator Willie P. Mangum of North Carolina complained, "My black family have been comparatively useless – the result, I think, of their profligacy and vices."[7]

The antislavery Harriet Martineau considered the slaveholders among the world's most patient people, willing to put up with inattentive service, dawdling, laziness, and dirty habits. She thought that patience with house servants made slaveholders more tolerant of ignorant field hands. Both house and field slaves demanded attention, constantly interrupting a mistress who was giving her children spelling lessons. Martineau thought that Northerners made bad masters because of unrealistic expectations, whereas southern-born mistresses proceeded "without the slightest hope of attaining anything like leisure and comfort." Mistresses muttered about slaves' demands but reveled in their own professed self-sacrifice. Martineau suffered abuse for her antislavery accounts of the South, but earned plaudits from Frederick A. Porcher of South Carolina for her understanding of the slaveholders' forbearance.[8]

Like slaveholders everywhere, Southerners congratulated themselves on being the kindest and most humane of masters. For the Presbyterian Reverend

Rufus William Bailey of South Carolina, not only did Southerners rank as the best of masters and Yankees and free people of color the worst, but the slaves knew as much. When slaves had a voice in their sale, they usually preferred a Southerner. Mary Boykin Chesnut, pointing to the New Jersey–born Ann Cooper Lee, grumbled about ignorant hard-driving Yankee émigrés. So did R. Q. Mallard, an elite slaveholder, William Wells Brown, who had escaped from slavery, Horace Cowles Atwater, an antislavery Yankee, A. J. L. Fremantle, an Englishman with the Confederate army, and Matilda Charlotte Houstoun, the English novelist. David Christy of Cincinnati, an agent for the American Colonization Society, berated Northerners for emancipating their slaves only to condemn them to misery in a hostile society. Christy thought Southerners much kinder and friendlier to blacks.[9]

The intellectually accomplished, northern-born Margaret Junkin married John T. L. Preston and assumed the responsibilities of a plantation mistress: "No time to myself in the multiplicity of the calls made on my attention" by slaves, by illnesses among blacks and whites, by the never-ending social calls and guests. John S. Wise, son of the governor of Virginia, said about his mother: "No one knows how much that sense of duty to her slaves contributed to her death." Eleanor Baker of Massachusetts described house slaves of rich Charlestonians as "a lazy, pampered set." Confessing to "perfect wonder at the indulgences & patience of Southern housewives," she offered a qualification: "Then again you see the reverse treatment." Northerners easily picked up the word "pampered" from plantation mistresses like Catherine Edmondston, who, during the War, cried out that the most pampered were the first to desert to the Yankees. The antislavery Catherine Stewart reported to northern women that a slave mistress did not enjoy enviable "luxurious leisure." Rather, "cares and vexations, in the midst of wealth, often plant a furrow on her brow."[10]

Thomas W. Gee of Virginia, who had served as a Christian missionary to the poor of New York City, owned a tobacco plantation of about sixty-five slaves. Frederick Law Olmsted thought that Gee felt like a parent to his slaves, who accepted him as such: "At dinner he frequently addressed the servant who waited on us familiarly, and drew him into our conversation as if he were a family friend, better informed on some local and domestic points than himself." Gee had to leave the dinner table three times to attend to slaves with one problem or another. Gee and Olmsted did not have ten consecutive uninterrupted minutes. Edmund Kirke, a northern businessman, discovered that the affection of some slaves for their masters "would have gladdened the heart of even the bitterest opponent of the peculiar institution." Kirke could hardly believe the indulgence shown to slaves who did half as much work as northern free laborers. He snapped at a planter friend: "You waste enough in one day, to feed the whole North for a week. It's a sin – the unpardonable sin – for you know better." His friend replied softly, "Well, it *is* wrong; but how can we help it? We can't make negroes anything but what they are – shiftless, and careless about everything but their own ease." Of the planter's kind and admirable wife, Kirke remarked, "She knew nothing – thought nothing – about the right or the wrong of slavery; but cheerfully and prayerfully, never wearying and never doubting, she went on in the rounds of duties allotted her, leaning on the arm of the GOOD ALL-FATHER, and looking steadfastly to HIM for guidance and support."[11]

Concerned ladies prayed individually and in groups for the strength to resist their slaves' provocations. Priscilla ("Mittie") Munnikhuysen of Maryland, marrying into a family of big sugar planters in Louisiana, prayed to be able to treat "*servants*, or *those* not my equals, by birth, with all kindness, and consideration, knowing as I do, they are creatures of feeling and have souls to save. That I may never treat anyone with contempt. For if *I* treat others with contempt, how will my Father in Heaven treat me?" Lucilla McCorkle reported from a women's prayer meeting in Alabama in 1847: "Mrs White, Mrs Cater, Mrs Orrs, Mrs Gore, Mrs Jackson, Miss Lizzy Riddle came up with fervor." McCorkle offered a prayer at the meeting:

> Grant me grace to perform my duty as a WIFE O make me conscientious in it. Thou knowest the infirmities I have to contend with but thy grace is sufficient. As a MOTHER I hourly need divine assistance and thou has promised – for the child is thine by dedication.... As a MISTRESS I so need patience forbearance meekness mercy.[12]

The *Richmond Enquirer* chided northern-born slaveholders for demanding that black laborers work as hard as white. An unidentified – possibly northern – agricultural writer observed that lowcountry slaves worked at a pace to give "a quick-working Yankee the convulsions." James Loring Baker affirmed that northern employers did not match the patience shown by southern planters toward their laborers' slow pace. Catherine Cooper Hopley, an Englishwoman, held blacks responsible for the pace of southern life: "You never see a negro in a hurry, and the masters and mistresses are inured to slowness." Southern gentlemen refused to rush around like Yankees or brisk Englishmen. "Are they to move with more celerity or less dignity than their slaves? Even the clerks in the stores are too well bred to be in a hurry, whatever their customers may be." Hopley, ignoring the effects of temperature and humidity, thought southern ladies ineffectual with brooms and cooking utensils but willing to put up with "inconveniences" imposed by slaves: "It is well that either by nature or education, the Virginians are of so easy and tranquil a mood, for they would otherwise enjoy no peace in their lives, with their lazy, unreflecting, childlike servants, the negroes." Garland Harmon, an articulate overseer of uncommon ability, could not read at night "without being bedeviled with 40 niggers – here after everything you can mention." Let a rainstorm come and Mary Jones of Georgia spent hours providing hot coffee and tending to drenched slaves. Here, a slave pleaded with her mistress to fix her dress. There, the whole slave force cajoled master for a holiday. Elsewhere, masters and mistresses spent an evening without help so that house servants could go to some social event. Amelia Murray, an Englishwoman, met six black slaves on their way to the theater. In England, three white servants would go one night and the other three the next. Not so in New Orleans. Slaves insisted on having each other's company all at once. The vast majority of slaves probably laughed at the notion that they received such indulgences. But a great many masters and mistresses took pains with one or more favorites, priding themselves on their generosity and attention to duty, and expecting boundless gratitude. William Faux of England, among others, remarked on masters who took their slaves' gratitude for granted.[13]

Did masters and mistresses devote time because of a sense of duty, because they cared, or because they feared pecuniary loss? One way or the other, they endured a constant drain on their time and energy. Even indifferent masters and mistresses had to attend to the medical needs of their human investments. William Howard Russell, the antislavery English newspaper correspondent, observed a planter who spent the whole night in attendance upon the birth of a slave: "Such kindly acts as these are more common than we may suppose; and it would be unfair to put a strict or unfair construction on the motives of slave owners." Plantations had a daily roster of slaves who needed medical attention. Eliza Magruder of Mississippi made at least three trips to the quarters in one day to attend to the sick. John Davidson's day was ruined when a falling tree almost killed an old servant. Thomas Linthicum, his wife, and their children held a constant vigil to try to save a dying slave. Beyond pecuniary considerations, sick slaves caused considerable inconvenience to those constantly on call. Masters and mistresses, attending to the sick, frustrated their children and visitors, who expected attention. Mary Carmichael's boys came to dinner but were disappointed not to see Mr. Edgar and Anna: "They having a very sick servant could not leave her." Especially for a favorite, masters and mistresses dropped everything. Stephens, hearing that a slave had fallen ill, quit work to arrange for a doctor: "So goes the world."[14]

Unlike overseers and millions of peasants and laborers the world over, southern slaves had Sunday off. In early eighteenth-century Virginia, William Byrd beat Anaka for various offenses but did not burden her and the other house servants by receiving guests on Sunday. To the end of the slave regime, considerate mistresses had cooks prepare meals on Saturday to be eaten cold on Sunday or dined early to give the house staff the rest of Sunday off.[15]

Masters who took pains on behalf of servants won praise; masters who denied servants consideration fell into bad odor. Edmund Ruffin – planter, prominent soil scientist, and secessionist firebrand – visited Governor Letcher of Virginia, to be greeted by Mrs. Letcher at the door since the servants had their customary Sunday off: "I was pleased to see this absence of all pretension, & simplicity of manners, induced as it was by kind indulgence to the servants." Bennet Barrow of Louisiana, a tough task master, asserted his right to every slave's time, arguing that a slave who claimed his own time made plantation order impossible. Yet he resented the several "Sunday gentlemen" who showed up to hunt: "Nothing provokes me more – Sunday being a day of rest to the negroes." He spent Sundays looking after his people: "I like to be about – allowance day – & they frequently want things not convenient to get any other day – & My orders for every negro to come up every Sunday morning cleaned and head combed." The Methodist Bishop H. N. McTyeire of Tennessee appealed for greater consideration for cooks and carriage drivers who needed rest and time to attend religious services. He was appalled to see carriage drivers outside church, caring for horses, while their masters attended services. Still, some masters and mistresses walked to church or made special arrangements to allow coachmen to attend their own churches.[16]

Slaves had holidays to themselves unless assigned essential services. The same could not usually be said for masters and mistresses, who had the sick to look after. Considerable numbers suffered during winter's waves of respiratory ailments. Slaves translated the masters' largesse and condescension into "rights" for themselves, but they usually expressed themselves indirectly through actions. Their silence reinforced the masters' sense of noblesse oblige and of being kind, considerate, burdened, and self-denying Christians. Solon Robinson, the northern agricultural reformer, writing from a plantation of 150 slaves in Jefferson County, Mississippi, reported that Colonel Dunbar refused to place his slaves on a second plantation, "keeping the aged and the children close by so that he could look after them personally."[17]

"As for your attempting to control an estate like one of ours," James H. Sheppard of Louisiana wrote to Abraham Sheppard, Jr., "it is out of the question." No one could adjust to the "trouble & vexation" of managing 150 slaves. Justice Ebenezer Starnes of the Supreme Court of Georgia believed that the slave who produced a profit for his master ought to have the benefit of counsel as well as succor. But oh, how some planters whined. The Baptist Reverend Iveson Brookes mentioned "the (to me irksome task)" of spending much time riding and walking over plantations to see that all was in order. Catholic Bishop John England of Charleston, no sentimentalist, lauded plantation mistresses for their selfless attention to their slaves' needs. A planter wrote in the *Southern Agriculturalist* that a record of slave conduct would be "nothing short of a series of violations of the laws of God and man." He expected no great reformation in their conduct, but, referring to the Bible, he added, "We are bound under many sacred obligations to treat them with humanity at all times and under all circumstances." Thirty years later, Catholic Bishop Augustin Verot of Florida, who protested abuse of slaves and free blacks, reproached masters for erring on the side of permissiveness.[18]

Elizabeth Curtis Wallace of Virginia assured her sister that runaways did not plague kind and forbearing masters, but her patience waned during the War: "That nigger Mahala has broke another china plate and saucer. If she would only confine herself to destroying the stone china I could bear it better, but she always breaks my french china." She wanted to replace her slaves with white servants, but the Bible convinced her that God sanctioned slavery. On a trip to New Orleans in 1845, B. Ballard wrote to a friend upriver in Louisiana, "I shall get through my business as quickly as I can, and return to the miserable occupation of seeing to negroes, and attending to their wants and sickness and to making them do their duty – and after all have no prospect of being paid for my trouble." William Gilmore Simms explained to a New Yorker, "With family cares, I have those which follow the keeping of 70 slaves, the most ignorant & troublesome children in the world." He distributed a molasses allowance: "Thus, I feed, physic, clothe, nurse, & watch some 70, and have to live from hand to mouth myself – the mere steward of my negroes." The Methodist Reverend R. H. Rivers of Mississippi, a college professor of moral philosophy, wrote, "I have known the slaveholder [to] surrender the pleasures and ease and luxury of home and give himself to the laborious and self-denying work of a Christian missionary." Dolly Burge, a plantation mistress of Middle Georgia, mused in 1864, "Many a Northern housekeeper has an easier time than a Southern matron with her hundred negroes."[19]

Mutual Dependency and Manipulation

"We hold the negroes and they hold us." Thus spoke Episcopal Bishop Leonidas Polk of Louisiana – big planter and Confederate general. "They furnish the yoke, and we the necks. My own is getting sore, it is the same with those of my neighbors, in church and state." Louisa McCord of South Carolina objected to receiving more slaves from her father's estate: "I am almost out of my senses with those that I have." As the War ended in Georgia, Eliza Frances Andrews's mother expected to enjoy her own emancipation more than the blacks enjoyed theirs. Colonel Wood of Kentucky told Henry Yates Thompson of England that he wanted to give up slavery because of its low returns. Thompson reacted skeptically, until others insisted that Colonel Wood was the greatest slave on his plantation.[20]

Proslavery ideologues pounced on every slave's pronouncement of reciprocal ownership. The editors of Emory and Henry College's *Southern Repertory and College Review* reveled when Jupiter, asked if he belonged to the Wilkerson family, replied: "No master, old Mr. Wilkerson belong to me." The editors commented: "He knew well enough that the benefits of his relation to his master were all on his – the servant's – side." The Reverend John Adger of South Carolina declared: "*They belong to us.* We also belong to them." An old black man in South Carolina refused to leave the plantation when emancipation came, explaining that his missus belonged to him, much as he belonged to her. Variations from Georgia: In the 1840s, the celebrated British geologist Charles Lyell asked a black woman whether she belonged to a family of his acquaintance. She replied merrily: "Yes, I belong to them, and they belong to me." J. A. Turner, a planter and agricultural reformer, remarked that slaves shared their masters' dread of having "our" cotton "getting in the grass." A. L. Hull of Georgia reminisced: "The negro claimed an ownership in everything on the place. It was 'our' cotton and 'our' cows. My father's riding horse was 'Mas Henry's horse,' but the carriage was 'our' carriage and the team was 'our' horses."[21]

Numerous stories fueled the slaveholders' belief that their slaves loved them dearly. Nathaniel Beverley Tucker saw slaves choose to remain rather than be sent to live with spouses. Cora Mitchel of Florida recalled her Connecticut-born father as an antislavery merchant who bought several slaves at their request to prevent their being sold away from their homes. In Louisiana, Sarah Morgan's female servants always took her part in quarrels, and she acted as arbiter in their quarrels. When the Yankees arrived, Morgan's favorite chose to remain with her mistress. In Arkansas, James Cazort charged his slave Ben with the training of his son: "Teach him to ride, to shoot, to hunt, to fish. Above all teach him to be honest in word and deed. Take care of him. If need be die for him." Louise Wigfall never forgot "little Emmeline," her companion who died at age eight: "She loved me with a devotion that I have never seen excelled." When Emmeline died, Louise Wigfall grieved and thereafter could not think of her "without a pang."[22]

Hopes for – and pretensions to – mutual love had a rational core in countless cases of reciprocal affection. A slave saved the lives of white family members under attack by a deranged slave. Slaves deeply moved Eliza Pinckney when they traveled thirty or forty miles to attend the funeral of her husband, their master. Roswell King, Jr., who managed several plantations, believed that a master or overseer "should be the kind friend and monitor to the slave, not the oppressor." Episcopal Bishop John Stark Ravenscroft of North Carolina retained a lifelong affection for the servants who, when he was a boy, risked their lives to save him from an enraged bull. Henry F. Pyle told of his stepfather, a slave who had run off to a black federal regiment during the War and returned to work for the Republican Party. His old master saved him from a lynching, declaring that the loss of his son during the War earned him the right to have his "nigger" left alone.[23]

Before, during, and especially after the War, Southerners cited examples of warm feelings between whites and blacks in the household. Even hard-driving lowcountry planters told themselves that they cared for their slaves much better than capitalists cared for their workers. They especially reveled in stories – true so far as they went – of affection for favorites who directly touched their lives. A. Flournoy, Jr., son of a big planter, off to war in 1861, wrote to his wife, Docy, "Tell all the negroes I think of them every day.... Tell them if I live to get home, I will bring home five boxes of the best tobacco for them." Reuben Allen Pierson, with the Confederate army in Virginia, wrote to his father in Louisiana, "Tell old Jack I have not forgotten him.... Few men so honest and faithful are to be found in these trying times."[24]

Expressions of affection by "old family servants" bolstered a sense of close ties. Slaveholders, Eliza Clitherall of South Carolina wrote, "vibrated to the depth of feeling" upon receiving a friendly message from a slave they had had to sell. Clitherall heard from "my old body servant, Evelina, whom I had rais'd from a little child to womanhood – & one of those who were taken away from me & sold at public auction – whose loss to me was irreparable." Clitherall spoke of "the poor things" who sadly parted from her when sent back to her mother-in-law. Genuine ties of affection did exist between some slaves and slaveholders, who extrapolated an imaginary love affair with all their slaves. The Presbyterian Reverend Charles Colcock Jones of Georgia said of a good

Christian mistress: "She shall be praised by her servants; for they cannot forget her condescension, her kindness, her instruction, and her care."[25]

Occasionally a slaveholder, feeling oppressed by his slaves, began to think the game not worth the candle – an attitude that justified slavery by implying that it was for the slaves' good. Said Colonel James Morgan, a small planter at Galveston Bay in Texas, "I am the slave for my negroes – while they are happy and content I am unhappy and the loser by them." Other slaveholders responded with good humor. In Simms's novel *Woodcraft*, Tom rejects emancipation, declaring that he owns Porgy, his master, and will not emancipate him. After the War, an embittered John S. Wise proclaimed, "I give, devise, and bequeath all my slaves to Harriet Beecher Stowe."[26]

The slaveholders wailing about their suffering, indeed oppression, invites laughter. Countless blacks doubtless mixed laughter with indignation. But the worst part of this apparent charade is that it was not a charade. Ownership of slaves trapped even halfway responsible masters and mistresses in constant demands on time and energy. Yes, the slaveholders, having brought it on themselves, did not qualify as candidates for martyrdom. Whether they inherited or bought slaves, they assumed responsibility for human beings who did not consent. They profited economically from slave labor and emotionally from the subjugation of others to their will. Yet the burdens they assumed wore them down in ways more easily felt than fathomed. Slaveholders took their slaves for granted as dependents, but some recognized that they depended on those dependents in matters physical and spiritual. Mistresses had only to take care of themselves to acknowledge that their comfort – and sanity – required performances by the slaves whose efficiency they often denigrated. Mary Boykin Chesnut considered Ellen a poor maid: "But if I do a little work, it is quite enough to show me how dreadful it would be *if I should have to do it all.*" With a commercial convention about to begin in Savannah, Harriet Cummings, like other ladies, opened her home to delegates. All would go well if Cora, her recently ill cook, held up. If not, Miss Harriet planned to get sick herself.[27]

In the 1770s, George Austin of South Carolina asked Josiah Smith, his plantation manager, to explain the greater financial success of other planters. Smith replied that they enriched themselves "by the hard Labour & Sweat of wretched slaves." He thought that their rigor would eventually undo them. Ebenezer Pettigrew of North Carolina had no qualms about slaveholding but worried about himself: "I am not willing that any thing living shall labour unto death or shall have its days shortened an hour for my aggrandizement or ease." The twenty-three year-old Everard Green Baker of Mississippi promised to be careful with earnings drawn from the hard labor of his slaves. Dr. John Stainbach Wilson of Georgia wrote, "Our slave labor is the source of all our wealth and prosperity; from this we enjoy all the necessaries and luxuries of life, and it is the basis of the most desirable social and political system the world has ever seen."[28]

Foreign travelers testified. Josiah Quincy of Massachusetts, visiting John Randolph at Roanoke, saw black men and women who "rushed toward him, seized him by the hand with perfect familiarity, and burst into tears of delight at his presence among them." E. L. Magoon, a popular northern contributor to southern literary journals, observed that Randolph shook hands with his slaves but not with plebeian whites. John Davis reported from Virginia about 1800, "The negroes of the plantation beheld the coming of Mr. *Wilson* with joy; old and young of both sexes came to the landing place to welcome his approach." An Illinoisan wrote from South Carolina in 1831, "I have never seen elsewhere, and I fear I never shall, such an outgushing of affection as I have seen on the arrival of 'young master' or mistress." In the 1850s, Olmsted reported from Virginia: "Black and white met with kisses, and the effort of a long-haired sophomore to maintain his supercilious dignity was quite ineffectual to kill the kindness of a fat mulatto woman, who joyfully and pathetically shouted, as she caught him off the gang-plank, 'Oh Massa George, is you come back!'" Olmsted filed a qualification: The field hands stood by, stolidly observing.[29]

Mistresses and their daughters frequently visited the quarters and occasionally the white poor. Sarah Rootes Jackson reported that the ladies went down to the quarters to give Old Aunt Sarah a pair of stockings and a hemmed handkerchief. Often black women reciprocated with garden produce. Sarah Wadley and her sister, visiting relatives in Vicksburg, were delighted by servants who "screamed out, 'Miss Mary and Miss Sarah, I declare!'" Juliana Margaret Connor, ending a visit in North Carolina, went to the quarters "to bid farewell to the negroes whom we found anxiously expecting us." Kate Carney of Tennessee mentioned how glad the blacks were to see Sister Mary, Brother Watson, and their servant Betsy when they visited and brought presents for all. From numerous everyday incidents the ladies found evidence that their slaves loved them as much as they loved their slaves. Gleeful plantation girls, on their way to becoming "young ladies," welcomed the opportunity to make clothing for newborn black babies and to fill Christmas stockings for the quarters. Letitia A. Burwell of Virginia, her mother, and her sister were received like princesses when they visited slave cabins. The slaves of Dolly Lunt Burge and Cornelia Jones Pond poured out affection when mistresses and masters returned home. It was not enough for Mary Telfair of Savannah to report that the slaves "looked well & happy." She had to tell herself that they "seemed disposed to *worship* me." Memoirs of nostalgic Southerners beamed with certainty of their slaves' love. For one, Belle Kearney of Mississippi found "deeply touching" the loyalty of plantation slaves to her father, their master. For another, Thomas Joseph Macon had no doubt that the slaves "revered" his mother.[30]

At the end of the nineteenth century, the Methodist Reverend I. E. Lowery of South Carolina lamented that before the War masters and slaves had lived together with tenderness and affection, whereas emancipation had produced "intense bitterness and alienation." And in truth, during and after the War, plantation mistresses increasingly used terms for black men seldom heard in earlier years – "ape-like," "gorilla," "orang-outang." Had they unleashed their true attitude, suppressed before the War? Or did the disillusionment and disappointment and defeat harden attitudes long manifest in softer form? Probably, some of both.[31]

Sally Baxter of New York, visiting South Carolina in 1855, sympathized with mistresses, not with their ostensibly well-treated and contented slaves: "The responsibility of slave holding and the care and anxieties of a mistress, particularly seem almost an impossible burden." Shortly thereafter, she married into the Hampton family and learned about the "burden" firsthand. Sally McDowell, daughter of Virginia's Governor James McDowell, told her fiancé in the 1850s to thank God that he did not suffer the "responsibility & distresses connected with slavery.... a "heavy evil." Myrta Lockett Avary heard her mother say, "Had slavery lasted a few years longer, it would have killed Julia, my headwoman, and me. Our burden of work and responsibility was simply staggering."[32]

Moses Liddell of Mississippi purchased more goods for his slaves than he had intended: "But I trust that they will feel a disposition to appreciate what we give them & behave accordingly." Archibald D. Murphey of North Carolina, struggling with indebtedness, as usual, thought to sell some of his sixty slaves, who were more than he could manage: "But Altho' Others treat their Negroes as well and perhaps better than I do, mine are attached to me, and I did not know Until the Time came, what Pain it would give me to sell them." Farish Carter, a many-sided businessman and planter – perhaps the wealthiest man in Georgia – wanted to move his family and investments to the Midwest. His wife, Eliza, who considered slaves a great nuisance, would not hear of selling them. Mary Jones, contemplating a move from Georgia to Philadelphia, asked her husband who would attend to their servants' temporal and spiritual needs: "It cannot be duty to leave them to live and die like the heathen."[33]

Obituaries and eulogies of slaveholders frequently conveyed assurances of their slaves' love. J. H. Hammond – a wretched and ungrateful son, unfaithful husband, lecherous uncle, bullying father – whimpered: "I have not a Christian's hopes nor feelings.... I love my family, and they love me. It is my only earthly tie. It embraces my slaves, and there to me the world ends." The ideal of loving slaves took strange forms. As a boy, Benjamin Franklin Hawkins of Tennessee, son of a small slaveholder, went hunting at night: "When I got tired, negroes would carry me on their shoulders for hours because they loved me well enough to care for me." To hear Joseph LeConte tell it, slave boys thought it a "Great honor" to carry Little Massa's books and lunch to school and to run his errands. (Slaves recalled their chores less cheerfully.) Sarah Alexander of Hopewell, Georgia, wrote to her daughter that her daily "little favors" to the servants "are received with such thankfulness and so prized as our up country servants know nothing of, and every one seems to think it a privilege to wait upon us." Leathy, an old servant in Virginia, asked Mary Campbell to send greetings to master and hoped to be well enough to cook and sew for him when he returned. An enraptured Mrs. Campbell wrote to her husband, "How much I love to hear such sentiments from an old family servant. In them, when faithful, you meet with true affection. Indeed we sometimes find them more sincere than near relatives. WELL – she at least shall have to say, that one poor slave hath found a friend." Mary Jones wrote her to son, "If it be dreadful to have the cry of the poor and the oppressed rising up to God against us, how sweet like incense poured forth their tributes of gratitude and affection, their prayers and benedictions." At school in Texas, Henry Percy asked his father to send love to the servants he had known since childhood, adding, "I know they all love me well."[34]

Less crudely, "Philom" urged, "We should love our slaves in order to make them love us." St. George Tucker and his family counted slaves "friends" without concessions to equality. Littleton Waller Tazewell wrote to John Randolph of a slave in the family for seventy years: "My faithful friend and servant John departed life a few hours before I reached home." Tazewell neither knew "a better man" nor had a "truer friend." Linton Stephens of Georgia, according to James D. Waddell, his confidant, had no greater friends than his faithful servants. Frederick A. Porcher insisted that the slaveholder saw the slave as "our friend, our dependence, our hope." Yet Elizabeth Perry, the wife of the unionist leader Benjamin Perry, and Tryphena Fox, the northern-born wife of a small slaveholding physician in Mississippi, agreed that the better masters treated slaves, the worse slaves behaved: "If any one is entitled to good, faithful, contented, grateful servants, *we are*." The chatter about "faithful friends" lingered long after the War. Nancy Bostick DeSaussure of the Georgia low country, sickened at the damage done by portrayals of slavery in *Uncle Tom's Cabin*, recounted stories of the slaves' love and loyalty. Rebeca [*sic*] Latimer Felton of Georgia remembered her mammy as a dear friend and, admitting slavery's evils, stressed close relations between mistresses and female slaves. Self-respect and self-love impelled slaveholders to believe that their slaves loved them, but then, so did consciousness of material interest. Thus, "P. T." advocated good treatment of slaves as necessary for good profits, and a planter in South Carolina advised every master to show his slaves that their interests and his rose together.[35]

Southerners mused about friendship in a manner that recalled their favorite ancient and early modern predecessors. Aristotle taught that friendship is a single soul in two bodies that links equals, not masters and slaves. Masters (despots, tyrants) see their slaves as extensions of themselves and cannot tolerate their independence. "Tyrants befriend only the base, especially flatterers who are more like slaves than friends." Southerners admired Aristotle, but on this matter their behavior suggests greater attention to Cicero and Francis Bacon. Friendship, Cicero wrote, can exist only among good men. A man must first be good himself and then seek another like himself. Cicero declared the first law of friendship: Ask of your friends only what is honorable and do for friends only what is honorable: "In friendship, those who are superior should lower themselves, so, in a measure should they lift up their inferiors." Southerners likely agreed with Lord Bacon's argument that friendship occurred much more often between superiors and inferiors than among equals.[36]

Fawning, gushing, dissembling slaves "put-on ole massa," turning whites' racial superstitions to advantage. Eighteenth-century Virginians judged newly imported Africans stupid when they broke hoes or feigned inability to use them.

In fact, those "stupid" slaves had used hoes competently in Africa. Amelia Murray heard a black gardener reply to his master, who said a hired Irishman did three times as much work: "White man use to work. You can't 'spect me – a nigger – demean myself like he." These stories testified to black ingenuity but confirmed the masters' conviction of black inferiority. Young mothers among the Fearns' slaves in Louisiana brought their babies to receive presents from a master who hardly distinguished one baby from another. Mothers exchanged babies to collect more than one present for each. Whites laughed good-heartedly at such clever servants. E. J. Pringle of South Carolina expressed a common thought: "There is more manliness in acknowledged obedience to superior power, than in the smiling subserviency of the sycophant, which makes the whole life a lie." All experience, Mary Howard Schoolcraft of South Carolina wrote, "proves that you cannot overwork a negro. He will do his task, and no human power can make him do any more." Dr. A. P. Merrill of Memphis offered a scientific rationale, repeated in medical and agricultural journals: The physical constitution of blacks prevented their being driven to excessive labor. This racial diagnosis provided slaves with an opportunity to wrest some control over the pace of work; simultaneously, it reinforced the masters' sense of superiority.[37]

Slaves did not deceive every master, and not every master deceived himself. Augustus Baldwin Longstreet, appealing to common sense, scoffed at the sham that had slavery weigh more on masters than slaves. Edmund Ruffin lashed out at the hypocrisy of slaves who pretended ignorance of matters they understood well. He told masters to stop acting like fools and hold slaves responsible for their actions. Planters learned as much during the War, when slaves balked or deserted. "I am done with nigger labour," Joseph Acklen of Louisiana wrote to Ade Franklin, his fiancée. "I never had much fancy for it as you Know but now I am fully satisfied I have suffered all Kinds of deprivations and then subjected to all Kinds of lies and slanders that malice could invent." Lucy Rebecca Buck of Virginia held forth: "I believe the servants despise their deliverers [Union troops] from the bottom of their hearts. Bah! They're greatly their superiors in good breeding." Then the dawn broke. She saw a mulatto in Union uniform: "The boy a short time since had fled from the best of masters and joined these miserable hypocrites." After the War, Augustin L. Taveau acknowledged having been deceived in believing slaves attached to their masters. They behaved as badly toward good masters as toward bad.[38]

Prone to self-deception, slaveholders grasped at every expression of slaves' goodwill. Slaves exchanged testimonies of affection and gifts with white children away at school or in the Confederate army. Nothing pleased masters and mistresses more than to receive cheerful greetings from slaves. Confederate troops welcomed greetings especially when they came – as Elise Young assured William N. Mercer – "with tears in their eyes." Whites' letters to relatives at home routinely returned greetings to slaves. Greetings ranged from Henry Graves of Georgia's stereotyped, "Give a howdy to the Darkies" to Susan D. Witherspoon of South Carolina's dignified, "Remember me to the servants of both houses." Away at school, Isaac Barton Ulmer of Alabama sent "love" and "respects" to the servants, whereas Susan Henry of Clarksville, Tennessee, sent greetings to the "Niggers." And Private Edward McGehee Burrus, C.S.A., wrote to his sister Kate: "Always remember me kindly to the negroes, at least such as deserve it – I can't remember who are the *black* sheep."[39]

When mistress had a baby, the slaves would likely be happy for her – unless they hated her. Black and white women considered children God's gifts and feared for each other in childbirth. "Servants all pleased," the Presbyterian Reverend Charles Colcott Jones wrote to his wife Mary, "and send their congratulations to Missy and the baby." Varina Howell Davis beamed when, at the birth of her first child, every slave came up to the house with chickens, eggs, and other gifts, thanking her for "little massa to take care of we." Eliza Quitman had been ill since giving birth: "I came down stairs on Sunday, and was greeted with smiling faces all around, both white and black."[40]

Keziah Brevard of Tennessee protested when Ned and Dick were sent to the fields: "I miss them & really do not like to make them do such hard work – they are house boys & can not stand the sun as the field hands do." Exasperated, she wrote, "I wish to be kind to my negroes, but I receive little but impudence from Rosanna & Sylvia." She rued speaking harshly to them: "Oh my God give me the fortitude to do what is right." Ann Hardin did not get to bed until 1:30 A.M. because a servant woman "did not do well." She too prayed for strength. George Richard Browder of Kentucky, a Methodist minister and farmer, thanked God for peace and good order: "We have no quarrels – no fighting & but little scolding – good servants & good masters live in peace. I have tried & prayed to do my duty by my servants & often met with ingratitude, dissatisfaction, insolence & insult."[41]

High expectations of slave loyalty led to traumatic clashes. From the earliest days, astonished slaveholders ranted against ungrateful slaves who repaid kindness by running off or turning on them. Servants stole one to two hundred dollars from the Carmichaels. "It is a hard trial to do your duty," moaned Miss Mary, when "the better you treat them the more unkindness they show you." During the War, Henry Yates Thompson expressed wonder that so many slaves deserted kind masters. "Ah, Sir," replied a planter, "you don't know the ungratefulness of the negro. Why, some of my negroes rested far more than I do; they had plenty to eat and drink." It did not help when black deserters displayed not hatred but indifference. If slaves intended to wound their masters deeply, they could not have done better.[42]

Ellen House found it "perfectly disgusting to see a man touch his hat to every negro he meets," but her outburst came during federal occupation. The white men whose behavior she complained of had long dominated the southern scene. When George Washington's slaves bowed to the visiting Louis-Philippe, the future king of France, he and his party bowed in return. The Presbyterian Reverend William Graham of Lexington, Virginia, smarted when asked why he had removed his hat in response to a bow from a black man: "What! would you have me outdone in politeness by a negro?"[43]

The handshake had been practiced during the ancient, medieval, and early modern eras, but with changing significance. By the nineteenth century, it had become a gesture of equality or friendship. Hence, racial loathing made casual hand shaking rare in the North. Nathaniel Macon of North Carolina, speaking in Congress during the Missouri crisis, explained the southern view of hand shaking as evidence of mutual affection. He did not mention that interracial hand shaking rarely occurred on the streets or in public places. But he did mention that slaveholders conversed much more easily with their slaves than Northerners conversed with their laborers and servants, for Southerners recognized no civil or other equality. Southern senators quoted General William Moultrie of South Carolina on the kind greetings he received from his slaves upon returning to his plantation after the Revolutionary War. George Tucker recounted how cheerily the slaves greeted Jefferson when he returned to Monticello, pouring out cares and troubles and expecting his personal attention. In the 1850s, the easy hand shaking of whites and blacks astounded Catherine Cooper Hopley: "It was a miracle my wrist was not dislocated in the ordeal." Fremantle observed "extraordinary familiarity and kindliness" in the readiness of masters to shake hands with their slaves. George S. Sawyer of New Orleans and other proslavery theorists challenged Yankees to visit the South and see the wonderful greetings. To no avail: Abolitionists saw only deceit. In the jaundiced view of the *Anti-Slavery Record*, joy at the return of massa from a trip or of young massa from college simply meant that the slaves welcomed an excuse for a holiday.[44]

Southern slaveholders imbibed something – how much remains unclear – of the Greco-Roman view of curiosity as characteristic of slaves, especially of domestics who had access to their master's bedrooms and intimate matters. But they showed little of the Greco-Roman fear of that curiosity, which seems to have gripped northern and foreign observers. Edmund Ruffin finally confessed to being a poor judge of character, easily deceived by slaves, but most masters, setting their slaves at a racial distance, did not grasp how much their slaves knew about them. Citing Juvenal, Samuel Johnson remarked, "The danger of betraying our weakness to our servants and the impossibility of concealing it from them may be justly considered one motive to live a regular and irreproachable life." Southerners much admired Johnson, but most ignored his warning.[45]

Souls

An irritated North Carolinian exploded in 1861, "What sophist first propagated that folly about the master having a property in the soul of the slave, I do not know." Yet well-intentioned slaveholders did assume responsibility for their slaves' souls. Eliza Clitherall spent $600 for "a little maid, whom I henceforth feel it to be my duty as I trust thro' divine assistance to be enabled to train her, Religiously and usefully – feeling myself responsible for her soul and well doing." Year after year, Lucilla McCorkle prayed for strength to be a good wife, mother, and mistress, who treated her slaves as rational human beings with souls as precious as her own. She had a hard time caring properly for her husband and child "and servants who have immortal souls – the responsibility is greater than I can bear." J. H. Ingraham of Natchez quoted a southern lady as saying that her slaves constituted a greater responsibility than her children since God held her directly accountable for their souls.[46]

Mistresses, worrying about their slaves' salvation, lectured house servants on chastity but rarely intervened since they considered black women naturally loose. Susan Nye Hutchinson of North Carolina "had much solemn talk" with her cook, Maria, whose "habits in respect to personal purity are a continual violation of the 7th Commandment." Hutchinson did not have much luck: "How truly does it illustrate that the Ethiopian cannot change his skin nor the Leopard his spots." Abolitionists played into proslavery hands by stressing the sexual exploitation of black women. By arguing that slavery degraded all participants, they conceded the charge that black women submitted in return for favors.[47]

Pious masters and mistresses read the Bible to their slaves, taught the catechism, and prayed with them. Here and there, a planter invited slaves to join in family prayers in the Big House. The Reverend Shaler Grandy Hillyer led family prayers in the dining room and invited, but did not require, his slaves to attend. Some house servants and drivers assisted in preaching and proselytizing. After emancipation, ex-slaves, including some who became ministers, condemned slavery but expressed gratitude to masters and mistresses who had led them to Christ.[48]

Especially in the Carolina/Georgia lowcountry, big planters – Aikens, Cuthberts, Hamptons, Hartwells, Mikells, Moores, Rhetts – built family chapels and "praise houses" primarily for their slaves. Dr. William N. Mercer of Mississippi, a notable planter, spent $30,000 on a chapel and rectory for some four hundred slaves, paying the Episcopal rector $1,200 a year. Edmund Ruffin, conducting an agricultural survey of South Carolina, admired the imposing chapels attended by slaves from neighboring plantations. Whites who attended church on Sunday, leaving slaves to worship on the plantation, worshiped with them during the week or on occasional Sundays. Chapels drew large numbers, notwithstanding Mary Howard Schoolcraft's annoyance at slaves who passed up Sunday chapel to see friends in town. W. H. Ravenel and the Baptist Reverend William P. Hill testified that slaves attended chapel, listened, and prayed fervently. Several slaves thanked Hill for his sermon, and he thought them "contented, well-fed, and moderately worked, which is the general character of the neighborhood." Alicia Hopeton Middleton described the chapel on her family's Pon Pon River plantation as "of Gothic, though simple, construction." The master held services regularly and once a month paid a minister to preach and administer communion. The Reverends W. P. Harrison, J. L. Moultrie, and John H. Cornish, among others, pronounced plantation chapels tasteful. In coastal South Carolina, the Reverend Alexander Glennie thought some chapels superior to parish churches.[49]

Ebenezer Jones of Tennessee instructed son and daughter to look ahead to Judgment Day: "To your slaves be always very kind. [Christ] will not ask if folks are black or white." John Rogers, near death in Charleston, charged his three children "to give all the indulgence possible to the negroes, in going to Church, and making them repeat their questions, for this reason that if neglected we will have to answer for the loss of their souls." The courageous Henrietta Shuck of Virginia, off to Asia as a missionary, inquired about her servants in Virginia, hoping that they were good Christians whom she would meet in heaven. "Pray for me, and for the heathen, whose minds are very dark." Judge Robert Raymond Reid of Georgia, a Unitarian, prayed to God "to make me a virtuous man; to protect my children and friends and servants, and to make *all* good and faithful servants of his will.... If *He* does not help me, I am lost." David Gavin of South Carolina, recovering from illness, prayed, "Grant thy blessings O Lord, Grant them to my brothers, friends, and relatives, to our negroes, enable them to be good and faithful servants and us kind and just masters and mistresses."[50]

John Walker of Virginia, a devout Methodist planter, praised God for His many gifts: "Kind Father be pleased to remember thine poor worm my dear wife and children & servants.... Oh blessed Master bless our dear children & servants." Walker, having lost his faithful Phil and Billy, both about eighty, prayed that they had entered Heaven. Learning of the death of Lewis, a slave he had rented out, Walker prayed, "I humbly hope and trust his soul rests in Heaven." A year later he lamented the accidental death of little Henry, a great favorite whom he had hoped to make his body servant. In 1834 he prayed for a dangerously ill Eliza: "Oh that Lord Jesus Christ our Master will give us grace at all times to bare up against the trouble of this world and finally take us all to rest with him is my most humble prayer." In 1839: "One of our family have died (a little negro child named Martha)." Six months later he lost his second daughter – the third of his four children: "Father I feel as much determined to serve Thee as ever I have been – help thine poor worm to hold out to the end of it please thine Goodness – bless my dear Peggy [his wife], child, the servants. My heart's desire and prayer to God is that we may all meet in Heaven."[51]

Bishop McTyeire, supported by Bishop Andrew, condemned "infidel and unchristian masters," adding, "Many a Christian master is ready to grant that among his servants are better Christians than himself." Episcopal Bishop William Meade of Virginia quoted a poor white man who observed the entrance examination of an African-born black man into the church in 1837: "I see, sir, that though some men are white, and some are black, true religion is all of one color." In South Carolina, when Mary Boykin Chesnut attended services for slaves on Mulberry plantation, she sometimes felt closer to the pure meaning of Christianity than at white services. The staunchly proslavery Mary Moragné did not take umbrage when two old slave women lectured her on prayer and challenged her religious commitment: "I was struck dumb – I felt that I was but a 'babe in Christ' before two poor old ignorant Africans. God had revealed himself to them – 'he has chosen the weak things of the world to confound the wise'; & when I went away I felt that they too were my sisters." Two years later she "had my feelings very much lifted up in humble adoration by hearing a negro at the quarter singing 'Come humble sinner.'" The slave had taught himself to read, "& though he is considered the worst negro on the plantation, he may be yet a chosen vessel of grace." She wept because "I am able to do nothing for the souls of these poor creatures."[52]

Mistresses prayed for the strength to do their duty to their slaves. Eliza Pinckney of South Carolina resolved to become a Christian mother, wife, and mistress: "I am resolved to be a good Mistress to my Servants, to treat them with humanity and good nature . . . to Encourage them when they do well, and pass over small faults; not to be tyrannical peevish or impatient towards them, but make their lives as comfortable as I can." Anne Tuberville Davis of North Carolina prayed to God to bless her husband, adding, "Lord bless me also and make us mutual blessings to each other and our children and servants." Lucilla McCorkle pleaded, "Domestic cares engross my mind to the exclusion of all religious & social duties. Our servants are a source of discomfort." She was "getting too hard in my manner toward Lizzy – too impatient toward her foibles. God forgive me." A year later she was still praying ardently for God's grace "to control my self and thus the authority to control others." Lizzie roused her ire on the Sabbath, "but I endeavored to defer anger till Monday." In Texas, Ann Raney Coleman felt terribly guilty when Eliza, her servant, died, because in a fit of anger she had wished her dead. Susan Nye Hutchinson, worn down by demands on her time, called on the consciences of mistresses to do their duty, on which slaves desperately needed to rely. Many mistresses who resorted to violence against black women prayed for forgiveness and control of their tempers. They asked a great deal of God. Thavolia Glymph, in *Out of the House of Bondage*, provides a chilling account of mistresses' frequent violence against slaves, which she aptly describes as "a kind of warring intimacy" between mistresses and slave women. According to John Brown of Georgia, a former slave, blacks believed that whites died in fright because of their sins.[53]

Belle Edmondson of Tennessee saw a conflict between duties to slaves and to her husband: "I am put here to be Patrick's companion and help-meet, and I cannot spend all Sunday preaching, teaching, & missionizing without evident neglect of that my plain duty." Her difficulties "beset many a well intentioned mistress" who, discovering that she could not do what she ought, did nothing. The wife of Judge William F. Tucker of Chickasaw County, Mississippi, pleaded that, in taking pains to care for sick slaves, he risked exposure to their diseases. And, although "ashamed" for having lost her temper with two servants, she cried, "Nobody knows what I have to try me sometimes."[54]

In providing slaves with religious instruction, slaveholders did not usually distinguish between two responsibilities: to save souls and to enhance social control. Clarissa Town of Louisiana taught the catechism to her slaves and exulted in their conversions: "I rejoice because it makes them happier here, and a promise of bliss hereafter. And it makes them better servants and more easily managed." A pleased Eliza Magruder wrote about slave conversions: "I pray God they may be sincere in their profession." Mary Jeffreys Bethell went into a rhapsody when Betty, her baby's thirteen-year-old nurse, and another slave professed religion: "I felt very thankful, I hope God will convert all of my negroes. I am praying for it.... All my children should become christians, my *servants* also." J. H. Greenlee of North Carolina spent a great deal of time in religious instruction and gave his slaves time off to observe fast days: "O Lord incline them to study what is for them external peace, make them thy servants, may they repent of sin and trust in Christ as their saviour." Greenlee hoped that religious instruction would lead his slaves to eventual emancipation and their emigration to Africa as Christian missionaries. Everard Green Baker reveled in the baptism of blacks and whites in his Baptist church. He traded some land with neighboring planters in order to get his slaves out of a swamp, announcing his reasons: "Not the least of which is that they will have the opportunity of going to church." Baker prayed to God to enable him to be "a faithful husband, a kind father & master & an exemplary Christian."[55]

Grief and Money

Edward Thomas Herriot of South Carolina owned nearly 400 slaves: "The majority love me and would defend my family – many will weep at my death as I have wept at many of theirs." Slaves did weep when a member of the white family died. Some put on a good act; others grieved for a master, mistress, or child whom they admired, liked, or just did not hate. William Grimes of King George County, Virginia, spoke bitterly for many slaves: "She is dead, thank God." Yet how was a decent slave to react when a mistress on her deathbed asked, "Lu, I'm dying, but you be good to my children"? And slaves had reason to freeze at the death of any master, which threatened to have the black community scattered by a division of his property.[56]

Edgar Allan Poe and John Reuben Thompson, two intellectuals who rarely descended to absurdities, joined the "Our Slaves Love Us" chorus. Poe singled out deathbed scenes as evidence that the master-slave relation rested on love. Thompson recommended Ann Rose Page's sentimental *Sketches of Old Virginia Family Servants* as refutation of abolitionist propaganda. After the War, Cynthia Coleman of Virginia, N. B. Tucker's daughter, wondered, "Do our Northern friends think that we felt this defection only in our pockets? No, a thousand times no, our hearts were wrung by the loss of our [black] friends, those we loved, and those who loved us." Her mother considered her slaves her children and suffered a blow of "crushing weight" when they left: "She had thought for them, worked for them, denied herself for them, watched over them in sickness and health." And Mammy did return to nurse Cynthia Coleman's mother as she lay dying.[57]

Read the record as you will – as tenderness, grief, affection, satire, or puttin'-on-ole-massa. Whites rarely distinguished between slaves' genuine grief and their own political point scoring. Neither John Hartwell Cocke of Virginia nor James Henley Thornwell of South Carolina was a fool or a dissembler. Cocke commented that blacks "nurse us in infancy . . . watch around our languishing beds in sickness; share in our misfortunes, weep over us when we die." Thornwell preached in Charleston in 1860, "From infancy to age, they attend on us – they greet our introduction into the world with smiles of joy, and lament our departure with heartfelt sorrow." Cocke and Hartwell were not the kind of men who would feign grief they did not feel. Neither were they men who could resist expressing their grief in a manner that, in effect, warded off what they saw as abolitionist slander. Especially after the sectionally volatile years of the Mexican War, Southerners found themselves unable to express even private emotions outside an intensifying politically charged context.[58]

When slaves died, all masters and mistresses rued the loss of their investment, and a discernibly large if immeasurable number felt the loss of a member of the household. Certainly, there were plenty of James Henry Hammonds, who focused on financial losses: "Have lost another negro child. Did ever one poor mortal have so many deaths around him?" Others fit the pattern described by an ex-slave woman in Tennessee. She described how her mistress cried like a baby over the death of a slave she had whipped often: "Huh, crying because she didn't have nobody to whip no more." Few people lived at the extremes. Typically, slaveholders simultaneously felt the loss of money and of a member of their household. The exigencies of attending to dependents provided welcome distraction to slaveholders who were grieving over the death of a husband, wife, or child of their own. Then too, slaveholders felt entitled to affection, loyalty, and devoted service. Unintentionally, they echoed the medieval aristocrats who, seeking salvation, wrote wills that asked for the prayers of the poor.[59]

Forget self-serving public apologetics. Listen to private communications. John Palfrey of Louisiana sent his grandson news of the death "of your favorite little Tom" despite attendance of a doctor. "I know you will regret his loss very much." When Ginney, a favorite servant, lay dying in 1829, Mira Lenoir of North Carolina wrote to her niece, "a good many of the neighbours came to see her while she lay sick & she was treated with as much respect by white & black as if she had been white." In Maryland, Martha Ogle Forman's "favourite woman," Lydia, an excellent, versatile, pleasant worker, died: "I shall long lament her loss and often think of her excellent qualities." Twenty years later, she lost another favorite and penned the longest – by far – eulogy for either white or black in her thirty-year diary. With the recovery of two endangered servants, George Swain of North Carolina thanked God in language he might have used for his wife or son.[60]

"Our old friend and faithful servant Sandy Maybank died," Charles Colcott Jones wrote to his daughter, Mary Mallard. "We feel his death, and will miss the cheerful and faithful man always. He has been with us 27 years!" Two months later, Eliza Roberts wrote to Jones and his wife of her "constant anxiety of mind about our poor servant Hannah," who had died after months of terrible pain and suffering. "I feel as if we had lost a friend in the family, she was such a good servant." Although Roberts acknowledged substantial monetary loss, she wrote, "I feel her death more as a friend. You both know what that feeling is." Shortly thereafter, Roberts asked to be excused for going on about Hannah. "But you have the same sympathies for these members of our household as we have.... When we lose our servants, the loss of their services is the last thing we think of; it is the shadow on our household when an attached faithful one is removed." C. C. Jones, Jr., followed with an expression of pain at the death of Dinah: "She was a faithful servant, and her loss to her little family and to the circle on the plantation must be severely felt."[61]

Rachel O'Connor of Louisiana carefully calculated pecuniary losses at the death of her slaves but mourned deeply, at least for favorites and mothers of dead children. Little Isaac was dying: "The poor little fellow is lying at my feet, sound asleep – I wish I did not love him as I do, but it is so, and I cannot help it." For O'Connor, the master-slave relation indissolubly united interest with sentiment. On the death of a slave's baby, she lamented the "poor mother's distresses." Two years later she had her hands full tending to sick slave children. Seven-year-old Sam died: "Oh, my dear sister, no pen can convey to you my distresses." The death of several of Eliza Bowman's slaves "don't appear to cost her a thought. Why cannot I be so?" Maria Bryan Harford of Georgia shared her mother's sorrow when Patty, a favorite, died. On a trip north, she received word that Ned had died. She felt his warm remarks about his master and his display of piety as the end approached. Nine months later she received word that the faithful Robert had died: "I feel as if I had lost myself a humble friend whom I have known and loved from my childhood." Weeping, she reflected on the common fate of all humanity. Counterpoint: A few years earlier her favorite cow had died. Harford regretted the pecuniary loss, "But it is not that, but a feeling of pain at the death of a creature to whom I had become really attached as to a faithful domestic."[62]

Tests of Faith

The death of a slave diminished the household. Masters and slaves lived too close to death not to feel that they might be next. The death of a black child reminded whites that their own children lived at high risk. The death of an old slave snapped ties to older generations, white and black. David Gavin of South Carolina lost eighty-year-old Friday, who had served his grandparents and parents, carrying keys and managing much of the plantation. Friday "seemed like a connecting link between me and grandfather and grandmother Gavin, for he could talk to and tell me of the actings and doings of them and others of the olden time, about the connections of the family, their names and where they lived and moved to or from." Reverence for those ties constituted an essential part of the meaning of life and its continuity. One or more slaves, especially among those in the Big House, were perceived as old friends. Times changed, but those currents continued to run.[63]

There were innumerable cases of genuine callousness, but also cases that only seemed so. The laconically recorded deaths of whites and blacks by, among others, Francis Terry Leak and Everard Green Baker of Mississippi, Mittie Munnikhuysen Bond of Louisiana, and Malinda Ray of North Carolina did not imply callousness. Masters and mistresses prayed that dying slaves had reconciled themselves to God and that God graced those whose repentance seemed in doubt. Dr. Samuel Leland took the loss of his patient, the slave Jacob, as a hard personal blow, and he feared that Jacob had not made peace with God. Dr. Charles Hentz felt "deep emotions of sadness" at the death of little Betsey, but he reminded himself that he practiced medicine as his contribution to the process of life, death, and salvation. Dr. M. W. Philips of Mississippi moaned at the financial losses when slaves died but commented on the death of Peyton, "I wish we could hope for his eternal state." Emily lost her boy Scott – "a remarkable child of his age, a pet of us all." Philips cried, "I feel as if I had lost some dear relative. We know he is the better by the change. May God make us all resigned and able to say, 'Thy will, O God, be done.'" [64]

George DeBerniere Hooper of Alabama described a deceased slave as "my friend" and my "Brother in Jesus Christ." Hooper, pleased by the conversion of a number of his slaves, wrote to his wife, "I verily believe that God has a *high* place prepared for them." David Campbell lost the pious, Bible-reading Leathy, a family servant for fifty-five years. Facing impending death, she commended her soul to Christ, inspiring all around her. Eliza, a faithful if high-tempered servant, died at age thirty-three after a painful, lingering illness that reduced her to a skeleton. "I hope God has blotted out/pardoned all her transgressions and that she may enjoy the happiness of the good." Campbell and his wife "feel her loss and grieve for her as they would for a relation whom they loved.... God has willed, and no doubt for good purposes, that she should be taken away – and we bow to his chastisement with humble resignation." Greenlee delighted in his slaves' progress in religious instruction, praying, "Oh that they may seek the Lord & be his servants and follow the blessed savior." When Jane's child died, he prayed in words reminiscent of those he invoked on the death of his own daughter and the children of his white neighbors: "Oh Lord sanctify every dispensation of thy providence to the good of thy creatures." [65]

Judith Rives thanked God that her poor Mammy had suffered little pain from a life-ending paralytic stroke, and that she had joined in family prayers, expressing faith in her Savior's love and pardon. "Every mark of respect was shown to this good and faithful servant, who, I trust, has entered into the joy of her Lord." Eliza Clitherall wrote in good times, "Hagar, my faithful old Hagar came down from Tuscaloosa. We commenc'd life's journey together, & I trust in the mercy of god we may end it together." Four years later Hagar died: "Her last words were 'Glory! Glory!'" Elizabeth Allston Pringle watched over a dying Pompey. Her father called out Pompey's name. Pompey opened his eyes "and a look of delight replaced the one of pain." He exclaimed, "My marster! Ye cum! O I tu glad! I tink I bin gwine, widout see yu once more.... I kin res' better now, but, my marster, I'm goin'! I want you to pray fur me." Her father knelt and "offered a fervent prayer that Pompey, who had been faithful in all his earthly tasks, should receive the great reward, and that he might be spared great suffering and distress in his going." [66]

Ministers frequently held up the Christian resignation of dying slaves as exemplary: "I have done but little except help nurse, *Mary* – who is sinking," George Richard Browder recorded in 1854. The next day: "Alas, alas the cruel grave should hide forever – one who was so attached to us & whom we regarded more as a friend & as a child than a servant." He considered Mary an amiable, trustful, and kind-hearted little girl who loved him and his family. "The pecuniary loss we do not regard – but our social loss is great – & our affliction sad." Browder had instructed her in the ways of the Lord: "We hope to see little *Mary* again, for she often spoke of Jesus & Heaven during her illness & seemed to trust in Christ. Her place in our family will never be fully supplied." Browder visited Lewis, his uncle's dying slave: "Yet feels happy at the thought of death – prays for his master & speaks confidently of a home in Heaven. The freedom & wealth of his master would be a poor exchange for the peace & comfort of this poor African slave!"[67]

Hugh Lawson Clay of Alabama wrote to Susanna Clay on the death of Jim, his body servant: "You know how devotedly attached and faithful he was to me, and know what must be my feelings in writing, the melancholy intelligence of his death." Then, Clay said too much: "No other servant in the place would have been attended in sickness with as much care and constancy as he was. . . . I feel desolate – my most devoted friend is gone and *his place* can never be supplied by another placed in his situation." Guy Bryan of Texas responded to the grief expressed in a letter from his half-brother, Stephen Perry, at the loss of Simon: "I too felt & felt deeply his loss for a thousand associations clustered around his name, he was the favorite body servant of uncle [Stephen F. Austin] & then of mother & afterward of your father & lastly of yourself." Simon was "a good member of society & you & I need not think it weakness to weep over his grave."[68]

Complacency at the death of a baby or child or indifference to a mother's suffering required a hard heart. There were plenty of hard-hearted slaveholders, even if not as many as legend has it. W. C. Harrison of Shelby County, Tennessee, hired a group of blacks from William H. Taylor and wrote a long, pained letter to Taylor on the sudden death of a little girl: "She died after suffering more than any little thing I ever saw." The cholera epidemic swept off many children from the two Manigault estates in South Carolina. Manigault felt the pecuniary loss but was "filled with melancholy" as he recalled sad scenes. Poignant references need not be extensive: "My little Negro babe is dead," Rachel O'Connor wrote to her sister Mary. Kate Stone saw Malona, her slave, "in great distress" over the loss of a third child. In 1858, Linton Stephens lost a number of slaves as well as his overseer. "I do feel most deeply for them, and particularly for poor old Abram and Charlotte, who have lost two children, and now have another at death's door."[69]

Slaveholders sent condolences to white families stricken by the death of esteemed slaves. Francis Taylor of Virginia, a big planter, noted the deaths of his neighbors' slaves along with the deaths of his own. John Houston Bills of Tennessee carefully recorded the deaths of his servants, sometimes with paeans to their virtues. He provided an account of "faithful" Sarah, a laundress "much lamented by all of us, esteeming her as one of the family." That account was much fuller than his accounts of the deaths of white friends. During the War, Bills responded sorrowfully over the death of Felix, a "faithful servant, *honest*, & intelligent," who died of disease at the front with Bills's son Leonidas. The death of "poor old Sue" saddened Susan Nye Hutchinson. Only two days earlier Mrs. Bell had remarked that Sue had been more of a mother than a servant to her.[70]

Condolences and consolation also flowed from blacks to whites. In Louisiana, slaves consoled a young planter distraught over the death of his trusted and beloved eighty-year-old manservant. During the War, Richard Willis received a moving letter from Washington, his fallen son's body servant, who regretted not having been at young master's side at the fatal moment: "Master Richard, I say to you it is good to be religious. . . . I believe it as much as I ever believed anything in my life that he is at rest. My heart believes it. I desire to be a better Christian I want to go to Heaven."[71]

Consciously or not, slaveholders could not easily resist turning their grief into ideological point scoring. Eliza Roberts wrote to Mary Jones, her niece: "I am sorry to hear of the death of your servant Eve. We feel those losses more than Northerners think; the tie is next to our relatives." Mary Jones's son commiserated with her on the sad death of Sina and the bereavement of her children: "There is much to be said, however, that with kind masters the orphans are always cared for, which is more than can be affirmed of many poor persons not occupying a similar relation in life. Their children are left to public charity, which is too often meager and beggarly." Less dramatically, slaveholders felt the deaths of slaves they perceived to have been loyal, faithful, and honest, for every such testified to masters and mistresses worthy of respect and deference. William Valentine of North Carolina mourned for Old Isaac, a neighbor's faithful slave admired throughout the county. Bennet Barrow said when George died: "a very great loss – one of the best negroes I ever saw." When the hundred-year-old Orange died, Barrow said, "A more perfect negro never lived, faithful honest & purely religious, never knew him guilty of a *wrong*." These scenes of grief reinforced the slaveholders' conviction that slaves were part of their households – that they lived with them, in contrast to the physical and emotional racial separation in the free states.[72]

Southern newspapers sometimes ran obituaries of "good" slaves more glowing than those they ran for most whites. On rare occasions planters paid deceased slaves the highest possible compliment, referring to them as "ladies" and "gentlemen." In Alabama, Richard Powell described Mary Skipworth, a seamstress and dining room attendant on J. H. Cocke's plantation, as "in truth a lady." W. H. Holcombe viewed a large funeral procession in Natchez for an aged Negro he described as "'a good and faithful servant' – a Christian and a gentleman." Holcombe recounted the scene at which the master "wept like a child at his bed-side, hand in hand with the poor old slave." He added, "I knew the old man well and there was a moral dignity about him which rendered him immeasurably superior to the miserable abolitionists who pretend to commiserate with his race, the most of whom are unworthy to have felt the grasp of his manly, honest hand. Requiescat in pace."[73]

Pious masters expressed joy when their slaves found Jesus. James Matthews of Mississippi, writing to his sister Hannah in Texas, sent family news, commenting that Sukey, a slave, "thanks you for sending her a few lines showing you still remember. Suckey is in poor health, but rich in Christian hope and I think ever ready to meet her Lord with joy." Elizabeth Early of Virginia reported that Til, her sick slave, "was powerfully converted in my room." Anna Matilda King wrote, "Old cupid, honest & true to his earthly owner, departed this life at 4 AM 20 Jan 1857." King added the death of "her good and faithful servant Harriet after years of suffering. . . . For her honesty, her moral character, her usefulness & perfect devotion to her owners she had not her equal." She sighed with relief that Hannah and Old Cupid died in Christ.[74]

W. H. Robbins lost his son, sister, and cook in quick order. Writing to the Reverend Dr. Thornwell, he expressed confidence that his son and sister had been saved, "But I do feel deeply an apprehension in regard to Sarah our Cook – Would that I have seen her & talked to her. . . . She had joined the Methodist Church, but this alone cannot relieve my anxiety about her." Mary Jeffreys Bethell tried to convert her dying slave: "Poor woman I hope she was saved." When Old Dick died at about eighty, Bethell fretted that he had not professed the faith, "but he is in the hands of a merciful God." Everard Green Baker penned a slightly longer obituary for his slave Jack than the one he had penned for the wife he deeply loved. Jack, an exemplary husband and father, had been reared by Baker's mother: "I never knew him to steal nor lie & he ever set a moral & industrious example to those around him. . . . I regret that he did not see his family before death." Jack had not professed Christianity, "Yet no man white or black I have ever known was more exemplary in his conduct. He was kind – moral – sober – industrious, obedient – & honest – I never knew one who kept closer to the path of rectitude." Baker solemnly promised to cherish Jack's memory and "repay to those he has left behind & who were dear to him, the kindness & gratitude which his services on earth have merited. He deserves a better reward than can be given in this world. Requiescat in pace." Waldon Edwards of North Carolina sustained "an irreparable loss," for Candace, who had waited on white folks faithfully: "I am sure I shall never be able to supply her place with one half so dutiful." Antonia Quitman informed her father, John A. Quitman, Mississippi's powerful politician, of the sadness occasioned by the death of Charles, who "has been such a faithful servant" to their cousins. "I know how hard it would be for us if Aunt Dicey or Harry should die."[75]

When the slaveholders paid tribute to their slaves, they were no less complimenting themselves. Near Savannah, Olmsted saw the headstone on the grave of Reynolds Watts, who had died in 1829 at age twenty-four: "To record the worth, fidelity, and virtue of Reynolds Watts. . . . Reared from infancy by an affectionate mistress and trained by her in the paths of virtue, she was strictly moral in her deportment, faithful and devoted in her duty and heart and soul."

That handsome tribute, directed at least as much to mistress as to slave, implicitly underscored the slaveholders' concept of organic household. Yet it often centered on a favored few and could be taken as indifference to others. A planter in St. Mary's Parish, Louisiana, wrote in 1849:

> I have been sad, sad today. I have had a greater misfortune than I have experienced since my father's death. I lost this morning the truest and most reliable friend I had in the world – one whom I had been accustomed to honor and respect since my earliest recollections; he was the playmate of my father's youth and the mentor of mine; a faithful servant, an honest man, and sincere Christian. I stood by his bedside today, and with his hands clasped in mine, I heard the last words he uttered; they were, "Master, meet me in heaven.".... I have a hundred others, many of them faithful and true, but his loss is irreparable.[76]

Dangerous Wishes

Like slave masters everywhere, Southerners sought to instill a sense of inferiority in their slaves, who – in fear, trembling, and awe – were expected to embrace their masters as absolute others. To the limited extent to which masters succeeded, they ruined themselves. For in order to inspire fear, the absolute other had to stand as the embodiment of arbitrariness and even cruelty. For those who provided protection and succor, the symbiosis that engendered love – or what passed for love – often turned into hatred and violence. As masters learned, fear provided a precarious foundation for the order and predictability on which rational economic and social life depended.

A telling shift of emphasis occurred in North Carolina. In the 1790s, the Reverend Charles Pettigrew left his sons "a most troublesome form of property." Since slaves had little reason to concern themselves with their masters' interests, he solemnly enjoined his children as a matter of Christian duty: "Endeavor to treat your negroes well." Some forty years later James Patton admonished his children in a spirit that combined moral duty with a questionable reading of slaves' response: "Be humane to your servants; give them plenty of nourishing diet and clothing. This will make them esteem you and cause them to do their duty with cheerfulness." So masters told themselves. But consider a passing matter during the War. Lowcountry planters developed a taste for family portraits and sought the best artists to paint them. When Yankee troops arrived, some slaves took revenge. They nailed the portraits to the walls of their cabins, gave them away, let them rot outside in the rain. Charles Manigault groaned that they thus showed "their hatred of their former master & all of his family." Manigault gave voice to an ancient theme, expressed by St. Jerome: "Sons love, slaves fear."[77]

During the late 1840s, D. W. Mitchell, an Englishman, attended a party in Virginia and found servants "on much more pleasant terms with the guests than any white servants I have ever observed." But southern slaveholders did not intend to replicate the unforgettable account of Fotis, the seductive slave girl, whom Apuleius blithely described as insolent toward her master's guests.

If a number read Apuleius, many more read Samuel Johnson, who observed, "Chains need not be put upon those who will be restrained without them." Chains or no chains, measures or no measures, masters grasped the limits of the "more pleasant terms." During the War, William Henry Trescot explained his insistence on speaking French at a dinner party: "We are speaking French against Africa. We know the black waiters are all ears now."[78]

The slaveholders sang paeans to their own virtue. Henry Bibb, an ex-slave, replied on behalf of the slaves in 1852 in a letter to Albert G. Sibley, a slave-holder. You slaveholders, he wrote, boast of caring for us, providing food and clothing and the like, but just who takes care of whom. "Let me ask you who is it that takes care of the slave holders and their families? Who is it that clears up the forest, cultivates the Land, manages the stock, husbands the grain, and prepares it for the table? Who is it that digs from the cotton, sugar, and rice fields, the means with which to build southern Cities, Steamboats, School houses and churches?" Bibb answered his own questions: The slaves perform that labor, and yet they and their children are deprived of its fruits.[79]

Slaveholders saw matters differently. John Martin Bolzius, visiting Jonathan Bryan's plantation in 1743, was certain that the slaves so loved their master and mistress that they did not desire freedom. Generations of white Southerners were no less certain. Who could doubt that slaves loved their masters and, for that matter, loved the soil on which their common household rested? Certainly not the "Gentleman" who wrote the poem on a "Liberian Emigrants' Farewell" that appeared in a flyer for a public meeting in Lexington, Virginia, in 1839:

> From our old home, now we sever
> From our mountains and our vales,
> To forget them, never – never,
> Till all life – all feeling fails.
> Dear Virginia! Dear Virginia!
> Loved, Oh loved wher'er we roam,
> Dear Virginia – loved Virginia!
> Farewell – farewell, dear old home.[80]

Even the intellectually accomplished Margaret Junkin of Virginia, reporting on fierce quarrels over *Uncle Tom's Cabin*, fell back on the clinching proslavery argument: Why, just look at how contented the slaves are. The Reverend C. C. Jones spoke for many, if more cautiously than most: "*Intercourse* with the people will be made more pleasant by kindness and condescension, without too great familiarity or sacrifice of becoming dignity and self-respect." Jones and the many for whom he spoke partially foreshadowed insights offered by Friedrich Nietzsche during the nineteenth century and by Albert Memmi, the Tunisian anticolonial theorist, during the twentieth. Nietzsche: "The familiarity of superiors embitters one, because it may not be returned." Memmi: "The oppressed are not filled solely with resentment against their oppressors, they also admire them and would even actually love them, with a kind of love, if they could."[81]

Countless whites lamented the passing of the beautiful days that ended sadly in 1865. In 1816, William Alexander MacCorkle, ex-governor of West Virginia, reflected on the master-slave relation: "Can a single being be found, who, after viewing the working of this patriarchal system, would desire to break it up, founded as it is upon reciprocal affection, mutual interest and perfect protection?" Edward Thomas admitted slaveholders' cruelty to slaves but judged it no worse than cruelty to wives and children in all countries: "Plantation life on the seaboard of Georgia was master and slave in its prettiest phase." Isaac DuBose Seabrook: "The days are well nigh past when Southern parents teach their children the duty of personal respect toward family servants or encourage them to visit their homes and minister to their wants." H. M. Hamill: "I cannot dismiss this passing glance at the social life of the Old South without a sense of abiding regret that it is gone forever." John S. Wise: "No more the happy darkey greeted us with smiles."[82]

5

The Blacks' Best and Most Faithful Friend

The negro has never yet found a sincere friend but his master.

– George M. Troup[1]

Greater self-deception is hard to imagine than that displayed by Governor George M. Troup in his address to the Georgia legislature in 1824. Self-deception, not hypocrisy. Troup expressed a long-gestating and widespread conviction. As the slaves' self-anointed friend, the master offered protection against the slaves' incompetence and emotional fragility. Privately as well as publicly, Southerners insisted that the slave recognized his master as his "best and most faithful friend." Proslavery northern public opinion helped. Southern newspapers relished and republished the frequent accounts from northern newspapers about the fine conditions and contentment of the slaves and about the urban misery of emancipated blacks who expressed a wish to be enslaved and return to the South. Beyond the principal newspapers of Richmond, Charleston, and New Orleans, small cities and towns reprinted directly from northern newspapers or from such southern newspapers as the *Fayetteville Observer, Semi-Weekly Mississippian, Mobile Tribune, Daily Alabama Journal, Macon Daily Telegraph, Texas State Gazette, Arkansas Gazette*, and *Weekly Raleigh Register*.[2]

As the South moved toward secession, assertions of slaves' loyalty and friendship grew louder, echoing long after the demise of slavery. They proceeded, especially among women, in tandem with notions of blacks' racial inferiority and general incompetence. The Massachusetts-born Tryphena Fox, married to a Louisiana slaveholder, wrote to her mother in 1856, "Negroes are so slow that they put me out of patience, not doing in all day what a good white man would do in an hour." A year later: "Talk about *freeing* negroes, some of them couldn't take care of themselves *ten* days." Adelaide Stuart Dimitry of Mississippi cried that emancipation dissolved the bonds of kindness between master and slave, depriving blacks of their staunchest friends: "Poor black dupes." Planters urged freedmen to stay with their old masters, since other whites cared nothing for them and would exploit them to the hilt. At the beginning of the War, Grace Brown Elmore of South Carolina asked, "Who but devils would seek to destroy the pleasant relations existing between Master & servant?" Elmore rated blacks the lowest of races: "What can the poor, uneducated, stupid, negro expect in the competition with white labor, which must sooner or later come?" And again: "The Negro as a hireling will never answer." With emancipation, "His and the Master's interests are now separate and there is no bond but dollars and cents between them." In 1895, Letitia A. Burwell of Virginia wrote, "Never again will the Negroes find a people so kind and true to them as the Southerners have been."[3]

The intellectually redoubtable Louisa S. McCord of South Carolina wrote to Henry C. Carey, the northern political economist, that withdrawal of white protection would doom an improvident black race: "You believe the negro to be an oppressed race, while we believe him to be a protected one.... We are convinced that we are his only safeguard from extermination, at least in this country." Obedient to her father's wish to emancipate several slaves, she exploded: "I am not even certain they will be willing to release *me* from the ownership." Thus did Southerners defend their ownership of slaves as a moral obligation.[4]

A Stagnant Race

In the Senate of Confederate Virginia, Robert Ruffin Collier introduced a resolution that declared southern blacks to be "in a higher condition of civilization than any of their race has ever been elsewhere." He recalled Napoleon's opinion that blacks had never created a civilization despite proximity to the great empires of Carthage and Egypt. Collier's resolution called slavery "the fundamental doctrine of southern civilization." In 1830, the proslavery Reverend Henry Bidleman Bascom – later bishop of the Methodist Episcopal Church, South – raised a contrary voice, praising black contributions to the building of ancient Egyptian civilization: "Africa has been degraded, insulted, and wronged for many centuries." Bascom spoke those words in New York. During the next twenty years the denigration of Africans became an easy ploy in both North and South.[5]

The peoples of Africa had never built a civilization, said "E. G." in 1845, deducing that the extinction of American blacks would follow the abolition of slavery. John C. Calhoun lectured the U.S. Senate in 1848 on a "remarkable fact": Never in human history have the colored races shown a capacity for free government. A year later Solon Robinson, a northern journalist and social reformer, won southern plaudits for saying that whites prevailed over Africans whenever they met. Black inability to progress reverberated in southern newspapers and provided a principal theme for such popular proslavery spokesmen as the Reverend William C. Buck, the editor of the *Baptist Banner* in Kentucky; T. W. Hoit of the St. Louis Literary and Philosophical Association; William H.

Holcombe, a prominent physician and literary figure in Natchez; and George P. Elliott and David J. McCord of South Carolina.[6]

Harrod C. Anderson of Tennessee fumed, "Negroes must be *made* to work when the seasons come on, for they seem not to see the present but are always putting off for some future day." Whitemarsh B. Seabrook, the future governor of South Carolina, believed that improvident blacks thought nothing of the future. Dr. Samuel Cartwright of Louisiana, friend of and physician to Jefferson Davis and a celebrated racial theorist, developed a wonderful alternative theory: The physical and mental constitution of blacks made them resist overwork and hard driving. Cartwright also invented "Drapetomania" – a mental disease that accounted for the blacks' penchant for running away. His theory did not account for the blacks' attachment to neighborhood and an unwillingness to migrate attested by Union soldiers found during the War. Yet medical practitioners in southern and northern ports used whites – the poor, transients, immigrants, and seamen – in experiments. Southern physicians paid scant attention to racial theories and assumed that the test results from blacks applied to whites. Josiah Nott of Mobile, an extreme scientific racist, used white and black prostitutes as guinea pigs.[7]

Ironically, the scientists and physicians who constructed a medical theory for limited black capacity strengthened the case for humane treatment. Dr. John Stainback Wilson joined Cartwright in urging planters to feed blacks vegetables, milk, and molasses. M. W. Philips of Mississippi advised planters to allow slaves plenty of time to eat, since they required much more than whites did. According to a physician ("Citizen of Mississippi"), everyone agreed that blacks had weak constitutions, could not work as hard or as long as whites, and had to be kept out of the rain. Mary Howard Schoolcraft of South Carolina thought so, too: "All experience in the South proves that you cannot overwork a negro. He will do his task, and no human power can make him do any more." An agricultural committee in South Carolina observed, "Negroes lack the motives of self-interest to make them careful and diligent." Exercise great patience with them: "Do not, therefore, notice too many omissions of duty." Dr. A. P. Merrill of Memphis, in an essay reprinted in medical and agricultural journals, stressed blacks' weak physical constitutions. Whites nonetheless considered black women physically stronger than white and better equipped for childbearing. In fact, childbed deaths were proportionately higher among blacks than whites. But most racial characterizations unintentionally encouraged slaves to manipulate white self-deception and wrest some control over the pace of work. After all, if black people were incompetent, not to say stupid, there would be no point in whites' pushing them too hard. Such racial characterizations encouraged masters' forbearance but simultaneously reinforced their sense of superiority.[8]

William Winans, a controversial Methodist pastor in Mississippi, believed blacks improvable, yet he endorsed much of Cartwright's work as scientifically sound. Samuel Galloway of Georgia, a Pennsylvania-born political economist, added a charming twist: "The Negro has a physical structure for enduring a tropical sun, for rendering a Southern plantation a delightful residence." To anyone who protested that slaves might not have found the residence delightful, Galloway had a reply: "The dark races, who possess the acutest senses, display insensitivity to moral beauty, manly virtue and elevated sentiment." The slaveholders had trouble getting their story straight. The slave trader A. J. McElveen wrote that no one who bought a slave need confine him: "He will go with them anywhere. The Boy cannot bear Punishment or Confinement."9

From every side and with endless assertions, a theme arose and prevailed: Non-Caucasians lacked the capacity to govern themselves. Hence, the white race must rule the world. President Thomas Roderick Dew of the College of William and Mary contrasted the "grinding despotisms" of Asia and Africa with the long struggles for liberty in Europe, attributing the difference to racial characteristics. Waddy Thompson of South Carolina, an American envoy to Mexico, contrasted Teutons and Anglo-Saxons with Mexicans, among others: "Our race has never yet put its foot upon a soil which it has not only not kept but has advanced." In the 1850s, W. R. Aylett of King William County, Virginia, a planter and grandson of Patrick Henry, repeatedly spoke of Latin Americans as unfit for self-rule but fit for an "Americanization" that established order. The theme and its corollary emerged with full force after the War.10

Black Incapacity

John S. Brisbane of South Carolina, the president of the St. Andrew's Ashley and Stono River Agricultural Association, urged careful study of slaves: "They are our impelling power." Study slaves the planters did, although not always successfully. Stolid black reactions to a cholera epidemic in 1849 led Dr. William A. Booth to remark: "All Negroes are fatalists." Yankee troops and officials in the Sea Islands commented on the "fatalism" of the blacks. The notion of black fatalism fed various white evaluations of black life and work.11

The need for specifics to demonstrate inherent black incapacity sometimes proved entertaining. Ariela J. Gross notes that masters everywhere insisted on the racial inferiority and childishness of slaves and yet became furious when they performed poorly. The Southern Agriculturalist and Register of Rural Affairs judged Joseph Ingraham's racially biased *South-West, by a Yankee*, an accurate portrayal of blacks as natural slaves. Tom, Charles Manigault's bricklayer, carried a letter from Louis Manigault but did not deliver it: "Negro like, I suppose he is keeping your Letter until he happens to see me, instead of leaving it at this house." The Presbyterian Reverend C. C. Jones, Jr., of Georgia did not contradict such denigration when a slave saved himself from the effects of a snakebite: "His presence of mind was remarkable for a Negro." As racial and class attitudes merged, whites left room for exceptions. A contributor to the *Southern Literary Journal* declared that emancipated blacks did not improve their condition, but then, neither did British laborers. After the War, Eliza Frances Andrews of Georgia sighed, "The negro is something like the

Irishman in his blundering good nature, his impulsiveness and improvidence." The English-born Amelia Barr had trouble with hired slaves in Texas: "I did not understand the negro women then, any better than I understand the Finnish or Irish women now. I thought right was always right and that all women of whatever race ought to do right." Accordingly, she found disagreeable her Scots husband's advice to make allowances.[12]

Few white Southerners – or Northerners – believed blacks capable of survival in a competitive free-labor society. In the 1790s, John Cooper, in his will, decided not to distribute his slaves widely among relatives: "To some it would be but burthening their conscience to hold them as slaves or they must liberate them, which in my opinion would be a very great disadvantage to the slaves." The theme persisted. Writing in the mid-1830s for widely circulating religious publications, the Presbyterian Reverend Rufus William Bailey of South Carolina saw black progress as preparation for eventual colonization. "Uncle Dunbar sold Mr. Noble a little negro boy to be free at one and twenty," Eliza Magruder of Mississippi wrote in 1846. "I am doubtful whether freedom will be a benefit to him." James H. Hammond seemed genuinely distressed over the possible fate of his slave mistress and mulatto children. To free them and send them to the North would be an act of wanton cruelty. He pleaded with his son, "Do not let Louisa or any of my children or possible children be slaves of Strangers. Slavery *in the family* will be their happiest earthly condition." In the 1850s a plantation mistress, speaking to the antislavery Barbara Leigh Smith Bodichon of England, categorically ruled out emancipation because Louisiana could not absorb the freedmen and the North would not receive them. Richard B. P. Lyons, British envoy extraordinary, alerted Foreign Secretary Earl Russell that Southerners considered slavery ordained by God to lift the African peoples.[13]

Slaveholders had to consider blacks unfit to support themselves. How else justify their enslavement? Edward Tayloe wrote to his brother from the University of Virginia in 1832, "I cannot but feel great uneasiness for the colored population of the State, where [cholera] has appeared it has proved very fatal.... Imprudent as negroes are, and destitute of many comforts, this effect was to have been expected." Wrote another slaveholder: "Negroes are a thriftless, thoughtless people. Left to themselves they will over eat, unseasonably eat, walk half the night, sleep on the ground, out of doors, anywhere." Dr. Bennet Dowler concluded that the good treatment Africans received as slaves saved them from catastrophe. Black abolitionists saw as especially dangerous the charges that blacks could not take care of themselves and that their conditions were worse in the North than in the South. Racial discrimination in the North as well as the South became a principal subject for blacks who lectured in Britain, Canada, and the United States in support of emigration to Haiti, Jamaica, or Africa. Confronting the argument of black unfitness for freedom, Peter Randolph, who had been a slave in Virginia, scoffed, "All I have to say is, give them an opportunity, and then see how close they will stick to their *beloved masters*."[14]

The notion of innate black incapacity upset southern clergymen, for it implied that slavery's ostensibly greatest accomplishment – the Christianization of Africans – had produced paltry results. During the politically inflamed 1850s, clerical and lay contributors to leading journals assailed polygenesists for branding Africans incapable of improvement. As evidence of black capacity, prominent clergymen cited impressive progress made by Africans before the white incursions. These included Episcopal Bishop William Meade, the Presbyterian Reverend George Howe, the Presbyterian Reverend John Leighton Wilson, for years a missionary to West Africa, and "J. M. W.," a Georgia planter. As Christopher Luse has recently demonstrated, these counterpoints did not shake widespread racial assumptions. Allegedly, Christian slavery civilized Africans but only within narrow limits.[15]

Scientific racism infected the North with its principal thesis that blacks were inherently, not just culturally, inferior to whites. Visiting Rhode Island in the 1730s, a distressed Dean (later Bishop) George Berkeley found that many whites pushed the thesis to its extreme, considering blacks a separate species. In New England, Cotton Mather and Jonathan Edwards felt required to defend man's common origin in Adam. In South Carolina, Anglican priests faced no such problem. Educated Southerners, like many Englishmen and Northerners, read or at least knew of Edward Long's *History of Jamaica* (1748), which viewed blacks as a species halfway between men and apes. By the 1830s fear of miscegenation had gripped some leading southern proslavery theorists. Miscegenation horrified Henry Hughes of Mississippi. John Fletcher of Louisiana proposed enslavement of whites who sired slave children, although he faulted social floaters more than slaveholders. The Presbyterian Reverend T. C. Thornton of Mississippi simultaneously raged against miscegenation and pled for humane treatment of slaves. The theologically liberal Episcopal Reverend James Warley Miles of South Carolina envisioned miscegenation as the probable root of original sin. The idea of miscegenation-as-sin, heard in slavery days, became wildly popular after the War. The prospect of "the *mongrelization* of our noble Anglo-Saxon race" sickened the Baptist Reverend Jeremiah Jeter of Virginia, who preached that God had separated the races.[16]

Dr. William B. Carpenter, Fellow of the Royal Society, in a letter to Boston's *Christian Examiner and Religious Miscellany*, challenged the notion of blacks' inherent inferiority but conceded deterioration of their racial stock. Polygenesists like Dr. Samuel H. Dickson of Charleston pounced on Carpenter's concession. By the 1850s much of the northern Democratic Party and its press had embraced polygenesis and scientific racism, which denied the unity of the human race and which the southern churches denounced as heresy. The British envoy extraordinary routinely referred to the Democratic Party as the "Pro-Slavery Party." Debating Abraham Lincoln in 1858, Stephen Douglas declared: "I positively deny that [the black man] is my brother or any kin to me whatever."[17]

In the South, racial arguments from history and culture prevailed over arguments from biology, but the gap was narrowing. In Virginia, William Byrd remarked casually, in his *History of the Dividing Line*, that all races have equal talents and that superiority stemmed from access to improvement. George Tucker of Virginia, who as a boy had been taught arithmetic by a black playmate, rejected as nonsense theories of racial superiority, and so did the historian David Ramsay and the diplomat Joel Poinsett of South Carolina. Sam Houston of Texas told Alexis de Tocqueville that blacks and Indians were as intelligent as whites and that education made the difference in performance.[18]

No critic irritated Nott more than the Presbyterian Reverend W. T. Hamilton of Mobile, who upheld the unity of mankind, attacked scientific racism in his book, *"Friend of Moses,"* and repelled accusations of black inferiority, which he traced to the secular Enlightenment and German Higher Criticism. Nott won a cheap victory when Hamilton left Mobile under a cloud in 1854, charged with the sexual molestation of a boy in his congregation. Nott wisecracked, "The friend of Moses attempted to thrust the Christian Religion in *per ano*." Despite Hamilton, rejection of the idea of separate species did not imply rejection of black inferiority. Matthew Estes of Mississippi suggested that a peculiar historical evolution had rendered blacks fit only for labor in uncultivated parts of the world. Fletcher argued that the evolution of some races accompanied the devolution of others. From the South Carolina elite, E. J. Pringle, William J. Grayson, and Henry William Ravenel accepted the possibility of black improvement under white tutelage, and lauded slavery for raising blacks to the highest point of civilization they could achieve. And they attacked scientific racism for encouraging maltreatment of slaves. With scientific issues hard to fathom, most Southerners deferred to their preachers. The Presbyterian Reverend Thomas Smyth of Charleston noted that Africans, like Europeans, varied considerably in color and traits and that all races were intermixtures. He argued that the degradation of the black race, having been historically and culturally determined, could be reversed. Calvin Wiley of North Carolina, a prominent educational reformer, declared, "The negro has been torn from his savage associations & introduced into families of the world's most intelligent, active, energetic, moral & Christian families."[19]

Black Thoughts, According to White Critics

Slaveholders maintained that their slaves, knowing that they required protection and support, preferred slavery to freedom. In 1797, the Presbyterian Reverend Henry Pattillo of North Carolina, declaring well-treated black slaves better off than poor whites, concluded that no friend would put the idea of freedom in their heads. A year later, Ramsay wrote that slavery had rendered blacks unfit for freedom, and that emancipation would be "ruinous" to both master and slave. In later decades, a Virginia planter assured John Finch, the British geologist, that his hundred or so slaves were happier than they would be if emancipated. George Shortridge of Alabama thought blacks "by nature lazy, listless, and indifferent" and easily enslaved. Representative Benjamin F. Perry of upcountry South Carolina simultaneously denounced the secessionists of 1850 and the "great evil" that would impose freedom on civilized and happy slaves. John Fletcher appealed to God's power and wisdom: "All in civilized and Christian life and practice, from the king upon the throne down to the slave, are rendered equally happy and contented with their condition.... He is not a correct philosopher who measures the happiness of a lower grade in life by his own feelings."[20]

In Parliament in 1775, Edmund Burke, delivering his prophetic speech on conciliation with America, opposed punishment of rebellious Americans by emancipation of their slaves: "Slaves are often much attached to their masters. A general wild offer of liberty would not always be accepted.... It is sometimes as hard to persuade slaves to be free, as it is to compel freemen to be slaves." Burke eschewed racial argument: "Slaves as the unfortunate black people are, and dull as all men from slavery, must not they a little suspect the offer of freedom from that very nation which has sold them to their present masters." Governor John Drayton of South Carolina and Jefferson Davis claimed that "happy and contented" slaves lived better than European peasants and Russian serfs and were so attached to their masters that they often refused liberation when offered. *The Southern Cultivator* exclaimed in 1852 that abolitionists could never persuade blacks to leave W. H. Huntingdon's "model plantation" on which well-fed and housed slaves worked reasonable hours, not the twelve to fourteen hours imposed on northern industrial workers.[21]

In the 1820s, *The Southern Review* reported (questionably) that southern state legislatures were burdened by petitions from blacks who had moved to the North and wished to return, and Seabrook maintained (plausibly) that the North considered free blacks "a nuisance of incalculable magnitude." Extreme poverty and police harassment motivated a handful in Alabama, Mississippi, Texas, and South Carolina to seek re-enslavement. Louisiana officially invited petitions for self-enslavement, but without result. Many of the blacks who went to Liberia did so in response to the persecution that followed the Nat Turner insurrection and frequent local insurrectionary scares. Increasingly, Americans heard about destitute northern blacks ready to sell themselves into slavery.[22]

De Bow's Review singled out Philadelphia as a showcase of the degradation of free blacks and claimed that in New York blacks begged to return to slavery. Carl David Arfwedson of Sweden heard about an old slave, traveling with his master in Philadelphia, who refused abolitionist entreaties to desert and chose to remain with his master after seeing the wretchedness of the free blacks. Mary Howard Schoolcraft investigated the suffering in Philadelphia, rummaging through northern and southern newspapers for signs of blacks' willingness to return to slavery in the South. She probably knew that William Lyon Mackenzie, the Canadian revolutionary, had dismissed American claims of equality, reinforcing the British abolitionist Joseph Sturge's account of virulent hostility to blacks in Philadelphia. James Johnston Pettigrew of the Carolina low country, who saw a crude performance of *Uncle Tom's Cabin* in Philadelphia, chuckled at actors who declaimed about equality while blacks sat in a segregated gallery.[23]

Said a slaveholder: "There are few slaves, we believe, in the Southern country who would change their present condition, which is one of dependence, for all the advantages which freedom would bring." Said another of runaways to the North: "Many a poor fugitive has wept to return to the indulgent master, and well filled corncrib." In one story, slaves deserted masters on a trip to England and then begged to return. Beverley Tucker of Virginia and William C. Buck in Kentucky doubted that many slaves favored emancipation. Nimrod Farrow of South Carolina wrote to Calhoun about a slave who, after being sold, traveled two thousand miles on foot to get to his "proper master." Harrison Berry, a literate slave in Georgia who did not question black aspirations for freedom, said that slaves distrusted the abolitionists in part because of the ill–treatment of free blacks at the North. And unconditional unionists claimed that East Tennesseans shrugged off emancipation because they expected blacks to work for old masters who treated them well.[24]

In the 1850s, Margaret Johnson Erwin of Mississippi freed her slaves. Nettie, a favorite, hurt and angry, demanded to know why Erwin no longer wanted her. A few years later, Erwin grieved deeply when her beloved Nettie died. The historian William S. Forrest of Norfolk wrote that many blacks in Virginia rejected "unqualified freedom," preferring to remain as slaves and be taken care of. J. S. Buckingham, William Chambers, and other foreign travelers reported the prevalent belief that blacks had little interest in a change of status. Prominent Northerners reinforced the belief. Lillian Foster had proof that the slaves rejected freedom. What "proof"? Why, they said so, when she asked. Leander Ker did not think that one slave in twenty would accept emancipation. He added that the depressing condition of northern free blacks proved their incapability. In later years, elite women like Susan Dabney Smedes of Mississippi and Letitia Burwell of Virginia pointedly recalled slaves who had remained with kind masters rather than accept freedom. In sober moments, whites discerned that blacks wore masks to disguise true feelings. Even the Reverend C. C. Jones, an experienced missionary to the slaves, admitted uncertainty about what he heard and saw.[25]

Yet all too many moments proved other than sober. Judge Garnett Andrews offered an ostensibly irrefutable argument at the Southern Central Agricultural Society of Georgia: "If unfitted for the relation, the African would – as any other race would – instead of affection, have the greatest hostility to those whose immediate rule he serves." James Warley Miles wrote, "Certain races, although for a time enslaved, will emancipate themselves ultimately; other races only flourish in subjection to superior races." He singled out blacks as a prime example of the latter. The high civilizations of Asians and Europeans proved "the germs of that civilization in their original nature." For Miles, Indians and Pacific Islanders perished under slavery, whereas blacks became "elevated" by participation in civilization and Christianity. George Sawyer of Louisiana provided a twist. Were the slaves faithful to their masters, as most Southerners claimed? Yes, but with a fidelity that flowed not from intellect or morals but from "an instinctive impulse, possessed even to a higher degree by some of the canine species." For Sawyer, too, black acceptance of slavery proved their inferiority. In 1865 Belle Boyd, the flamboyant Confederate spy, spoke for countless white Americans: "Can it be urged that a race which prefers servitude to freedom has reached that adolescent period of existence which fits it for the latter condition?"[26]

Views of Emancipation

When slaveholders proclaimed friendship with their slaves, they accurately stated that freedmen had few white friends in the North. In the early nineteenth century several thousand American blacks went to Haiti, only to return disillusioned. Abolitionists, on the defensive, charged that only the worst blacks had gone and only in expectation of a dole. In the late 1850s, V. Moreau Randolph, the captain of the schooner *Ontario*, reported to antislavery relatives in Virginia that emancipated blacks in Haiti and the British West Indies were veering back toward barbarism. Rafael Semmes, the Confederacy's talented naval commander, the Unitarian Reverends Charles A. Farley and Charles M. Taggart, and Daniel Lee, the editor of *Southern Cultivator*, were among many who agreed. Replying with heavy sarcasm, the American Anti-Slavery Society pointed to West Indian freedmen who cultivated family farms. The proslavery spokesmen easily turned the argument aside. They did not deny that blacks could sustain themselves – if poorly – outside the world market; they attributed to blacks an inability to survive marketplace competition.[27]

Some white Southerners, having gone north to escape slavery, joined the abolitionists. Others went north with proslavery attitudes and opposed abolitionism. In 1819, Allen G. Thurman of Virginia moved to Chillicothe, Ohio, with the blacks his parents had emancipated. He thereupon established a national reputation as one of the Democratic Party's strongest defenders of white supremacy. In 1857, a delighted Edmund Ruffin heard that Ellwood Fisher, a proslavery ideologue, had been raised a Quaker: "His grandfather & father had emancipated their slaves & made every other incidental sacrifice to perform what they deemed their religious & moral duty in that respect." Other antislavery émigrés had the wrenching experience of seeing their children return to the South or remain in the North as proslavery Negrophobes. In the early 1820s, Governor Edward Coles, Thomas Jefferson's protégé, freed his slaves and led the fight to keep slavery out of Illinois. Coles, who braved his neighbors' wrath when he settled former slaves on farms, reported that, although harassed, they did well. Yet Coles's son Robert returned to Virginia to fight for the Confederacy. The Indiana-born George Cary Eggleston, author of *Rebel's Recollections*, came from a family that freed its slaves and left the South. He too returned to Virginia as a young man and fought for the Confederacy.[28]

In 1836 the Reverend George Addison Baxter, the president of Hampden-Sydney College, maintained that Virginia had emancipated thousands of slaves in the post-Revolutionary years, only to have them fail as free men. He pointed to Ohio as compelled to legislate against burdensome free blacks. Sad stories abounded. The Reverend Tobias Gibson of Mississippi freed his slaves, most of whom, according to a Methodist historian, became vagabonds. In subsequent decades, distinguished Southerners – James Madison, J. L. Petigru, the Reverends Moses Hoge and J. L. Wilson – told similar stories. Maria Edgeworth, the antislavery British novelist, wrote to Rachel Mordecai Lazarus of North Carolina that she had seen the Reverend William Buell Sprague, a prolific and esteemed northern minister who had visited Mount Vernon. He reported that the slaves emancipated by George Washington had proved as worthless and wretched a lot as he had ever beheld. George Washington Parke Custis remarked, "They succeeded very badly as freemen."[29]

In Virginia, the Presbyterian father and mother of James and William Holcombe converted to Methodism. Their father became a preacher, and they freed their slaves. They moved to Indiana in order to raise their children away from the sinful and stultifying atmosphere of slavery. The sons chose sin and stultification. William settled in Natchez, where he became a prominent homeopathic physician, author, and Swedenborgian. James returned to Virginia, where he became a successful lawyer and political and legal theorist. Both became proslavery southern-rights men, repudiating their parents' philosophy and politics, although not their persons. William discussed his father respectfully and warmly and described his mother as an "old-fashioned Methodist of very strong religious propensities." One day, William accidentally received a copy of the New York *Tribune*, which carried a report of an antislavery speech by Henry Ward Beecher. He protested, "I have no patience with such ignorant, fanatical and seditious tirades concocted in falsehood and delivered in malice." He acknowledged "the real evils of slavery" and supported reform but denounced Beecher's speech as "a coarse calumny in tendency." William Holcombe upheld "a political axiom of very great wisdom – 'never disturb an *established* evil until you have a prompt and infallible remedy at hand' – Never shake a man's faith in his religion, whatever complexion it may be of, until you have better one to give him. Paganism is preferable to infidelity, slavery to anarchy." William Holcombe considered slavery the only possible relation between an advanced and an inferior race: "Freedom and competition with the white man would ultimately annihilate the negro race in the South." Yet he departed from racial argument: "He who works under a master and receives nothing but a subsistence is a slave." The capitalists of the North depressed labor: "The Democrats of the North were therefore the Natural allies of the South as remarked by Mr. Jefferson."[30]

The Baptist Reverend Richard Fuller mentioned a minister in Virginia who had prepared a family of slaves to provide for themselves, sent them to Pennsylvania, and then yielded to entreaties to take them back. Fuller, renowned for his defense of slavery in a debate with Francis Wayland, transferred to Baltimore, where he supported colonization. He lauded black progress under Christian auspices but doubted that whites would accept even the most accomplished blacks. As a matter of conscience, the Cumberland Presbyterian Reverend Ephraim McLean freed his slaves and provided them with a farm, implements, and stock. Within a few years they became idle, drunken, and miserable. They begged him to take them back, and he did. John Triplett Thom, a big planter in the Virginia piedmont with qualms about slavery, decided on an experiment. He freed some slaves and provided them with farms and necessaries in Pennsylvania. Discouraged within a year, they returned to his plantation. The Methodist Reverend Gilbert D. Taylor of Tennessee regretted having freed his two slaves, who fell into dissipation. Samuel Gist of Virginia settled hundreds of emancipated slaves in Ohio without sufficient capital. Fleeced by speculators and creditors, they faced violence from hostile white farmers. William Capers of South Carolina, before becoming a Methodist bishop, turned his farm over to his slaves to prepare for freedom. They failed miserably. Gerritt Smith of New York, an abolitionist and philanthropist, established a program for the distribution of land to blacks in New York State. A fiasco: Most of the land had to be surrendered for nonpayment of taxes. John England, the Catholic bishop of Charleston, asserted that he knew "many freedmen who regretted their manumission." Richard H. Wilde, a congressman and fine poet, left Georgia for New Orleans only to receive entreaties from his slaves to return to look after them.[31]

John Randolph of Roanoke emancipated some four hundred slaves by will. The record remains cloudy, but most seem to have ended as poor, landless laborers. Proslavery spokesmen assumed the worst and harped on it. In 1850, M. R. H. Garnett of Virginia chided northern philanthropy for welcoming fugitive slaves but not free blacks, and the Methodist Reverend Samuel Dunwoody preached in Marietta, Georgia, about the hostility that Ohioans showed toward John Randolph's freedmen. Whatever the truth about those and other emancipated blacks, Letitia A. Burwell expressed the general white sentiment when she declared that they went to seed. Richard Randolph, John's brother, freed his slaves but settled them at home. H. A. Garland commented: "It proved in the end to be a mistaken philanthropy. Left in the county where they had been slaves, these negroes soon became idle and profligate vagabonds and thieves; a burthen to themselves and a pest to the neighborhood." Some Virginia Quakers freed their slaves and converted them into tenants, but they stole more than they worked. Thomas Jefferson, in one of his more generous moments, attributed their failure to the lingering effects of slavery rather than to racial incapacity, but others thought differently. John Hartwell Cocke, a cofounder of the University of Virginia and a big planter who admired *Uncle Tom's Cabin*, taught some slaves to read, trained them in trades, and sent them to his Alabama plantation to prepare for freedom. Their disappointing behavior made him an object of ridicule. Cocke's aversion to slavery waned, much to the delight of his proslavery son. And everyone heard that the slaves emancipated by Bishop William Meade of Virginia became beggars. (Poor Meade: In 1847 he published a volume devoted to the "fidelity and piety" of "old Virginia's family servants.") John MacGregor, an antislavery Scot, wrote of a northern community that included some two thousand escaped slaves, whom critics described as being in miserable condition. Still, MacGregor thought them better off than many whites in Kentucky. The southern press regaled readers with reports of emancipated blacks who had come to a bad end. Ensuing debacles proved blacks either incompetent or shut out by hostile northern whites. The alternatives were not mutually exclusive. Each reinforced the slaveholders' sense of being the only real friends blacks had.[32]

Freedmen's failures were bruited about, but not their successes. Chief Justice Roger B. Taney, having freed his slaves in Maryland, expressed pleasure at their achievements in freedom. All across the South free blacks developed skills and accumulated money to buy their freedom and that of family members. By 1830 some 80 percent of the blacks in Baltimore were free, and by 1860 free blacks outnumbered slaves in Maryland. Blacks made heroic efforts to buy themselves out of slavery after accumulating funds as skilled workers whose masters found it profitable to let hire their own time. An unusual feature of the transition in Baltimore was the largely informal system – partly sanctioned at law – that resembled the old Roman *peculium* and Cuban *coartación*: Slaves bought their freedom a little at a time, in effect converting themselves from slaves-for-life into "term-slaves." Bishop Bascom, defending southern withdrawal from the Methodist Church, pointed to the substantial number of literate and intelligent free blacks in Baltimore. Proslavery polemics ignored thousands of slaves who, against all odds, earned money to buy freedom for themselves and their families.[33]

Northerners gave aid and comfort to proslavery Southerners. Solon Robinson referred to the supposed loyalty of slaves during the Revolution and the War of 1812: "The truth is that the slaves of the South do not desire to be freed from their servitude." Samuel Seabury, citing northern freedmen who regretted their emancipation, reasoned that southern slaves seemed content and therefore implicitly submitted to enslavement. The *Indiana Sentinel* gushed about a manumitted slave who, having tasted freedom in California, wished he were still a slave in Texas. Hinton Helper, the southern abolitionist, wrote from California about disillusioned freed blacks who wanted to return to slavery. Many slaves rejected freedom if it meant leaving home and community for life in Liberia – for a dangerous voyage to a strange, far-off land and, possibly, a life of deprivation. Stephen Douglas came under fire when he agreed to manage his wife's plantation in Alabama. But what could he do? His father-in-law's slaves had rejected freedom and transportation to Liberia. The American Colonization Society preached to blacks that their lives would be much better in Liberia. Unfortunately, too many emigrants, finding life especially hard, returned in bitterness or sent word to southern blacks that slavery was preferable to what they had.[34]

Wilkes Flagg, a slave in Milledgeville, Georgia, single-handedly demonstrated the error of conflating a refusal of freedom under discrete circumstances with an attitude toward freedom in principle. Flagg had a benevolent master, Tomlinson Fort, whose children had taught him to read. For unknown reasons Flagg refused Fort's offer of freedom. If the story had ended there, proslavery men would have rejoiced. But when Flagg thought the moment propitious, he bought himself and his family out of slavery. Reputedly the finest headwaiter in Georgia, as well as a successful blacksmith and Baptist preacher, he supervised dinner for a succession of governors. By 1860 his assets totaled $25,000. Flagg privately favored abolition.[35]

The Reverend Rufus William Bailey of South Carolina wrote to his Christian brethren in Maine in the mid-1830s, "The Negro has as firm friends here as any where. There are many men at the South who have made themselves poor for the benefit of the slaves." He taunted New Englanders: "Who at the North has done this?" Asserting the superior condition of southern slaves relative to northern free blacks, he maintained that "intelligent slaves" grasped the discrepancy. Belle Boyd considered irrefutable the superior condition of the southern "helot" relative to the northern "free Negro." Judge John Richter Jones of Pennsylvania wrote in 1861: "The *political* servitude of the negro race is as complete [here] as where the constitution acknowledges none but *white* citizens as it is in Virginia." Philip Schaff, the Mercersburg theologian, spoke of "the miserable condition of the unfortunate African race both in the free and in the slave States."[36]

Reports circulated of slaves who accompanied masters to free states, spurned a chance to claim freedom, and returned with their masters – that is, returned to their mates, children, and the only homes they knew. William Hobby of Georgia regaled Southerners with stories of slaves, traveling with masters, who shrank from the miserable condition of northern free blacks. When an occasional black claimed the right to return to his family in the South, abolitionists denied that anyone had a right to choose enslavement. President Thomas Cooper of South Carolina College retorted that blacks had a right to choose slavery in order to improve their chances of survival. During the War, slaves who escaped to or were taken by the Yankees and found their way back to their owners described horrible mistreatment, which masters chose to believe. Texans boasted that their slaves could easily escape across the Rio Grande if they wanted to. That few blacks refused emancipation or asked for re-enslavement did not matter. Overwhelming evidence of a desire for freedom could be suppressed or interpreted as evidence of Yankee tampering or rebellion against constituted authority. Proslavery Southerners, like people in other circumstances, heard what they wanted to hear. Southerners acknowledged that a slave's refusal of freedom might testify to the discrimination and wretchedness he faced as a pariah in either the North or the South. They concluded that blacks, shut out from ordinary institutions of northern life, needed the personal protection slavery offered.[37]

News from Africa

In Richmond, the Reverend Charles A. Farley told his Unitarian congregation that blacks emancipated before preparation for freedom "would relapse into barbarism" and "iron despotism." Newspapers across the South foresaw "relapse" and, in the words of the *Weekly Mississippian*, the transformation into "a blighted race" unable to sustain itself. Adelaide Stuart Dimitry of New Orleans gave relapse short shrift, describing plantation slaves as "dull, ignorant, semi-barbarous." In contrast, *abolitionists,* convinced of the superiority of free labor, had enormous expectations for Sierra Leone and Liberia. By the late 1790s dreams of profitable investment had faded, and in 1807 the near-bankrupt Sierra Leone Company asked the crown to take over the colony. Thomas Foxwell Buxton, the antislavery parliamentary leader, conceding failure, reproved the British government for an overly generous policy that undermined incentives and encouraged dependency. Seymour Drescher concludes his historical study: "The abolitionists silently distanced themselves from the idea of Sierra Leone as a labor experiment in competition with West Indian slavery."[38]

Accounts of Liberia as fiasco spread across the South. In Missouri, Judge William Barclay Napton circulated a report from the Richmond *Enquirer* on newly emancipated slaves sent to Liberia: Two-thirds had died of disease, and others had returned to Virginia sick and emaciated. Traveling in the Southwest, Matilda Charlotte Houstoun of England reflected on Liberia as the latest proof of black inadequacy. W. W. Wright, in *De Bow's Review*, regaled readers with accounts of complicity in slavery and the slave trade by residents of Sierra Leone and Liberia. Southerners ignored contrary voices from antislavery men like the border state Presbyterian Reverend Robert J. Breckenridge and Philip Schaff of Pennsylvania, who declared Liberia and Sierra Leone in good order and progressing well.[39]

Some twelve thousand blacks went to Liberia between 1820 and 1861 – about half recently emancipated and all but a thousand or so from the South. Emigrants faced a hard "seasoning." Before 1844, 21 percent of the arrivals died in their first year. The struggle to build a viable economy proved painful, giving rise to acute privation. An emerging Liberian leadership engaged in frequent wars with the native Africans whose land they were occupying. Black Americans sought to promote Christianity, build schools, and suppress the native slave trade; they also sought to "civilize" the natives and seize their land. Southern slaveholders combined disgust, mirth, and smug satisfaction upon learning that settlers had oppressed natives and recapitulated the white conquest of Indian lands. A southern naval officer, appalled by hardship in Monrovia, commented on a state dinner full of pompous talk: "I imagined myself among a collection of house servants who were closely imitating their masters." In 1931, an international commission on conditions in Liberia reported that "the ruling Americo-Liberians have inflicted virtual slavery upon the natives of the interior," replete with raiding, kidnapping, flogging, torture, and daily cruelties.[40]

Some blacks simply touched base, expressing affection for their "white family"; others, with or without affection, wanted something. Phillis Jennings, having been sold to Guadeloupe, sent Mary Pettigrew, her old mistress, condolences on the death of a member of the white family, addressing her as "My Dear Mother." She closed with "your affectionate daug[h]ter – and always-ready to send all Service – but – do not forget – Masr Jacke – whom I nurse – tell him I hope he has not forgot me." She requested nothing but, instead, sent two jugs of gin. Other expressions of affection seem intended to send regards through the white family to their own black relatives and friends. Still, whites took every expression of affection straight, as some were doubtless meant to be taken.[41]

Appeals for help deluged Virginians. Albert Fairfax trained his slaves in trades and settled them in Liberia. Failing miserably, they asked to return. A steady stream of letters from Liberia, pleading hardship, recalled former masters to their old paternal obligations. They asked for money and supplies, including books, writing paper, and quills to assist in the education of their children. Settlers asked for whipsaws, shoes, medical supplies, and "any other thing you think proper," as York Walker put it. Occasionally, settlers promised to reciprocate by sending coffee or skins. The deferential tone and frequent references to "father" or "dear friend" strengthened slaveholders' self-images. Frequent reports in the southern press usually put Liberians in the worst possible light. In 1858, a plantation mistress in Louisiana assured Bodichon that Southerners rejected the cruelty of sending blacks to Liberia. A gentleman she knew had received letters from his former slaves in Liberia, many of whom were starving. She commented: "That plan is a failure."[42]

A few proslavery Southerners defended the Liberians. In 1836, the *Southern Literary Messenger* published a generous account of their intellectual and material progress and of their leading newspaper, the *Liberia Herald*. In 1848, the Virginia Historical Society welcomed Liberia's progress, praising Virginia's special contribution. The Episcopal Reverend Philip Slaughter of Virginia and the Lutheran Reverend Boston Drayton of South Carolina depicted Liberia as overcoming adversity. In 1857, even Edmund Ruffin noticed when Bishop Thomas Atkinson of North Carolina applauded the success of ex-slaves in Liberia.[43]

Gilbert Hunt bought his freedom, went to Liberia, and returned to a warm welcome from whites and an easier life as a blacksmith in Richmond. The crowning proslavery moment came in 1859. Joseph Mackintosh accumulated $1,600 in Culpeper County to pay his way to Liberia, where, although serving as a judge and moving in high circles, he found himself almost penniless. He went to Canada, only to encounter deplorable conditions for blacks. He returned to Virginia to work as a bath keeper and attendant at White Sulphur Springs, where white gentlemen crowded around to hear his story. A gentleman in Richmond, who remembered him, made the necessary legal arrangements. Mackintosh said that if Virginia expelled free blacks, he would ask Jeremiah Morton to accept him as his slave and body servant. Peter Randolph, a black man of different temperament, wrote a bitter account of his life as a slave in Virginia; yet he observed that news of cruelty to blacks in the North kept many southern slaves from fleeing there. Thomas Smallwood, an ex-slave, organized fugitive slaves to go to Canada. He praised the accomplishments of most American black settlers but complained about a shiftless minority. He arraigned American abolitionists for encouraging ne'er-do-wells to tell negative stories about black life in Canada in order to persuade others to settle in the northern states, where, ostensibly, perfect freedom reigned.[44]

Ex-slaves interviewed by Benjamin Drew in Canada turned in generally favorable but nonetheless disturbing reports about white racial attitudes and practices. Aaron Siddles emigrated with $10,000, accumulated in Indiana. Despite economic success in Indiana, he chafed under discriminatory laws and attacks by white hoodlums. Samuel Ringgold Ward, a black abolitionist, left an unflattering picture of Canadian racism, especially among lower-class whites. Blacks had secured political rights but little social acceptance. Notably, schools remained racially segregated. Emancipated in Norfolk, Virginia, Elijah Jenkins heard that blacks needed the care of white people, but when he arrived in Canada, he found them doing well without masters. On balance, black abolitionists held Canada up as a beacon of freedom, but few white Southerners paid attention.[45]

The supposed inability of blacks to survive in freedom became common coin among white Americans. British scientists, including Charles Lyell, supported the notion of black inability to compete with whites in the marketplace. The Presbyterian Reverend J. C. Mitchell of Mobile cited the autodidact Hugh Miller to argue that inferior races cannot survive competition with superior races. Wayne Gridley of South Carolina invoked Lyell to argue that emancipation would end in a mass slaughter of blacks. From Philadelphia in 1845, Eliza Middleton Fisher reported to her mother in the low country a conversation with her friend Frances Kemble, who thought her slaveholding husband, Pierce Butler, had an uneasy conscience. Fisher protested that most Southerners honestly believed that the slaves would suffer if emancipated. In agreement, J. D. B. De Bow cited *Things as They Are in America* by William Chambers, the Scots publisher. South Carolina's E. S. Dargan pressed that view in an address to Alabama's secession convention. After emancipation, New York newspapers – *Daily News*, *Day-Book*, *Journal of Commerce* – and such Northerners as Richard H. Colfax, J. K. Paulding, and Solon Robinson thought that the worsening conditions of blacks demonstrated their vulnerability – which they interpreted as helplessness – in competition with white workers.[46]

The Fate of the Indians

William J. Grayson spoke for most white Americans when he avowed that blacks would fare no better under emancipation than Indians had under white conquest. Divines assumed moral responsibility for the survival of black brothers in Christ. Contempt for and condescension to Indians strengthened a sense of general white racial superiority. Calhoun credited peoples of mixed race with the overthrow of Spanish rule in Latin America, saying that future progress depended on the white element in their nature. Henry S. Foote of Mississippi, justifying American occupation of Texas, stressed the incompatibility of the white and Indian races and the unfitness of the Mexicans ("unlettered rabble," "demi-savages") for political freedom. After the War, the Presbyterian

Reverend Robert Lewis Dabney of Virginia contrasted the traditional bravery
of the British with the vengefulness of the Indians. Dabney thought God had
probably predestined most humans for salvation, with whites as His chosen
instruments.[47]

In 1838, the Unitarian Reverend Theodore Clapp of New Orleans asserted
that emancipation spelled destruction of the black race: "It would be equivalent
to deliberate and cold-blooded murder." Presbyterians especially sounded the
alarm. In 1834, the Reverend C. C. Jones asserted that only the protection of
white masters kept the black race alive. The New School Presbyterian Reverend
Joseph C. Stiles wrote that the northern states legislated, often unjustly, on the
assumption of black inferiority; yet they demanded abolition of the slavery
that provided blacks with protection and tutelage. Stiles asked what kind of
love wrathfully plunged dependents into darkness and slaughter. He answered:
The abolitionist "hates the master more than he loves the slave." W. R. Aylett
of Virginia called free blacks a class that spurned work. Waving logic aside,
he called for their expulsion because the work he said they spurned competed
with that of white men, driving down the price of labor. Similarly, Francis
Pickens of South Carolina worried about blacks' driving white workers out
of the labor market by working for a "bottle of rum and twist of tobacco."
Dabney, James Henley Thornwell, and religious leaders expected emancipation
to condemn blacks to follow the Indians to destruction. During the War, J. A
Lyon's "Report to the General Assembly of the Presbyterian Church" called
for a thorough reform of the slave codes. "Constitutionally kind, affectionate,
imitative, and contented," the black man could not take care of himself, "as
facts do but too sadly prove, in the midst of a superior people, who had no
interest in his person."[48]

In the 1840s, the Reverend Dr. William Capers of South Carolina advised the
General Assembly of the Methodist Church that even if slavery deserved opprobrium, those who pushed blacks into freedom under current circumstances were
betraying them and would earn their curses. Other Methodists followed suit.
In Mississippi, Winans damned most abolitionists as *incendiaries, cutthroats,
and, therefore, hydra-headed monsters of inhumanity*" whom the slaves knew
to be their enemies. The Reverend Augustus Baldwin Longstreet, in *A Voice
from the South* (eight editions by 1848), predicted that abolition would lead
to the deprivation and starvation of black children, the elderly, and the infirm
and set the race on the road to extinction. A decade later he reiterated the message at South Carolina College, referring to "an abject race of negroes, who
never knew freedom and never can attain it." For the Baptists, the Reverend
Thornton Stringfellow of Virginia acknowledged the possibility of eventual
emancipation under the direction of masters, but he worried about the extermination of people "utterly unprepared for a higher civil state." They would
"die out by inches, degraded by vice and crime, unpitied by honest and virtuous
men, and heart-broken by sufferings without a parallel." African colonizationists joined in warning that blacks risked replication of the fate of the Indians. In
1855, the pro-colonization *Western Journal and Civilian* of St. Louis credited

enlightened philanthropists with knowing that emancipation meant "a curse instead of a blessing to both races."[49]

During the secession crisis, Episcopal Bishop J. H. Otey of Tennessee, a unionist, agreed with Bishop Stephen Elliott of Georgia, a secessionist, that emancipation would cast the blacks into a no-man's-land. Otey wrote a northern clergyman in 1861:

> The party that elected Mr. Lincoln proclaimed uncompromising hostility to the institution of slavery – an institution which existed here and has done so from its beginning, in its patriarchal character. We feel ourselves under the most solemn obligations to take care of, and provide for, these people who cannot provide for themselves. Nearly every Free-soil State has prohibited them from settling in their territory. Where are they to go?

Similarly, Catholic Bishop John Hughes of New York asked: "Where are they to go, gentlemen abolitionists? You would have destroyed the relations between them and their masters.... You could not expect their masters to still provide them with food, clothing, and medicines and medical attention. Whose business will it be to see to all this?"[50]

In 1844, Secretary of State Calhoun, writing to Richard Pakenham, Britain's minister to Washington, taunted the transatlantic antislavery forces with the wretched condition of northern free blacks. Calhoun knew that, during the "Dorr War" in Rhode Island, the antislavery Thomas W. Dorr, who personally supported black suffrage, had led a radical democratic movement that opposed it, whereas his conservative opponents had supported it. A few years later, Calhoun got an earful from Henry Lewis Morgan – the anthropologist whom Karl Marx and Friedrich Engels much admired. Morgan said that the southern intention to preserve the black race disgusted Northerners: "The feeling towards that race in the North is decidedly that of hostility. There is no respect for them; no wish for their elevation; but on the contrary a strong desire to prevent the multiplication of the race so far as it is possible to do so." In 1849, the Episcopal Reverend Francis Wharton of Philadelphia wrote to Calhoun of having spent some time in South Carolina and finding blacks much better regarded there than in the North. That year, Fitzwilliam Byrdsall of New York, a radical democrat ("Loco-Foco"), wrote to Calhoun that in the Northern states, "Dogs-cats, any kind of animal may ride in stages & rail cars with white people here but not the negro." John L. O'Sullivan of Young America and *The Democratic Review* accused abolitionists and Republicans of hypocrisy for promoting emancipation, observing that the free states severely discriminated against blacks and wanted no part of them. From conservative circles, James A. Dorr of New York charged that the North had abolished slavery primarily to get rid of its own blacks. Southerners also heard about northern hostility to other nonwhites. Reports circulated in Beaufort, South Carolina, of an outrage committed against visiting Japanese dignitaries in Philadelphia by hoodlums who called them "niggers" and tried to drag them from their carriages.[51]

In southwestern Virginia, G. W. M. Simms reminded students at Emory and Henry College of the experience of the Indians, concluding, "Freedom is the black man's foe." Joseph and Jefferson Davis allowed the possibility of preparing blacks for some measure of freedom, but they envisioned horror if blacks were thrown into the marketplace. Bryan Tyson of Maryland, in a wartime pro-Union pamphlet, said that most white Southerners thought emancipated blacks would go the way of the Indians. Alexander Stephens, Robert Toombs, and Edmund Ruffin emphatically agreed. So did William Gilmore Simms, for whom hired labor and slave labor differed only in name. He thought a southern slave would be a fool to trade his position for that of an English factory operative. Leading southern clergymen and jurists, including those most anxious to protect slaves from abuse, had long agreed that freedom hurt emancipated blacks. After the War, southern women novelists pictured slaveholders as having protected blacks from the dire results now under way.[52]

During the agitation over the annexation of Texas, Secretary of State Abel Upshur, Duff Green, and other leading Southerners charged that British success – in their alleged machinations to abolish slavery in Texas – was encouraging a race war that blacks would not survive. In the 1850s, John Johnson of the University of Virginia referred to abolitionism as "a bitter competition for labor – a war of races." James P. Holcombe asked: Since the descendants of European serfs are now struggling to survive in the new industrial system, what chance would racially inferior blacks have? Replying to Mrs. Stowe and other abolitionists, E. J. Pringle of South Carolina, Albert Taylor Bledsoe of Virginia, George Sawyer of Louisiana, J. A. Turner of Georgia, and "A North Carolinian," among many, invoked the laws of political economy to warn that without the protection of humane masters, economic competition would "crush" emancipated blacks, plunging them into poverty and crime. Northerners would use them like so many machines.[53]

That emancipated blacks faced a greater evil than slavery became a common theme. The Lutheran Reverend John Bachman of Charleston suggested that whites should have enslaved the Indians to save them from destruction. During the War, William Russell, the British correspondent, discerned much hand wringing among Marylanders over the prospects for emancipated poor blacks. The fiercely proslavery and paternalistic Chief Justice Lumpkin of Georgia spoke for much of the southern bench in demanding that the courts protect black slaves against market pressures: "What friend of the African or of humanity would desire to see these children of the sun brought into close contact and competition with the hardy and industrious population . . . northwest of the Ohio, and who loathe negroes as they would so many lepers?" In Ohio, Judge Frederick Grimke of Chillicothe, brother of Sarah and Angelina Grimké, doubted that blacks would end better than the Indians. But then, so did Episcopal Bishop John Henry Hopkins of Vermont. Passing through Ohio in June 1861, Jason Niles of Mississippi overheard a raucous discussion of the War and a demand that fugitive slaves and free blacks be expelled to Kentucky.[54]

The Specter of Barbarism

Slaveholders wrung their hands over another grim prospect – that emancipation would propel blacks toward barbarism or, as the Reverend George A. Baxter of Virginia put it, "a savage state." Proslavery polemics from St. Louis to Charleston claimed that Jamaicans, Haitians, and Africans progressed while under white control but regressed afterward. Keziah Brevard of Tennessee considered slavery a God-ordained burden that she and her fellow Southerners would be better off without. But she doubted that blacks could sustain themselves and feared their extermination in a race war. The legendary Jubal Early believed that southern slavery had civilized Africans, created as happy and content a class of laborers as found anywhere, and prevented racial devolution. Dr. Elijah Millington Walker, a nonslaveholder in rural Mississippi, read about the experience of British Guiana, concluding that blacks behaved well under slavery but, once freed, deteriorated rapidly. In the 1850s, William Elliott of South Carolina saw Africans with "savage" expressions: "You can readily believe what Captain [Theodore] Canot has said of them – 'that before their transportation from Africa, the greater portion were cannibals!'" As such, Elliott said, they stood in stark contrast to the civilized demeanor of southern blacks. Southern missionaries reported cannibalism in West Africa, specifically the eating of criminals and captives. James Martin of Alabama reflected on West Indian emancipation: "You cannot educate or civilize [the black] without restraint, and so soon as that restraint would cease he would return to barbarism." But then, the Reverend T. H. Cunningham of Boston took much the same view. He confessed antipathy to blacks, deplored slavery, and opposed abolitionism: "They cannot hold their own" and "would relapse into African barbarism." After the War, Frances Fearn of Louisiana dreaded emancipation because she feared a black lapse into savagery without the master's firm and guiding hand.[55]

In 1862, Episcopal Bishop Alexander Gregg of Texas declared that if the South lost the War, blacks faced extinction, ground down by a *"heartless servitude"* imposed by "strangers to any other feeling than that which a hireling relation, the slavery of capital inspires." Mary Virginia Hawes Terhune (Marion Harland) and former governor Francis Pickens of South Carolina reiterated that Southerners relied on the loyalty of their slaves but believed that emancipation would strip away their newly acquired elements of civilization. A decade earlier, Pickens had cried out, "The West Indies, free, yet poor – miserable – wretched, in degradation and ruin. And this is what the world called humanity."[56]

At the beginning of the twentieth century, Frank Alexander Montgomery of Mississippi and Thomas Hughes of Virginia were sure that blacks recognized slaveholders as their "best friends," who provided them with greater care, health, and happiness than they enjoyed in freedom. Hughes believed that the slaves "led an almost ideal life," not thinking much about freedom or desiring it. In 1906, Myrta Lockett Avery of Georgia wrote that freedom had propelled backward "an alien race, an ignorant race, half-human, half savage," which would have died out like the Indians if whites had not retaken power and needed their labor. Sam Aleckson, born a slave in Charleston, brought a different yet not contradictory perspective: "If the Negro had emerged from slavery in a sullen and vindictive frame of mind he would unquestionably have shared the fate of the American Indian."[57]

The relation of the fate of the Indians to the likely fate of emancipated blacks troubled every decade. In the 1830s and 1840s slaveholders, especially those whose families had migrated to the Southwest, remembered the danger the Indians had posed. They knew that their families had benefited from Indian removal. But once white military power prevailed, many Southerners permitted themselves to regret the violent displacement of a noble people. That the regret amounted to little more than sentimentality testified to a persistent determination to consolidate the fortunes and positions of white families. Its persistence, however diluted, testified to a nagging consciousness that the victorious whites had secured their most deeply cherished material goods and cultural achievements at the expense of a people whose souls enjoyed the same standing as their own in the eyes of God.

6

Guardians of a Helpless Race

We, above all, ... were guarding the helpless black race from utter annihilation at the hands of a bloody and greedy "philanthropy," which sought to deprive them of the care of humane masters only that they might be abolished from the face of the earth, and leave the fields of labor clear for that free competition and demand-and-supply, which reduced even white workers to the lowest *minimum* of a miserable livelihood, and left the simple negro to compete, as best he could, with swarming and hungry millions of a more energetic race, who were already eating one another's heads off.

– E. A. Pollard[1]

Justifications for slavery rested on a general belief in black racial inferiority and on a specific belief in black inability to compete with whites in the marketplace. Personal correspondence, diaries, plantation record books, agricultural periodicals, and sermons trumpeted variations of those beliefs. Proslavery spokesmen proclaimed widespread agreement in the North as well as the South that without vigilant masters, blacks would die like flies and revert to some alleged African barbarism, paganism, even cannibalism. Hence, considerations of humanity and interest required masters to rule their plantation households with an iron hand, intervening to keep blacks from hurting themselves, each other, and whites.

Blacks as well as whites commented on the frequency with which slaves sought protection from masters against the abuse of hostile whites, especially the lower-class roughs who served on slave patrols. When slaves dreaded their own master or lacked access to him or expected a severe beating, many ran off to the woods, but more than a few ran to a neighboring slaveholder to ask for his intercession, which they often got. The heroic Solomon Northup, who became a prominent abolitionist after enduring slavery in Louisiana, fled to a kind former master when his current master threatened his life. Was a slave about to be hanged for killing another slave? His master petitioned for commutation. Did a slave stand accused of raping a white woman? The master provided legal counsel, demanding an inquiry into the woman's character and reputation. Was the overseer a brute? The responses of masters varied, but he risked dismissal. In Georgia, an overseer shot a locally prominent planter who had fired him for abusing slaves. Did white mechanics try to prevent slaves from hiring their own time? Masters made sure that the laws remained largely unenforced. All such instances invited slaveholders' self-congratulation.[2]

Vindication from the Free States

In the early 1820s, Isaac Harby of Charleston challenged New Englanders to acknowledge Southerners' kind treatment of their slaves and New Englanders' unkind racial discrimination. In 1828, a contributor to the *Southern Review* speculated that, unlike southern slaves, northern blacks experienced contempt and felt the gap between pretensions to equality and the reality of subordination. In the 1830s, the Unitarian Reverend Charles A. Farley of Richmond refused to recognize freedom as a blessing when it meant deprivation and starvation. He depicted northern free blacks as being in an untenable position – told they were free, knowing they were not. During the famous Webster–Hayne debate of 1830, Senators Robert Y. Hayne and William Smith of South Carolina and John Rowan of Kentucky rebuked Daniel Webster for ignoring the miserable condition of northern free blacks. In 1854, B. F. Stringfellow of Missouri described the northern free black as having no chance for social equality and as suffering a worse fate than a slave: "His political privileges are in fact the worst species of oppression." When, therefore, the abolitionist Theodore Weld urged slaveholders to visit the North to see how well blacks progressed under freedom, he met derision and appeals to extensive contrary evidence.[3]

Southerners smiled as blacks withdrew from avowedly antislavery northern churches that subjected them to discrimination and humiliation. Southerners smiled again when black clergymen denounced the Presbyterian Reverend Nathan S. S. Beman and other abolitionists for preaching equality in segregated churches. When the black Presbyterian Reverend Samuel Cornish of New York asked white ministers whether they considered racial segregation in church sinful, they answered affirmatively but admitted that they yielded to the prejudices of congegants. The story of the Catholic Church's first nonwhite bishop was telling. In the 1840s, an Irish planter in Georgia sent his mulatto son, James A. Healey, to a Quaker school in New York. Young Healey encountered meanness and discrimination from schoolmates and insufferable condescension from teachers who paraded their abolitionism. For good measure, Healy writhed under anti-Irish and anti-Catholic bigotry. To his relief, his father transferred him and his brothers to Catholic schools.[4]

Proslavery intellectuals complained angrily about the use of northern textbooks in southern schools, but their complaints concerned slavery rather than race. Southern and northern schools taught geography as a standard subject, most frequently assigning Morse's *American Geography* (1789, many editions thereafter). Morse condemned slavery as impolitic, inefficient, and wrong, but also denigrated blacks. Nineteenth-century textbooks, including *A System of Geography* by Sidney Morse, Jedidiah's son, ranked races in a presumably natural order, with blacks at the bottom.[5]

In 1837, Gabriel Capers of Georgia, speaking primarily to white yeomen, argued that northern free blacks suffered much more than southern slaves. British travelers offered confirmation. In 1835, Richard Cobden, a pillar of English liberalism, reported on the widespread defamation of blacks in the North; in 1859, he returned to find that denigration worse. Andrew Bell of Southampton, England, prefaced a scathing indictment of southern slavery with a no less scathing indictment of northern discrimination against blacks. Sir Charles Lyell agreed. R. R. Madden, an antislavery Irish Catholic and judge on the Britain's Mixed Commission in Havana, made several trips to the United States, including one on which he served as a witness in the *Amistad* trial. Northerners' hatred of blacks appalled him. When Dr. Elijah Millington Walker of Mississippi heard that Californians wanted to exclude blacks, he concluded that most white Americans shared the sentiment.[6]

The southern press reveled in reports of black protests in the free states. In 1839, "A South Carolinian," writing to Charlestonians on behalf of free blacks who had gone north, railed against the rampant immorality, degradation, and misery in New York and Philadelphia. Austin Steward, a fugitive slave, powerfully limned black reaction to discrimination in Ohio and across the North. An indignant Samuel Ringgold Ward protested the contempt that he and fellow blacks encountered in New York City. Hosea Easton, an associate of the famous black radical David Walker, recalled a vicious campaign in New England in the 1820s that portrayed blacks as subhuman. By contrast, in 1859, James M'Cune Smith hailed the racial equality of Maine, Massachusetts, and Rhode Island. Yet blacks faced antagonism as soon as the northern states abolished slavery. After the War, Connecticut voted down black suffrage. Since white workers and artisans in the free states objected to competition from slaves, many supported emancipation. In consequence, in northern cities and Baltimore, white artisans and workers pushed skilled blacks out of their trades. When New Jersey ended slavery, it did not emancipate all slaves; it still held 326 black slaves in 1850, 18 in 1860.[7]

Northern railroads imposed more severe racial segregation than did southern railroads, which accommodated black servants. In 1853, free blacks who entered Illinois had to pay a heavy fine or face indenture to work it off. The *New Orleans Bee* called the measure "an act of special and savage ruthlessness." In Illinois, blacks suffered extensive mob violence and could not testify against whites in court. Antislavery mobs in Chicago rescued blacks arrested under the Fugitive Slave Law, but Southerners continued to accuse Northerners of having sold many slaves southward when preparing to abolish slavery.[8]

Southern journals stepped up exposés during the 1850s. Mann Butler of Kentucky referred to "the utter failure of the free colored race in the nonslaveholding States to confirm the hopes of their white friends by improved virtue and industry." Butler attributed the Northwest's unwillingness to welcome blacks in part to the reputation for crime and idleness that free blacks carried from the Northeast. In the *Southern Literary Messenger*, "J. A. W." and "B." deplored the oppression of free blacks in the North, singling out New England. Another contributor, who thought that whites in Massachusetts discriminated against free blacks as a means of self-protection, deplored a pretense of freedom that caused bitterness and impaired morals. In 1860, yet another contributor declared, "The whole war against slavery has grown out of the hatred of the [northern] white to the black." *De Bow's Review*, reminding Harriet Beecher Stowe of racial prejudice in Massachusetts, outlined the North's discriminatory laws. In 1853, William S. Forrest devoted the better part of a chapter in his *Historical and Descriptive Sketches of Norfolk and Vicinity* to contrasting the security of blacks, slaves and free, in Virginia with the misery of the blacks in the North. T. R. R. Cobb of Georgia published a state-by-state report on the condition of northern blacks.[9]

The treatment of blacks in the North disgusted the antislavery Margaret Johnson Erwin of Mississippi and the proslavery Sally McDowell of Virginia. Both believed southern slaves fared much better. The Southerners' view of conditions in New England deserved heavy qualification. In colonial New England, especially Massachusetts, blacks approached equality with whites more closely than anywhere else – at least at law. Hostility toward blacks increased in the United States during the nineteenth century, but Vermont and Maine probably displayed greater racial harmony than other states. John Wood Sweet suggests: "White claims to racial preeminence became more urgent, rigid, and consistent in the 1820s and 1830s, just as new democratic ideals were becoming established and new class divisions were becoming entrenched." Indeed, in the 1830s, Alexis de Tocqueville found the greatest prejudice against blacks in states that did not have slavery. Thereafter, the long-standing opposition of northern radical democrats to black rights, including suffrage, intensified.[10]

Overwhelmingly, Northerners and Southerners believed in innate white superiority and the need to defended white supremacy. With few exceptions, free blacks in 1860 could not vote, testify against whites in court, request poor relief, attend school with white children, serve in state militias, or marry whites. At the time of the Reconstruction Acts, only six northern states allowed blacks to vote. Yet the legal restrictions on blacks in the North had less effect than widespread economic and social bigotry. Irish and other immigrants were blamed for the antiblack riots and the vicious measures that drove blacks out of the trades in northern cities, but riots and discrimination had long preceded their arrival. Beginning in the late 1840s the growing strength of antislavery and of black militancy led to some improvement, but daily indignities, discrimination in employment, and segregation in churches and public schools continued.[11]

After 1840, racial discrimination intensified in the Midwest. Ohio's first constitutional convention (1802) attempted to protect black servants and apprentices from enslavement, but, subsequently, the legislature imposed severe Black Codes. Ohio, Wisconsin, and Michigan responded to the Fugitive Slave Law of 1850 with Personal Liberty Laws but did not curb discrimination or allow blacks to vote. In fact, many free-soilers and Republicans advocated expulsion of blacks from their states and territories. In the 1850s the Free-Soil Party, which held the balance of power between Democrats and Whigs, won repeal of some of the more obnoxious features of the Black Codes and extended blacks rights in the courts and schools. Blacks nonetheless remained pariahs.[12]

Antislavery loomed large in early Iowa, supported by the Presbyterian and Congregational Churches. By 1838, southern emigrants had become politically ascendant, and Iowa's first state legislature enacted a Black Code. In reaction, strong elements of the Free-Soil and Republican parties opposed not only slavery but also racial discrimination. But they too despaired of changing racial attitudes, and the prospect of miscegenation made whites apoplectic. Throughout the Midwest, antislavery and Republican leaders endorsed white supremacy. Representative James Henry Lane of Indiana, who emerged as a ferocious antislavery leader in Kansas, announced, "I would as soon as leave sell a negro as a mule." Ruefully, the abolitionist George W. Julian of Indiana conceded: "Our people hate the Negro with a perfect if not a supreme hatred." Julian worried that emancipation, which he unequivocally supported, might lead to extermination of blacks. In 1862, William Stuart, a British representative in Washington, reported deep divisions in western public opinion on the future of emancipated blacks but virtual unanimity on the unacceptability of their moving north. In 1863, responding to British criticism, Robert Trimble painted a roseate picture of New England but a harsh picture of repression in Indiana and Illinois, for which he blamed Southerners. In France, too, public opinion condemned racial discrimination in the North.[13]

Although Pennsylvania's delegates to the federal Convention warned of Northerners' revulsion at the prospect of racial equality, prejudiced Northerners exhibited little systematic belief in inherent black inferiority before 1830. Joanne Pope Melish observes that in New England, the discourse of slavery became a discourse on race – that is, shifted from a focus on the behavioral effects of enslavement to a focus on assumed black biological traits. Thereafter, scientific racism grew apace. In the 1850s, the *Mississippian and State Gazette* of Jackson deadpanned, "In our Northern States, where the Negro finds not a genial home, they have 'PROFESSED to abolish slavery.'" Frank F. Steel, from a Republican family in Ohio, spending time on a large plantation in Mississippi, confessed to having a Northerner's prejudice against "the colored element." Discriminatory laws slackened somewhat, but northern blacks faced lynching and the burning of their homes. Henry L. Benning and Joseph E. Brown of Georgia, pouncing on such reports, called for secession in order to save blacks from impoverishment or extermination. The colonizationist *African Repository* gave the charge a curious twist, accusing slave states of pressuring their free blacks to go to an unreceptive North.[14]

During the 1850s, northern blacks intensified their resistance to segregation in schools and churches, but they had their hands full. When free blacks in South Carolina contemplated emigration in the face of repressive measures in 1860, they thought twice about going to a North that reeked of Negrophobia.

In 1860, an appalled John S. C. Abbott of New York, an antislavery historian, described Negrophobia as worse in the North than in the South. A slaveholder in Virginia assured a British traveler that, even among abolitionists, he had seen evidence of northern distaste for blacks. Congress created segregated schools in the District of Columbia while fashioning the Fourteenth Amendment. Yet black freedom in the North caused considerable uneasiness in the South. In 1808, racial mixing in New York City appalled Captain Henry Massie of Virginia. In the 1820s, John Pendleton Kennedy bristled when a stagecoach driver made him relinquish his seat to a black woman; in Philadelphia, he almost got a beating from a black man whose wife he had told to relinquish her seat to a white woman. In 1838, William Shepard Pettigrew of North Carolina chafed at the "equality" of whites and blacks in Ohio, which extended to their eating and drinking together.[15]

Abolitionism Indicted for Racism

For decades, Southerners pummeled abolitionists and free-soilers as advocates of a vicious ideology that threatened blacks with a life-and-death competitive struggle for which they lacked the intelligence and resourcefulness. Southerners especially caviled at the gross hypocrisy of some Republicans who claimed that blacks preferred a warm climate and would depart the North for a post-emancipation South. A. H. H. Stuart of Virginia, a unionist, invoked the West Indies to accuse Northerners of knowing that blacks could not survive as free workers and that emancipation would prostrate the South. Curtis M. Jacobs of Maryland charged that abolitionism "looks to the entire destruction of the negro race in this country." The Presbyterian Reverend W. A. Hall, addressing Confederate troops in Virginia, attributed to William H. Seward espousal of an infidel doctrine of black extermination. John Berrien Lindsley of Tennessee acknowledged the good intentions of abolitionists but considered free-soilers advocates of racial extermination. Charles Eliot Norton of Harvard, among other eminent men, did not welcome extermination but did support free soil in order to "confine the Negro to the South." Southern journalists recognized that the Negrophobic Hinton Helper of North Carolina advocated emancipation as a measure to get rid of blacks. The courageous Reverend Peter Cartwright, who left the South for the free states, lashed out at fellow Methodists, notably the fiery abolitionist Reverend Orange Scott, for preaching destructive radicalism. The abolitionists, Cartwright cried, cared nothing for blacks. Their opposition to colonization ignored American realities and threatened an emancipation that invited catastrophe for the emancipated. Some Northerners made that point in order to justify slavery, but Cartwright made it to support gradual emancipation.[16]

With undue severity, both slaveholders and black abolitionists assailed anti-slavery whites for promoting extermination. Yet by no means did all abolitionists assume that people released from slavery could compete on equal terms without preparation, assistance, and equal protection under the law. Noah

Webster and other early conservatives advocated gradual, carefully guided emancipation to allow blacks time to overcome the debilitating effects of slavery. Some Republicans made a good faith effort to protect freedmen and confront the difficulties. Caught between free market ideology and paternalistic impulses, they remained at sea.[17]

When Southerners taunted Northerners for loathing blacks, they ranked abolitionists among the worst offenders. However guilty some abolitionists were, their movement carried the banner of racial equality virtually alone, combating racial stereotypes at enormous personal risk. In the 1790s, Morgan Rhees defended blacks against racist aspersions, cited African achievements in the ancient world, and claimed that Africans personified the Devil by painting him white. Charles Elliott made much of African accomplishments in his *Sinfulness of Slavery* (1850). The Congregationalist Reverend Abram Prynne of New York defended racial equality in his debate with the proslavery Methodist Reverend William G. Brownlow of Tennessee. Occasionally, a politically moderate Northerner protested the distortions of African history and society. Alexander Everett, the editor of the *North American Review*, dismissed notions of racial superiority as unsubstantiated, noting the high quality of ancient Ethiopia and the black element in Egyptian civilization. After a paean to the black African contributions to ancient Palestine – the cradle of Judaism and Christianity – he turned to West Africa, deriding those who accused its peoples of stupidity and viciousness without knowledge of the languages and cultures: "This reasoning proved the stupidity and degradation of those who thought it satisfactory, and not of the Africans."[18]

Efforts to repel the charge of African barbarism encountered unexpected difficulties. In 1787, the Quakers sought to promote favorable images of Africans. They adopted as a symbol a kneeling slave in supplication: "Am I not a Man and a Brother?" In the words of Hugh Honour, the art historian, "Despite the good intentions of the originators, it had the effect of depersonalizing and degrading blacks." So did the widely circulated picture of helpless Africans aboard a slave ship. Painters, with the notable exception of William Blake, showed no black heroes, although, like Eastman Johnson in "Life at the South" and Thomas Waterman Wood in "A Southern Cornfield," they did capture the slaves' thirst for freedom. The irony deepened during the nineteenth century. Prominent antislavery Northerners slid into the romantic depiction of whites as excessively aggressive and of blacks – ostensibly to their credit – as naturally humble Christians. This imagery inadvertently strengthened the notion that racially inferior blacks could not compete in a competitive free labor society with whites who were superior in work ethic, productivity, business acumen, and entrepreneurship.[19]

In Georgia, the Milledgeville *Federal Union* protested that some large cotton planters cynically supported the Compromise of 1850 in expectation of ten years of high profits, after which blacks could go to the devil. A decade later, an eighteen-year-old South Carolina belle assured a visiting Englishman that blacks would remain loyal to their masters in wartime, but she quickly added, "If the slaves rose, we should kill them like so many snakes." In every part of the South, those with a "devil take the hindmost" view showed even greater indifference to human suffering than the bourgeois whom proslavery ideologues reviled. John H. Claiborne, the director of the military hospitals in Petersburg, Virginia, sounded like a Yankee in 1864 when he said that emancipation might not prove bad, since blacks could not survive outside slavery. S. P. Richards of Georgia, having had to whip "our woman Caroline," expressed disgust for all blacks. He wished them back in Africa: "To think too that this cruel war should be waged for them."[20]

In agreement with Frances Kemble, Frederick Law Olmsted acidly remarked, "I begin to suspect that the great trouble and anxiety of Southern gentlemen is: How, without quite destroying the capabilities of the negro for any work at all, to prevent him from learning to take care of himself." Olmsted had seen for himself living refutations of southern notions of black incapacity. He admired the deportment and moral and intellectual qualities displayed at the Colored National Convention in Rochester, New York, in 1853. He understood the theory of black incapacity as a variant of the theory advanced by the propertied classes of Europe: "That there must be, in every country, a large class that is unfitted, by the necessity that is imposed upon them to labor, for the forethought and reflection necessary for the comfortable support of their families, much more for taking any part in the control of their commonwealth." Olmsted accurately espied the growing strength of "slavery in the abstract" – the extreme proslavery theory that every society had to subject the mass of its people of all races to personal servitude. Adherents believed, Olmsted wrote, that "the laboring class is better off in slavery, where it is furnished with masters who have a mercenary as well as a humane interest in providing the necessities of a vigorous physical existence to their instruments of labor, than it is in Europe, or than it will be in the North." The widespread southern view was "identical" to that of the "aristocratic party of the Old World."[21]

In 1855, the socially prominent Amelia Murray of England dined in Washington with the Democratic Governor Horatio Seymour of New York and the Republican U.S. Representative Hamilton Fish. Both gentlemen agreed that the inherent weaknesses of the black race forecast its disappearance. Fish cited his own family in New York, which had freed its slaves and provided for them – to no avail. He added that a few retained a deep attachment to his family. President Julian M. Sturdevant of Illinois College, a Republican, assured workers that emancipated blacks posed no threat because they could not compete and would perish if released from their masters' protection. Charles Francis Adams and other prominent Republicans agreed. The radical Thaddeus Stevens, a racial egalitarian, had few illusions about the effects of enslavement and the probable consequences of emancipation. He urged Congress to divide the plantations and give every freedman and poor white forty acres and a mule: "If we do not furnish them with homesteads and hedge them around with protective laws . . . we had better have left them in bondage." Northern businessmen supported efforts to infuse Puritan virtues and help freedmen become productive citizens. But they charged that land distribution encouraged self-sufficiency and undermined cotton production for market.[22]

William Lloyd Garrison, Wendell Phillips, Owen Lovejoy of Illinois, Senator James Harlan of Iowa, and some prominent antislavery businessmen expected blacks to succeed if given a chance. Lydia Maria Child wrote in 1862, "What can we do with the slaves? is a foolish question. Take them away from Mr. Lash and place them with Mr. Cash settles that imaginary difficulty." But Ralph Waldo Emerson, George Ticknor, Horace Bushnell, Theodore Parker, and Samuel Gridley Howe advocated colonization or amalgamation or threw up their hands. Horace Greeley, unsure that blacks could survive if given the opportunity, chose not to lose sleep, since, like whites, they would have a chance to "root hog or die." In *Appeal to Caesar*, Albion Tourgee wrote that most Northerners expected freedmen to be left to survive or die, as fate might have it. Senator Henry Hubbard of New Hampshire, opposing abolition in the District of Columbia, wanted no influx of emancipated blacks to compete with northern free labor, adding that, besides, southern slaves lived better than northern free blacks.[23]

Persistent Fears of Black Extermination

In the South, the conviction that emancipation spelled extermination grew during the 1850s and well after. The Reverend Joseph B. Jackson of New Orleans summed it up, maintaining that under the federal emancipation, blacks would "perish before races of superior civilization." When the War began, the bishops of the Protestant Episcopal Church reiterated their long-standing view. Bishop Stephen Elliott told the faithful in Savannah, "We are fighting to protect and preserve a race who form a part of our household, and stand with us next to our children." And, he told that annual convention of the Diocese of Georgia, "We can not permit our servants to be cursed with the liberty of licentiousness and infidelity, but we will truly labor to give them the liberty wherewith Christ has made us all free." A year later, he invoked West Indian emancipation to underscore blacks' need for protective white masters. In 1865, Elliott took the oath of allegiance to the United States and urged communicants, "Be good citizens and above all do the best for the poor unfortunate negroes." He elaborated:

> The whole race will now go out before civilization (so-called) and competition, as the Indians are doing. We can survive the change, and one day flourish again; but not they; their fate is sealed; and the edict of puritanism has already gone forth. "If you cannot and will not work, you must die." The furthest I can go in behalf of these fanatics is to cry, "Father forgive them, for they know not what they do."

When Elliott died, Bishop R. H. Wilmer of Alabama recalled that he had never expected emancipated blacks to withstand the rigors of the marketplace and survive as a race.[24]

In 1861, the Presbyterian Reverends George Armstrong of Norfolk, James A. Lyon of Mississippi, and Benjamin Morgan Palmer of New Orleans agreed: To survive, blacks required Confederate protection against the Yankees. The eloquent Palmer appealed to the legislatures of Georgia and South Carolina to shield blacks from the rigors of a merciless market. The Presbyterian Reverend William S. White of Lexington, Virginia, a strong unionist who accepted biblical sanction for slavery, asked antislavery Northerners what would happen to emancipated blacks. They stunned him by replying that blacks would not be their problem and could go to the devil. During the federal occupation of Vicksburg, the Catholic Bishop William Henry Elder could not contain himself. Blacks were dying in the streets, but the Federals did nothing, pleading short supplies. Irate, Elder asked several federal officers about their government's intentions. "Everyone whom I have asked has lamented that he thinks there is no policy in their regard, except to deprive the masters of their services & their belief is that as far as the Fed. Govt. & Army prevail, the race will die out like that of the Indians. They throw the blame on the South." The letters of Union troops reveal that few showed interest, although an increasing number grew more sympathetic as they viewed the blacks' hardships firsthand. At that, the officers whom Elder confronted may have misunderstood the attitude of their government, for more humane voices emerged amid the wild confusion of the time. Elder's concern also stemmed from his fears about the blacks' "weakness of mind," which accounted for his difficulty in teaching them the truths of Christianity. He nonetheless thought that the Catholic Church had a wonderful opportunity to convert people with a natural tendency toward dependence. Still, Father Joseph B. O'Hagan, a Union Army chaplain, winced as "the soldiers vented all their spleen" against blacks.[25]

During the War, Catherine Edmondston and Judith McGuire thought that poor deluded blacks faced misery and death. John Wilkes Booth raged that Lincoln's war on the South "is only preparing the way for their annihilation." Eliza Frances Andrews of Georgia saw Yankee-induced extermination or reduction to a new form of servitude. Ministers and laymen had much to worry about at home. In Alabama, the nonslaveholding families of Confederate deserters and dissenters – especially the "corn women" – directed their bitterness at the Confederacy and the blacks. William King of Georgia concluded that most Yankee troops hated blacks, believed them better off in slavery, and wanted their expulsion from the country. The Confederate Congressman Warren Akin of Georgia charged that Union troops rounded up blacks for shipment to slaveholding Cuba. Emilie Riley McKinley, a proud rebel, quoted a Union officer as taunting freedmen: "You think you are free, but you are in greater bondage than you were before." For Emmala Reed of upcountry South Carolina, blacks "are being freed to *die*." She continued to refer to the duties and responsibilities of maintaining "our large household white and black." When Maria returned "half-starved" after a week's absence, Reed wondered, "Where else can they go for sustenance but to their Masters." Although Richard Malcolm Johnston of Georgia accepted slavery, its demise relieved him of "responsibility for their care."[26]

Before and after the War, the Pennsylvania-born Josiah Gorgas of Alabama, the Confederacy's master of ordnance, considered emancipated blacks destined for calamity. Edmund Ruffin expected emancipation to inflict endless cruelties and shrink the number of blacks by 50 percent in ten years. Henry Craft of Memphis knew that the War, whichever side won, had delivered a "death blow" to slavery. "I believe that it will soon be demonstrated that free negroes in large numbers cannot live with white people. I believe too that a very large number of the negroes will not accept their freedom & that by one name or another, pretty much the old relations will be re-established." And if not? "The negroes must leave the Country, or the whites must." In the aftermath of Confederate defeat, Varina Davis reiterated her concern that the blacks faced the fate of the Indians.[27]

Touring the South in 1866, John Richard Dennett – lawyer, educator, and special correspondent for the *Nation* – met Southerners of every type who agreed that white immigrants would displace blacks. Racial incapacity, not slavery, had rendered blacks unfit to compete; cradle-to-grave security provided by masters had sustained the race. Dennett thought freedmen worked tolerably in the disorder of the moment, but white perceptions remained firm. The Associate Reformed Presbyterian Reverend Samuel Agnew of Mississippi saw the change from slavery to freedom as "fraught with sore evils to the poor negroe." John Houston Bills of Tennessee, arranging contracts with his former slaves, mused about their pitiable condition. He had lived easily with slavery before the War, thinking its redeeming feature the protection of blacks, whose "slothful nature" put them at risk. He wished them success and expected a few to do well. "But as a race they will degenerate and finally become Extinct as the Indians." In "Memoranda" for 1866, he wrote: "I found the institution here when I came upon the stage of life. I have bought Many & sold few; never bought one but that I thought I bettered his or her condition & most of those I bought I done so at their own request. May they do better for themselves is the only wish I have, but fear the result."[28]

During the War, southern newspapers forcefully reiterated the presumed inability of emancipated blacks to compete with whites in free society. T. W. MacMahon of Virginia, grounding his defense of southern slavery on black inferiority, nonetheless concluded, "Slavery was the universal and invariable superstructure of all social and political systems." Well after the War, Charles Colcott Jones, Jr., of Georgia, P. T. G. Beauregard of Louisiana, and Philip Alexander Bruce of Virginia told large audiences that blacks would fade away or revert to barbarism. Edward King reported from Louisiana in 1875 that intelligent and sympathetic whites believed – without evidence – that emancipated blacks were already dying off. Judge Junius Hillyer of Georgia, who considered whites destined to rule other races, never wavered in his view of emancipation as a terrible crime against blacks. Conservatives in South Carolina asserted that they alone protected blacks, and Wade Hampton appealed for white-black friendship. But the blacks whom whites thought loved them were in no mood to reciprocate. For George Fitzhugh of Virginia, blacks deserved an equal chance to compete in the new capitalist order, but he doubted they could. Robert E. Lee remarked after the War, "I have always observed that wherever you find the negro, everything is going down around him, and wherever you find the white man, you see everything around him improving." Some old devotees of slavery resisted self-fulfilling prophecy: Among them were Governor James L. Orr of South Carolina; Andrew B. Martin, a former governor of Alabama; J. L. M. Curry of Alabama, a prominent politician and educator; and the Methodist Bishop Holland N. McTyeire. They pleaded for the education of blacks to make them solid, conservative citizens. They assumed that Christianity and Christian masters were civilizing blacks, who, however, would probably never reach the level of civilization achieved by whites.[29]

White Recognition of Black Achievement

That white seamen, including those on slavers, exhibited skill, fortitude, and courage did not deter their employers from treating them as inferior beings. Ship captains had little difficulty in transferring their brutality toward transported black slaves to their white sailors – and vice versa. Slaveholders, notwithstanding their endless proclamation of black incapacity, supplied abundant evidence to the contrary, crowing that they encouraged black self-improvement.[30]

Slaves supplemented the tables of their masters and overseers with wild turkeys, rabbits, and other game, as well as chickens and eggs. Especially in the rice districts, slaves raised bees and sold honey and beeswax to their masters. Planters preferred beeswax mixed with turpentine as polish for their status-laden mahogany furniture. Slaves caught opossum, raccoon, and terrapins, which sold high when converted into bacon. To discourage trading at country stores, some masters established plantation stores at which slaves could buy calicoes, handkerchiefs, tin ware, molasses, sugar, and tobacco. Henry William Ravenel described the slaves' initiative and skill and yet considered them improvident – a racial trait "probably encouraged and strengthened by the condition of slavery." Proslavery polemicists cited newspaper reports of large sums earned by slaves. Masters commonly allowed slaves to sell chickens, eggs, and even corn to respectable neighbors, doing their best to check petty trade with strangers and disreputable elements. Some slaves had permission to hawk their wares in town. In 1858, an Alabaman fumed that payment of thirty to forty dollars a year to a slave "is not uncommon here." Loren Schweninger, the leading historian of black property ownership in the South, has identified an impressive number of slaves whose masters paid them for extra work or allowed them to hire their own time. The economist Stephen Crawford has estimated that between 10 and 24 percent of plantation slaves earned money by "extra" work.[31]

Without legal claim to property, a slave had to depend on his master's honesty. Daniel Hundley of Alabama expressed the ideal: A master who robbed a slave of his earnings "would be pelted with rotten eggs out of the community" and find no "resting-place for the soles of his feet south of Mason's and Dixon's line." The hyperbolic Hundley did not name anyone pelted. Still, most masters had to behave honestly. The slaves, not being stupid, did not enter into agreements with dishonest masters known to have broken promises. Character and conscience aside, masters dealt honestly because the arrangements corresponded to their interests.[32]

A danger arose from the heirs of a master who had established an informal *peculium*. When John Curtis of Alexandria, Louisiana, bequeathed hundreds of dollars to a slave family, the editor of the *Republican* assured the public that, although the transaction lacked standing at law, it would be carried out faithfully. Indeed, family honor dictated strict respect for the master's wishes, although not everyone upheld the code. Assorted rationalizations poured forth, but a disrespect for the claims of a slave easily combined with greed to produce violations of trust and ugly court fights. Court records identified cheaters. Solomon Northup paid tribute to legal procedures designed to protect slaves against cheating.[33]

Masters observed that slaves who raised their own corn, chickens, or pigs not only reduced trade with storekeepers and dissolute poor whites but also made them less likely to steal. J. D. Wilson of South Carolina explained that having their own crops "infused into them a greater regard for the rights of others." Moses Liddell of Louisiana suffered the inconvenience and high cost of shipping slaves' produce in order to reduce outside contact. Masters took perverse satisfaction from their largesse, twisting slaves' responses to reinforce their own racial prejudices. A planter in Georgia explained: "I give my negroes as much money as I am willing to see them throw away in the indulgence of a childish fancy." Slaves played a game of their own. The press in Mississippi growled that slaves gouged townspeople with inflated prices for chickens and eggs. Probably so, but why not? They were not gouging members of their plantation households.[34]

Every southern state had slaves and free blacks whose contributions to technology and agricultural development caught the public eye. Governor Albert Gallatin Brown of Mississippi praised a slave mechanic's double plow and scraper as "way ahead" of northern versions. Governor Henry Wise of Virginia, excoriating the laziness and inefficiency of whites, fumed that he had learned more about agriculture from "old Negroes" than from whites. J. S. Buckingham of Britain reported from Macon, Georgia, that Solomon Humphries had purchased his and his family's freedom and made a fortune as a well-respected merchant. Horace King, born a slave, served in the Georgia legislature during Reconstruction after a career as a builder of bridges, courthouses, and public buildings in three states. Nejar Scott, a slave carpenter, built several plantation homes in Mississippi and Louisiana, some of which still stand. In 1857, Jesse Crowell, a skillful slave carpenter of Washington County, Mississippi, carved the communion rails with ferns of Delta plants for the Episcopal Church. Robert Harlan of Kentucky, a barber and then a grocer, earned enough to travel to Canada, England, and California; purchasing his freedom, he settled in Cincinnati. And as historians now recognize, slaves contributed significantly to the technology of rice planting and sugar, hemp, and other machinery.[35]

The skill of black boatmen on the Mississippi River and Atlantic coast became proverbial. On the Mississippi River, the well-known Simon Gray was only one of a large, widely noticed group of highly skilled boatmen. Blacks made up half the crews on the riverboats in Arkansas, and some rose to become engineers. On the Atlantic coast, planters chose as master of the boats a slave who knew the channels, shoals, snags, and tides and supervised the manning of sails, oars, and poles. From Maryland to Georgia, slaves worked at catching fish, shrimp, and oysters and selling them to their masters and to whites in nearby towns. The laws acknowledged the special importance of fishermen by granting them greater leeway to buy and sell than slave mechanics and others. Railroad owners, too, acknowledged the talent of skilled slaves. Owners and passengers alike praised black firemen. Much of the economic strength of the slave system arose from reliance on the intelligence, initiative, and managerial skill of ostensibly incompetent or deficient slaves.[36]

Joseph E. Davis of Mississippi, brother of Jefferson Davis, encouraged the intelligent, literate, resourceful Benjamin Montgomery to engage in a variety of business relations on his plantations. Montgomery accumulated a great deal of money through his plantation store, which served neighboring whites as well as blacks. He left with the Yankees during the War but returned to become a a founder of Mound Bayou in the Mississippi Delta, the largest black township in America. When Davis lost his property, Montgomery helped him out. Yet Jefferson Davis shook his head when Joseph sold land to Montgomery, a superb manager and businessman, for he believed that even the best of blacks would become tyrannical with prosperity. Andrew Durnford, a free mulatto, became a business associate and intimate friend of the wealthy John McDonough of Louisiana, who prepared his slaves for emancipation and emigration. A slave gardener on Oak Alley Plantation near Donaldsville, Louisiana, reputedly performed the first successful pecan grafting. Among free blacks, Frank McWhorter of Kentucky set up a saltpeter factory in Pulaski County in 1812 and succeeded in producing gunpowder. Robert Gordon of Virginia worked in his white father's coal yard, accumulated money from selling the slag, invested in his own business, and bought his freedom in 1846. Benjamin David of Bennettsville, South Carolina, built a successful construction business. Anthony Weston of South Carolina, having built an outstanding rice mill, was worth $40,000 by 1860. Thomas Day, a free black cabinetmaker in Milton, North Carolina, had a white clientele that included state leaders, and he trained whites in the trade. A master craftsman, he and his work remained popular among whites for some forty years. These are only a few of the better-known cases.[37]

A number of big planters in the upper South preferred slave managers to white – among them, George Washington, A. H. Bernard, the Carters, Littleton Waller Tazewell, Charles Pettigrew, Chief Justice Frederick Nash of North Carolina's Supreme Court, and Henry Clay. On Sapelo Island, Georgia, Thomas Spaulding, a big rice planter, eschewed white overseers for black drivers (foremen). Women from the low country to Texas entrusted plantations to the management of experienced slaves, especially during the War. Up country, David Dickson kept an overseer on one of his places but trusted the others to drivers. Alexander Stephens, who trumpeted black inferiority in his famous "Cornerstone Speech," trusted his plantation to drivers when he traveled to Washington. In Alabama, Charles Tait and Hugh Davis were among leading planters who relied on the managerial skills of drivers. In Louisiana, R. R. Barrow escaped notice in 1857 for having a black overseer, but five planters in Iberville paid fines. Louisiana also had some twenty-five free black overseers. Josiah Henson proudly recalled that he had served for many years as his master's quasi-overseer and "factotum." In Texas, cattle raisers trusted heavy managerial responsibilities to slaves.[38]

Intelligent slaves surprised planters by mastering agricultural innovations. James Cuthbert of James Island, South Carolina, remarked that many planters relied on blacks to plan and carry out important functions. Edmund Ruffin, when off on long trips, left his plantation in the care of Jem Sykes, his able driver, who recognized the connection between agricultural innovations and larger crop yields. D. E. Huger Smith, who considered blacks inferior, recognized the efficiency of Tom Bellinger, a driver, with "supreme control" of the plantation, and his wife, who provided admirable hospitality. Huger Smith lauded the trunk minders, upon whose skill and intelligence a successful rice crop depended. Overseers supposedly remained at their posts at all times, but some slipped away for days, leaving drivers in charge.[39]

Who knows how many planters felt as did the Virginian who told Olmsted that he wished the law permitted use of black overseers? Unusual cases may have been less unusual than they seem. Mingo, a slave in North Carolina, received sixty dollars a year for managing a plantation from the 1820s until 1849. Here and there an inexperienced mistress turned over her money matters to a slave woman. Some slaveholders' sons casually revealed, without resentment, that they worked under the direction of a slave foreman or "boss," as they called him.[40]

Southern planters boasted of the intelligence of one or more of their slaves. In 1845, the Hillsborough (N.C.) *Recorder* published the work of the slave poet George Moses Horton. T. C. Thornton, the president of Centenary College in Mississippi, in a proslavery polemic, praised black intelligence and management skills, comparing them favorably to those of European laborers. Thornton referred to Plato Hutt, a slave who saved enough from his poultry raising and garden to buy thirty or forty dollars' worth of books at a time; to a black preacher who attracted hundreds of whites to his sermons and scientific discourses; and to Dr. Gowen, a black physician in Port Gibson who had studied with Benjamin Rush. In Alabama, Lyell heard of a slave blacksmith who was self-taught in Greek and Latin and was learning Hebrew; the Presbyterians planned to send him as a missionary to Liberia. Ellis, the unnamed blacksmith, was ordained in Tuscaloosa and went to Liberia, as did George M. Erskine, another talented black Presbyterian preacher.[41]

From colonial days planters had called on the skills of black herbal doctors. Some whites understood that blacks brought a heavy reliance on "magic" to their practice: With their own version of psychosomatic medicine, Africans believed that illness and death stemmed from spiritual as well as physical causes. Ailing whites called on the medical skills of slaves and free blacks more than they cared to admit. Some highly regarded physicians trained slaves to assist in the treatment of white and black patients. Many plantation mistresses relied on black midwives and called in white physicians only for difficult cases. Both blacks and whites learned some of their herbal medicine from Indians, and vice versa. "Tattler," in the *Southern Cultivator*, strengthened a plea for Christian instruction of slaves by warning of the perfidious effects of black "doctors" with pretensions to magical powers.[42]

In 1709, John Lawson praised the "admirable Cures performed by these Savages, which would puzzle a great many graduate Practitioners." Governor Gooch of Virginia reported in 1729 that a slave had cured venereal diseases with herbs. An old slave discovered a valuable medicinal herb that led the government of Virginia to emancipate him. A century later, planters in Alabama drew criticism for accommodating African "superstitions," but Martin Marshall, among others, did well with the homemade cures he learned from African and Indian lore. In 1833, John Walker of Virginia had a slave who was going blind. White physicians failed to cure him, but for ten dollars "Old Man Docr. Lewis," a neighbor's slave, cured him with herbs. Frances Kemble reported on a slave's herbal cure for ear infections and on a planter's admission that the only help for his rheumatism came from a white doctor taught by blacks in Virginia. Dr. David Worth, who established what was probably the first hospital in North Carolina, relied on his servants as well as his wife to nurse recuperating patients.[43]

Planters and overseers lauded nurses and drivers for their care of black patients. John Hamilton of Williamsport, Louisiana, heard that his brother was losing slaves: "Your doctors are a rough set – They give too [much] medicine. It is seldom that I call in a physician. We Doctor upon the old woman slave and have first-rate luck." Supposedly under supervision, slave nurses administered medicine in the quarters. Virginia tolerated black doctors until 1748, when stories spread about their poisoning of white patients. Some states passed laws to prohibit treatment of the sick by black medical practitioners, but there is little evidence of enforcement. Masters profitably hired out slaves as plantation physicians. Midwives with reputations as experts in herbal medicine hired their own time. Slaves also worked as dentists on plantations, and a few had successful practices in towns. The white dentists of Atlanta complained in 1859 that Roderick D. Badger was hiring his own time and acquiring wide popularity. Badger, born a slave and apparently freed, was trained in dentistry by his white father and practiced in Atlanta in the 1850s despite efforts to suppress his practice. During the War, he served as a military aide to a Confederate colonel and afterward continued his successful practice for whites and blacks.[44]

In the eighteenth and early nineteenth centuries, blacks won acclaim from whites for their preaching to interracial congregations. "Black Harry" Hosier, a free black, traveled with Bishop Asbury and Dr. Coke, sometimes taking the pulpit. George Liele, a slave in Georgia, preached so powerfully that his master freed him. Liele went to Savannah, where he preached in town and country and trained Andrew Bryan, a slave, who trained Andrew Marshall. These men preached primarily to slaves but drew large white audiences. The celebrated Lot Cary took Richmond by storm and ended as a missionary in Liberia. The black Baptists Liele and David George left America with the British at the end of the Revolution, but in 1783 Jesse Peter became pastor at Silver Bluff, South Carolina – the first black Baptist church in the United States. In 1798, the South Carolina–born Joseph Willis preached in the Mississippi Territory. After Nat Turner's insurrection, states and communities restricted the activities of black preachers, and fewer whites heard them. The Princeton-educated John Chavis gained social acceptance among whites by teaching Greek and Roman literature to members of such prominent families as the Mangums and Manlys, at whose table he dined. Chavis, a good friend of Senator Willie P. Mangum of North Carolina, ingratiated himself with conservatives by his strong support for Federalist-Whig policies and opposition to abolitionism. Bishop William Capers of South Carolina described Henry Evans, an early nineteenth-century free black Methodist preacher, as "confessedly the father of the Methodist Church, white and black, in Fayetteville [North Carolina] and the best preacher of his time in that quarter." Every distinguished visitor, Capers added, went to hear him.[45]

Even at segregated camp meetings, whites flocked to spellbinding black preachers and attended the funerals of well-liked slaves at which respected black preachers conducted services. Certain black preachers became legends in their localities and beyond. In 1832, at the height of the post–Nat Turner repression, the state legislature of North Carolina exempted Ralph Freeman from the prohibition against free black preachers, noting that blacks and whites required his services in his thinly populated section. Freeman preached the funeral service for his friend the white Baptist Reverend Joseph Magee. George M. Erskine of East Tennessee and the blacksmith Ellis of Alabama preached so effectively to mixed congregations that they were sent to Liberia as missionaries. Described as "black as a crow," the eloquent Caesar McLemore, purchased in 1828 by the Alabama Baptist Association, preached primarily to slaves but drew a large white audience. The church raised money to free him. Dock, another slave, refused manumission in order to stay with his master but continued to preach to whites and blacks. He saw no reason to quit his master, thinking that if he were free, slaves would pay less attention to his preaching. To the end of the old regime, whites praised the eloquence, rhetorical power, and piety of black preachers.[46]

Evidence of black accomplishment – even when proudly acknowledged by whites – availed little. Every case could be celebrated as an exception that proved the rule. Pseudo-reconciliation of blatant contradictions abounded. A contributor to the *Southern Quarterly Review* argued that since an intelligent slave was worth more than a stupid one, masters cultivated the expansion of their slaves' intelligence. He then asserted that the condition of northern free blacks revealed them to have low intelligence. Exceptional black individuals, remarked Waddy Thompson of South Carolina, showed great talent, but, since the whole world agreed on their race's baseness, they were condemned to misery. A slaveholder blurted out in an agricultural journal (republished in other journals): "You must provide for him yourself, and by that means create in him a habit of perfect dependence on you. Allow it once to be understood by a negro that he is to provide for himself, and you that moment give him an undeniable claim on you for a portion of his time to make this provision." The slave will perceive an encroachment on his time, and his "disappointment and discontent are seriously felt."[47]

An Incongruity

White belief in black incapacity ran up against "free Negroes" (usually mulattoes or "people of color") who succeeded as slaveholders. Most owned a spouse, children, or other relatives, for the laws required the expulsion of emancipated slaves. Often successful mechanics or tradesmen bought their wives and children and then invested in other slaves for their labor. But by the end of the eighteenth century some free people of color held slaves strictly for profit, and in Louisiana and South Carolina a few became substantial planters. Most slaveholding people of color in South Carolina – about two-thirds of whom were women – held slaves as a source of labor with no intention of manumitting them. Those who rose to planter status generally met acceptance by whites as persons of wealth and prestige. Here and there, acceptance went the limit. South Carolina accepted racial intermarriage at law. Some especially fair-skinned children of well-to-do colored slaveholders married into white families. James Pendarvis of the Charleston District (3,000 acres and 113 slaves) married a white woman, and his daughter married a white man. In 1850, Reuben Robertson of Turkey Creek, South Carolina, a free person of color, owned 50 slaves and 700 acres of land valued at $5,000. He was the son of a white farmer and the colored mistress he had emancipated with their four children. Reuben Robertson, a successful farmer, steadily increased his slaveholdings and wealth and married a white woman. In Louisiana, Eliza Robertson found the black slaveholding Decuirs "excellent good people, and many a white man might envy them their reputation for honesty." Horace Cowles Atwater, an antislavery northern traveler, was surprised to find so many colored planters in South Carolina and especially Louisiana, who accepted slavery and its mores and held social views close to those of white planters. In Florida, Anna

Kingsley (Anta Majigeen Ndiaye), the beautiful daughter of a wealthy African slaveholder and the emancipated wife of Zephaniah Kingsley, slave trader and planter, owned a dozen slaves and knew that her father had been killed during a slave raid. Yet she voiced no objection to slavery per se or to her husband's multiple wives. She had, after all, been raised in a slaveholding, polygamous society. She proved an excellent manager, slaveholder, and businesswoman.[48]

Free people of color who sought to increase their income had a simple choice: They could acquire slaves or leave the South. By 1800 black slaveholding had reached noticeable proportions across the lower South as well as in Virginia and Maryland. In the Charleston District in 1790, one-third of the 155 free black families owned slaves, and some such proportion appears to have obtained in Savannah, Pensacola, Mobile, and New Orleans. Some mulatto and quadroon small slaveholders in town and country had been emancipated by white fathers or descended from those who had been. In the 1830s, southern state legislatures expressed concern over the 3,600 free "black" slaveholders. Virginia deprived free blacks of the right to own slaves other than spouses and children. Many white Virginians praised free black craftsmen as superior to white. The more successful craftsmen owned slaves and taught them their trades. The high quality of their work helps to account for the firm resistance of whites of all classes to proposals for the expulsion of free blacks despite their performance of needed services. Indeed, the ease with which slaves learned skilled trades during the colonial period led to a pronounced decline in the importation of skilled white indentured servants. In 1860, Charles Campbell, the historian, provided an ironic twist. He claimed that colonial Virginians, seeing white servants treated wretchedly, did not fret over blacks.[49]

In 1830, nine free persons of color with more than fifty slaves each ranked as substantial planters. By 1860, the number had dropped to seven with an average of more than eighty slaves. Auguste Debucet, the largest, had an estate worth more than $200,000. Alabama had a good many free blacks who owned relatives and a few who invested in slaves. The largest owned between fourteen and twenty-seven slaves in 1850. William Ellison of South Carolina, born a slave, bought his freedom in 1816 and ended as the largest slaveholding person of color outside Louisiana. Having learned to make gins as a slave, he built his own successful manufactory in the Fairfield District. Planters considered Ellison's gins of superior quality, and his customers extended to Mississippi. In 1845 he was rich enough to buy the home of former governor Stephen D. Miller. While a manufacturer, he presided over a cotton plantation and owned more than sixty slaves. Ellison, who had sexual relations with and children by his slaves, freed none and broke up families by sale.[50]

Black slaveholding yielded some unpleasant stories. Professor Francis Lieber of South Carolina College raised his eyebrows when a free black cook refused to buy her husband, explaining, "He is not over good, and might not behave after I have bought him." Any free black who owned a wife or children risked dying in debt and having creditors seize them. In Savannah in the 1830s, a white planter coveted the daughter of a rich black who owned his own wife and children. In love with a man of color, she defied her father's wishes and refused the planter. Her father sold her to the planter. George Wright of Alabama had to sell his five sons when he could not meet obligations. Fortunately, another free black and some sympathetic whites bought them and treated them well. Dick, a free black in Mississippi, took a two-year $1,000 loan from W. N. Mercer, a big planter, with his son as collateral, but paid it back. In Baltimore, freedmen held their children as slaves in order to protect them, but in bad times they might have to apprentice the children to whites.[51]

The testimony of whites, reinforced by that of ex-slaves, identified people of color as harsh masters. Examples there were: For one, Jacob Guillard, a blacksmith in Baltimore, treated his slaves roughly and had a severe problem with runaways. Few of those who made the charge offered evidence, but neither did sentimentalists who characterized free people of color as especially humane masters. As masters, free people of color ran the same gamut as whites. Loren Schweninger's thorough study concludes that they differed little in their treatment of slaves.[52]

The success of nonwhite slaveholders did not make whites reconsider southern slavery's racial basis. Instead, they wondered aloud if re-enslavement of free blacks might not be a good idea. John Taylor of Caroline opposed "the policy of introducing by law into society, a race, or nation of people, between masters and the slaves, having rights extremely different from either, called free negroes or mulattoes." For Taylor, southern society rested on slave labor. He accused free blacks of encouraging dissatisfaction and insubordination among slaves, of disrupting the rural economy, and of constituting an unproductive class that burdened society. Worse, being depraved and lawless, they stole and traded in goods stolen by slaves: "Cut off from most of the rights of citizens, and from the allowances of slaves, it is driven into every species of crime for subsistence; and destined to a life of idleness, anxiety, and guilt." Taylor discouraged free blacks from accumulating property or trying to sink or swim in a well-policed market society. He did not rail against the poor whites whom other Southerners denounced as dissolute; rather, he called for the removal of the "free negroes." In gentle moments, Taylor wanted the government to pay for resettlement in the western territories or in Africa. In harsh moments – in the same book – he suggested ruthless methods of repression. He demanded that slaves convicted of stealing be sold out of Virginia – that is, dumped on other slave states, which did not respond cheerfully. Several newspapers in North Carolina advocated an ingenious way to get rid of free blacks: Southerners who visited the North should take one or more free black servants with them. The abolitionists, assuming they were slaves, would seize and "emancipate" them, thereby ridding North Carolina of these "nuisances." In the 1850s the southern press stepped up demands for expulsion or enslavement. It was only one step from John Taylor's outbursts to George Fitzhugh's modest proposal to enslave free blacks for their own good.[53]

7

Devotion unto Death

Nine-tenths of the Southern masters would be defended by their slaves, at the peril of their own lives.

– Thomas R. R. Cobb[1]

General Thomas Williams spoke for many Union officers when he expressed confidence that the Confederacy would face servile insurrections as his troops moved south. A great many Southerners thought differently. In South Carolina during the 1830s, Senator William Smith and Representative William Drayton proudly proclaimed that, if war came, southern slaves would fight shoulder to shoulder with their masters. In the 1840s, Matilda Charlotte Houstoun, the British novelist, reported that sugar planters in Louisiana believed their slaves willing to die for them. Yet those same planters shuddered at the prospect of a war in which England sent black troops to incite slaves to repeat the horrors of Saint Domingue. Houstoun belittled the notion that Englishmen would resort to the barbarism of inciting race war, but she thought that slaves might desert even the best of masters in a crisis.[2]

Armed Slaves: Friends or Foes?

Southerners had selective memories and never did strike a balance between confidence in slave loyalty and foreboding over slave revolt. A historically minded people, they knew that armed slaves and free people of color had helped to tame the frontier, defending farms and plantations against Indian raids. Nathaniel Bacon recruited black as well as white troops during his rebellion in Virginia in 1676. From the early settlements until the Yamassee War in the lower Southeast in 1715–17, probably as many blacks as whites served as front-line troops – until the sight of armed slaves frightened whites as much as the prospect of Indian attacks. During the eighteenth century, South Carolina manumitted slaves who saw battle in militia service. Charles Pinckney, a delegate to the federal Constitutional Convention and afterward governor of

South Carolina, extolled slaves' military contributions to the patriot forces in the Revolution. In New Orleans, free men of color cheered American annexation, and Governor W. C. C. Claiborne lauded their militia. During the War of 1812, Andrew Jackson and Zephaniah Kingsley hailed the performance of free colored militias in Florida, especially against Indians. Counterpoint: George Tucker, Virginia's fine statistician, recorded significant slave flight to the British. In 1818, the antislavery James Turner Morehead, speaking at the University of North Carolina, declared impolitic the establishment of a colony for emancipated blacks in the Northwest, warning that in time it would grow into a formidable hostile force.[3]

In 1850, General Felix Huston of Mississippi told the Nashville Convention that years of study and experience had convinced him that slavery strengthened the South militarily relative to the North because its laborers provided a source of economic strength. Not all Southerners agreed. The influential Baptist Reverend Richard Fuller of Baltimore and Senator John J. Crittenden of Kentucky, among many, believed that slavery would weaken the South in war, much as they thought it had weakened the Roman state in ancient times. Benjamin F. Perry, South Carolina's prominent unionist, recalled the defection of slaves to the British during the Revolution, foretelling a repetition if the South seceded in 1850. Secession meant war. The laboring classes, instead of providing troops as in Europe, would require troops to overawe them. Jonathan Worth of North Carolina, opposing secession in December 1860, predicted a South surrounded by enemies, "all hating us." Southerners would have "to cut the throats of our negroes or have our own throats cut." A northern invasion would trigger slave insurrection, and "the poor negroes will be killed." By May 1861 a resigned Worth explained that Lincoln's course had left North Carolina no choice. Apparently forgetting his dread of slave insurrection, he declared, "Our white population *and our slaves* will resist to the death." James W. Drane of Mississippi said of northern employers, "Their servants hate them; ours love us. My niggers would fight for me and my family. They have been treated well, and they know it." Drane called on Mississippians to follow the example of the biblical patriarch Abraham and lead their armed slaves in battle. Touring the South, John S. C. Abbott, the antislavery New Englander, gasped: "Surely, you do not expect an intelligent man to accept this statement."[4]

The works of ancient Greek and Roman historians and modern scholars like Augustus Boeckh taught southern politicians, intellectuals, and clergymen about the frequent recruitment of slave troops. Robert E. Lee, well read in Greek history and literature, noted that ancient and modern slaves were accustomed to firm discipline. But as Lee and other educated Southerners knew, Xenophon and Demosthenes warned that slaves bore masters natural enmity and presented them with physical danger. Cato the Elder had a pithier version – "Our slaves are our enemies" – and the Romans had a proverb, *quot servi, tot hostes* [all slaves are enemies]. Yet Southerners had access to another point of view, notably from Seneca, one of their favored authors, who challenged received wisdom: "They are not all enemies when we acquire them; we make them enemies" by "excessively haughty, cruel, and insulting" treatment. George Sawyer of Louisiana, recognizing the "frequent insurrections among the slaves," denounced Roman slavery as brutal and concluded that Roman masters had dreaded violent retaliation. In particular, he cited the sadistic treatment meted out by Roman ladies to female attendants and Tacitus' account of four hundred slaves put to death after one of them murdered Pedanius Secundus, their master.[5]

The Greeks preferred not to use slaves and helots as soldiers, but they had to recruit large numbers in order to defend their cities. Spartans relied on soldiers from among helots and *neodamodeis* (helots previously emancipated for military service), but they showed their apprehension by arranging the disappearance of two thousand helots who had distinguished themselves during the Peloponnesian War. Southern slaveholders found the Roman experience difficult to interpret. In Appian's account, Hannibal armed slaves, but Tiberius Gracchus and his supporters, protesting a swelling slave force and a declining yeomanry, depicted slaves as faithless and militarily useless. Yet Tiberius, who won distinction in the storming of Carthage (147–146 B.C.), was the grandson and son of men who had, respectively, organized slaves to fight for Rome during the Punic Wars and in the campaign in Spain. Gaius Marius, among others, offered freedom to slaves recruited during the civil wars. Then and afterward, some slaves responded, whereas others did not. Freedom was a high reward, but the danger of execution for treachery to masters provided a strong counterweight. Tacitus told of slaves who gave up their lives to protect masters but also told of Clemens – "the daring of a single slave" – who almost brought down the Roman state with "a design beyond a slave's conception." Writing on the Second Punic War, Livy made much of the Romans' willingness to arm slaves rather than ransom prisoners of war, whom they considered cowards for having surrendered. Livy praised slave warriors for their discipline and reliability. Educated Southerners during the War recalled from Plutarch that Caesar's march on Rome had frightened some senators into proposing to liberate and arm slaves. Cato the Younger – a hero to Southerners – denounced the proposal as unjust and unlawful, yet he encouraged voluntary emancipation for slaves ready to join the army. In Senegal, Zephaniah Kingsley of Florida learned firsthand that the fierce and dreaded warriors who filled the standing army of the slave-raiding Amari Ngoone Ndella, king of Kajoor, were his slaves.[6]

In Congress in the 1830s, James H. Hammond dismissed as "all a flourish" a Virginian's suggestion that slaves frightened their masters. "In no part of the world have men of ordinary firmness less fear of danger from their operatives than we have." He recounted worker and peasant risings in France and England, troubles in Ireland, and riots in the North as "appropriate illustrations of the peace and security of a community whose laborers are called free." The South had no such problems. Nat Turner's *coup de main* qualified as the South's only real slave insurrection, although no more than a "bloody outbreaking of six drunken wretches." Hammond wrote to the antislavery Thomas Clarkson of Britain that the slaves would happily hang abolitionists and help crush any black troops sent against the South. In 1835, the citizens of Pendleton, South Carolina, resolved in a public meeting, "We feel confident that a very large majority of the Slaves would support their masters and die by their sides, even in a servile conflict."[7]

Proslavery apologists, floating a romantic version of the American Revolution, claimed that blacks as well as Indians had fought for the Patriots in the bloody struggle for South Carolina's backcountry. Whites remembered them as wonderfully loyal to their masters, whereas, in fact, many slaves had proved defiant, absconded to the British, or taken up arms against the Patriots. "Perhaps the world cannot exhibit a history," wrote William Gilmore Simms in the 1830s, "more remarkable, or more worthy of a grateful remembrance, than the conduct of the serviles of the South during the war of the revolution." A decade later, Augustus Baldwin Longstreet, in a widely circulated pamphlet, acclaimed slave loyalty, arguing that the British had forced slaves to go with them. Even the historian Robert R. Howison of Virginia, an emancipationist, referred to slaves who had gone with the British during the Revolution and the War of 1812 as "seduced" and "enticed." For spice, Howison found Nat Turner's uprising "unprovoked." In the Southwest, figures as prominent as Dr. Samuel A. Cartwright and the historian Albert James Pickett maintained that slaves had stood by their masters during the American Revolution and the War of 1812. Yet, as Patricia Bradley concludes, black efforts to gain sympathy and respect by serving in the Revolutionary armies did little to alter prevailing images and conditions. Black contributions drew little attention until the abolitionists emerged.[8]

In 1837, John C. Calhoun told Attorney General James T. Austin that Massachusetts suffered more deaths from mobs than South Carolina suffered from slave insurrections. Some of South Carolina's most distinguished citizens in effect supported Calhoun. Chancellor William Harper dismissed the thought of a general slave insurrection, arguing that a talented and energetic revolutionary leader could not become so widely known as to combine and direct disgruntled slaves. Dr. John S. Wilson told planters, "I am confident that there is enough affection and fidelity in every neighborhood to ensure the disclosure of any scheme of insurrection." Loyal slaves exposed incipient slave revolts in Tennessee, Louisiana, and elsewhere. Hugh Legaré wrote: "We have no uneasiness at all about the event of any servile war unless it be complicated by some other kind of war." The slaves always proved loyal unless misled by Jacobins, and if they rose, they would be exterminated.[9]

From Virginia, Nathaniel Beverley Tucker, who expected slaves to guard the plantations, contrasted their "proud humility" with the "servile sulkiness" of northern free blacks. President Thomas Roderick Dew of the College of William and Mary said that "many" slaveholders had armed their slaves to resist Nat Turner. Southern unionist warnings against self-deception had little effect. Slaveholders, echoed by northern sympathizers, remained certain that their slaves would not only fight for their masters but also reject freedom at the hands of Yankee invaders. And Livy provided comfort with an account of a faithful slave woman who exposed a conspiracy of a considerable number of Roman women to poison their husbands.[10]

During the War, E. A. Pollard of Virginia, among other Southerners, claimed that the paucity of slave revolts proved blacks fit for slavery. They found support from northern "Copperheads," who ranted against black "savagery." Yet proslavery paeans to black courage in defense of their masters proceeded *pari passu* with the denigration of blacks as cowards. And with cowardice went the tyrannical disposition associated with bullies. "Negroes," Robert Collins of Georgia wrote in 1854, "are by nature tyrannical in their disposition, and if allowed will often abuse the weaker." Slaveholders had a responsibility to rein them in. During the War, Gustave A. Breaux of Louisiana observed the conduct of his slaves as liberation neared: "Overbearing to all who fear them, as they are crouching to those who show no fear." Apparently, blacks were cowards except when they protected masters and mistresses. The slaveholders found a wonderful model for such dreams in Plutarch. Marc Antony ordered his slave Eros to kill him. Instead, Eros threw himself upon the sword. Antony, who then committed suicide, commented, "It is well done, Eros. You show your master how to do what you had not the heart to do yourself.[11]

"We sleep soundly at night and have no fear of our slaves." So ran the refrain, which had some substance behind it. Simms confidently asserted, "Men retire to their beds at night, on plantations surrounded with slaves, without locking a door or bolting a window." H. W. Ravenel added that lowcountry planters did not have to lock their doors because they suffered no "heavy robberies." Richard Taylor, receiving Victoria Stuart-Wortley on his plantation in Mississippi in 1848, boasted of reliable slaves against whom no doors had to be locked or special security measures taken. She was deeply impressed by Taylor's valet, who had taught himself to read and whom Taylor encouraged.[12]

Slaveholders distrusted their slaves much more than they let on even to themselves. The most deadly consequences surfaced during reports of insurrectionary plots. Whites responded quickly and often savagely to any rumor – no matter how weakly grounded – with summary execution of the innocent along with the guilty. Sometimes the more sober planters proved strong enough to protect the slaves by reining in white hysteria. More often, they availed little and had to confine their disgust to diaries and private correspondence. Revulsion at the inhumanity of panicky neighbors deepened with suspicions that lower-class whites used reports of plots as an excuse to vent racial hatred and humiliate planters. Planters contended with a public opinion manipulated by politically ambitious demagogues.[13]

"The present is replete with danger." With those words Light Horse Harry Lee summoned the Virginia militia in the 1790s when some hundred and fifty blacks in Norfolk joined whites in a pro-French demonstration. For decades hostilities with France and Britain aroused apprehensions of slave rebellion, nowhere more tellingly than in the Southwest. Although some slaves remained staunchly loyal to their masters during Louisiana's great slave revolt of 1811, planters never doubted that the mass of slaves constituted a dangerous domestic enemy. Especially in heavily black parishes, whites looked to the United States Army to guarantee their security. During the War of 1812 planters in the Southwest, anticipating defection of slaves to the British, discussed humane reform of slave codes to render the slaves more content.[14]

In 1811, John Randolph of Roanoke, opposing war with Britain, charged that French revolutionary ideology threatened to unleash massive slave revolts. The slaves had remained loyal during the Revolution, but now: "The night-bell never tolls for fire in Richmond that the mother does not hug the infant more closely to her bosom." In 1835, Senator William Campbell Preston of South Carolina echoed Randolph's words in an address on petitions to abolish slavery in the District of Columbia. In the midst of sectional struggles in the 1850s, Josiah Quincy strove to rally the North by ruffling the South with Randolph's words. Even Moses Stuart of Massachusetts, who faced northern opprobrium for denying the sinfulness of slavery, ridiculed the southern pretense that their slaves' insurrectionary potential did not frighten them.[15]

In 1829, General Joseph W. Allston of South Carolina took charge of troops sent from Charleston to put down an incipient slave revolt. He received a letter from J. L. Petigru, the acknowledged head of the South Carolina bar, who often defended blacks in court: "I am afraid you will hang half the country. You must take care and save negroes enough for the rice crop. It is to be confessed that your proceedings have not been bloody as yet, but the length of the investigation alarms us with apprehension that you will be obliged to punish a great many." Across the South, lynching awaited whites suspected of aiding rebellious blacks. During the panic in Mississippi in 1835, William H. M. Thompson wrote to his wife that the repression promised to become a greater evil than that it was intended to correct: "It is supposed the Governor will have to call out the militia to restore order."[16]

The worst panics came with Nat Turner in 1831 and the insurrectionary plot attributed to slave ironworkers of Tennessee in 1856. Frightened whites tortured and killed numerous blacks. Nat Turner shook much of the South, especially North Carolina. In Salisbury, a preacher reported turmoil when his parishioners took a trivial accident as an indication of slave rebellion. In Wilmington, Rachel Lazarus described Turner's impact as having caused a deep change in local sentiments: "To be necessarily surrounded by those in whom we cannot permit ourselves to feel confidence, to know that unremitted vigilance is our only safeguard, & that soon or late we or our descendants will become the certain victims of a band of lawless wretches who will deem murder & outrage, just retribution is deplorable in the extreme." Mrs. Coleman Freeman reported from Canada on her experiences as a slave in North Carolina. Nonslaveholders, she said, would have killed blacks indiscriminately if masters had not intervened, sending slaves to jail to isolate the violent ones but also to keep innocent slaves safe. Yet writing during the War, Sarah Clayton, from a wealthy planter family in Georgia, recalled that she and her peers knew about Nat Turner but "were spared additional terror by our ignorance of all particulars." In South Carolina, prominent men like James Henley Thornwell recoiled from the hysteria and brutality that swept the South after Nat Turner's revolt and lesser events, but they said little in public.[17]

An insurrectionary scare jarred Tennessee in 1856 and spread across the South. After widespread arrests, white vigilantes lined the roads of Stewart County with the spiked heads of suspected rebels. Benjamin Allen commented to William Trousdale on the hanging of four blacks at Gallatin: "The whole thing was grossly exaggerated, and no doubt had its origins in the late Presidential canvass, the negroes hearing so much of Fremont began to think that if he was elected they would all be free, but I have no idea there was any organized plan for insurrection." Moncure Conway, the Virginia-born abolitionist, identified an important aspect of the panic when he wrote that Southerners of the generation of the 1850s had not experienced a serious slave revolt: "That is the very reason why there is such a horror and panic about it: it is a vague, mysterious, and unknown evil." M. D. Cooper, a planter, offered a caustic interpretation:

> We are trying our best in Davidson County, to produce a negro insurrection, without the slightest aid from the negroes themselves. . . . The rack, the thumbscrew and the wheel are looked upon, it is true, as instruments of justice belonging to the dark ages of barbarism – but then the lash properly administered is quite as efficient. It breaks no bones while it satisfactorily elicits whatever confessions in disclosures the ministers of extra-legal justice are anxious to procure. . . . There is, in sober seriousness, no shadow of foundation for any belief of domestic plot in insurrection. But the popular mind is in that excited state requiring the most trivial cause to set everything in a blaze. Our better citizens are at work and I hope will succeed in preventing an outbreak – among the whites.[18]

Even men troubled by excesses refused to take chances. When panic gripped Alabama, William Procter Gould called his slaves together. They denied ever having heard of such troubles. "This may or may not be so – but from nothing I have noticed in their conduct can I bring myself to believe that any of them are looking forward to a change in their situation. What they might have done if there had been an actual outbreak must remain unknown to us." *The Southern Watchman* of Athens, Georgia, expressed disgust: "We were not amongst those who apprehended any danger. First, because the great mass of the negroes are well treated and are so much 'better off' than the [poor?] whites, that they have no excuse for making such an attempt." Besides, the editors added, the slaves understood the relation of forces and knew they would be massacred if they rose. The editors nonetheless called for increased vigilance as well as more stringent laws against free persons of color and against slaves who hired their own time. Frederick Law Olmsted, horrified by the grisly torture of suspected rebels, acknowledged that slaveholders generally went to bed unafraid. But he too explained that the slaves recognized the overwhelming military power of their masters. Cooler southern heads measured the plot in

Tennessee and the danger of its replication elsewhere. They wanted greater vigilance but expressed anxiety about destructive overreaction. M. Gillis of Louisiana recounted the disgust of big planters with the popular response to "a sham insurrection." During the secession crisis of 1859, William Tecumseh Sherman, the superintendent of the Louisiana Military academy, remarked, "The mere dread of [slave] revolt, sedition or external interference makes men ordinarily calm almost mad."[19]

The self-deception of those who denied the possibility of slave revolt puzzled Edmund Ruffin. He observed that newspapers systematically suppressed reports of plots and that prominent men opposed secession in horror of a war in which abolitionists triggered slave revolts. Ruffin credited reports from the ironworks in Tennessee, but not reports from Virginia. He lamented the execution of innocent blacks in a wave of white hysteria. General Huston urged northern newspapers to end abolitionist agitation. The South had the power to crush any slave insurrection, but if insurgents "do damage to a single neighborhood, and destroy the lives of a few women and children," whites would have to kill large numbers of the "misguided wretches" as at Southampton.[20]

The Reverend James Furman of South Carolina, in a militant speech to a secessionist meeting, recited the litany of blacks as "a tractable, docile, affectionate class of dependants" who could nonetheless easily be misled. Emancipation would turn them into thieves, marauders, and – he hinted – rapists. A curious litany it was, recited in some essentials by men with vastly different attitudes toward slavery, blacks, and the Union. Fitzgerald Ross, a prosouthern Scot with the Confederate army, thought blacks "a very affectionate race." Their attachment to their masters reminded him of the interclass bond in the clans of Highland Scotland in bygone days. The abolitionist Thomas Wentworth Higginson, commanding black troops in the Union army, testified to their courage, but added, "They are simple, docile, and affectionate almost to the point of absurdity."[21]

Concern for White Women

The uneasiness of slaveholding women mocked protestations of white serenity and trust in slave loyalty. In Mississippi in the 1830s, J. H. Ingraham of Natchez recounted an incident: A runaway entered the room of a white woman about midnight. In a commanding voice, she ordered him to stop. He obeyed. "This conduct betrayed no uncommon nerve or resolution in the lady, for southern ladies would laugh at the idea of being afraid of a negro." Ingraham, who saw little likelihood of a slave uprising, added, "The negro has a habitual fear of the white man,... combined with a fearless contempt the white man has for him." Catherine Carson, a young mistress on a large plantation near Natchez, soothed her nervous father in Kentucky: "So far from being afraid of them I feel they would be a protection." After work, the slaves went to see how she was doing and to collect the apples, flour, molasses, and other treats she had for them: "This little kindness they have not known for a long time and I assure you they appreciate it."[22]

These heartwarming stories did not reassure those afraid of an individual act of violence or the slitting of a few throats. From personal experience, gentlemen portrayed their ladies as uneasy and in need of protection. William W. Freehling has recently noted that Nat Turner's rebels killed fewer than ten white men but twice as many women and some forty children. It is not surprising, then, that the female antislavery petition campaign of 1831 in Virginia – organized primarily by John Hartwell Cocke – attracted several hundred women, but that post–Nat Turner soul searching ended the agitation. On the eve of secession, President James Buchanan told Congress, "Many a matron throughout the South retires at night in dread of what may befall herself and her children before the morning."[23]

Slaveholding women struggled to maintain their composure. Mary Jane Chester, a student at Columbia Female Institute in Tennessee, complained to her mother that fire regulations prevented her from locking her door at night. The election of William Henry Harrison had convinced slaves that their day had arrived: "There is great talk of an insurrection and I am frightened to death every night." Her mother assured her that Harrison would do nothing to liberate the slaves, but that when the slaves learned differently, "We may look for trouble." In Georgia, a mistress on a plantation that had experienced a slave plot kept an axe next to her bed in her husband's absence. Kate Stone of Louisiana observed mistresses unable to hide their dread of strong, recalcitrant black women. Stone remarked during the War, "We would be practically helpless should the Negroes rise, since there are so few men left at home. It is only because the negroes do not want to kill us that we are still alive." The citizens of Culpeper County, Virginia, doubled patrols during the insurrection scare of 1856, citing apprehension among the ladies. Mary Owen Sims of Arkansas did not sleep a wink during the presidential election of 1856 because of rumors of an impending slave insurrection. During the War, Anita Dwyer Withers of San Antonio, Texas, praised certain servants but admitted that others had her "worried to death." Mary Boykin Chesnut of South Carolina described white women's terror upon learning of slaves who had murdered reputedly kind and indulgent masters or mistresses.[24]

Mounting Crises

Jefferson Davis denied that abolitionist demagogy and intrigue turned the slaves' heads: "I have no fear of insurrection; no more dread of our slaves than I have of our cattle. Our slaves are happy and contented." In 1860, Senator Louis Wigfall of Texas, claiming that slaves had toiled quietly and loyally during the Mexican War, predicted the same if war followed secession. Davis and Wigfall expressed a view widely held, but so did John W. H. Underwood, a future congressman, who wrote to Howell Cobb in 1844 to demand repression of abolitionist agitation: "Sir the negroes in Georgia are already saying to each other that great men are trying to set them free and will succeed. . . . If the agitation of the subject is continued for three months longer we will be compelled to arm our Militia and shoot down our property in the fields."[25]

In 1858, James Sparkman told Benjamin Allston, his fellow South Carolinian, that intelligent Northerners often questioned him about slavery. They thought that armed slaveholders chained and guarded their slaves. "In answer I stated that my negroes locked me up and my family every night and frequently went off with the keys in their pockets." For years, Edmund Ruffin, refusing to believe that his slaves had set four big fires on his plantation, blamed local poor whites. With the fifth fire he considered the probable truth. "We all know that if our slaves so choose, they could kill every white person on any farm, or even through a neighborhood, in any night." Communities that faced Yankee invasion took firm measures to prevent outbreaks by slaves who were ostensibly content but vulnerable to tampering. In response to a conspiracy in 1861, J. D. L. Davenport of Mississippi wrote to Governor J. J. Pettus, "Nothing but eternal Vigilance will keep down the enemy at home." When the Yankees arrived at New Orleans, Clara Solomon dreaded slave violence more than violence from the hated Yankees.[26]

And yet when slaveholders went to war in 1861, they appealed to trusted slaves to protect the white women and children. The *Natchez Courier* gushed over a report from Port Gibson that James Seldon, who had voluntarily become the slave of James S. Mason, had been the first person to sign up for a Confederate loan and that free people of color in Vicksburg were contributing generously. Emma Holmes of Charleston thought the free colored men of Charleston "very creditable" when they raised $450 for the Confederacy's Soldier Relief Society. In 1863, she reported that a trustworthy old black man sent to spy on the Yankees had returned with valuable information. Louisa Lovell of Mississippi and many others credited slaves' claims of loyalty to the Confederacy. They took satisfaction from authentic reports of some blacks, slave and free, who offered to fight for the Confederacy in response to harsh treatment received from Yankee invaders. Some ex-slaves and their descendants took pride in blacks who defended humane masters and mistresses when the Yankees arrived. But the realistic A. M. Keiley, CSA, while extolling loyal slaves, thought them small in number. These accounts went hand in hand with accounts of black unrest, defection, and sedition.[27]

Priscilla Bond of Louisiana, the young mistress of a sugar plantation, cheerfully announced, "I made the negroes a Confederate flag. . . . I presented it to them and told them they must not let the Yankees get a hold of it." That they appreciated the gift remains problematical, but they might have done so for reasons Priscilla Bond did not glimpse. Jeff Hamilton, a slave who revered Sam Houston, his master, noted that many slaves sincerely cheered the young men who marched off to war despite wishing for the freedom they expected from a Union victory: "When you are living with people all around you who are kind and good to you and whose sons are fighting, you can't help but get some of their enthusiasm."[28]

The slaves cheered the raising of the Stars and Bars, much as they later cheered the raising of the Stars and Stripes. Peoples everywhere, especially poor people, keep two or more flags in their pockets, knowing that the mighty warriors who speak in their name consider them pawns. People who desperately need to feel loved by those for whom they presume to speak have always hailed the flag-waving as proof of deeply felt loyalty. In November 1860, the northern-born-and-reared Reverend John Hamilton Cornish of South Carolina witnessed "a Torch Light Procession in which Abe Lincoln, the supposed President Elect of the U. S. was carried in effigy by two negroes – and finally hung on a gibbet & burnt." Upcountry, Floride Calhoun knew that her slaves supported secession. She had heard them say that the Yankees wanted to starve and destroy black people, just as they were doing to their white workers. Jackson, her slave, had run up to her, shouting, "Good news, good news, another state has seceded, Georgia is with us." In Virginia, "Uncle Dick," hoping Lincoln would not be elected, did not understand the Yankees' refusal to leave southern folk alone and have the Union as it used to be.[29]

Southern newspapers boasted in 1861 that slaves would take up arms, if necessary, to repel a Yankee invasion. Planters in Alabama and Mississippi petitioned Confederate state governments to arm their slaves. "Our slaves will repel your armies," a Methodist minister proclaimed at Natchez in 1861, "for they are not tempted by your offers of freedom. They know that they must labor, and that, too, as a subordinate people." White churches took black prayers for the Confederacy as proof of loyalty and devotion; they do not seem to have considered the possibility that those blacks were praying, not for a Confederate victory, but for the safe return of the soldiers, the sparing of lives, and the consolation of widows and fatherless children. Blacks' affection for their masters, wrote Samuel Galloway of Georgia, "is so ardent that they will execute the most hazardous office to demonstrate their zeal and attachment." John Berrien Lindsley of Tennessee mused over the blacks' reluctance to rise when Yankee troops drew near. He saw the "goodness of the African race" and its "mild, amicable, passive temperament." Counterpoint: Captain John Franklin Godfrey, a strong abolitionist, sadly observed the naïve enthusiasm of the freedmen in the Southwest: "Their happiness was to be of such short duration." Counterpoint: Slaves in Virginia caught southern whites off guard when they boldly sang "John Brown's Body."[30]

Body Servants in War and Propaganda

During the first two years of the War – less so afterward – masters brought body servants to the front. Even nonslaveholders rented slaves to do their washing and cooking and attend to their horses. Body servants may have had as strong a desire for freedom as other slaves, but their fidelity to particular masters cannot be gainsaid. Yeomen troops complained that they went without shoes and blankets while their officers provided for body servants. A few servants took up arms and killed Yankees; many more proved skillful "foragers" – a polite word for those who stole for their masters. They provided much of the music and entertainment in camp. Confederate officers cited examples like that of Charles Porter Strothers, who won the admiration of Stonewall Jackson and Richard Taylor for braving enemy fire to stay with masters. Suddenly, whites appreciated the masculine pride displayed by the black men usually perceived as "boys." Poignant stories were told of slaves who risked their lives to nurse wounded masters on battlefields or to retrieve their bodies.[31]

Some body servants absconded or defected to the Yankees, but many – perhaps most – proved loyal to their masters, some heroically so. The Reverend T. V. Moore, among other preachers, extolled body servants who volunteered to shoulder rifles for the CSA. Coleman Davis Smith went to war with a young master, a Captain Davis, whom he described as "always good and kind to me." When Union troops arrested Davis and hanged him for refusing to provide information, Smith lamented, "I begged him to tell what the Yankees wanted him to but he said no. I asked him to let me but he said no.... Then the trap was sprung and it broke my heart. I cant stand to think of it now." Early in the War some blacks fought as Confederate troops, although unrecognized as such. On numerous occasions servants picked up weapons and fought alongside their masters, and some black sharpshooters took a notable toll on Yankee troops. At least three black men rode with William Clarke Quantrill's ferocious Confederate guerrillas in Missouri, enjoying the respect of white comrades as men among men.[32]

The courage, resourcefulness, and loyalty of body servants became proverbial. For that very reason, when a trusted body servant deserted to the Yankees, morale in the ranks took a hard blow. Edgeworth Bird wrote glowingly of Sam, who remained steadfast through dangers and privations, but wrote ruefully of the desertion of Colonel James Waddell's Antony and a "great many" others. Meanwhile, the mere presence of body servants stirred class resentments in the army, the strength and extent of which remains unclear. Southerners ignored a lesson from ancient history: Alexander the Great allowed horsemen only one servant each and restricted infantrymen to one servant for every ten.[33]

The Confederacy Opts for Black Troops

The War put perception and self-deception to the test. Toward the end, a desperate Confederacy decided to recruit black troops for a last-ditch attempt to defeat the Yankee invasion. The War ended before the experiment could be tried, but the debate reopened long-standing controversies over the character of blacks and the policy of arming slaves of any race. The constant refrain that blacks lacked the courage and resourcefulness to make good soldiers flew in the face of experience. The slaveholders sought to control the distribution of guns to slaves but had limited success. Slaves shot wild game for their masters' tables and supplemented their own diets. Selected slaves had the privilege of carrying guns and other weapons for guard duty as well as hunting. In South Carolina, planters routinely assigned an armed slave to hunt ducks, and rice planters armed slaves to kill birds. In Louisiana, armed slaves stood guard in two shifts to protect expensive sugar machinery.[34]

In 1864, a group of officers in the Army of Tennessee, led by General Patrick R. Cleburne, called for black recruitment. Jefferson Davis, who had long opposed it as unwise and inexpedient, left the door open if military conditions deteriorated. With the war effort near collapse, Davis joined Judah Benjamin and Robert E. Lee in calling for black troops. Although the measure came too late, General Cleburne's arguments remain arresting. Exponents refuted notions that blacks could not make good soldiers by replying that blacks were fighting well for the Union, much as they had fought well for Toussaint Louverture's army in Saint-Domingue. Opponents like General H. T. Walker of Georgia argued that recruitment of blacks recognized them as equals. Edmund Ruffin encapsulated the widespread tension among Southerners. He considered blacks incompetent soldiers and generally craven. Then again, he reflected on their inexperience, certain that they remained affectionate and loyal. As for slaves who deserted to the Yankees, Ruffin wanted them shot not merely for desertion but for "ingratitude" and as "traitors to the government." For all that, he reluctantly supported the proposal to enlist slaves in the army.[35]

The campaign to enlist slaves had to overcome decades of myths, propaganda, and blithe assumption. Harriet Martineau and other critics of slavery had long taunted: If slavery was good for blacks, as whites asserted, why reward them with freedom for special service? In reply, whites tripped over themselves. In the 1780s, Ariel, a slave, earned his freedom by performing heroically during the fire at St. Philip's Church in Charleston. He became a local legend, remembered by the white press a half-century later. Subsequently, other blacks won commendations and rewards for bravery during great fires, but after 1820 rewards no longer included manumission.[36]

The desperate attempt to recruit blacks ran into widespread opposition in Lee's Army of Northern Virginia. Belief in black cowardice ran deep. Indeed, the cowardice of slaves, regardless of race, became proverbial during the ancient and medieval ages. On the eve of secession, a "Daughter of South Carolina" wrote in the *Charleston Mercury*, "They are arrant cowards, these dear dark friends of ours. Some of you will remember how in '22 they would shrink away at the gleam of their masters' sword as he armed for nightly patrol." Events often compelled those who assumed black cowardice to wonder. In the 1790s, southern Federalists insisted that war with France would bring an invasion by black as well as white troops, triggering massive slave revolts. Emancipation in the British West Indies confronted Southerners with the possibility of invasion by black troops in the event of an Anglo-American war. Robert Monroe Harrison, the American consul in Jamaica, repeatedly warned that abolitionists were preparing blacks for action if war came.[37]

In the 1830s, Chancellor Harper explained:

> Though morally timid, they are by no means wanting in physical strength of nerve. They are excitable by praise; and directed by those in whom they have

confidence, would rush fearlessly and unquestioning upon any sort of danger. With white officers and accompanied by a strong white cavalry, there are not troops in the world from whom there would be so little reason to apprehend insubordination or mutiny.[38]

Without contradicting the common depiction of blacks as the Jacobins of the South, some intelligent and well-read Southerners, who did not ordinarily slip into blather, convinced themselves of the natural timidity of blacks. Contradictory evidence did not matter.

The New School Presbyterian Reverend Frederick Ross considered blacks the gentlest of races: the men docile, the women affectionate. T. R. R. Cobb noted that the ruling classes of Egypt, Babylon, and Persia had armed slaves to defend their regimes. He cited ancient monuments to support his contention that 1,600 years before Christ, black slaves in Egypt "were the same happy negroes of this day." Maria (Mrs. John) Bachman of Charleston took a trip to the North in the 1850s and commented on "genteel niggers," whose natural qualities made them barbers and waiters. Sarah Henry Bryce of South Carolina attributed true Christian feeling to blacks who refused to follow John Brown. The antislavery Margaret Johnson Erwin of Mississippi freed her slaves. Alone in her family, she supported her uncle, Richard Mentor Johnson of Kentucky, who had two black mistresses and married an octoroon. Yet Erwin considered blacks "children, primitive children, and a hundred years will not take care of that." During the War, an antislavery unionist woman recalled the many times Atlantans had quaked in expectation of a black uprising that would open the city to the Yankees. But in districts drained of white men, the slaves made no move: "The Negroes go along with the same submission that characterizes the race."[39]

On the eve of the War, some respected slaveholders refused to succumb to the propaganda about black cowardice and militarily incompetence. Henry Watkins Allen, a big sugar planter who became war governor of Louisiana, witnessed the return of Louis Napoleon's army from Italy in 1859, judging its blacks to be "admirable soldiers." Realistic appraisals increased, but respect and admiration for black military qualities did not necessarily pass into thoughts of emancipation. In Kentucky, the Presbyterian *Danville Quarterly Review* commented that the War demonstrated how wrong Southerners had been to denigrate blacks, who were proving fine soldiers capable of freedom. The worldly Judah Benjamin characterized a slave as prone to revolt and ever ready to conquer his liberty. Benjamin's words came in a call for tougher measures to police the slaves.[40]

In August 1863, Benjamin described the cost of compensating owners for black recruits as prohibitive. He spoke for a great many when he predicted that whites would desert from the army if asked to fight alongside blacks, and he added that slaves were most useful as laborers. Almost everyone understood that enlistments required emancipation of troops and their families and wondered how slavery could survive. Whites could not easily contradict Howell

Cobb when he declared: "You cannot make soldiers of slaves, nor slaves of soldiers.... If slaves will make good soldiers, our whole theory of slavery is wrong." The Episcopal Reverend James Warley Miles of South Carolina, predicting the defection of armed blacks to the Yankees, thought the proposal mocked the South's contention that blacks lived in the condition best suited for them. Robert Barnwell Rhett fumed that the Confederacy had waged a bloody four-year war to sustain slavery, and that its leaders now wanted to surrender what it had fought for. The Richmond *Examiner* reminded readers that southern slaveholders had long thought of themselves as the blacks' best friends, but now they heard that emancipation would reward military service: "Slavery, then, in the eyes of Mr. Davis, keeps the Negro out of something which he has the capacity to enjoy.... If the case be so, then slavery is originally, radically, incurably wrong and sinful, and the sum of barbarism." A congressman from Virginia declared, "If we offer the slaves freedom as a boon we confess that we are insincere and hypocritical in saying that slavery was the best state for the negroes themselves." Among militant women, Catherine Edmondston of North Carolina seethed that the Confederacy surrendered a principle by offering freedom to black recruits, since Southerners had always promoted slavery as their best condition.[41]

Expediency confronted principle. Sergeant William Pitt Chambers, from a small farm in Covington County, Mississippi, opposed black enlistment "on higher ground than expediency – it is not right." By contrast, although the arming of slaves made Walter Herron Taylor, Lee's adjutant, nervous, he bowed to the judgment of his superiors. "It makes me sad, however," he wrote to his wife Bettie, "to reflect that the time honoured institution will be no more, that the whole society is to be revolutionized. But I suppose it is all right and we will have to be reconciled."[42]

How far could self-deception go? "It is said the Negro regiments fought there like demons," Kate Stone responded to the news from Milliken's Bend in 1863, "but we cannot believe that. We know from long experience they are cowards." The notion of black cowardice spread in the unlikeliest of quarters. The black abolitionists John Rock and Frederick Douglass had to reply to charges by Theodore Parker, among others, that blacks showed inherent cowardice by refusing to fight for their freedom and that John Brown's raid had failed to spark a slave revolt. Wartime southern spokesmen and newspapers ridiculed Yankees for thinking that blacks could make reliable soldiers, and a good many antislavery men in the North agreed. Probably, most Union soldiers initially opposed recruitment of blacks, considering them worthless as soldiers, but black performance in battle noticeably softened attitudes. Hostility among border-state Southerners who fought for the Union and among Yankees who fought for the Confederacy ran deeper, but it too ebbed as the War progressed. Marcus Woodcock of Middle Tennessee of the Union's 9th Kentucky Infantry, commenting on Yankee hostility to the enlistment of black troops and acknowledging his own antipathy to blacks, understood the military necessity and swallowed hard. Slowly, he came to see racial prejudices as irrational. He ended as a radical Republican and supported black rights.[43]

Mrs. James H. Loughborough left a gripping account of the siege of Vicksburg, in which she praised the behavior of her family's servants, who "seemed to possess more courage than is usually attributed to negroes." William Pitt Ballinger, a prominent Texas lawyer, advocated recruitment of slaves but saw no need to offer special incentives, since they would willingly fight for their masters. Confederate commanders proved more realistic. In Florida, they expected serious defections and expected Thomas Wentworth Higginson's black troops to electrify the slaves, exposing their pro-Union feelings.[44]

James Alexander Seddon, the Confederate secretary of war, glowed about the slaves' having "the homes they value, the families they love, and the masters they respect and depend on to defend and protect against the savagery and devastation of the enemy." Seddon's romantic flourish had a point, for, initially, blacks hesitated. Charles Wesley, in his study of Confederate black recruitment, remarked, "To the majority of the Negroes, as to all the South, the invading armies of the Union seemed to be ruthlessly attacking independent states, invading the beloved homeland and trampling upon all that these men had held dear." The complexity Wesley discerned had some tragic consequences. In 1856, William E. Davis armed his slaves and those of his brother, Jefferson Davis, to enforce his property claims against neighbors he thought were cheating him. The gambit worked, and Davis got his way. During the War, Joseph Davis armed slaves against Yankee encroachments, but when the Confederates arrived and saw armed blacks, they opened fire on sight, killing some.[45]

Slaves effected work slowdowns on plantations, deserted when Union troops approached, and seized opportunities for freedom. But their complex response often inadvertently fed a post-War southern white myth of loyalty and docility. "The world had never seen such a body of slaves," Governor David Shelby Walker of Florida cried in 1865. After the War, Jefferson Davis and a host of Confederate leaders lavishly praised the loyalty of the slaves, who continued to labor in the fields and as manual laborers for the army, and who eschewed rebellion. In a number of cities, free blacks offered to fight for the Confederate army. The army and state militias enlisted thousands of blacks, although, apparently, they did not participate in important battles. The Presbyterian Reverend Robert Franklin Bunting, chaplain of Terry's Texas Rangers (CSA), cut through the debate while reasserting the divine sanction of slavery: "One fact is past argument, viz: The negro will be the future soldier of the war: If not on our side, then against us."[46]

Lewis Clarke, having experienced enslavement firsthand, uttered a last thought that encompassed everything necessary: "There is nobody deceived quite so bad as the masters down South; for the slaves deceive them, and they deceive themselves."[47]

Notes

Introduction

1. "Harper on Slavery," in *The Pro-Slavery Argument, as Maintained by the Most Distinguished Writers of the Southern States* (Philadelphia, 1853), 94.
2. "Domestic" slavery has two meanings: It grounds slavery in state rather than national law, and it locates slavery in the household. See Mark V. Tushnet, *Slave Law in the American South: State v. Mann in History and Literature* (Lawrence, Kans., 2003), 22–23.
3. For an in-depth analysis of the planters' westward emigration, see James David Miller, *South by Southwest: Planter Emigration and Identity in the Slave South* (Charlottesville, Va., 2002), esp. 10–11, 135–136; Foby, "Management of Servants," *SC*, 11 (Aug. 1853), 226–227; also, M. W. Philips, "Preserving Health," *South-Western Farmer*, 2 (Aug. 1843). Among recent contributions to the discussion of paternalism, see esp. Mary R. Jackman, *The Velvet Glove: Paternalism and Conflict in Gender, Class, and Race Relations* (Berkeley, Calif., 1994), 14, 346; also, Charles F. Irons, *The Origins of Proslavery Christianity: White and Black Evangelicals in Colonial and Antebellum Virginia* (Chapel Hill, N.C., 2008), 86–88.

   William E. Wiethoff, an able historian who should know better, asserts that stern punishment of slaves exposed paternalism as a myth – a formulation that misunderstands everything of importance: *The Insolent Slave* (Columbia, S.C., 2002), 135, 162. Similarly, Richard Follett, in a strong book, treats paternalism as a mask, not to say a fraud, if it proceeds with profits for the master: *The Sugar Masters: Planters and Slaves in Louisiana's Cane World 1820–1860* (Baton Rouge, La., 2005), Chapter 5. For our view, see Elizabeth Fox-Genovese and Eugene D. Genovese, *Fruits of Merchant Capital: Slavery and Bourgeois Property in the Rise and Expansion of Capitalism* (New York, 1983); Elizabeth Fox-Genovese, *Within the Plantation Household: Black and White Women of the Old South* (Chapel Hill, N.C., 1988); and Eugene D. Genovese, *Roll, Jordan, Roll: The World the Slaves Made* (New York, 1974).
4. [George McDuffie], *Governor McDuffie's Message on the Slavery Question* (New York, 1983 [1835]), 8; "Omo," "Negro Houses – Plantation Hospitals," *SC*, 14 (Jan. 1856); Waddy Thompson, 24th Cong., 1st Sess., *Congressional Globe*, Dec. 21, 1835, Appendix, 15; Robert L. Dabney, *Defence of Virginia (and through Her*

of the South) in Recent and Pending Contests against the Sectional Party (New York, 1969 [1867]), 305–306.

5. Elizabeth Fox-Genovese and Eugene D. Genovese, *Slavery in White and Black: Class and Race in the Southern Slaveholders' New World Order* (New York, 2008).

6. J. S. Buckingham, *The Slave States of America*, 2 vols. (New York, 1968 [1842]), 1:65; George P. R. James, "Virginia Country Life," in Eugene L. Schwaab and Jacqueline Bull, eds., *Travels in the South: Selected from Periodicals of the Time*, 2 vols. (Lexington, Ky., 1973), 2:523; John Palfrey to William T. Palfrey, July 16, 1833; also, George H. Hepworth, *Whip, Hoe, and Sword: Or, The Gulf-Department in '63* (Boston, Mass., 1864), 49–50.

7. Thomas Colley Grattan, *Civilized America*, 2 vols. (London, 1859), 1:184; Tucker quoted in Maude Howlett Woodfin, "Nathaniel Beverley Tucker: His Writings and Political Theories with a Sketch of His Life," *Richmond College Historical Papers*, 2 (1917), 21.

8. *SQR*, 11 (1847), no. 22, vii; James O. Andrew to Leonore Andrew, May 26, 1844, in George G. Smith, *The Life and Letters of James Osgood Andrew, with Glances at His Contemporaries and at Events in Church History* (Nashville, Tenn., 1882), 359; Clemson to Calhoun, Aug. 12, 1845, in *JCCP*, 22:71–72; *DNCB*, 2:238 (Freeman); B. W. McDonnold, *History of the Cumberland Presbyterian Church* (Nashville, Tenn., 1899), 413; Steven Rowan and James Neal Primm, eds., *Germans for a Free Missouri: Translations from the St. Louis Radical Press, 1857–1862* (Columbia, Mo., 1983), 125; Garland quoted in William Lee Miller, *Arguing about Slavery: The Great Battle in the United States Congress* (New York, 1996), 30; T. C. Thornton, *An Inquiry into the History of Slavery* (Washington, D.C., 1841), 171; Henry St. G. Tucker, *Commentaries on the Laws of Virginia*, 3rd. ed. (Charlottesville, Va., 1844), 2:73–75; Tucker, *A Few Lectures on Natural Law* (Charlottesville, Va., 1844); Tucker, *Lectures on Government* (Charlottesville, Va., 1844).

1. "Boisterous Passions"

1. Augustine, "On the Trinity," tr. Arthur West Hadden, rev. and annotated by William G. T. Shedd, in Philip Schaff, ed., *Nicene and Post-Nicene Fathers*, 1st ser., 14 vols. (Peabody, Mass., 1995), 3:176.

2. Thomas Jefferson, *Notes on the State of Virginia*, ed. William Peden (Chapel Hill, N.C., 1955), 155.

3. Thomas L. Pangle, *The Spirit of Modern Republicanism: The Moral Vision of the American Founders and the Philosophy of Locke* (Chicago, 1988), 180–181; Baron de Montesquieu, *The Spirit of the Laws*, tr. Thomas Nugent, 2 vols. in 1 (New York, 1975 [1748]), 1: Bk. 15.1; George Mason, "Scheme for Replevying Goods and Distress for Rent," in Robert A. Rutland, ed., *The Papers of George Mason*, 3 vols. (Chapel Hill, N.C. 1970), 1:61–62; Mason in James Madison, *Notes of the Debates in the Federal Convention of 1787* (Athens, Oh., 1966), 504; Ellsworth–Mason exchange in Robert Allen Rutland, *George Mason: Reluctant Statesman* (Williamsburg, Va., 1961), 88; H. Roy Merrens, ed., "A View of Coastal South Carolina in 1778: The Journal of Ebenezer Hazard," *SCHS*, 73 (1972), 190.

4. St. George Tucker, ed., *Blackstone's Commentaries*, 5 vols. (Philadelphia, 1803), 1 (pt. 2), App. Note H., 63, 69; Ezekiel Birdseye, "To the Editor," Feb. 23, 1837, and Birdseye to Gerrit Smith, June 25, 1841, in Durwood Dunn, *An Abolitionist in the Appalachian South: Ezekiel Birdseye on Slavery, Capitalism, and Separate Statehood*

in East Tennessee, 1841–1846 (Knoxville, Tenn., 1997), 130, 162. See also the antislavery Quaker in Virginia: *Memoirs of Samuel M. Janney* (Philadelphia, 1881), 208–209. On Ramsay's shift, see Arthur H. Shaffer, *To Be an American: David Ramsay and the Making of the American Consciousness* (Columbia, S.C., 1991), 176–177; Shaffer, "David Ramsay and the Limits of Revolutionary Nationalism," in Michael O'Brien and David Moltke-Hansen, eds., *Intellectual Life in Antebellum Charleston* (Knoxville, Tenn., 1986), 73–75; J. H. Ingraham, *Sunny South; Or, The Southerner at Home* (New York, 1968 [1860]), 52–53; Clement Eaton, *The Freedom-of-Thought Struggle in the Old South* (New York, 1964), 220 (Gaston).

5. James Sidbury, *Ploughshares into Swords: Race, Rebellion, and Identity in Gabriel's Virginia, 1730–1810* (New York, 1997), 257; John Hersey, *An Appeal to Christians, on the Subject of Slavery*, 2nd ed. (Baltimore, 1833), 43–45; Sarah M. Grimké, *An Epistle to the Clergy of the Southern States* (New York, 1836), 19; William Goodell, *Views of American Constitutional Law, in Its Bearing upon American Slavery*, 2nd ed. (Utica, N.Y., 1845), 11; John S. C. Abbott, *South and North; or, Impressions Received during a Trip to Cuba and the South* (New York, 1969 [1860]), 83–84, 100; La Roy Sunderland, *Anti-Slavery Manual: Containing a Collection of Facts and Arguments on American Slavery*, 3rd ed. (New York, 1839), 31; Rufus W. Clark, *A Review of the Rev. Moses Stuart's Pamphlet on Slavery, Entitled Conscience and the Constitution* (Boston, 1850), 73–74; Charles K. Whipple, *The Family Relation as Affected by Slavery* (Cincinnati, 1858), 19; Wayland in Richard Fuller and Francis Wayland, *Domestic Slavery Considered as a Scriptural Institution in Correspondence*, 5th ed. (New York, 1847), 120; Len Gougeon and Joel Myerson, eds., *Emerson's Antislavery Writings* (New Haven, Conn., 1995), 17, 38, 48, also, 74; Grimké, quoted in Ronald G. Walters, *The Antislavery Appeal: American Abolitionism after 1830* (Baltimore, 1976), 71; Josiah Quincy, *Address Illustrative of the Nature and Power of the Slave States and the Duties of the Free States* (Boston, 1856), 6, 18; January 1862 in Adam G. de Gurowski, *Diary*, 3 vols. (Boston, 1862–65), 1:143.

6. Wesley quoted in Walter J. Fraser, Jr., *Charleston! Charleston!: The History of a Southern City* (Columbia, S.C., 1989), 54; H. S. Fulkerson, *Random Recollections of Early Days in Mississippi* (Vicksburg, Miss., 1885), 16, 144; Frederick Law Olmsted, *A Journey in the Back Country* (New York, 1970 [1861]), 269; Olmsted, *A Journey Through Texas; Or, a Saddle-Trip on the Southwestern Frontier* (Austin, Tex., 1978 [1857]), 116–117; Robert Everest, *A Journey through the United States and Part of Canada* (London, 1853), 106; Daniel Blake Smith, "In Search of the Family in the Colonial South," in Winthrop D. Jordan and Sheila L. Skemp, eds., *Race and Family in the Colonial South* (Jackson, Miss., 1987), 35–36.

7. David Macrae, *The Americans at Home* (New York, 1952 [1870]), 46–48; Frances Trollope, *Domestic Manners of the Americans* (Gloucester, Mass., 1974 [1832]), 208, n. 1; Mrs. [Matilda Charlotte] Houstoun, *Hesperos: Or, Travels in the West*, 2 vols. (London, 1850), 2:222; Catherine Cooper Hopley, *Life in the South from the Commencement of the War*, 2 vols. (New York, 1971 [1863]), 2:244; in general, see Jane Louise Mesick, *The English Traveller in America, 1785–1835* (New York, 1922), 141–144.

8. Harriet Martineau, *Society in America*, 2 vols. (New York, 1837), 2:128; Fredrika Bremer, *Homes of the New World: Impressions of America*, tr. Mary Howitt, 2 vols. (New York, 1853), 1:337, 2:233–234; Thomas L. Bayne "Autobiographical

Sketch" (ms.), 20; also, Thomas Tisdale, *A Lady of the High Hills: Natalie Delage Sumter* (Columbia, S.C., 2001), 121.

9. Committee of the Synod of Kentucky, *Address to the Presbyterians of Kentucky* (Newburyport, Ky., 1836), 7–8; Kendall quoted in Clement Eaton, *Henry Clay and the Art of American Politics* (Boston, 1957), 66; Mary Jane Chester to Elizabeth Chester, Jan. 7, 1841, in Mary Jane Chester Papers; John Evans to George Noble Jones, April 15, 1852, in Ulrich Bonnell Phillips and James David Glunt, eds., *Florida Plantation Records from the Papers of George Noble Jones* (St. Louis, Mo., 1927), 65; Arney R. Childs, ed., *Planters and Businessmen: The Guignard Family of South Carolina, 1795–1930* (Columbia, S.C., 1957), 15; *TCWVQ*, 1:300.

10. Elisabeth Muhlenfeld, *Mary Boykin Chesnut, A Biography* (Baton Rouge, La., 1981), 19 (she was five); Anna Matilda King to Thomas Butler King, Dec. 24, 1844, Aug. 8, 1858, in T. K. Butler Papers; T. Michael Parrish, *Richard Taylor: Soldier Prince of Dixie* (Chapel Hill, N.C., 1992), 55; Mary D. Robertson, ed., *Lucy Breckinridge of Grove Hill: The Journal of a Virginia Girl, 1862–1864* (Kent, Oh., 1979), 211.

11. Solomon Northup, *Twelve Years a Slave* (New York, 1970 [1854]), 261–262. For a sampling of black testimony, see Benjamin Drew, ed., *A North-Side View of Slavery: The Refugee* (New York, 1968 [1856]), 156; *AS: Ind.*, 6, pt. 2:28; *Okla.*, 7, pt. 1:77; *S.C.* 2, pt. 2:178. The nostalgic R. Q. Mallard recalled a slaveholder who punished white and black children for playing together: *Plantation Life before Emancipation* (EE: 1998 [1892]), 10.

12. Francis Black in *AS: Tex.*, 4, pt. 1:88; Feaster in *S.C.* 2, pt. 2:50, 130, 178; Pennington in Arna Bontemps, ed., *Great Slave Narratives* (Boston, 1969), 208; D. E. Huger Smith in Alice R. Huger Smith, *A Carolina Rice Plantation of the Fifties* (New York, 1936), 81, 83.

13. D. F. Jamison, "Annual Address," in *Proceedings of the State Agricultural Society of South Carolina* (Charleston, S.C., 1856), 352.

14. Edmund Burke, *Conciliation with the Colonies*, ed. Cornelius Beach Bradley (Boston, 1894), 21.

15. Robert Dawidoff, *The Education of John Randolph* (New York, 1979), 217–218; William Cabell Bruce, *John Randolph of Roanoke, 1773–1833*, 2 vols. (New York, 1970 [1922]), 1:140, 239; 2:675; Kenneth Shorey, ed., *Collected Letters of John Randolph of Roanoke to Dr. John Brokenbrough, 1812–1833* (New Brunswick, N.J., 1988), xvii; "Letter from Mr. Wirt to a Law Student," *SLM*, 1 (1834), 35; [Daniel K. Whitaker], "English Views of the Literature and Literary Men, and of the Political and Domestic Character of the People of Ancient Greece and Rome," *Southern Literary Journal*, 1 (1836), 426; James P. Holcombe, *The Election of a Black Republican President* (Richmond, Va., 1860), 9; Nathaniel Beverley Tucker, "Moral and Political Effect of the Relation between the Caucasian Master and the African Slave," *SLM*, 10 (1844), 747; May 14, 1863, in *ERD*, 2:656; George Fitzhugh, "Southern Thought," *DBR*, 23 (1857), 349. For Burke's impact, see Elizabeth Fox-Genovese and Eugene D. Genovese, *The Mind of the Master Class: History and Faith in the Southern Slaveholders' Worldview* (New York, 2005), 18, 39, 76, 728.

16. Henry W. Miller, *Address Delivered before the Philanthropic and Dialectic Societies of the University of North-Carolina, June 3, 1857* (Raleigh, N.C., 1857), 8; Jasper Adams, *Elements of Moral Philosophy* (Philadelphia, 1837), 101–102;

Robert Y. Hayne, Jan. 25, 1830, in Herman Belz, ed., *The Webster-Hayne Debate on the Nature of the Union: Selected Documents* (Indianapolis, Ind., 2000), 49–50; [William Drayton], *The South Vindicated from the Treason and Fanaticism of the Northern Abolitionists* (Philadelphia, 1836), 104–108; Robert Toombs, "Slavery – Its Constitutional Status and Its Influence on Society and on the Colored Race," *DBR*, 20 (1856), 604; Basil Manly, "An Address on Agriculture Delivered before the Alabama Historical Society," *SA*, 2 (1842), 339; John Perkins, Jr., *An Address Delivered before the Adelphic and Belle-lettres Societies, of Oakland College . . . On the Duty of Drawing from the History and the Theory of Our Government Just Views of Individual and National Life* (Port Gibson, Miss., 1853), 17–18; "Address at the University of Georgia, 1871," in *Senator Benjamin Hill of Georgia: His Life, Speeches and Writings* (Atlanta, Ga., 1893), 342, n.; J. L. M. Curry, *The South in the Olden Time* (Harrisburg, Pa., 1901), 5; D. J. McCord, "How the South Is Affected by Her Slave Institutions," *DBR*, 11 (1851), 351–352, 357. Also, Edward C. Bullock, *True and False Civilization: An Oration Delivered before the Erosophic and Philomathic Societies of the University of Alabama* (Tuscaloosa, Ala., 1858), 26–27.

17. John Taylor, *Arator: Being a Series of Agricultural Essays, Practical and Political: In Sixty-Four Numbers* (Indianapolis, Ind., 1977 [1818]), 121–123.

18. John Chester Miller, *The Wolf by the Ears: Thomas Jefferson and Slavery* (New York, 1977), 32; Jefferson quoted in Dumas Malone, *Jefferson and His Time*, 6 vols. (Boston, 1948–81), 1:87, also, 6:329–330; for Smith, see Glover Moore, *The Missouri Controversy, 1819–1821* (Lexington, Ky., 1953), 125.

19. George Tucker, *The Life of Thomas Jefferson*, 2 vols. (London, 1837), 1:10–11, 120, 122–123; "A Few Thoughts on Slavery," *SLM*, 20 (1854), 198; John Randolph Tucker, "The Great Issue," *SLM*, 32 (1861), 164. George Tucker reiterated these themes after he removed to Philadelphia: *Political Economy for the People* (Philadelphia, 1859), 86–87.

20. [M. R. H. Garnett], *The Union, Past and Future: How It Works, and How to Save It*, 4th ed. (Charleston, S.C., 1850), 36–38; Samuel A. Cartwright, *Essays . . . in a Series of Letters to the Rev. William Winans* (Vidalia, Miss., 1843), 67; Joseph T. Durkin, *Stephen R. Mallory: Confederate Navy Chief* (Chapel Hill, N.C., 1954), 104; Pleasant A. Stovall, *Robert Toombs: Statesman, Speaker, Soldier, Sage* (New York, 1892), 137–138; Norman D. Brown, *Edward Stanly: Whiggery's Tarheel "Conqueror"* (University, Ala., 1974), 92; "Remarks in the House of Representatives, Dec. 18, 1845," in Haskell M. Monroe, Jr., James T. McIntosh, et al., *The Papers of Jefferson Davis*, 11 vols. (Baton Rouge, La., 1971–2004), 2:390; Winston quoted in James Benson Sellers, *Slavery in Alabama* (University, Ala., 1964), 34; Wharton Jackson Green, *Recollections and Reflections: An Auto* [sic] *of Half a Century and More* (EE: 1998 [1906]), 52–53.

21. Thomas R. Dew, *An Address Delivered before the Students of William and Mary at the Opening of the College* (Richmond, Va., 1836), 17; Henry Howe, *Historical Collections of Virginia* (Charleston, S.C., 1845), 158; Mr. Smith, "Character of the American People," *SQR*, new ser., 2 (1857), 404; Chancellor Harper, "Slavery in the Light of Social Ethics," in E. N. Elliott, ed., *King Cotton Is King and Pro-Slavery Arguments* (New York, 1969 [1860]), 597; "Slavery and the Abolitionists," *SQR*, 15 (1849), 198–202. In *SLM*, see W. [of Westmoreland Co., Va.], "Slavery in the Southern States," 9 (1843), 739–740; Nathaniel Beverley Tucker, "Moral

and Political Effect of the Relation between the Caucasian Master and the African Slave," 10 (1844), 333; Sigma, "Southern Individuality," 38 (1864), 370; also, C., "Servility," 1 (1834), 6.

22. Robert F. W. Allston to James Hammond, July 24, 1846, in J. H. Easterby, ed., *The South Carolina Rice Plantation, as Revealed in the Papers of Robert F. W. Allston* (Chicago, 1945), 95, 27 (sons).

23. Edward A. Pollard, *Black Diamonds Gathered in the Darkey Homes of the South* (New York, 1968 [1859]), 107; W. H. Trescot, "Oration Delivered before the South-Carolina Historical Society," in *Collections of the South-Carolina Historical Society* (Charleston, S.C., 1859), 3:29–32, quote at 32; T. R. R. Cobb, *An Inquiry into the Law of Negro Slavery* (New York, 1968 [1858]), cxviii, ccxix, 35; A. B. Meek, *Romantic Passages in Southwestern History, Including Orations, Sketches and Essays* (Mobile, Ala., 1857), 58–59; Daniel R. Hundley, *Social Relations in Our Southern States* (Baton Rouge, La., 1979 [1860]), 70–71; William L. Breckenridge, "Moral View of Slavery," *Georgia Telegraph* (Macon), May 31, 1849.

24. F. W. Pickens, *An Address Delivered before the State Agricultural Society of South Carolina* (Columbia, S.C., 1849), 13–15; *Anniversary Discourse of E. H. Barton, A.M., M.D., President, before the New Orleans Academy of Sciences* (New Orleans, La., 1856), 22.

25. D. W. Mitchell, *Ten Years in the United States: Being an Englishman's Views of Men and Things in the North and South* (London, 1862), 182, 195; John Mitchel, "A Tour in the South-West," *Southern Citizen*, Feb. 6, 1858.

26. Adams, *Elements of Moral Philosophy*, 150; William Meade, *Old Churches, Ministers, and Families of Virginia*, 2 vols. (Berryville, Va., 1978 [1857]), 1:90–91.

27. A. A. Porter, "North and South," *SPR*, 3 (1850), 365; Iveson L. Brookes, *A Defence of Slavery against the Attacks of Henry Clay and Alex'r Campbell* (Hamburg, S.C., 1851), 40–42; Thornton Stringfellow, "Bible Argument" and "Statistical View," in Elliott, ed., *Cotton Is King*, 483, 523.

28. Haigh Diary, Jan. 23, 1842; R. H. Rivers, *Elements of Moral Philosophy* (Nashville, Tenn., 1859), 356; H. N. McTyeire, *Duties of Christian Masters*, ed. Thomas O. Summers (Nashville, Tenn., 1859), 128; [George Howe], "The Raid of John Brown, and the Progress of Abolition," *SPR*, 12 (1860), 788; *Sermons by the Rt. Rev. Stephen Elliott, D.D., Late Bishop of Georgia, with a Memoir by Thomas M. Hanckel, Esq.* (New York, 1867), xv.

29. Sterling Ruffin to Thomas Ruffin, Sept. 8, 1803, in *TRP*, 1:46.

30. John Fletcher, *Studies on Slavery, in Easy Lessons* (Natchez, Miss., 1852), 25, 206–207; James O. Andrew, *Family Government: A Treatise on Conjugal, Parental, Filial and Other Duties*, 3rd enl. ed. (Nashville, Tenn., 1882), 79–80.

31. Thomas R. R. Cobb, *"Historical Sketch of Slavery,"* in *An Inquiry into the Law of Negro in the United States* (New York, 1968 [1858]), lxx; "Against Timarchus," in *Speeches of Aeschines*, LCL, §§7–8, 11–15, 29, 51, quotes at 8, 51. For an extensive treatment of the case against Timarchus with special attention to attitudes toward homosexuality, see K. J. Dover, *Greek Homosexuality* (Cambridge, Mass., 1978), ch. 2. *Lives of the Twelve Caesars*, tr. Joseph Cavore (New York, 1931), 31.

32. Gilberto Freyre, *The Masters and the Slaves: A Study in the Development of Brazilian Civilization*, trans. Samuel Putnam (New York, 1956), 75.

33. *DHE*, 4:155; Jennifer R. Green, *Military Education and the Emerging Middle Class in the Old South* (New York, 2008), 3, 21–22, 31; Cottrell Diary, Nov. 9, 1855;

Diane B. Jacob and Judith M. Arnold, *A Virginia Military Institute Album, 1839–1910* (Charlottesville, Va., 1982), 4; Mark T. Carleton, "Louisiana State Seminary and Military Academy," *EC*, 3:957.

34. John Peyre Thomas, *The History of the South Carolina Military Academy* (Columbia, S.C., 1991 [1893]), 74–75, 78, 243, quote at 278; J. Hardeman Stuart to Oscar Stuart, Feb. 15, 1857, in Mayes-Dimitry-Stuart Papers; William Dusinberre, *Them Dark Days: Slavery in the American Rice Swamps* (Athens, Ga., 2000), 288 (Allston); John Bowers, *Stonewall Jackson: Portrait of a Soldier* (New York, 1989), 79; Otey to Cook, Jan. 8, 1862, in Otey Papers; Richard Yeadon, *Address on the Necessity of Subordination in Our Academies and Colleges, Civil and Military* (Charleston, S.C., 1854), 16n, 21–23.

35. Hunter Dickinson Farish, ed., *Journal and Letters of Philip Fithian: A Plantation Tutor of the Old Dominion, 1773–1774* (Charlottesville, Va., 1957), Dec. 1, 1773; "Extract from the Autobiography of J. Allen Hill," in W. W. Sweet, *Religion on the American Frontier. The Presbyterians, 1780–1840: A Collection of Source Materials* (New York, 1936), 816–817. Students at the University of Virginia reported alcoholism a serious problem by 1860: Peter S. Carmichael, *Lee's Young Artillerist: William R. J. Pegram* (Charlottesville, Va., 1995), 24; also, John N. Waddel, *Historical Discourse Delivered on the Quarter Centennial Anniversary of the University of Mississippi* (Oxford, Miss., 1873), 12.

36. *TSW*, 5:130; Lynn A Nelson, *Pharsalia: An Environmental Biography of a Southern Plantation, 1780–1880* (Athens, Ga., 2007), 194; Lucius Salisbury Merriam, *Higher Education in Tennessee* (Washington, D.C., 1893), 34; George Washington Paschal, *History of Wake Forest College*, 2 vols. (Wake Forest, N.C., 1935), 1:350. For servants on campuses: Robert F. Pace, *Halls of Honor: College Men in the Old South* (Baton Rouge, La., 2004), 47–51. On venereal diseases, see Felice Swados, "Negro Health on the Ante-Bellum Plantation," *Bulletin of the History of Medicine*, 10 (1941), 471–472; Marie Louise Marshall, "Samuel A. Cartwright and States' Rights Medicine," *New Orleans Medical and Surgical Journal*, 90 (1940–41), 4; Eugene D. Genovese, "The Medical and Insurance Costs of Slaveholding in the Cotton Belt," *Journal of Negro History*, 45 (1960), 151; Physician's Account Book, 1830–1831; Physician's Fee Book, 1847–1850; Physician's Record Book, 1855–1862; Physician's Book, 1852, in Minis Collection; Turner Account Book, March 15, 1851, July 30, 1855, Feb. 10, 1858; Weymouth T. Jordan, ed., *Herbs, Hoecakes and Husbandry: The Daybook of a Planter of the Old South* (Tallahassee, Fla., 1960), 67, 73, 108, 111.

37. D. E. Huger Smith, *A Charlestonian's Recollections, 1846–1913* (Charleston, S.C., 1950), 15; Parrish, *Richard Taylor*, 24; Brian Steel Wills, *A Battle from the Start: The Life of Nathan Bedford Forrest* (New York, 1992), 10–11. On manual labor schools, see, e.g., R. L. Dabney, *Life and Campaigns of Lt. Gen Thomas J. (Stonewall) Jackson*, (Harrisonburg, Va., 1983 [1865]), 19; George Washington Paschal, *History of Wake Forest College*, 2 vols. (Wake Forest, N.C., 1935), 1:70–91; George Lee Simpson, Jr., *The Cokers of Carolina: A Social Biography of a Family* (Chapel Hill, N.C., 1956), 43; Damon R. Eubank, *In the Shadow of the Patriarch: The John J. Crittenden Family in War and Peace* (Macon, Ga., 2009), 4.

38. Stuart Noblin, *Leonidas Lafayette Polk: Agrarian Crusader* (Chapel Hill, N.C., 1949), 22; John Albert Feaster Coleman Diary, May 25, June 7, 1849, in Stephen Berry, ed., *Princes of Cotton: Four Diaries of Young Men in the South, 1848–1860* (Athens, Ga., 2007), 328, quote at 330; James C. Bonner, *Milledgeville: Georgia's*

Antebellum Capital (Athens, Ga., 1978), 151 (Browns); *Senator Benjamin H. Hill of Georgia: His Life, Speeches and Writings* (Atlanta, Ga., 1891), 12, 342n; also, H. P. Griffith, *The Life and Times of Rev. John G. Landrum* (Charleston, S.C., 1992 [1885]), 26–27; James Russell Lowell, ed., "A Virginian in New England Thirty-Five Years Ago," *Atlantic Monthly*, 26 (1870), 164.

For prominent men who worked with slaves in the fields, see "Memoir of Langdon Cheves and Fragments," in Richard C. Lounsbury, ed., *Louisa S. McCord: Poems, Drama, Biography, Letters* (Charlottesville, Va., 1996), 248; Carmack Diary, "Account of Life for His Children" (ms.); Reuben Davis, *Recollections of Mississippi and Mississippians* (Oxford, Miss., 1972 [1889]), 4; Joel Crawford to Gen. Duncan L. Clinch, Nov. 17, 1844, in Henry Thomas Shanks, ed., *The Papers of Willie Person Mangum*, 5 vols. (Raleigh, N.C., 1955–56), 4:241; J. Marion Sims, *The Story of My Life* (New York, 1884), 71; Aiken "Autobiography," 2–3 (ms.); Thomas Tilestone Wells, *The Hugers of South Carolina* (New York, 1931), 11–12; Emmaline Eve's account of her family in Carmichael Papers. For sons of small slaveholders, see *TCWVQ*, 1:337, 2:824, 3:1314; Augustus Longstreet Hull, *Annals of Athens, Georgia, 1801–1901* (Danielsville, Ga., 1906), 79; Joshua W. Caldwell, *Sketches of the Bench and Bar of Tennessee* (Knoxville, Tenn., 1898), 156; "Hon. William L. Sharkey of Mississippi," *American Whig Review*, 15 (1852), 427; William Henry Hoyt, ed., *The Papers of Archibald D. Murphey*, 2 vols. (Raleigh, N.C., 1914), April 13, 1807 (1:11); *Autobiography of Col. Richard Malcolm Johnston* (EE: 1997 [1900]), 27–28. For planters' respect for the yeomen's pride in hard work, see Carl R. Osthaus, "The Work Ethic of the Plain Folk: Labor and Religion in the Old South," *JSH*, 70 (2004), 745–782.

39. William Wirt, *Sketches of the Life and Character of Patrick Henry* (Philadelphia, 1817), 13–14; Philip Graham, *The Life and Poems of Mirabeau B. Lamar* (Chapel Hill, N.C., 1938), 11; Archie Vernon Huff, Jr., *Langdon Cheves of South Carolina* (Columbia, S.C., 1977), 21–22; Vincent H. Cassidy and Amos E. Simpson, *Henry Watson Allen* (Baton Rouge, La., 1964), 9–10; Robert Douthat Meade, *Judah P. Benjamin: Confederate Statesman* (New York, 1943), 8–12; ed.'s intro. to Shanks, ed., *Papers of Willie P. Mangum*, 1:xv; John Hebron Moore, *The Emergence of the Cotton Kingdom in The Old Southwest: Mississippi, 1770–1860* (Baton Rouge, La., 1988), 240–241, and for salaries in Mississippi, 252–253; Walter Prescott Webb, ed., *The Handbook of Texas*, 3 vols. (Austin, Tex., 1952–76), 2:89; John W. Green, *Law and Lawyers: Sketches of the Federal Judges of Tennessee, Sketches of the Attorneys-General of Tennessee, Legal Reminiscences* (Jackson, Tenn., 1950), 32 (Baxter); John W. Green, *Lives of the Judges of the Supreme Court of Tennessee, 1795–1947* (n. p., 1947), 120; William S. Powell, ed., *Dictionary of North Carolina Biography*, 6 vols. (Chapel Hill, N.C. 1979–94), 2:23, 2:213, 5:52; *DGB*, 1:24, 178, 2:982; Catherine Cooper Hopley, *Life in the South from the Commencement of the War*, 2 vols. (New York, 1971 [1863]), 2:80; 1:104–105. Some well-to-do young men worked without wages to learn bookkeeping and other skills: Thomas Gaillard to John S. Palmer, Mar. 24, 1859, in Louis P. Towles, ed., *A World Turned Upside Down: The Palmers of South Santee, 1818–1881* (Columbia, S.C., 1996), 237; also, Edwin J. Scott, *Random Recollections of a Long Life, 1806 to 1876* (Columbia, S.C., 1884), 14.

40. Davis Blake Carter, *The Story of Uncle Minyard Told: A Family's 200-Year Migration Across the South* (Spartanburg, S.C., 1994), 48; on Russell's, see Paul. H. Hayne, "Memoir of Henry Timrod," in *The Poems of Henry Timrod* (New York,

1873), 327, 330; Alan Smith Thompson, "Mobile, Alabama, 1850–1851: Economic, Political, Physical, and Population Characteristics" (Ph.D. diss., University of Alabama, 1979), 36.

41. W. H. Holcombe, "Autobiography" (ms.), Part 2, chs. 2, 4–5, 21. Beverly Lafayette Holcombe worked in the field with his slaves so that his wife and daughter could spend gay winters in New Orleans.

42. John Belton O'Neall, *Biographical Sketches of the Bench and Bar of South Carolina*, 2 vols. (Charleston, S.C., 1859), 2:27; Reuben Davis, *Recollections of Mississippi and Mississippians* (Oxford, Miss., 1972 [1879]), 157–158; Hundley, *Social Relations*, 40–41; Amelia E. H. Barr, *All the Days of My Life: An Autobiography. The Red Leaves of a Human Heart* (New York, 1980 [1913]), 185–186.

43. In *TCWVQ*: For planters' sons who admitted to doing little or no work, see 1:317; 2:464, 494, 671, 694, 829; 3:1038, 1205, 1245, 1256; 4:1425, 1430, 1756; 5:1860, 1901, 1940, 1983, 2019, 2066, 2106, 2111, 2115, 2151, 2162. For those who worked in the fields when on vacation from school, see 1:192, 220, 225, 239, 286; 2:439, 441, 545, 603, 628, 865; 3:923, 985, 1060, 1179; 4:1523, 1667, 1774; 5:1833, 2137. For sons of small and middling slaveholders who worked when on vacation, see 1:363, 386; 2:460, 547, 550, 679, 684; 3:875; 3:923, 965, 995, 1065; 4:1771; 5:2005. For Dance, 2:630; for Gardner, 3:884.

44. For testimony by small and middling slaveholders' sons on working with slaves, see *TCWVQ*: 1:360, 399, 412, 413, 418; 2:704, 708, 711, 824; 3:88, 1037 (Hartsfield), 1078, 1083, 1110, 1163, 1240; 4:1361, 1596. 1708, 1769, 1777, 1780; 5:1797, 1958, 2025, 2030, 2037, 2205. For Adair, see 1:165, and for Reynolds, 5:1823. Also, William S. Price, Jr., "Nathaniel Macon, Planter," *NCHR*, 78 (2001), 199.

45. *TCWVQ*, 2:815 (Fisher). For planters' sons who did farm work in preparation for overseeing, see 3:921; 4:1370, 1670; 5:1980.

46. Catherine Thom Bartlett, ed., *"My Dear Brother": A Confederate Chronicle* (Richmond, Va., 1952), 21–22; for the low country, see Easterby, *South Carolina Rice Plantation*, passim; Dusinberre, *Them Dark Days*, 39.

47. Edward J. Pringle, "The People," *SQR*, n. s. 9 (1854), 52–55, quote at 52. For the text of the Lyon Report, see *SPR*, 16 (1863), 1–37.

48. Anthony Trollope, *North America*, ed. Donald Smalley and Bradford Allen Booth (New York, 1951 [1862], 10; *Speech of Lieut. Gov. Reynolds on the Preservation and Reconstruction of the Union* (St. Louis, Mo., 1861), 3; H. A. Tupper, *A Thanksgiving Discourse* (Macon, Ga., 1862), 4; John Forsyth, "The North and the South," *DBR*, 17 (1854), 361–378.

49. David J. McCord, "How the South Is Affected by Her Slave Institutions," *DBR*, 11 (1851), 349–363, quote at 357; W. R. Aylett speech on slavery, 1851–1854?, in Aylett Family Papers; F. A. Porcher, "Southern and Northern Civilization Contrasted," *RM*, 1 (1857), 98; Bledsoe quoted in Thomas L. Connelly, *The Marble Man: Robert E. Lee and His Image in American Society* (New York, 1977), 70.

50. William Garrott Brown, *A Gentleman of the South: A Memory of the Black Belt From the Manuscript Memoirs of the Late Colonel Stanton Elmore* (Kila, Mont., 1903), 128, 129; Harvey Toliver Cook, *The Life and Legacy of David Rogerson Williams* (New York, 1916), 24. A running theme of *A Treatise on the Patriarchal, or Co-Operative System of Society* (n. p., 1828) by the proslavery but antiracist Zephaniah Kingsley of Florida was that well-treated black slaves were more virtuous – much less corrupt – than the mass of poor laboring whites. For a critical

new edition, see Daniel Stowell, ed., *Balancing Evils Judiciously: The Proslavery Writings of Zephaniah Kingsley* (Gainesville, Fla., 2000).

51. *Memoir of William Ellery Channing, with Extracts from His Correspondence and Manuscripts*, 3 vols. (Boston, 1851) 1:83; and see Virginius Dabney, *Liberalism in the South* (Chapel Hill, N.C., 1932), 35, 39.

2. The Complete Household

1. Fredrika Bremer, *Homes of the New World: Impressions of America*, 2 vols. (New York, 1853), 1:385; Henry F. Pyles in *AS: Tenn.*, 7 (pt. 1), 253–255; Quintilian, *Institutio Oratoria*, 5 vols. (LCL), 2, Bk. 4, §2:121, 3, Bk. 7, §1:37–38; Orlando Patterson, *Slavery and Social Death: A Comparative Study* (Cambridge, Mass., 1982), 63.

2. Richard Beale Davis, ed., *William Fitzhugh and His Chesapeake World, 1676–1701: The Fitzhugh Letters and Other Documents* (Chapel Hill, N.C., 1963), 48; Charles W. Stetson, *Washington and His Neighbors* (Richmond, Va., 1956), 106; Gerald W. Mullin, *Flight and Rebellion: Slave Resistance in Eighteenth-Century Virginia* (New York, 1972), 22–33; *The Journal of John Harrower: An Indentured Servant in the Colony of Virginia, 1773–1776*, ed. Edward Miles Riley (Williamsburg, Va., 1963), June 14, 1774 (56); Anna McKnight to Thomas Jefferson, Oct. 29, 1802, in Jack McLaughlin, ed., *To His Excellency: Thomas Jefferson: Letters to a President* (New York, 1991), 104.

3. Randolph to John Brockenbrough, July 15, 1814, Aug. 1, 1814, Feb. 24, 1820, in Kenneth Shorey, ed., *Collected Letters of John Randolph of Roanoke to Dr. John Brokenbrough, 1812–1833* (New Brunswick, N.J., 1988), 11, 27; William Cabell Bruce, *John Randolph of Roanoke, 1773–1833: A Biography Based Largely on New Material*, 2 vols. (New York, 1970 [1922]), 1:624; also, Hugh A. Garland, *The Life of John Randolph of Roanoke*, 2 vols. (New York, 1969 [1859]), 2:43–44, 85, 100, 338; Sean Michael Lucas, *Robert Lewis Dabney: A Southern Presbyterian Life* (Phillipsburg, Pa., 2005), 31; McCord, "Negro and White Slavery," in Richard Lounsbury, ed., *Louisa S. McCord: Political and Social Essays* (Charlottesville, Va., 1995), 193. Also, *Speech of the Rev. Wm. H. Brisbane, Lately a Slaveholder in South Carolina* (Hartford, Conn., 1840), 6–7; G. Ingraham to Susan Fisher, June 20, 1841, in Fisher Papers; Bills Diary, Aug. 20, 1843, Jan. 1, 1867.

4. John Fulton, *Memoirs of Frederick A. P. Barnard* (New York, 1896), ch. 10.

5. Henry A. Murray, *Land of the Slave and the Free: Or, Cuba, the United States, and Canada*, 2nd ed. (London, 1857), 2:224; Earl E. Thorpe, *Eros and Freedom in Southern Life and Thought* (Durham, N.C., 1967), 45; also, A. Lipscomb, *The Social Spirit of Christianity* (Philadelphia, 1846), 21–22; Leslie Owens, *This Species of Property: Slave Life and Culture in the Old South* (New York, 1976), 115 and passim.

6. J. R. Wilson, *Mutual Relation of Masters and Slaves as Taught by the Bible* (Augusta, Ga., 1861), 7, 8, 9, 12–13; F. A. Ross, *Slavery Ordained of God* (Philadelphia, 1857), 118; William A. Hall, *The Historic Significance of the Southern Revolution* (Petersburg, Va., 1864), 13; J. C. Coit, *Discourse upon Governments, Divine and Human* (Columbus, S.C., 1853), 35; George D. Armstrong, *The Christian Doctrine of Slavery* (New York, 1967 [1857]), 57–59, 158; Armstrong, *The Theology of Christian Experience* (New York, 1858), 168–169, quotes at 168; Armstrong, *The Doctrine of Baptism: Scriptural Examinations* (New York, 1857), 305–311.

7. See esp. Gavin Wright, *Political Economy of the Cotton South: Households, Markets, and Wealth: The Nineteenth Century* (New York, 1978), chs. 2 and 3, and Elizabeth Fox-Genovese, *Within the Plantation Household: Black and White Women of the Old South* (Chapel Hill, N.C., 1988), ch. 1; Samuel Galloway, *Ergonomy; Or, Industrial Science* (Athens, Ga., 1853), 294 and 351, 357–358. For context, see George B. Forgie, *Patricide in the House Divided: A Psychological Interpretation of Lincoln and His Age* (New York, 1979), ch. 1, quote at 18; Thorpe, *Eros and Freedom*, 45. Jeffrey Robert Young, *Domesticating Slavery: The Master Class in Georgia and South Carolina, 1670–1837* (Chapel Hill, N.C., 1999) re-dates the emergence of paternalism.

8. Andrew P. Butler to Waddy Thompson, July 16, 1852, in Waddy Thompson Papers.

9. Memminger quoted in William S. Jenkins, *Pro-Slavery Thought in the Old South* (Gloucester, Mass., 1960), 210; William O. Prentiss, *A Sermon Preached at St. Peter's Church* (Charleston, S.C., 1860), 14; James O. Andrew, *Family Government: A Treatise on Conjugal, Parental, Filial and Other Duties* (Nashville, Tenn., 1882), 64–70.

10. P. A. Brunt, *Studies in Greek History and Thought* (Oxford, 1993), 360–363 (Plato and Aristotle) "To Demonicus," *Isocrates*, 3 vols. (LCL) (vols. 1–2 trans. and ed. George Norlin; vol. 3 trans. and ed. La Rue Van Hook), 1:#36; James Oscar Farmer, Jr., *The Metaphysical Confederacy: James Henley Thornwell and the Synthesis of Southern Values* (Macon, Ga., 1986), 161; Petronius, *The Satyricon*, tr. P. G. Walsh (Oxford, 1996), 38; Xenophon, *Memorabilia; Oeconomicus; Symposium; Apology*, trans. E. C. Merchant and O. J. Todd (LCL), Bk. 3, §§11–16, Bk. 7, §§1–7, 35–37, Bk. 8, §3:5, Bk. 13, §9.

11. Charles Colcock Jones, *The Glory of Woman Is the Fear of the Lord* (Philadelphia, 1847), 25; C. W. Howard, "Address before the Mnemosynean Society of Cassville Female College," *RM*, 4 (1858), 92–93; Israel Campbell, *An Autobiography: Bond and Free* (EE: 2001 [1861]), 7–13; Edward Everett Brown, *Sketch of the Life of Mr. Lewis Charlton and Reminiscences of Slavery* (EE: 2000), 1.

12. We have treated at length the extent of democratization in the North and the Southerners' misunderstanding of its pace: Elizabeth Fox-Genovese and Eugene D. Genovese, *The Mind of the Master Class: History and Faith in the Southern Slaveholders' Worldview* (New York, 2005), and Elizabeth Fox-Genovese and Eugene D. Genovese, *Slavery in White and Black: Class and Race in the Southern Slaveholders' New World Order* (New York, 2008).

13. In *TRP*: "*State v. Mann*," 4:256, 4:250 ("Rough Draft"), 4:251 ("Second Draft"). For Moore in *State v. Will*, see W. J. Peele, ed., *Lives of Distinguished North Carolinians* (Raleigh, N.C., 1898), 389–412, quote at 394; Mark V. Tushnet, *The American Law of Slavery: Considerations of Humanity and Interest* (Princeton, N.J., 1981), 54–65.

14. J. P. Holcombe, "Is Slavery Consistent with Natural Law?," *SLM*, 27 (1858), 403; J. P. Holcombe, "The Right of the State to Institute Slavery," *Southern Planter*, 19 (1859), 26. See also Peter Bardaglio, "'An Outrage upon Nature,'" in Carol Bleser, ed., *In Joy and in Sorrow: Women, Family, and Marriage in the Victorian South, 1830–1900* (New York, 1991), 34; James Benson Sellers, *Slavery in Alabama* (University, Ala., 1964), 226; and the letter of Thomas Bragg to Judah P. Benjamin, Nov. 25, 1861, in Rembert W. Patrick, ed., *The Opinions of the Confederate Attorneys-General, 1861–1865* (Buffalo, N.Y., 1950), 52.

15. Ruffin to Holt, March 4, 1854, in *TRP*, 2:420; "Address of Thomas Ruffin Delivered before the State Agricultural Society of North Carolina, Oct. 18, 1855," in *TRP*, 4:332–334; *Charleston Mercury*, September 14, 1859; also, Walter Clark, "Thomas Ruffin," in William Draper Lewis, ed., *Great American Lawyers*, 8 vols. (Philadelphia, 1907–09), 4:286. For a fascinating study of the ideological and technical legal implications of *State v. Mann* – together with a fine account of Ruffin – see Mark V. Tushnet, *Slave Law in the American South: State v. Mann in History and Literature* (Lawrence, Kan., 2003).

16. Dunbar quoted by J. F. H. Claiborne, *Mississippi as a Province, Territory, and State, with Biographical Notices of Eminent Citizens* (Spartanburg, S.C., 1978 [1880]), 145; Moses Liddell to St. John R. Liddell, Apr. 7, 1841; Weymouth T. Jordan, "System of Farming at Beaver Bend, Alabama, 1862," *JSH*, 7 (1941), 78.

17. See *State v. Reed* in Bryce R. Holt, *The Supreme Court of North Carolina and Slavery* (Durham, N.C., 1927), 72; "Domestic Slavery," *SLM*, 11 (1845), 513–528; *JCCP*, 13:24–25, 42, 145; *Remarks on the Subject of the Ownership of Slaves, Delivered by R. R. Collier of Petersburg, in the Senate of Virginia, October 12, 1863* (EE: 2000 [1863]), 20–21; Note in Barnsley Papers; "Channing's Duty of the Free States," *SQR*, 2 (1842), 163–164; 3 (1850), 342; [R. S. Breck], "Duties of Masters," *SPR*, 8 (1855), 268–270; [E. T. Baird], "Religious Instruction of Our Colored Population," *SPR*, 12 (1859), 350–351.

18. Thomas T. Stone, *Address before the Salem Female Anti-Slavery Society at Its Annual Meeting, December 7, 1851* (Ithaca, N.Y., 2006 [1852]), 14; Richard Fuller and Francis Wayland, *Domestic Slavery, Considered as a Scriptural Institution*, 5th ed. (New York, 1847), 9, 23, 140–141, 143, and Fuller's Letter Three. For an antislavery comment, see William Hosmer, *Slavery and the Church* (New York, 1969 [1853]), 10–11, 14, 33–43.

19. Henry Hughes, *Treatise on Sociology, Theoretical and Practical* (New York, 1968 [1854]); Simms to John Pendleton Kennedy, April 5, 1852, and Simms to William Porcher Miles, March 7, 1861, in Mary C. Oliphant et al., eds., *The Letters of William Gilmore Simms*, 6 vols. (Columbia, S.C., 1952–82), 3:174, 4: 343; E. A. Pollard, *Southern History of the War*, 2 vols. in 1 (n. p., 1977 [1866]), 2:202n; Alexander H. Stephens, *A Constitutional View of the Late War between the States*, 2 vols. (New York, 1970 [1868, 1870]), 1:539–540, 2:25; "The New Republic," *SLM*, 32 (1861), 394; T. R. R. Cobb, *An Inquiry into the Law of Negro Slavery in the United States* (New York, 1968 [1858]), 83, 103–104; George S. Sawyer, *Southern Institutes Or, an Inquiry into the Origin and Early Prevalence of Slavery and the Slave Trade* (New York, 1967 [1858]), 219–220, 312–314; "Speech on the Oregon Bill," July 12, 1848, in *JDP*, 3:335, 362; Jefferson Davis, *The Rise and Fall of the Confederate Government*, 2 vols. (New York, 1958), 1:515–519.

20. "Harper on Slavery," in *The Pro-Slavery Argument, as Maintained by the Most Distinguished Writers of the Southern States* (Philadelphia, 1853), 11–12; Alexander McCaine, *Slavery Defended from Scripture against the Attacks of the Abolitionists* (Baltimore, Md., 1842), 10–11; [Conway Robinson], *An Essay upon the Constitutional Rights as to Slave Property* (Richmond, Va., 1840), 1–19; *Raleigh Register, and North-Carolina Gazette*, Nov. 12, 1841; *Georgia Weekly Telegraph*, Feb. 7, 1861; *Speech of Hon. Sampson W. Harris on the Bill to Organize a Territorial Government for the Territory of Oregon* (Washington, D.C., 1848), 6; George P. Elliott, *An Oration, Delivered before the Artillery Company at Beaufort, South Carolina, July 5, 1852* (Charleston, S.C., 1852), 10; Sally McDowell to John Miller,

Apr. 1, 1856, in J. R. Wilson, *Mutual Relation of Masters and Slaves as Taught by the Bible* (Augusta, Ga., 1861), 5; Robert H. Smith, *An Address to the Citizens of Alabama, on the Constitution and Laws of the Confederate States of America* (Mobile, Ala., 1861), 19; John Fletcher, *Studies on Slavery, in Easy Lessons* (Natchez, Tenn., 1852), 81, 182–183, 187–188, 203.

21. *JHTW*, 4:409, 412, 415; H. B. Bascom, *Sermons from the Pulpit* (Louisville, Ky., 1849), 247; Sebastian G. Messmer, ed., *The Works of the Right Rev. John England, First Bishop of Charleston*, 7 vols. (Cleveland, Oh., 1908), 5:187, 194. On the divines' efforts to reform slavery, see Eugene D. Genovese, *A Consuming Fire: The Fall of the Confederacy in the Mind of the White Christian South* (Athens, Ga., 1998).

22. [S. J. Cassells], *Servitude and the Duty of Masters to Their Servants* (Norfolk, Va., 1843), 5; Robert L. Dabney, *Defence of Virginia (and through Her of the South) in Recent and Pending Contests against the Sectional Party* (New York, 1969 [1867]), 94; John Adger, "Human Rights and Slavery," *SPR*, 2 (March 1849), 579–582; William Pope Harrison, *The Gospel among the Slaves* (Nashville, Tenn., 1893), 39; C. C. Jones, *The Religious Instruction of the Negroes in the United States* (Savannah, Ga., 1842); Ferdinand Jacobs, *The Committing of Our Cause to God* (Charleston, S.C., 1850), 6n; "J. F. S.," "Longfellow's Poems on Slavery," *Randolph Macon Magazine*, 2 (1852), 292; Thornton Stringfellow, "The Bible Argument," in E. N. Elliott, ed., *Cotton Is King, and Pro-Slavery Arguments* (New York, 1969 [1860]), 462n, quote at 468. As late as 1897, Robert Lewis Dabney defined slavery as property in services: *The Practical Philosophy, Being the Philosophy of the Feelings, of the Will, and of the Conscience, with the Ascertainment of Particular Rights and Duties* (Harrisonburg, Va., 1984 [1897]), 403–419.

    For northern versions of property in services, see John Henry Hopkins, *A Scriptural, Ecclesiastical, and Historical View of Slavery from the Days of the Patriarch Abraham to the Nineteenth Century* (New York, 1864), 30–31; Samuel Seabury, *American Slavery Distinguished from the Slavery of English Theorists and Justified by the Law of Nature* (New York, 1861); and Herbert Anthony Kellar, ed., *Solon Robinson: Pioneer and Agriculturalist: Selected Writings*, 2 vols. (Indianapolis, Ind., 1936), 2:271; John Richter Jones, *Slavery Sanctified by the Bible* (Philadelphia, 1861), 9.

23. Committee of the Synod of Kentucky, *An Address to the Presbyterians of Kentucky, Proposing a Plan for the Instruction and Emancipation of Their Slaves* (Newburyport, Ky., 1836), 5, 14; H. Shelton Smith, *In His Image . . . But: Racism in Southern Religion* (Durham, N.C., 1972), 138–139; Jenkins, *Pro-Slavery Thought in the Old South*, 227–235; R. P. Stanton, *Slavery Viewed in the Light of the Golden Rule* (Norwich, Conn., 1860), 9. On judges' inability to isolate household relations, see Tushnet, *American Law of Slavery*, 33, and Laura Edwards, "Law, Domestic Violence, and the Limits of Patriarchal Authority in the Antebellum South," *JSH*, 65 (1999), 769–770.

24. Patterson, *Slavery and Social Death*, 22.

25. "A Practical Treatise: On the Duties of Christians Owning Slaves" (ms.), ch. 2:48–49, in Calvin Wiley Papers. For the thesis of the unity of capital and labor under slavery see Fox-Genovese and Genovese, *Slavery in White and Black*, 30–33.

26. Henry Ambler, *Sectionalism in Virginia from 1776 to 1861* (Chicago, 1910), 153; Drew R. McCoy, *The Last of the Fathers: James Madison and the Republican Legacy* (Cambridge, Mass., 1989), 245–246; William A. Smith, *Lectures on the*

Philosophy and Practice of Slavery (Nashville, Tenn., 1856), 39–40. By refusing to take seriously the concept of a slaveholding household, critics obscure an essential feature of proslavery ideology: See, e.g., Robin L. Einhorn's *American Taxation, American Slavery* (Chicago, 2006), 138–145, 161–169.

27. George B. Cheever, *Rights of the Coloured Race to Citizenship and Representation; and the Guilt and Consequences of Legislation Against Them* (New York, 1864), 26; on Phillips, see Louis S. Gerteis, *Morality and Utility in American Antislavery Reform* (Chapel Hill, N.C., 1987), 88–89; Dabney, *Defence of Virginia*, 300; for Dabney on hierarchy and family, see Lucas, *Robert Lewis Dabney*, ch. 1; Samuel C. Hyde, Jr., *Pistols and Politics: The Dilemma of Democracy in Louisiana's Florida Parishes, 1810–1899* (Baton Rouge, La., 1996), 70.

28. For the colonial problem, see James C. Ballagh, *A History of Slavery in Virginia* (Baltimore, Md., 1902), 39–40, 71. For the post-War reaction, see Gerald David Jaynes, *Branches without Roots: Genesis of the Black Working Class in the American South, 1862–1882* (New York, 1986), 30, n. 8. Joseph Story agreed that the three-fifths rule recognized slaves as persons and property but argued that slaves' status as property placed them in antagonism to masters: *Commentaries on the Constitution of the United States*, 2 vols. (2nd ed.; Boston, 1851), 1:440–441.

29. *Negroes and Religion: The Episcopal Church at the South Memorial to the General Convention of the Protestant Episcopal Church in the United States of America* (Charleston S.C., 1863), 2.

30. Elizabeth Thom to Lucy Lewis, Feb. 3, 1840, in Catherine Thom Bartlett, ed., *"My Dear Brother": A Confederate Chronicle* (Richmond, Va., 1952), 22–23; Harriet Martineau, *Retrospect of Western Travel*, 2 vols. (London, 1838), 1:221; *Plantation Life: The Narratives of Mrs. Henry Schoolcraft* (New York, 1969 [1860]), 153–154; "A Former Resident of Slaves States," *Influence of Slavery upon the White Population* (Boston, n. d.), 1–2; Holbrook Diary, Mar. 29, Aug. 23, 1852, in D. D. Hall, "A Yankee Tutor in the Old South," *New England Quarterly*, 33 (1960), 89; Craig Simpson, *A Good Southerner: The Life of Henry A. Wise of Virginia* (Chapel Hill, N.C., 1985), 72.

31. J. G. Clinkscales, *On the Old Plantation: Reminiscences of His Childhood* (Spartanburg, S.C., 1916), 9; George Lee Simpson, Jr., *The Cokers of Carolina: A Social Biography of a Family* (Chapel Hill, N.C., 1956), 40; Harold W. Mann, *Atticus Haygood: Methodist Bishop, Editor, and Educator* (Athens, Ga., 1965), 5–6.

32. Louis Morton, *Robert Carter of Nomini Hall: A Virginia Tobacco Planter of the Eighteenth Century* (Charlottesville, Va., 1969), 80; Lawrence S. Rowland et al., *The History of Beaufort County, South Carolina*, 2 vols. (Columbia, S.C., 1996), chs. 16–17; J. H. Hammond in *Pro-Slavery Argument*, 128; Elizabeth Silverthorne, *Ashbel Smith of Texas: Pioneer, Patriot, Statesman, 1805–1886* (College Station, Tex., 1982), 67; Maunsel White to Maunsel White II, Aug. 24, 1860; Susan Dabney Smedes, *Memorials of a Southern Planter* (New York, 1965 [1887]), 76; J. L. Bridgers, "Annual Address Delivered before the North Carolina State Agricultural Society," *Transactions, 1857* (Raleigh, N.C., 1858), 17. Also: Thomas Diary, June 12, 1852 (S.C.); Bills Diary, 1846 (Tenn.); Mercer Papers, 1830s, and E. G. Baker Diary, May 29, 1860 (Miss.); R. R. Barrow Residence Journal, 1857–1858, and Orange Grove Plantation Diaries, Dec. 25, 1849 (La.).

33. Charles E. Cauthen, ed., *Family Letters of the Three Wade Hamptons, 1782–1901* (Columbia, S.C., 1953), xv–xvi; Henry Papers, 1839; Leak Diaries, Nov.–Dec. 1835; Iveson Brookes to Cornelia Brookes, April 30, 1860; John W. DuBose,

The Life and Times of William Lowndes Yancey (New York, 1942 [1892]), 1:400; Joseph Karl Menn, *Large Slaveholders of Louisiana, 1860* (New Orleans, La., 1999), 97; Abigail Curlee, "The History of a Texas Slave Plantation, 1831–1863," *Southwestern Historical Quarterly*, 26 (1922), 79–127; Randolph B. Campbell, *An Empire for Slavery: The Peculiar Institution in Texas, 1821–1865* (Baton Rouge, La., 1989), 195; Frank L. Owsley, *Plain Folk of the Old South* (Baton Rouge, La., 1949), 88; J. Carlyle Sitterson, *Sugar Country: The Cane Sugar Industry in the South* (Lexington, Ky., 1953), 52.

34. Edmondston Diary, Mar. 32, 1862; H. N. McTyeire, *Duties of Christian Masters*, ed. Thomas O. Summers (Nashville, Tenn., 1859), 42, 219; J. O. Andrew, "Religious Instruction of the Negroes," New Orleans *Christian Advocate*, republished as appendix to McTyeire. A Planter, "Planters and Overseers: Management of Slaves," *SCTA*, Sept. 12, 1844; James A. Lyon et al., "Slavery, and the Duties Growing Out of the Relation" (Report to the General Assembly of the Presbyterian Church), *SPR*, 16 (July 1863), 1–37, esp. 21–22.

35. Angelina Grimké, in Theodore Dwight Weld, *Slavery as It Is: Testimony of a Thousand Witnesses* (New York, 1839), 53; Holman Hamilton, *Zachary Taylor: Soldier in the White House* (Indianapolis, Ind., 1951), 18–19, 30–31, and see Charles S. Sydnor, *Slavery in Mississippi* (Gloucester, Mass., 1965 [1933]), 69; Duncan Clinch Heyward, *Seed from Madagascar* (Chapel Hill, N.C., 1937), ix, 74, 97; Sitterson, *Sugar Country*, 96; Henry Edmund Ravenel, *Ravenel Records* (Atlanta, Ga., 1898), 47–48; Clinkscales, *On the Old Plantation*, 8–9. See newspaper advertisements in Freddie L. Parker, ed., *Stealing a Little Freedom: Advertisements for Slave Runaways in North Carolina, 1791–1840* (Westport, Conn., 2001), 22, 152, 153, 176, 280–281, 373, 469–470, 672; and in Lathan A. Windley, comp., *Runaway Slave Advertisements: A Documentary History from the 1730s to 1790*, 4 vols., (Westport, Conn., 1983), see, e.g., 1:48–49.

36. For sale of children in Africa, see Patrick Manning, *Slavery and African Life: Occidental, Oriental, and African Slave Trades* (New York, 1990), 90; for Western Europe to the fifteenth century, see Pierre Bonnassie, *From Slavery to Feudalism in South-Western Europe*, trans. Jean Birrell (Cambridge, 1991), 2, 36; Pierre Dockès, *Medieval Slavery and Liberation*, trans. Arthur Goldhammer (Chicago, 1982), 5; Ruth Mazo Karras, *Slavery and Society in Medieval Scandinavia* (New Haven, Conn., 1988), 54–55.

37. Armstrong, *Christian Doctrine of Slavery*, 120n; *ERD*, 3:825; "Uncle Tom's Cabin," in Richard C. Lounsbury, ed., *Louisa S. McCord: Political and Social Essays* (Charlottesville, Va., 1995), 255; D. J. McCord, "Life of a Negro Slave," *SQR*, n. s., 7 (1853), 209; Fitzgerald Ross, *Cities and Camps of the Confederate States*, ed. Richard Barksdale Harwell (Urbana, Ill., 1958), 32; William Dusinberre, *Them Dark Days: Slavery in the American Rice Swamps* (New York, 1996), 107; *Slave Life in Georgia: A Narrative of the Life, Sufferings, and Escape of John Brown, a Fugitive Slave* (Savannah, Ga., 1972 [1855]), 55.

38. "British Philanthropy," 305, in Lounsbury, ed., *McCord: Political and Social Essays*; [A North Carolinian], *Southern Slavery Considered on General Principles, Or, A Grapple with Abstractionists* (New York, 1861), 18–19; *SPR*, 16 (1863), 154–157; Joseph Jones to parents, Nov. 3, 1856, in Jones Collection. Robert H. Gudmestad properly ridicules slaveholders' apologetics: *A Troublesome Commerce: The Transformation of the Interstate Slave Trade* (Baton Rouge, La., 2003), 201. Judges skillfully interpreted slave-sale cases to support slavery: Jenny

Bourne Wahl, *The Bondsman's Burden: An Economic Analysis of the Common Law of Slavery* (New York, 1998), 47–48.

39. Douglas Ambrose, *Henry Hughes and Proslavery Thought in the Old South* (Baton Rouge, La., 1996), 136.

40. McTyeire, *Duties of Christian Masters*, 71; Marianne Palmer Gaillard to John S. Palmer, June 4, 1844, in Louis P. Towles, ed., *A World Turned Upside Down: The Palmers of South Santee, 1818–1881* (Columbia, S.C., 1996), 92; Elizabeth Randolph to Mary Braxton Randolph Carter, Apr. 12–23, 1825, in Joan E. Cashin, ed., *Our Common Affairs: Texts from Women of the Old South* (Baltimore, Md., 1996), 174; Amelia E. H. Barr, *All the Days of My Life: An Autobiography. The Red Leaves of a Human Heart* (New York, 1980 [1913]), 169–170; Rachel O'Connor to David Weeks, July 12, 1826, in A. B. W. Webb, ed., *Mistress of Evergreen Plantation: Rachel O'Connor's Legacy of Letters, 1823–1845* (Albany, N.Y., 1983), 18.

41. W. G. Bean, *Stonewall's Man: Sandie Pendleton* (Chapel Hill, N.C., 1959), 27; Corinna Brown to Mannevillette Brown, Aug. 2, 1840, in James M. Denham and Keith L. Huneycutt, eds., *Echoes from a Distant Frontier: The Brown Sisters' Correspondence from Antebellum Florida* (Columbia, S.C., 2004), 123; Brevard Diary, Sept. 18, 1861.

42. Charles Elliott, *Sinfulness of American Slavery: Proved from Its Evil Sources*, 2 vols. (New York, 1968 [1850]), 1:147; Douglas L. Wilson and Lucia Stanton, eds., *Jefferson Abroad* (New York, 1999), 179; Dusinberre, *Them Dark Days*, 48–83; Joseph B. Cobb, *Mississippi Scenes* (Philadelphia, 1851), ch. 7; John S. Wise, *The End of an Era* (Boston, 1900), 80–88.

43. "Speech of Rev. J. S. Martin," in Benjamin Quarles, ed., *Blacks on John Brown* (Urbana, Ill., 1972), 29.

44. Edwin Heriott, "Education at the South," *DBR*, 21 (1856), 655–656; Josiah Quincy, *Address Illustrative of the Power of the Slave States and the Duties of the Free States* (Boston, 1856), 6.

3. Strangers within the Gates

1. David Brown, *The Planter: or, Thirteen Years in the South, by a Northern Man* (Upper Saddle River, N.J., 1970 [1853]), 118; *HLW*, 2:289.

2. Daniel E. Sutherland, "The Servant Problem: An Index of Antebellum Americanism," *Southern Studies*, 18 (1979), 488–503; Sutherland, *Americans and Their Servants: Domestic Service in the United States from 1800 to 1910* (Baton Rouge, La., 1981), Prologue and chs. 2–3; *Incidents of My Life: The Autobiography of Rev. Paul Trapier*, ed. George W. Williams (Charleston, S.C., 1954), 9; "The Phases of Society," *SPR*, 8 (1854), 198–199; Elliott Ashkenazi, ed., *The Civil War Diary of Clara Solomon: Growing Up in New Orleans, 1861–1862* (Baton Rouge, La., 1995), June 18, 1861 (27), March 15, 1862 (quote at 87); Rosalie Roos, *Travels in America, 1851–1855*, trans. Carl L. Anderson (Carbondale, Ill., 1982), 95, quote at 141; Elmore Diary, Dec. 9, 1861, in Marli F. Weiner, ed., *Heritage of Woe: The Civil War Diary of Grace Brown Elmore, 1861–1868* (Athens, Ga., 1997), 23.

3. Thavolia Glymph, *Out of the House of Bondage: The Transformation of the Plantation Household* (New York, 2008), 52; for the North, see Noel Ignatiev, *How the Irish Became White* (New York, 1995); Letitia A. Burwell, *A Girl's Life in Virginia before the War*, 2nd ed. (New York, 1895), 53; Eliza M. Fisher to Mary

H. Middleton, July 10, 1839, in Eliza Cope Harrison, ed., *Best Companions: Letters of Eliza Middleton Fisher and Her Mother, Mary Hering Middleton, from Charleston, Philadelphia, and Newport, 1839–1846* (Columbia, S.C., 2001), 61; Thomas Low Nichols, *Forty Years of American Life* (London, 1864), 1:223; Mrs. [Matilda Charlotte] Houstoun, *Hesperos: Or, Travels in the West*, 2 vols. (London, 1850), 1:178–179.

4. Barbara Ryan, *Love, Wages, Slavery: The Literature of Servitude in the United States* (Urbana, Ill., 2006); Tera W. Hunter, *To 'Joy My Freedom: Southern Black Women's Lives and Labor after the Civil War* (London, 1997), 17; *Mississippi Free Trader and Natchez Gazette*, Oct. 10, 1846.

5. Chandos M. Brown, *Benjamin Silliman: A Life in the Young Republic* (Princeton, N.J., 1989), 165; Jefferson to John W. Eppes, Aug. 7, 1804, in Sarah N. Randolph, *The Domestic Life of Jefferson* (New York, 1871), 309; Maria Bryan Harford to Julia Ann Bryan Cumming, Sept. 25, 1839, in Carol Bleser, ed., *Tokens of Affection: The Letters of a Planter's Daughter in the Old South* (Athens, Ga., 1996), 263; James Russell Lowell, ed., "A Virginian in New England Thirty-Five Years Ago," *Atlantic Monthly*, 27 (1871), 680–681; Sarah Mytton Maury, *An Englishwoman in America* (London, 1848), 193–196, 212; Amelia M. Murray, *Letters from the United States, Cuba, and Canada* (New York, 1856), 194–195, 198–199, 218; Sara Agnes Rice Pryor, *My Day: Reminiscences of a Long Life* (EE: 1997 [1909]), 61.

6. David Macrae, *The Americans at Home* (New York, 1952 [1870]), ch. 6; Daniel Sutherland, *The Confederate Carpetbaggers* (Baton Rouge, La., 1988), 72–73.

7. Wadley Private Journal, Nov. 28, 1860; Aug. 8, 1858, ERD, 1:219; Elizabeth W. Allston Pringle, *Chronicles of Chicora Wood* (New York, 1976), 14; W. Kirk Wood, ed., *A Northern Daughter and a Southern Wife: The Civil War Reminiscences and Letters of Katherine H. Cumming, 1860–1865* (Augusta, Ga., 1976), 2; Ernest McPherson Lander, Jr., *The Calhoun Family and Thomas Green Clemson: The Decline of Southern Patriarchy* (Columbia, S.C., 1983), 158; James Petigru Carson, *Life, Letters and Speeches of James Louis Petigru: Union Man of South Carolina* (Washington, D.C., 1920), 209; Frederick Law Olmsted, *A Journey in the Back Country* (New York, 1970 [1860]), 36; John S. C. Abbott, *South and North; or, Impressions Received during a Trip to Cuba and the South* (New York, 1969 [1860]), 210; B. W. Korn, "Jews and Negro Slavery in the Old South, 1789–1865," in Leonard Dinnerstein and Mary Dale Palsson, eds., *Jews in the South* (Baton Rouge, La., 1973), 94; Phillip Alexander Bruce, *History of the University of Virginia, 1819–1919*, 5 vols. (New York, 1920–22), 2:58; George J. Stevenson, *Increase in Excellence: A History of Emory and Henry College* (New York, 1963), 61.

8. Mrs. S. J. Hale, "An Appeal to American Christians on Behalf of the Ladies Medical Missionary Society," *Southern Lady's Companion*, 6 (1852), 27–30; James Norman to Orion Norman, Dec. 6, 1861, in Susan Lott Clark, *Southern Letters and Life in the Mid 1800s* (Waycross, Ga., 1993), 124–125; Ira Rosenwaike, "Further Light on Jacob Henry," in Dinnerstein and Palsson, eds., *Jews in the South*, 49. Also, Taylor Diary, July 25, 1786; Cornish Diary, Sept. 25, 1845; John Walker Diary, Jan. 13, 1830; April 16, Sept. 10, 11, 1834; and accounts for 1837; John A. Quitman to Reverend Frederick Henry Quitman, Jan. 29, 1826; Evans Diary, Oct. 7, 1857; Jean E. Schultz *Women at the Front: Hospital Workers in Civil War America* (Chapel Hill, N.C., 2004), 19.

9. Clement Eaton, *A History of the Southern Confederacy* (New York, 1961), 203; D. W. Mitchell, *Ten Years in the United States* (London, 1862), 101; Olmsted, *Back Country*, 36; James Adger to J. H. Thornwell, April 29, 1848, in Thornwell Papers; C. C. Jones, Jr., to Rev. and Mrs. C. C. Jones, July 4, 1860, in Robert Manson Myers, ed., *The Children of Pride: A True Story of Georgia in the Civil War* (New Haven, Conn., 1972), 592.

10. *Plantation Life: The Narratives of Mrs. Henry Schoolcraft* (New York, 1969 [1860]), 234–235; R. Q. Mallard, *Plantation Life before Emancipation* (Richmond, Va., 1892), 18.

11. Anna Maria Calhoun to John C. Calhoun, Jan. 24, 1846, in JCCP, 22:504; R. D. Arnold to Ellen Arnold, July 7, 1854, in Richard H. Shryock, ed., *Letters of Richard D. Arnold, M.D., 1808–1876* (Durham, N.C., 1929), 67; Margaret Junkin to J., Nov. 25, 1850, in Elizabeth Preston Allan, *The Life and Letters of Margaret Junkin Preston* (Boston, Mass., 1903), 57.

12. Ira Berlin et al., eds., *Freedom: A Documentary History of Emancipation, 1861– 1867, Series One: The Destruction of Slavery*, 3 vols. (New York, 1985–93), 3:446; Clyde Lottridge Cummer, ed., *Yankee in Gray: The Civil War Memoirs of Henry E. Handerson, with a Selection of His Wartime Letters* (Cleveland, Oh., 1962), 7–8, 21–28; Lucy Wood Diary, June 24, 1861, in Butler Papers; Suzanne L. Bunkers, *The Diary of Caroline Seabury, 1854–1863* (Madison, Wis., 1991), esp. 10, 47ff., 56, 59. Also, HLW: "Diary of Brussels, 1833: 1:17, 25, 39, 41, 48, 58; James Allen to Elizabeth Allen, Sept. 9, 1856; Dec. 13, 1857, in the Allen Collection; Carney Diary, Sept. 16, 1859; *Charles S. Sydnor, A Gentleman of the Old Natchez Region: Benjamin L. C. Wailes* (Durham, N.C., 1938), 282.

13. J. B. Grimball Diary, May 7, 1833; Daniel E. Sutherland, *Seasons of War: The Ordeal of a Confederate Community, 1861–1865* (New York, 1995), 12 (Kelly); Rembert W. Patrick, *Aristocrat in Uniform: General Duncan L. Clinch* (Gainesville, Fla., 1963), 60.

14. Mary Hering Middleton to Eliza Middleton Fisher, Apr. 18, 1841, in Harrison, ed., *Best Companions*, 178–179; for Clarke, see DNCB, 1:380–381. Margaret Law Callcott, ed., *The Mistress of Riversdale: The Plantation Letters of Rosalie Stier Calvert, 1795–1821* (Baltimore, Md., 1991), xi, 105; Bills Diary, December 1846. McNeal herself had thirteen slaves: April 3, 1847. For some exceptional white servants, see Pringle, *Chicora Wood*, 114; Cornish Diary, June 30, 1853; Gorgas, Jan. 12, 1857, in Sarah Woolfolk Wiggins, ed., *The Journals of Josiah Gorgas, 1857–1878* (Tuscaloosa, Ala., 1995), 5, 76–77; William Dusinberre, *Them Dark Days: Slavery in the American Rice Swamps* (New York, 1996), 38.

15. Anne Newport Royall, *Letters from Alabama, 1817–1822* (University, Ala., 1969), April 30, 1821 (202); R. F. W. Allston to Adele Petigru Allston, Nov. 27, 1853, in J. H. Easterby, ed., *The South Carolina Rice Plantation, as Revealed in the Papers of Robert F. W. Allston* (Chicago, 1945), 116–117; Pringle, *Chicora Wood*, 140; Woodward in AS: S.C., 3 (pt. 4), 254.

16. Edmund Kirke [James R. Gilmore], *My Southern Friends* (New York, 1863), planter quoted at 163; E. C. Wallace Diary, Sept. 12, Oct. 16, 19, 1863, in Eleanor P. Cross and Charles B. Cross, Jr., eds., *Glencoe Diary: The War-Time Journal of Elizabeth Curtis Wallace* (Chesapeake, Va., 1968), 59, 67; Constance McLaughlin Green, *Washington: Village and Capital, 1800–1878* (Princeton, N.J., 1962), 110–111. Also, Cathleen A. Baker, *The Enterprising S. H. Goetzel: Antebellum and Civil War Publisher in Mobile, Alabama* (San Diego, Calif., 2008), 24; E. L.

Phillips in Jacob Rader Marcus, ed., *Memoirs of American Jews, 1775–1865*, 3 vols. (Philadelphia, 1955), 3:163–196.

17. DHE, 40–42; Cornelius J. Heatwole, *A History of Education in Virginia* (New York, 1916), 19, 53–58; Richard Beale Davis, *Intellectual Life in the Colonial South, 1585–1763*, 3 vols. (Knoxville, Tenn., 1978), 1:307–308; W. J. Wells to Ebenezer Pettigrew, June 27, 1827, in Sarah McCulloh Lemmon, ed., *The Pettigrew Papers*, 2 vols. (Raleigh, N.C., 1971, 1988), 2:82; John Davis, *Travels of Four and a Half Years in the United States of America*, ed. A. J. Morrison (New York, 1909 [1803]), 91–92.

18. Valentine Diary, Oct. 26, 1838; EC, 1:26 (Allen); Paul. H. Hayne, "Memoir of Henry Timrod," in *The Poems of Henry Timrod* (New York, 1873), 19–22; Alberta Morel Lachicotte, *Georgetown Rice Plantations* (Columbia, S.C., 1955), 39–40 (Glennie); Preston Graham, Jr., *A Kingdom Not of This World: Stuart Robinson's Struggle to Distinguish the Sacred from the Secular during the Civil War* (Macon, Ga., 2002), 14–15; *Marion Harland's Autobiography: The Story of a Life* (New York, 1910), 95–97.

19. Leak Diary, Feb. 16, July 25, 1856 (Laughton); William C. Davis, *Jefferson Davis: The Man and His Hour* (New York, 1991), 16; Charles Dabney to Thomas Dabney, Aug. 2, 1849, in Susan Dabney Smedes, *Memorials of a Southern Planter*, ed. Fletcher M. Green (New York, 1965 [1887]), 120–121.

20. Dallas C. Dickey, *Seargent S. Prentiss: Whig Orator of the Old South* (Baton Rouge, La., 1945), 38–39; Catherine Cooper Hopley, *Life in the South from the Commencement of the War*, 2 vols. (New York, 1971 [1863]), 1:48.

21. Robert E. May, *John A. Quitman: Old South Crusader* (Baton Rouge, La., 1985), 114; Clement Eaton, *Henry Clay and the Art of American Politics* (Boston, Mass., 1957), 65; Adele Petigru Allston to Mrs. R. Hamilton, May 19, 1853, in Easterby, ed., *South Carolina Rice Plantation*, 115; D. J. McCord to W. P. Miles, Mar. 11, 1848, in Miles Papers; W. G. Simms to J. H. Hammond, Sept. 14, 1848, in Mary Oliphant et al., eds., *The Letters of William Gilmore Simms*, 6 vols. (Columbia, S.C., 1952–82), 2:444; Leak Diary, 1858; Wilma King, ed., *A Northern Woman in the Plantation South: Letters of Tryphena Blanche Holder Fox, 1856–1876* (Columbia, S.C., 1993), 6–8.

22. J. H. Ingraham, *Sunny South; Or, The Southerner at Home* (New York, 1968 [1860]), 271; [Ingraham], *The South-West. By a Yankee*, 2 vols. (n. p., 1966 [1835]), 1:170; "Remarks," July 1833, in David Rice Plantation Journal; Simms to Hammond, Sept. 14, 1848, in Oliphant et al., eds., *Letters of Simms*, 2:444; Charles Dabney to Thomas Dabney, Aug. 2, 1849, in Smedes, *Memorials of a Southern Planter*, 120–121; David F. Allmendinger, Jr., ed., *Incidents of My Life: Edmund Ruffin's Autobiographical Essays* (Charlottesville, Va., 1990), 47; Elizabeth R. Baer, ed., *Shadows on My Heart: The Civil War Diary of Lucy Rebecca Buck of Virginia* (Athens, Ga., 1997), Jan. 22, 1862 (19).

23. George A. Blackburn, ed., *The Life Work of John L. Girardeau* (Columbia, S.C., 1916), 24, 27; John Belton O'Neall, *Biographical Sketches of the Bench and Bar of South Carolina*, 2 vols. (Charleston, S.C., 1859), 2:317–318 (Hanford); Louisa C. Hillyer, Appendix to *The Life and Times of Judge Junius Hillyer: From His Memoirs* (Tignall, Ga., 1989), 131; Jean Bradley Anderson, *Piedmont Plantation: The Bennehan-Cameron Family and Lands in North Carolina* (Durham, N.C., 1985), 40 (Bryant); W. H. Davidson, "Oakbowery Census of 1860," in Chattahoochee Valley Historical Society, *War Was the Place: A Centennial Collection of*

Confederate Soldier Letters and Old Oakbowery, Chambers County, Alabama (n. p., Bulletin #5, 1961), 139 (Dolbert); also, Ellen Mordecai, *Gleanings from Long Ago* (Raleigh, N.C., 1974), 9.

24. Holbrook Diary, Mar. 29, Aug. 5, 1852, in D. D. Hall, "A Yankee Tutor in the Old South," *New England Quarterly*, 33 (1960), 87–88; *The Journal of John Harrower: An Indentured Servant in the Colony of Virginia, 1773–1776*, ed. Edward Miles Riley (Williamsburg, Va., 1963), xviii–xix, 48, xvii; Davis, *Four and a Half Years*, 53 ("drive"); W. A. Graham to Susan W. Graham, May 8, 1837, in J. G. DeRoulhac Hamilton, ed., *The Papers of William Alexander Graham*, 5 vols. (Raleigh, N.C., 1957–73), 1:498; Anna M. King to Thomas B. King, Dec. 27, 1844, in T. B. King Papers; William C. Warren to Ebenezer Pettigrew, Nov. 24, 1828, in Lemmon, ed., *Pettigrew Papers*, 2:107.

25. Charles East, ed., *The Civil War Diary of Sarah Morgan* (Athens, Ga., 1991), July 5, 1861 (105).

26. TCWVQ, 1:312, 360, 406, 2:829; 3:933; 4:1404, 1605, 5:2166, 2233, 2250, 2261, 2076. Ralph V. Anderson and Robert E. Gallman, "Slaves as Fixed Capital: Slave Labor and Southern Economic Development," *Journal of American History*, 64 (1977), 30–33, 38; for women slaveholders, see, e.g., Thomas Gaillard to John S. Palmer, Feb. 28, 1852, in Louis P. Towles, ed., *A World Turned Upside Down: The Palmers of South Santee, 1818–1881* (Columbia, S.C., 1996), 176–177; for the intensive work of white and black Appalachian women, see Wilma A. Dunaway, *Women, Work, and Family in the Antebellum Mountain South* (New York, 2008), 157; J. Carlyle Sitterson, "Hired Labor on Sugar Plantations of the Ante-Bellum South," *JSH*, 14 (1948), 201–203; Robert J. Breckenridge," Remonstrance . . . Against the Petition of the Late 'Slave-Holders' Convention,'" *Spirit of the XIXth Century*, 1 (1842), 138; Barbara Jeanne Fields, *Slavery and Freedom on the Middle Ground: Maryland during the Nineteenth Century* (New Haven, Conn., 1985), 19, 73–74, 77–78. On hired white labor, see John Seymour Erwin, *Like Some Green Laurel: Letters of Margaret Johnson Erwin, 1821–1863* (Baton Rouge, La., 1981), 105ff. Also, G. Melvin Herndon, "Elliott L. Story: A Small Farmer's Struggle for Economic Survival in Antebellum Virginia," *Agricultural History*, 56 (1982), 519; Frederick Law Olmsted, *A Journey through Texas* (Austin, 1978 [1857]), 14, 107, 114–115; William H. Williams, *Slavery and Freedom in Delaware, 1639–1865* (Wilmington, Del., 1996), 43. Dubiously, Jonathan D. Martin says that, probably, all slaves were hired out at least once: *Divided Mastery: Slave Hiring in the American South* (Cambridge, Mass., 2004), 2, 8, 103.

27. Hunter Dickinson Farish, ed., *Journal and Letters of Philip Vickers Fithian: A Plantation Tutor of the Old Dominion* (Charlottesville, Va., 1957), xxix; Edwin Morris Betts, ed., *Thomas Jefferson's Farm Book: With Commentary and Relevant Extracts from His Writings* (Charlottesville, Va., 1987), 456; Janet Sharp Hermann, *Joseph E. Davis: Pioneer Patriarch* (Jackson, Miss., 1990), 50; Wayne K. Durrill, *War of Another Kind: A Southern Community in the Great Rebellion* (New York, 1990), 14. For white tenants and landless laborers on slave plantations in Appalachia, see Wilma A. Dunaway, *Slavery in the American Mountain South* (New York, 2003), 42–43, 140. Massy Gwyn (white) taught St. George Tucker's slaves to make fine cloth: Phillip Hamilton, *The Making and Unmaking of a Revolutionary Family: The Tuckers of Virginia, 1752–1830* (Charlottesville, Va., 2003), 60. Early Kentuckians complained of white servants who expected invitations to

table: Harry Toulmin, *The Western Country in 1793: Reports on Kentucky and Virginia* (London, 1948), 65.

28. "Panola," in ACP, n. s. (1858), 76. On the preference for hired slaves, see Martin, *Divided Mastery*, 108; on preference for free blacks, see John H. Russell, *The Free Negro in Virginia, 1619–1865* (New York, 1913), 146–149; Carl A. Brasseaux, *Acadian to Cajun: Transformation of a People, 1803–1877* (Jackson, Miss., 1992), 10; J. William Harris, "Portrait of a Small Slaveholder: The Journal of Benton Miller," *Georgia Historical Quarterly*, 74 (1990), 8; Corinna and Ellen Brown to Mannevillette Brown, Aug. 1, 1836, in Denham and Huneycutt, eds., *Echoes from a Distant Frontier*, 39.

29. "Speech on Executive Powers," in Russell Kirk, *John Randolph of Roanoke: A Study in American Politics, with Selected Speeches and Letters* (Chicago, 1964), 358; "Speech on the Oregon Bill," June 27, 1848, in JCCP, 25:533; William W. Holden, *Address Delivered before the Duplin County Agricultural Society* (Raleigh, N.C., 1857), 7; William A. Smith, *Lectures on the Philosophy and Practice of Slavery* (Nashville, Tenn., 1856), 17–18, 53–54; William A. Smith, "The Relations of Capital to Labor, and of Slavery to the Workingmen and Non-Slaveholders," reported in Richmond *Daily Dispatch*, Feb. 4, 1861.

30. Cartwright, "South's Position in the Union," in J. D. B. De Bow, *The Industrial Resources, Statistics, &c. of the United States and More Particularly of the Southern and Western States*, 3rd ed., 3 vols. (New York, 1966 [1854]), 3:62; Dixon Diary, March 19, Sept. 6, 1860, in Stephen Berry, ed., *Princes of Cotton: Four Diaries of Young Men in the South, 1848–1860* (Athens, Ga., 2007), 53, 185.

    For white field laborers, see Taylor Diary, esp., 1786–1791, 1795; Brisbane Receipt Book, Feb. 2, 1797; Diaries, June 1, 1802; Mar. 15, 1803; Jan. 21, May 3, 1804, in Ravenel Records, 233–235; Mary Campbell to David Campbell, Jan. 8, 1822; John Walker Diary, Nov. 20, 30, 1826; Nov. 3, 1827; May 21, Sept. 22, 1829; April 6, 1834; May 4 and 14, 1830; Dec. 19, 1837; Diary, July 23, 1845, in Sturdivant Plantation Records; Stewart Account Books, 1841–1860; Allen Collection; John B. Lamar to Mrs. Howell Cobb, April 27, 1846, in Ulrich B. Phillips, ed., *Plantation and Frontier: Documents, 1649–1863*, 2 vols. (New York, 1969 [1910]), 2:38; Greenlee Diary 1848, Feb. 21, 1851, June 21, 23, 1853, Pitts Diary and Account Book, Jan. 21, Sept. 4, 1850; Dec. 1, 1855; Nov. 9, Nov. 5, 1856; M. King Diary, Oct. 5, 1853; Graves Papers, 1853; Fletcher M. Green, ed., *Ferry Hill Plantation Journal* (Chapel Hill, N.C., 1961), 25; E. G. Baker Diary, July 21, 1858; Cornelius O. Cathey, "Sidney Weller, Antebellum Promoter of Agricultural Reform," *NCHR*, 31 (1954), 4; William Harris Hardy and Toney A. Hardy, *No Compromise with Principle: Autobiography and Biography of William Harris Hardy in Dialogue* (New York, 1946), 27; Herbert Gambrell, *Anson Jones: The Last President of Texas*, 2nd ed. (Austin, Tex., 1964), 420; *Farmer and Planter*, 6 (Feb. 1858), 43; J. Carlyle Sitterson, "The McCollams: A Planter Family of the Old and New South," *JSH*, 6 (1940), 350; "A Tour in the Southwest," in Charles Capen McLaughlin et al., eds., *The Papers of Frederick Law Olmsted*, 2 vols. (Baltimore, Md., 1977, 1981), 2:289.

31. Massenburg Plantation Journal, 1836–44; Cornelia Greene to Margaret Cowper, May 3, 1800, in Mary R. Bullard, *Robert Stafford of Cumberland Island: Growth of a Planter* (Athens, Ga., 1995), 21; Hudson Diaries, May–June, 1853; March–Aug. 1855; Caesilius, "Chrysion," in E. H. Warmington, ed., *Remains of Old Latin*, 4 vols. (LCL), 1:§21.

32. B. H. Barrow Diary, March 20, 1840, in Edwin Adams Davis, ed., *Plantation Life in the Florida Parishes of Louisiana, 1836–1846, as Reflected in the Diary of Bennet H. Barrow* (New York, 1943), 186–187; Bennett H. Wall, "The Founding of the Pettigrew Plantations," *NCHR*, 27 (Oct. 1950), 408, and generally, Robert Starobin, "Privileged Bondsmen and the Process of Accommodation: The Role of House Servants and Drivers as Seen in Their Own Letters," *Journal of Social History*, 5 (1971), 61; Ebenezer Pettigrew to James Cathcart Johnston, Jan. 17, 1843, in Lemmon, ed., *Pettigrew Papers*, 2:548–549; Maria Bryan to Julia Ann Bryan Cumming, Jan. 1, 1827, in Bleser, ed., *Tokens of Affection*, 22–23. For a white worker who stole from a plantation: Mary E. Moragné Journal, July 15, 1839, in Delle Mullen Craven, ed., *The Neglected Thread: A Journal of the Calhoun Community, 1836–1842* (Columbia, S.C., 1951), 142.

33. Claudia L. Bushman, *In Old Virginia: Slavery, Farming, and Society in the Journal of John Walker* (Baltimore, Md., 2002), 62–69, 100, 185; Charles C. Bolton, *Poor Whites of the Antebellum South: Tenants and Laborers in Central North Carolina and Northeast Mississippi* (Durham, N.C., 1994), esp. 12; Carl H. Moneyhon, *The Impact of the Civil War and Reconstruction on Arkansas: Persistence in the Midst of Ruin* (Baton Rouge, La., 1994), 47–50; Brasseaux, *Acadian to Cajun*, 13. For Polk, see Chase C. Mooney, *Slavery in Tennessee* (Bloomington, Ind., 1957), 159. For tenancy, see Lori A. Cline, "Something Wrong in South Carolina: Antebellum Agricultural Tenancy and Primitive Accumulation in Three Districts" (M.A. thesis, University of South Carolina, 1996), ch. 1; Charles H. Faulkner, *The Ramseys at Swan Pond: The Archeology and History of an East Tennessee Farm* (Knoxville, Tenn., 2008), 87–88; William G. Shade, *Democratizing the Old Dominion: Virginia and the Second Party System, 1824–1861* (Charlottesville, Va., 1996), 44; Lynette Boney Wrenn, ed., *A Bachelor's Life in Antebellum Mississippi: The Diary of Dr. Elijah Millington Walker, 1849–1852* (Knoxville, Tenn., 2004), xv.

34. Sitterson, "Hired Labor on Sugar Plantations," 201–203; TCWVQ, 1:395; 4:1401 (Lusk); Caroline Couper Lovell, *The Light of Other Days* (Macon, Ga., 1995), 74. For class prejudices and contempt for white plantation workers, see Michael Wayne, *Death of an Overseer: Reopening a Murder Investigation from the Plantation South* (New York, 2001), esp. ch. 7; Olmsted, *Back Country*, 274–276; Kenneth W. Noe, *Southwest Virginia's Railroad: Modernization and the Sectional Crisis* (Urbana, Ill., 1994), 50–51.

35. Bolton, *Poor Whites*, 42–65; William Lee Miller, *Arguing about Slavery: The Great Battle in the United States Congress* (New York, 1996), 188 (Calhoun); Fred Arthur Bailey, *Class and Tennessee's Confederate Generation* (Chapel Hill, N.C., 1987), 35; TCWVQ, 4:1710. The Lipscomb plantation (thirty slaves) had a live-in white woman weaver paid by the piece.

36. Xenophon, "Hiero," in Xenophon, *Scripta Minora*, trans. E. C. Marchant (Cambridge, Mass., LCL, 1968), 9§3; Eugene D. Genovese, "'Rather Be a Nigger than a Poor White Man': Black Perceptions of Southern Yeomen and Poor Whites," in Hans Trefousse, ed., *Toward a New View of America: Essays in Honor of Arthur C. Cole* (New York, 1977), 79–96; "Address of James Barbour, Esq. President of the Agricultural Society of Albemarle," *American Farmer*, 7 (1825), 290–291; James Barbour, "Address to the Agricultural Convention of Virginia," *Farmers' Register*, 3 (1836), 685; T. Pollok Burguyn, "Agriculture in North Carolina," *American Agriculturalist*, 5 (1846), 158; J. J. Flournoy, "The Science of Good

Husbandry," SC, 3 (1845), 157. Also, Isaac DuBose Seabrook, *Before and After; Or, The Relations of the Races at the South*, ed. John Hammond Moore (Baton Rouge, La., 1967 [1895]), 59; Isaac Stephens to William Elliott, Oct. 22, 1849, in Elliott-Gonzalez Papers; "All about Overseers," *Southern Planter*, 18 (1858), 413; Charles G. Steffen, "In Search of the Good Overseer: The Failure of the Agricultural Reform Movement in Lowcountry South Carolina, 1821–1834," *JSH*, 63 (1997), 753–802. Sugar plantation overseers might make $1,000 a year or more: J. Carlyle Sitterson, "Hired Labor on Sugar Plantations," 195, 198.

37. Lewis Livingston, "To Christopher Quandry," *Southern Planter*, 16 (1856), 229–230; Acklen typescript in U. B. Phillips Papers; Eugene D. Genovese, *Roll, Jordan, Roll: The World the Slaves Made* (New York, 1974), 16–20; Martin, *Divided Mastery*, 160.

38. B. H. Barrow Diary, July 25, 1839, in Davis, ed., *Florida Parishes*, 154; on Massie, see Lynn A Nelson, *Pharsalia: An Environmental Biography of a Southern Plantation, 1780–1880* (Athens, Ga., 2007), 179–180, 250 n. 49; A. L. Brent to William Cabell, Nov. 12, 1858, in Cabell-Ellet Papers; "General Suggestions," in "A Practical Treatise: On the Duties of Christians Owning Slaves," in Wiley Papers; Daniel Coleman, "A Few Words about Overseers," *SC*, 7 (1849), 139–140, quote at 140; [J. A. Campbell], "Slavery among the Romans," *SQR*, 14 (1848), 403–404.

39. Julia A. Flisch, "The Common People of the Old South," *Annual Report of the American Historical Association*, 1 (1908), 135–136; Marty D. Matthews, *Forgotten Founder: The Life and Times of Charles Pinckney* (Columbia, S.C., 2004); John Randolph to Francis Scott Key, Oct. 17, 1813, in Hugh A. Garland, *The Life of John Randolph of Roanoke*, 2 vols. (New York, 1969 [1859]), 2:27; *Daily Alabama Journal* (Montgomery) May 26, 1852; Bill Cecil-Fronsman, *Common Whites: Class and Culture in Antebellum North Carolina* (Lexington, Ky., 1992), 62–63; Cline, "Something Wrong in South Carolina," 1–2.

40. R. F. W. Allston, "Obituary of Overseer Thomas Briton Hamlin," in Easterby, ed., *South Carolina Rice Plantation*, 263–264; Manigault Journal, 1864, in James M. Clifton, ed., *Life and Labor on Argyle Island: Letters and Documents of a Savannah River Rice Plantation, 1833–1867* (Savannah, Ga., 1978), 347–348; William Bell to William H. Otey, Jan. 25, 1860, in Wyche-Otey Papers; "Table Talk" (Nov. 28, 1861), in Lindsley Papers; Harry St. John Dixon Diary, Sept. 4, 1860, in Berry, ed., *Princes of Cotton*, 182. For an overseer's protest against planter insults, see "A Word to Overseers," *SC*, 7 (1849), 181–182. On overseers and elite, see William E. Wiethoff, *Crafting the Overseer's Image* (Columbia, S.C., 2006), ch. 5.

41. Sarah N. Randolph, *The Domestic Life of Jefferson, Compiled from Letters and Reminiscences* (New York, 1871), 35; Massenburg Farm Journal, March 5, 1835; Hudson Diary, Aug. 31, 1856; Susan R. Jervey and Charlotte St. J. Ravenel, *Two Diaries from Middle St. John's Berkeley, South Carolina, February–May, 1865* (EE: 1998), 15. A. M. Keiley reported that black troops looted poor whites in Virginia: *In Vinculis; or, The Prisoner of War. Being the Experience of a Rebel in Two Federal Pens* (New York, 1866), 84–85.

42. E. G. Baker Diaries, July 21, 1858; for rage, see George H. Hepworth, *Whip, Hoe, and Sword: Or, The Gulf-Department in '63* (Boston, Mass., 1864), 101; Weymouth T. Jordan, *Hugh Davis and His Alabama Plantation* (University, Ala., 1948), 50; John Q. Anderson, ed., *Brokenburn: The Journal of Kate Stone, 1861–1868* (Baton Rouge, La., 1955), 5; William Davis in John W. Blassingame, ed., *Slave Testimony: Two Centuries of Letters, Speeches, Interviews, and Autobiographies*

(Baton Rouge, La., 1977), 171; *Narrative of William Wells Brown, An American Slave, written by Himself* (Boston, 1847), 102–103.

43. "Professor Dew on Slavery," in *Pro-Slavery Argument*, 436; E. A. Knowlton's entries for Dec. 25, 1857, and April 21, 1858, in Barrow Residence Journal.

44. C., "Servility," *SLM*, 1 (Aug. 1834), 6; J. William Jones, *Personal Reminiscences of General Robert E. Lee* (Baton Rouge, La., 1989 [1875]), 163; John Spencer Bassett, *The Southern Plantation Overseer, as Revealed in His Letters* (Northampton, Mass., 1925), 2–3, 169; AS: South Carolina, 2 (pt. 1), 235; John G. Guignard to James S. Guignard, Sept. 30, 1828, in Arney R. Childs, ed., *Planters and Businessmen: The Guignard Family of South Carolina, 1795–1930* (Columbia, S.C., 1957), 49; John Evans to George Noble Jones, Sept. 9, 1854; July 2, 1855, in Ulrich Bonnell Phillips and James David Glunt, eds., *Florida Plantation Records from the Papers of George Noble Jones* (St. Louis, Mo., 1927), 100, 135; Ingraham, *South-West*, 100, 135; W. W. Supple to A. H. Arrington, May 21, 1860, in Arrington Papers; J. B. Grimball Diary, Nov. 22, 28, 1855.

45. J. B. Grimball Diary, Oct. 20, 1832; Linton Stephens to Alexander H. Stephens, June 8, 1858, in James D. Waddell, ed., *Biographical Sketch of Linton Stephens, Containing a Selection of His Letters, Speeches, State Papers, Etc.* (Atlanta, Ga., 1877), 151–152; Easterby, ed., *South Carolina Rice Plantation*, 27, quote at 114; Pringle, *Chicora Wood*, 204; Harvey Toliver Cook, *The Life and Legacy of David Rogerson Williams* (New York, 1916), 213; Archibald H. Arrington to Kate Arrington, Jan. 30, 1857.

46. John Otto and Augustus Marion Burns III, "Black Folks and Poor Buckras: Archeological Evidence of Overseer and Slave Living Conditions on an Antebellum Plantation," *Journal of Black Studies*, 14 (1983), 195–196; AS: S.C., 2 (pt. 2), 281; T. Reed Ferguson, *The John Couper Family at Cannon's Point* (Macon, Ga., 1994), 72–73. On slaveholding overseers, see William Kauffman Scarborough, *The Overseer: Plantation Management in the Old South* (Athens, Ga., 1966), 55–64.

47. Louis B. Wright, ed., *The Prose Works of William Byrd of Westover* (Cambridge, Mass., 1966), 342; E. Merton Coulter, *Old Petersburg and the Broad River Valley of Georgia: Their Rise and Decline* (Athens, Ga., 1965), 110; Carney Diary, Jan. 21, 29, 1861; William S. McFeely, *Frederick Douglass* (New York, 1991), 19, 24; Ralph B. Flanders, *Plantation Slavery in Georgia* (Chapel Hill, N.C., 1933), 140 (Walker); Moses Harris to John Christie, May 6, 7, 1853, in Hughes Family Papers; Anderson, ed., *Brokenburn*, 15. For a story of an ill-fated love affair between a planter's son and overseer's daughter, see Robert S. Inge, "The Overseer's Daughter," *Southron*, 1 (1839), 213–221.

48. Journal of John Harrower, Feb. 25, 1776 (138); *DGB*, 1:396–397; Orville W. Taylor, *Negro Slavery in Arkansas* (Durham, N.C., 1958), 161; letters, 1840s, in W. R. Smith Papers; Alice DeLancey Izard to Margaret Izard Manigault, Apr. 27, 1815, in Joan E. Cashin, ed., *Our Common Affairs: Texts from Women in the Old South* (Baltimore, Md., 1996), 125.

49. AS: S.C., 2 (pt. 1), 199; Cornish Diary, Nov. 20, 1839; Mary Granger, ed., *Savannah River Plantations* (Spartanburg, S.C., 1983), 18.

50. Pierre Marambaud, *William Byrd of Westover, 1674–1744* (Charlottesville, Va., 1971), 119; Ella Tazewell to Cameron Thom, May 7, 1863, in Catherine Thom Bartlett, ed., *"My Dear Brother": A Confederate Chronicle* (Richmond, Va., 1952), 94; A. M. Clemson to J. C. Calhoun, Jan. 24, 1846, in Lander, *Calhoun Family*, 32–33; see the letters between Skipwith and Cocke in Randall M. Miller, ed., *"Dear Master": Letters of a Slave Family* (Ithaca, N.Y., 1978), 188, 220, 221, 223, 226,

253; Bills Diary, Jan. 28, 1846; July 14, 15, 30, 1853; Sydnor, *Gentleman of the Old South*, 112; Riley, ed., "Diary of a Mississippi Planter," 475–476; Mary Chesnut, June 11, 1862, in C. Vann Woodward, ed., *Mary Chesnut's Civil War* (New Haven, Conn., 1981), 376; Charles Manigault to James Haynes, March 1, 1847, in Clifton, ed., *Argyle Island*, 49; M. D. Cooper to William Cooper, Nov. 22, 1842. For slave women assigned to overseers, see also Charles S. Davis, *The Cotton Kingdom in Alabama* ((Montgomery, Ala., 1937 [1974]), 46–47; Guion Griffis Johnson, *A Social History of the Sea Islands, with Special Reference to St. Helena Island, South Carolina* (Westport, Conn., 1969), 75.

51. Glenn and Virginia Linden, eds., *Disunion, War, Defeat, and Recovery: The Journal of Augustus Benners, 1850–1885* (Macon, Ga., 2007), 40; William Pope Harrison, *The Gospel among the Slaves* (Nashville, Tenn., 1893), 269; C. Hill, "On the Management of Negroes," in James O. Breeden, ed., *Advice among Masters: The Ideal in Slave Management in the Old South* (Westport, Conn., 1980), 52.

52. C. Carson to W. S. Waller, Jan. 26, 1836, in Carson Family Papers; W. M. Otey to Octavia Otey, Nov. 13, 1851, in Wyche-Otey Papers; Leak Diaries, Oct. 17, 1854; Holland N. McTyeire, *A History of Methodism* (Nashville, Tenn., 1886), 358–359; D. E. Huger Smith, *A Charlestonian's Recollections, 1846–1913* (Charleston, S.C., 1950), 16–17; Hudson Diary, June 31, 1852.

53. William Dosite Postell, *The Health of Slaves on Southern Plantations* (Gloucester, Mass., 1970), 137; for positive views of overseers' sons, see TCWVQ, 3:966; 5:1964, 2133; J. E. Craighead to John Craighead, Oct. 24, 1846, in Hynes Papers.

54. Conner Diary, Aug. 13, 1827; Anderson, ed., *Brokenburn*, 5, 15; Howell Adams to William Ruffin Smith, Nov. 20, 1846, in Smith Papers; W. Emerson Wilson, ed., *Plantation Life at Rose Hill: The Diaries of Martha Ogle Forman, 1814–1845* (Wilmington, Del., 1976), 175–176 (Feb. 20–21, 1824); also, Cornish Diary, Aug. 2, 1840; Mary E. Moragné Journal, July 18, 1837; Jan. 27, 1842; Craven, ed., *Neglected Thread*, 46, 226.

55. For legal matters, see *Henderson v. Warmack* (Mississippi, 1854) in Maxwell Bloomfield, *American Lawyers in a Changing Society, 1776–1876* (Cambridge, Mass., 1976), 115. For a "horrible murder," see Butler Diary, June 15, 1861.

56. William Cabell Bruce, *John Randolph of Roanoke, 1773–1833: A Biography Based Largely on New Material*, 2 vols. (New York, 1970 [1922]), 2:703–705; James Rowe to J. C. Cole, July 26, 1840, in Cole-Taylor Papers; Gavin Diary, May 3–6, 1859.

57. James Benson Sellers, *Slavery in Alabama* (University, Ala., 1964), 64 (Scott); *Narrative of James Williams, An American Slave, Who Was for Several Years a Driver on a Cotton Plantation in Alabama* (New York, 1838), 44–45. For deep attachments between overseers and slave women, see AS: S.C., 2 (pt. 1), 128; J. Carlyle Sitterson, *Sugar Country: The Cane Sugar Industry in the South* (Lexington, Ky., 1953), 107; James M. Clifton, ed., *Life and Labor on Argyle Island: Letters and Documents of a Savannah River Rice Plantation, 1833–1867* (Savannah, Ga., 1978), 250; Phillips and Glunt, eds., *Florida Plantation Records*, 25; Theodore Dwight Weld, *Slavery as It Is: Testimony of a Thousand Witnesses* (New York, 1839), 11. For court cases see Helen Tunncliff Catterall, ed., *Judicial Cases Concerning Slavery and the Negro*, 4 vols. (Washington, D.C., 1919–37), 3:405, 620; James Hugo Johnston, *Race Relations in Virginia and Miscegenation in the South, 1776–1860* (Amherst, Mass., 1970), 306–307. For sexual exploitation by overseers see Wiethoff, *Crafting the Overseer's Image*, 32–38.

58. Scarborough, *Southern Overseer*, 75–77; Tait quoted in Davis, *Cotton Kingdom in Alabama*, 50; Acklen, typescript of ms. (p. 13), in Phillips Papers; Journal of Araby Plantation, in Nutt Papers; also, Francis Johnson Scott, ed., "Letters and Papers of Governor David Johnson and Family," Appendix to *Proceedings of the South Carolina Historical Association* (1941), 25. For firings see David Duncan Wallace, *The Life of Henry Laurens* (New York, 1967), 67; Ulrich Bonnell Phillips, *Life and Labor in the Old South* (Boston, 1948 [1929]), 323; Joe Gray Taylor, *Negro Slavery in Louisiana* (Baton Rouge, La., 1963), 219, 233; Bell I. Wiley, *Southern Negroes, 1861–1865* (New Haven, Conn., 1958), 52; Rachel Weeks O'Connor to David Weeks, July 8, 1832; Nov. 16, 20, 1833; and O'Connor to A. T. Conrad, April 12, 1835, in Weeks Papers. For black testimony, see Virginia Writers Program, *The Negro in Virginia* (Winston-Salem, N.C., 1991), 84–85; AS: Ala., 6 (pt. 1), 46; Ark., 9 (pt. 3), 27, 10 (pt. 6), 103; Ga., 3 (pt. 4), 310; N.C., 15 (pt. 2), 132; Miss., 7 (pt. 2), 4.

59. J. T. Leigh to J. K. Polk, Aug. 13, 1839, in Bassett, *Southern Plantation Overseer*, 122; Charles Manigault to Louis Manigault, Feb. 28, Dec. 18, 1856, in Clifton, ed., *Argyle Island*, 211, 238.`

4. Loyal and Loving Slaves

1. Frances Fearn, *Diary of a Refugee*, ed. Rosalie Urquart (New York, 1910), 7–8; Annie Hawkins of Texas, quoted in Thavolia Glymph, *Out of the House of Bondage: The Transformation of the Plantation Household* (New York, 2008), 18.

2. Nathaniel Beverley Tucker, "An Essay on the Moral and Political Effect of the Relation between the Caucasian Master and the African Slave," *SLM*, 10 (1844), 333–335; John Coalter, quoted in Philip Hamilton, *The Making and Unmaking of a Revolutionary Family: The Tuckers of Virginia, 1752–1830* (Charlottesville, Va., 2003), 127; Lily Logan Morrill, ed., *My Confederate Girlhood: The Memoirs of Kate Virginia Cox Logan* (Richmond, Va., 1932), xi, 28. Also, James Logan [of Scotland], *Notes of a Journey through Canada, the United States of America, and the West Indies* (Edinburgh, U.K., 1838), 187–188.

3. Sarah Hicks to her parents, Oct. 10, 1853, in James C. Bonner, ed., "Plantation Experiences of a New York Woman," *NCHR*, 33 (1956), 389; Mary J. Windle, *Life at the White Sulphur Springs; or, Pictures of a Pleasant Summer* (Philadelphia, 1857), 45; Sarah Mytton Maury, *An Englishwoman in America* (London, 1848), 193; Ives, quoted in Marshall De Lancey Haywood, *Lives of the Bishops of North Carolina from the Establishment of the Episcopate in that State Down to the Division of the Diocese* (Raleigh, N.C., 1910), 99–100; James Stuart, "Bad Roads, Loose Morals, Sadism, and Racetrack Discipline, 1830," in Thomas D. Clark, ed., *South Carolina: The Grand Tour, 1780–1865* (Columbia, S.C., 1973), 162–163.

4. Max Weber, *Ancient Judaism*, trans. and ed. Hans H. Gerth and Don Martingale (Glencoe, Ill., 1952), 256–257; Cicero, *De Senectute*, trans. William Armistead Falconer (LCL), §11.37; T. R. R. Cobb, *An Inquiry into the Law of Negro Slavery in the United States* (New York, 1968 [1858]), lxxxvii; "The Hannibalic War," in *Appian's Roman History*, 4 vols. (LCL), 1:1.2; [John Archibald Campbell], "Slavery among the Romans," *SQR*, 14 (1848), 407. Lysias, however, insisted that slaves naturally disliked their masters: "Before the Areopagus: Defence in the Matter of the Olive-Stump," in *Lysias*, trans. and ed. W. R. M. Lamb (LCL), §35.

5. Abbé Robin in "Travelers' Impressions," *Journal of Negro History*, 1 (1916), 404; Gayarré quoted in John Herbert Nelson, "Charles Gayarré, Historian and Romancer," *Sewanee Review*, 33 (1925), 427–428.

6. James O. Andrew, *Methodist Magazine and Quarterly Review*, 13 (1831), 316; Marsh Diary; Thomas E. Schott, *Alexander H. Stephens of Georgia: A Biography* (Baton Rouge, La., 1988), 65; Victoria Alexandrina Maria Louisa Stuart-Wortley, *A Young Traveller's Journal of a Tour in North and South America During the Year 1850* (London, 1852), 132–133.

7. Carolyn Merrick, *Old Times in Dixie Land: A Southern Matron's Memories* (New York, 1901), 6, 19; Kate Mason Rowland and Mrs. Morris L. Croxall, eds., *The Journal of Julia LeGrand: New Orleans, 1862–1863* (Richmond, Va., 1911), Dec. 20, 1862 (56); Ernest McPherson Lander, Jr., *The Calhoun Family and Thomas Green Clemson: The Decline of Southern Patriarchy* (Columbia, S.C., 1983), 69–70; Henry Thomas Shanks, ed., *The Papers of Willie P. Mangum*, 5 vols. (Raleigh, N.C., 1955–56), 5:309, 19. For a romantic retrospective view of demands on mistresses, see Mary Norcott Bryan, *A Grandmother's Recollection of Dixie* (EE: 1998 [1912]).

8. Harriet Martineau, *Society in America*, 2 vols. (New York, 1837), 2:313–316, 336, 3:326–327 (leisure and comfort), 330; Harriet Martineau, *Retrospect of Western Travel*, 2 vols. (London, 1838), 1:215 (self-sacrifice); F. A. Porcher, "Southern and Northern Civilizations Contrasted," *RM*, 1 (1857), 101.

9. Rufus William Bailey, *The Issue: Presented in a Series of Letters on Slavery* (New York, 1837), 29; Chesnut Diary, Nov. 30, 1861, in C. Vann Woodward, ed., *Mary Chesnut's Civil War* (New Haven, Conn., 1981), 249; R. Q. Mallard, *Plantation Life before Emancipation* (EE: 1998 [1892]), 42–43; *Narrative of William W. Brown, an American Slave. Written by Himself* (London, 1849), 20; Horace Cowles Atwater, *Incidents of a Southern Tour: or, The South as Seen with Northern Eyes* (Boston, Mass., 1857), 25–26; note to entry for Apr. 24, May 7, 1863, in A. J. L. Fremantle, *Three Months in the Southern States: The 1863 Diary of an English Soldier, April-June 1863* (London, 1863), 48, 79; Mrs. [Matilda Charlotte] Houstoun, *Hesperos: Or, Travels in the West*, 2 vols. (London, 1850), 2:159–160, 208; David Christy, "Lecture on African Colonization," *AR*, 25 (1849), 325–351.

10. Mary Price Coulling, *Margaret Junkin Preston: A Biography* (Winston-Salem, N.C., 1993), 102; John S. Wise, *The End of an Era* (Boston, Mass., 1900), 36; E. J. W. Baker Journal, 1848, 16; Edmondson Diary, May 10, 1862, in Beth G. Crabtree and James Welch Patton, eds., *"Journal of a Secesh Lady": The Diary of Catherine Devereux Edmondston, 1860–1866* (Raleigh, N.C., 1979), 173; Catherine Stewart, *New Homes in the West* (Nashville, Tenn., 1843), 150–152.

11. "The South," in Charles Capen McLaughlin et al., eds., *The Papers of Frederick Law Olmsted*, 2 vols. (Baltimore, 1977, 1981), 2:182 (*New York Times*, Feb. 19, 1853); James R. Gilmore [Edmund Kirke], *My Southern Friends* (New York, 1863), 104–105, 113, 125.

12. Kimberly Harrison, ed., *A Maryland Bride in the Deep South: The Civil War Diary of Priscilla Bond* (Baton Rouge, La., 2006), Jan. 11, 1860 (139); McCorkle Diary, Sept. 9, 1847.

13. "Slaves, Free Negroes and Mulattoes," *Richmond Enquirer*, Feb. 9, 1832; "A South Carolina Rice Plantation," *SC*, 8 (1850), 85; J. L. Baker, *Slavery* (Ithaca, New York, 2006 [1860)]), 14; Catherine Cooper Hopley, *Life in the South from the Commencement of the War*, 2 vols. (New York, 1971 [1863]), 2:80; Harmon quoted in William Kauffman Scarborough, *The Overseer: Plantation Management*

in the Old South (Athens, Ga., 1966), 103; Mary Jones to C. C. Jones, Sept. 14, 1854, in Robert Manson Myers, ed., *The Children of Pride: A True Story of Georgia and the Civil War* (New Haven, Conn., 1972), 90; Bonner, ed., "Plantation Experiences of a New York Woman," 392; St. John R. Liddell to Moses Liddell, Dec. 28, 1851; Amelia E. Murray, *Letters from the United States, Cuba, and Canada*, 2 vols. in 1 (New York, 1968 [1856]), 273; W. Faux, *Memorable Days in America: Being a Journal of a Tour to the United States* (New York, 1969 [1823]), 68. Also, A. Flournoy, Jr., to Docy Flournoy, July 8, 1861, in M. F. Flournoy, ed., "From *History of the Flournoy Family*" (typed); Marsh Diary, Jan. 9, 1850.

14. William H. Russell, *My Diary North and South* (Boston, 1863), 75; William Henry Milburn, *Ten Years of Preacher Life: Chapters from an Autobiography* (New York, 1859), 325–326; Linton Stephens to Alexander H. Stephens, March 29, 1858, in James D. Waddell, *Biographical Sketch of Linton Stephens, Containing a Selection of His Letters, Speeches, State Papers, Etc.* (Atlanta, Ga., 1877), 142; Certificate of Dr. H. W. McCoun for T. L. Linthicum, Nov. 25, 1852, in "Slave Papers"; St. John R. Liddell to Moses Liddell, Feb. 14, 1852, in Liddell Papers; Rachel Weeks O'Connor to David Weeks, Oct. 14, 1824, in Weeks Papers; Fort Papers; Magruder Diary, May 21, 1846; Davidson Diary, April 19, 1853; Bethell Diary, April 17, 27, 29, 1862; Craft Diary, July 17, 1863; Journal of Sarah Rootes Jackson, Nov. 14, 1834, in Jackson-Prince Papers; Carmichael Diary, Oct. 14, 1837, March 2, 1838, July 27, 1845; Bills Diary, Sept. 11, 1845.

15. Louis B. Wright and Marion Tinling, eds., *The Great American Gentleman: William Byrd of Westover, His Secret Diary for the Years 1709–1712* (New York, 1963), Sept. 19, 1709 (39), July 23, 1710 (90); Hutchinson Diary, Jan. 6, 1828; Hilliard Diary, June 9, 1850; Carney Diary, April 28, 1861; John Q. Anderson, ed. *Brokenburn: The Journal of Kate Stone, 1861–1868* (Baton Rouge, La., 1955), 77; Charles L. Perdue, Jr., et al., eds., *Weevils in the Wheat: Interviews with Virginia Ex-Slaves* (Charlottesville, Va., 1976), 140; Withers Diary, Oct. 21, 186.

16. ERD, Feb. 19, 1860 (1:403); Edwin Adams Davis, ed., *Plantation Life in the Florida Parishes of Louisiana, 1836–1846, as Reflected in the Diary of Bennet H. Barrow* (New York, 1943), March 30, 1840 (188), and "Rules of Highland Plantation," 406–407; H. N. McTyeire, *Duties of Christian Masters*, ed. Thomas O. Summers (Nashville, Tenn., 1859), 47–48.

17. See, e.g., Newstead Plantation Diary, Jan. 16, 1859; Manigault Diary, Dec. 25, 1854; Solon Robinson, "Negro Slavery in the South," *DBR*, 7 (Nov. 1849), 381. *American Agriculturalist* of New York – read by many southern planters – serialized Robinson's report in 1849.

18. James H. Sheppard to Abraham Sheppard, Jr., July 31, 1822; Starnes in *Jim (a Slave) v. State* (1854), in Helen Tunnicliff Catterall, ed., *Judicial Cases Concerning Slavery and the Negro*, 4 vols. (Washington, D.C., 1919–37), 3 (pt. 1), 36; Iveson Brookes to Cornelia Brookes, April 30, 1860; Sebastian G. Messmer, ed., *The Works of the Right Rev. John England, First Bishop of Charleston*, 7 vols., (Cleveland, Oh., 1908), 3:258; B. McBride, "Directions for Cultivating Various Crops Grown at Hickory Hill," *SA*, 3 (1830), 238; Augustin Verot, *A Tract for the Times: Slavery and Abolitionism* (Baltimore, 1861), 12. For planters' complaints of excessive leniency, see Ariela J. Gross, *Double Character: Slavery and Mastery in the Antebellum Southern Courtroom* (Princeton, N.J., 2000), 110.

19. Elizabeth Curtis Wallace to her sister, undated, Wallace Diary, Apr. 7, 15, May 10, Dec. 12, 1863, in Eleanor P. Cross and Charles B. Cross, Jr., eds., *Glencoe*

Diary: The War-Time Journal of Elizabeth Curtis Wallace (Chesapeake, Va., 1968), Introduction (unpaginated), 24, 26, 33, 80. In Mary C. Oliphant et al., eds., *The Letters of William Gilmore Simms*, 6 vols. (Columbia, S.C., 1952–82) see B. Ballard to Lewis Thompson, Feb. 9, 1845, Simms to E. A. Duyckinck, May 28, 1860 (4:222), Simms to James Lawson, March 17, 1861 (353). R. H. Rivers, *Elements of Moral Philosophy* (Nashville, Tenn., 1859), 357; James I. Robertson, Jr., ed., *The Diary of Dolly Lunt Burge* (Athens, Ga., 1962), Nov. 8, 1864 (98).

20. Polk quoted in Joseph H. Parks, *General Leonidas Polk, C.S.A.: The Fighting Bishop* (Baton Rouge, La., 1962), 122; George Fitzhugh, "Frederick the Great by Thomas Carlyle," *DBR*, 29 (1860), 155–156; McCord to Langdon Cheves, Jr., Jan. 18, 1860, in Richard C. Lounsbury, ed., *Louisa S. McCord: Poems, Drama, Biography, Letters* (Charlottesville, Va., 1996), 353; Eliza Frances Andrews, *War-Time Journal of a Georgia Girl* (New York, 1907), 292; Christopher Chancellor, ed., *An Englishman in the Civil War: The Diaries of Henry Yates Thompson* (New York, 1971), 59–60.

21. *Southern Repertory and College Review*, 3 (1854), 250; John Adger, *The Religious Instruction of the Colored Population: A Sermon* (Charleston, S.C., 1847), 6, 13; review of Adger in *SPR*, 1 (1847), 139. Sir Charles Lyell, *Travels in North America, Canada, and Nova Scotia, with Geological Observations*, 2nd ed., 2 vols. (London, 1855), 1:169, 182, 185, quote at 189; Caroline R. Ravenel to D. E. Huger Smith, July 26, 1865, in Daniel E. Huger Smith et al., eds., *Mason-Smith Family Letters, 1860–1868* (Columbia, S.C., 1950), 225 (old man); J. A. Turner in Mills Lane, ed., *Neither More nor Less than Men: Slavery in Georgia* (Savannah, Ga., 1993), 49; Augustus Longstreet Hull, *Annals of Athens, Georgia, 1801–1901* (Danielsville, Ga., 1906), 289.

22. Hamilton, *A Revolutionary Family*, 188; Cora Mitchel, *Reminiscences of the Civil War* (EE: 1998 [1916]), 4–5; Morgan Diary, May 31, June 26, Sept. 3, 1862, in James I. Robertson, ed., *A Confederate Girl's Diary: Sarah Morgan Dawson* (Westport, Conn., 1960), 52, 88, 211–212; Gary J. Battershell, "Upcountry Slaveholding: Pope and Johnson Counties, Arkansas, 1840–1860" (Ph.D. diss., University of Arkansas, 1996), 94 (Cazort); Mrs. D. G. [Louise Wigfall] Wright, *A Southern Girl in '61: The War-Time Memories of a Confederate Senator's Daughter* (New York, 1905), 12. For the fear that runaways might return to previous masters, see Lathan A. Windley, comp., *Runaway Slave Advertisements: A Documentary History from 1730 to 1790*, 4 vols. (Westport, Conn., 1983), 1:3, 48, 77.

23. Harriott Horry Ravenel, *Eliza Pinckney* (New York, 1896), 182; King in Lane, ed., *Neither More nor Less than Men*, 100; Haywood, *Lives of the Bishops of North Carolina*, 44. For incidents of slaves who risked – sometimes lost – their lives while protecting the plantation from trespassing runaways, see Lathan Algerna Windley, *A Profile of Runaway Slaves in Virginia and South Carolina from 1730 through 1787* (New York, 1945), 8.

24. William Dusinberre, *Them Dark Days: Slavery in the Rice Swamps* (Athens, Ga., 2000), 46–47; A. Flournoy, Jr., to Docy Flournoy, July 8, 1861, in M. F. Flournoy, ed., "Excerpts from 'History of the Flournoy Family'"; Reuben Allen Pierson to William H. Pierson, Jan. 15, 1864, in Thomas W. Cutrer and T. Michael Parrish, eds., *Brothers in Gray: The Civil War Letters of the Pierson Family* (Baton Rouge, La., 1997), 225.

25. Clitherall Autobiography (ms.), Feb. 2, 1860, and Book 6 (1813); Charles Colcock Jones, *The Glory of Woman, in the Fear of the Lord* (Philadelphia, 1847), 43.

26. Morgan quoted in William R. Hogan, *The Texas Republic: A Social and Economic History* (Austin, Tex., 1969), 24; William Gilmore Simms, *Woodcraft* (New York, 1856), 509; Wise, *End of an Era*, 461.

27. Woodward, ed., *Mary Chesnut's Civil War*, Feb. 26, 1865 (733); Harriet Cumming to Sister Clifford, Dec. 6, 1856, in Marion A. Boggs, ed., *The Alexander Letters, 1787–1900* (Athens, Ga., 2002), 194–195; also, Thomas Diary, March 29, 1865; Susan Dabney Smedes, *Memorials of a Southern Planter*, ed. Fletcher M. Green (New York, 1965 [1887]), 34.

28. Josiah Smith, Jr., to George Austin, July 31, 1774, in J. Smith Lettercopy Book; Ebenezer Pettigrew to James Cathcart Johnston, July 16, 1836, in Sarah McCulloh Lemmon, ed., *The Pettigrew Papers*, 2 vols. (Raleigh, N.C., 1971, 1988), 2:378; E. G. Baker Diary, Feb. 13, July 8, 1849; J. S. Wilson, "The Peculiarities & Diseases of the Negro," *ACP*, as reprinted in Breeden, ed., *Advice among Masters*, 136.

29. Russell Kirk, *John Randolph of Roanoke: A Study in American Politics, with Selected Speeches and Letters* (Chicago, 1964), 129 (Quincy); E. L. Magoon, *Orators of the American Revolution* (New York, 1850), 448; John Davis, *Travels of Four and a Half Years in the United States of America*, ed. A. J. Morrison (New York, 1909 [1803]), 107–108; G. M., "South-Carolina," in Eugene L. Schwaab and Jacqueline Bull, eds., *Travels in the Old South: Selections from Periodicals of the Times*, 2 vols. (Lexington, Ky., 1973), 1:234; Frederick Law Olmsted, *A Journey in the Seaboard Slave States* (New York, 1968 [1856]), 135.

30. Sarah Rootes Jackson Journal, May 21, 1834, in Jackson-Prince Papers; also, James Benson Sellers, *Slavery in Alabama* (University, Ala., 1964), 128; Wadley Private Journal, Dec. 29, 1860; Conner Diary, Aug. 13, 1827; Carney Diary, June 16, 1859.
    For visits to the quarters, see Marsh Diary, Jan. 9. 1850; Carney Diary, Feb. 3–4, 1861; Letitia A. Burwell, *A Girl's Life in Virginia before the War*, 2nd ed. (New York, 1895), 2–3; Robertson, Jr., ed., *Diary of Dolly Lunt Burge*, ix; Ralph B. Flanders, "Two Plantations and a County of Antebellum Georgia," *Georgia Historical Quarterly*, 12 (1928), 13 (1928), 11–12; Isaac DuBose Seabrook, *Before and After; Or, The Relations of the Races at the South*, ed. John Hammond Moore (Baton Rouge, La., 1967 [1895]), 69; Josephine Bacon Martin, ed., *Life on a Liberty County Plantation: The Journal of Cornelia Jones Pond* (Hinesville, Ga., 1983), 58; Belle Kearney, *A Slaveholder's Daughter* (EE: 1997 [1900]), 13; Charles J. Johnson, Jr., *Mary Telfair: The Life and Legacy of a Nineteenth-Century Woman* (Savannah, Ga., 2002), 330; Thomas Joseph Macon, *Life Gleanings* (Richmond, Va., 1913),7; N. B. De Saussure, *Old Plantation Days: Being Recollections of Southern Life before the War* (New York, 1909).

31. I. E. Lowery, *Life on the Old Plantation, in Ante-Bellum Days; Or, A Story Based on Facts* (Columbia, S.C., 1911), 10–11; and see, e.g., Andrews, *War-Time Journal*, 70–71; Anderson, ed., *Brokenburn*, 10.

32. Sally Baxter to George Baxter, Apr. 15, 1855, in Ann Fripp Hampton, ed., *A Divided Heart: Letters of Sally Baxter Hampton, 1853–1862* (Spartanburg, S.C., 1980), 23; Sally McDowell to John Miller, Oct. 4–5, in Thomas E. Buckley, S. J., ed., *"If You Love that Lady Don't Marry Her": The Courtship Letters of Sally McDowell and John Miller, 1854–56* (Columbia, Mo., 2000), 816; Myrta Lockett Avary, *Dixie after the War* (New York, 1968 [1906]), 179. For Northerners on the warm welcome house servants gave mistresses, see Mary Norcott Bryan, *A Grandmothers Recollections of Dixie* (New Bern, N.C., 1912), 15.

33. Moses Liddell, Dec. 28, 1851; Murphey to William Polk, Feb. 18, 1820, in William Henry Hoyt, ed., *The Papers of Archibald D. Murphey, 1777–1832*, 2 vols. (Raleigh, N.C., 1914), 1:158; on Carter, see Ralph Betts Flanders, *Plantation Slavery in Georgia* (Chapel Hill, N.C., 1933), 192, 228; Mary Jones to C. C. Jones, June 5, 1850, in Robert Manson Myers, ed., *A Georgian at Princeton* (New York, 1976), 26.

34. Jan. 29, 1848, in Carol Bleser, ed., *Secret and Sacred: The Diaries of James Henry Hammond, a Southern Slaveholder* (New York, 1988), 188; for a typical obituary, see M. F. Ingersoll, "Excepts from *History of the Flournoy Family*" (typescript); Hawkins in *TCWVQ*, 3:1052; William Dallam Armes, ed., *The Autobiography of Joseph LeConte* (New York, 1903), 33; Sarah Alexander to her daughter, Feb. 20, 1853, in Boggs, ed., *Alexander Letters*, 177; Virginia Campbell to David Campbell, April 5, 1837, in Campbell Family Papers; Mary Jones to C. C. Jones, Jr., July 7, 1858, in Myers, ed., *Children of Pride*, 427; Percy quoted in Elizabeth Silverthorne, *Plantation Life in Texas* (College Station, Tex., 1986), 49.

35. "Philom," "Moral Management of Negroes," *SC*, 7 (May and July 1849), excerpted in James O. Breeden, ed., *Advice among Masters: The Ideal in Slave Management in the Old South* (Westport, Conn., 1980); Hamilton, *Revolutionary Family*, 152; Waddell, *Linton Stephens*, 95; Norma Lois Peterson, *Littleton Waller Tazewell* (Charlottesville, Va., 1983), 129; F. A. Porcher, "Southern and Northern Civilization Contrasted," *RM*, 1 (1857), 103; Elizabeth Perry Diary, Mar. 11, 1844 (141), in Benjamin F. Perry Papers; Tryphena Fox to Anna Rose Holder [mother], June 29, 1856, in Wilma King, ed., *A Northern Woman in the Plantation South: Letters of Tryphena Blanche Holder Fox, 1856–1876* (Columbia, S.C., 1993), 31; Nancy Bostick DeSaussure, *Old Plantation Days: Being Recollections of Southern Life before the War* (EE: 1997 [1909]), 17–18; Rebeca (sic) Latimer Felton, *Country Life in Georgia in the Days of My Youth* (New York, 1980 [1919]), 99–100; P. T., "Judicious Management of the Plantation Force," and A Planter, "On the Management of Negroes," *SA*, 10 (1837), 10 (1838), 626.

36. Aristotle as quoted by Mary P. Nichols, *Citizens and Statesmen: A Study of Aristotle's Politics* (Savage, Md., 1992), 208, n. 44, and for related matters see 21, 23, 82; also, P. A. Brunt, *Studies in Greek History and Thought* (Oxford, U.K., 1993), 367; Cicero, *De Amicitia*, trans. William Armistead Falconer (LCL), §§19.72.

37. Murray, *Letters from the United States*, 272; Fearn, *Diary of a Refugee*, 4–5; [E. J. Pringle], *Slavery in the Southern States, by a Carolinian* (Cambridge, Mass., 1852), 28; *Plantation Life: The Narratives of Mrs. Henry Schoolcraft* (New York, 1969 [1860]), 49; Merrill in Breeden, ed., *Advice among Masters*, 178–188. For slaves' manipulation of the idea of black incompetence, see Roger D. Abrahams, *Singing the Master: The Emergence of African American Culture in the Plantation South* (New York, 1992). On northern black responses, see, e.g., Edward Scott's speech in Providence, Oct. 6, 1857, in C. Peter Ripley et al., eds., *The Black Abolitionist Papers*, 5 vols. (Chapel Hill, N.C., 1985–91), 4:366.

38. John Donald Wade, *Augustus Baldwin Longstreet: A Study of the Development of Culture in the South* (New York, 1924), 49; *Farmers' Register*, 5 (1837), 32; Joseph A. S. Acklen to Ada Franklin, Aug. 20, 1863; Apr. 27, May 3, 1862, in Elizabeth R. Baer, ed., *Shadows on My Heart: The Civil War Diary of Lucy Rebecca Buck of Virginia* (Athens, Ga., 1997), 56, 59–60; Thavolia Glymph, *Out of the House of Bondage: The Transformation of the Plantation Household* (New York, 2008), 137 (Taveau). For similar accounts, see Jacob Thompson to James M. Howry,

Oct. 8, 1867, in P. W. Rainwater, "Letters to and From Jacob Thomson," *JSH*, 6 (1940), 106; and Paul Cameron in Jean Bradley Anderson, *Piedmont Plantation: The Bennehan-Cameron Family and Lands in North Carolina* (Durham, N.C., 1985), xviii, 111.

39. Anna Matilda King to Lord King, Sept. 28, 1848, in T. B. King Papers; Elise Young to W. N. Mercer, Dec. 28, 1853, in Mercer Papers; Henry Graves to Aunt Hattie, Nov. 17, 1862, in Graves Papers; Susan D. Witherspoon to Susan McDowall, May 11, 1837, in Witherspoon-McDowall Papers; Isaac Barton Ulmer to Abigail Ulmer, Apr. 14, 1859; Susan Henry to Marion Henry, Oct. 11, 1850, in Henry Papers; Edward McGehee Burrus to Kate Burrus, Jan. 1, 1864, in Lester Papers.

40. E. Grey Dimond and Herman Hattaway, eds., *Letters from Forest Place: A Plantation Family's Correspondence* (Jackson, Miss., 1993), see esp. the correspondence in chs. 6, 8; C. C. Jones to Mary Jones, May 2, 1860, in Myers, ed., *Children of Pride*, 577; Davis quoted in Eli N. Evans, *Judah P. Benjamin: The Jewish Confederate* (New York, 1988), 77; Eliza Quitman to John A. Quitman, Jan. 20, 1836.

41. Brevard Diary, Sept. 18, Oct. 10, 1860; Hardin Diary, Mar. 25, 1851, in Stuart and Family Papers; Browder Diary, Mar. 24, 1857, in Richard L. Troutman, ed., *The Heavens Are Weeping: The Diaries of George Richard Browder, 1852–1886* (Grand Rapids, Mich., 1987), 95–96. Also, Parthenia Antoinette Hague, *A Blockaded Family: Life in Southern Alabama during the Civil War* (Boston, Mass., 1888), 120; Mary Ann Cobb to John B. Lamar, Nov. 11, 1865, in Kenneth Coleman, ed., *Athens, 1861–1865* (Athens, Ga., 1969), 28.

42. Carmichael Diary, Apr. 9, 1838; Chancellor, ed., *Diaries of Henry Yates Thompson*, 104.

43. Daniel E. Sutherland, ed., *The Civil War Diary of Ellen Renshaw House* (Knoxville, Tenn., 1996), Oct. 10, 1863 (74); Louis-Philippe, King of France, *Diary of My Travels in America*, trans. Stephen Becker (New York, 1976), Apr. 5, 1797 (32); Graham quoted in Henry Ruffner, *History of Washington College* (Lexington, Va., 1893), 61.

44. Herman Roodenburg, "The 'Hand of Friendship': Shaking Hands and Other Gestures in the Dutch Republic," in Jan Bremer and Herman Roodenburg, eds., *A Cultural History of Gesture* (Ithaca, N.Y., 1991), ch. 7; Macon's speech in W. J. Peale, ed., *Lives of Distinguished North Carolinians* (Raleigh, N.C., 1898), 109; also, Robert M. Calhoon, *Evangelicals and Conservatives in the Early South, 1740–1861* (Columbia, S.C., 1988), 168; for references to Moultrie, see Glover Moore, *The Missouri Controversy, 1819–1821* (Lexington, Ky., 1966), 125, n. 149; George Tucker, *The Life of Thomas Jefferson*, 2 vols. (London, 1837), 1:336–337; Hopley, *Life in the South*, 1:112–113; A. J. L. Fremantle, *Three Months in the Southern States: The 1863 Diary of an English Soldier, April–June 1863* (London, 1863), May 4, 1863 (73–74); George S. Sawyer, *Southern Institutes* (New York, 1967 [1858]), 230; "A Fact with a Short Commentary?," *Anti-Slavery Record*, 2 (Jan. 1836), 3.

45. Allmendinger, ed., *Incidents of My Life*, 44. For ancient views of slaves' curiosity, see the "spying slaves" in Aristophanes' *Frogs* and William Fitzgerald, *Slavery and the Roman Literary Imagination* (Cambridge, UK, 2000), 105, Juvenal and Johnson, quoted at 19.

46. [A North Carolinian], *Slavery Considered on General Principles, Or, A Grapple with Abstractionists* (New York, 1861), 21; Clitherall Autobiography (ms.),

Apr. 2, 1853; McCorkle Diary, Nov. 29, 1846, Jan. 24, June 6, Aug. 8, 1847; J. H. Ingraham, *Sunny South; Or, The Southerner at Home* (New York, 1968 [1860]), 210.

47. Hutchinson Journal, Sept. 6, 1829; Ronald G. Walters, *The Antislavery Appeal: American Abolitionism after 1830* (Baltimore, 1976), ch. 5.

48. *The Life and Times, of Judge Junius Hillyer: From His Memoirs* (Tignall, Ga., 1989), 135–136; Perdue, Jr., et al., eds., *Weevils in the Wheat*, 313; Eve Carmichael's account of her father, 103, in Carmichael Papers; Hutchinson Journal, Oct. 3, 1831; Sarah Alexander to Clifford Alexander, Feb. 20, 1853, in Boggs, ed., *Alexander Letters*, 176. On the planters' preaching, see: Greenlee Diary, 1840s–1850s, esp. Dec. 31, 1848; Bethell Diary, Dec. 3, 1856; McCorkle Diary, June 26, 1846; Clitherall "Autobiography" (ms.), June 25, July 18, Aug. 1, 15, 1852; Magruder Diary, July 12, 1857; Hanson Diary, Sept. 15, 26, 1858; Mar. 30, 1860. For the low country, see Henry William Ravenel, "Recollections of Southern Plantation Life," ed. Marjorie Stratford Mendenhall, *Yale Review*, 25 (1936), 765. For accounts by ex-slaves, see *AS*: Reverend W. E. Northcross, in *Ala.*, 6 (pt. 1), 299–305, 381; Alonza Fantroy Toombs, in *Ga.*, 6 (pt. 1), 383; *Tex.*, 4 (pt. 1), 52.

49. Hill Diary, Nov. 24, 1846; also, Louisa M. Smythe, ed., *For Auld Lange Syne: Collected for My Children* (Charleston, S.C., 1900), 4; George C. Rogers, Jr., *The History of Georgetown County, South Carolina* (Columbia, S.C., 1970), 358–359; Guion Griffis Johnson, *A Social History of the Sea Islands, with Special Reference to St. Helena Island, South Carolina* (Westport, Conn., 1969), 146–148; Charles Joyner, *Down by the Riverside: A South Carolina Slave Community* (Urbana, Ill., 1984), 73; A. Middleton, "Family Record," in Alicia Hopton Middleton et al., *Life in Carolina and New England during the Nineteenth Century* (Bristol, R.I., 1929), 79; W. P. Harrison, *The Gospel among the Slaves* (Nashville, Tenn., 1893), 270; Moultrie, *ACP*, 2 (1854), 253; Cornish Diary, Jan. 8, 1845; Albert Sidney Thomas, *A Historical Account of the Protestant Episcopal Church in South Carolina, 1820–1857: Being a Continuation of Dalcho's Account, 1670–1820* (Columbia, S.C., 1957), 382 (Glennie); Joseph Blount Cheshire, *The Church in the Confederate States: A History of the Protestant Episcopal Church in the Confederate States* (New York, 1912), 121–122. For Mississippi, see Walter Brownlow Posey, *Frontier Mission: A History of Religion West of the Southern Appalachians to 1861* (Lexington, Ky., 1966), 200 (Mercer). For plantation chapels in various states, see Joe Gray Taylor, *Negro Slavery in Louisiana* (Baton Rouge, La., 1963), 149; John S. Grasty, *Memoir of Rev. Samuel B. McPheeters, D.D.* (St. Louis, Mo., 1871), 74; Caleb Perry Patterson, *The Negro in Tennessee, 1790–1865* (Austin, Tex., 1922), 124, 146; Anson West, *A History of Methodism in Alabama* (Spartanburg, S.C., 1983 [1893]), 504. On the condition of chapels, see John Michael Vlach, *Back of the Big House: The Architecture of Plantation Slavery* (Chapel Hill, N.C., 1993), 145–148; Pierce Butler, *The Unhurried Years: Memories of the Old Natchez Region* (Baton Rouge, La., 1948), 16.

50. Jones quoted in Chase C. Mooney, *Slavery in Tennessee* (Bloomington, Ind., 1957), 92; John Rogers to "My Dear Children, Sarah, Eliza, and Rosannah," Apr. 5, 1842, in Renwick Papers; Shuck quoted in J. B. Jeter, *Memoir of Mrs. Henrietta Shuck: The First American Female Missionary to China* (Boston, Mass., 1846), 193–194; Reid Private Journal, July 19, 1833, in Stephen F. Miller, *The Bench and Bar of Georgia: Memoirs and Sketches*, 2 vols. (Philadelphia, 1858), 2:217; Gavin Diary, Nov. 21, 1857; also, Agnew Journal, Dec. 31, 1856.

51. John Walker Diary, July 29, Aug. 13, 1839; May 28, Aug. 9, 1832; Mar. 25, June 24, 1833; May 3, 1834; Aug. 13, 1839; Feb. 22, 1840.

52. McTyeire, *Duties of Christian Masters*, 140, 181, 235; William Meade, *Sermons, Dialogues and Narratives for Servants, to Be read to Them in Families* (Richmond, Va., 1831), 75; Elisabeth Muhlenfeld, *Mary Boykin Chesnut: A Biography* (Baton Rouge, La., 1981), 52; Moragné, June 13, 1839; Sept. 21, 1841, in Delle Mullen Craven, ed., *The Neglected Thread: A Journal of the Calhoun Community* (Columbia, S.C., 1951), 135–136, 212–213.

53. Ravenel, *Eliza Pinckney*, 118; Davis Diary and Meditations, June 28, 1840; McCorkle Diary, June 14, Nov. 22, 1846; Oct. 10, 1847; C. Richard King, ed., *Victorian Lady on the Texas Frontier: The Journal of Ann Raney Coleman* (London, 1972), 102–103; Hutchinson Journal, Nov. 12, 26, 1826; Glymph, *Out of the House of Bondage*, 37; *Slave Life in Georgia: A Narrative of the Life, Sufferings, and Escape of John Brown, a Fugitive Slave* (Savannah, Ga., 1972 [1855]), 167–168.

54. Edmondson Diary, Dec. 12, 1860; Feb. 26, 1864; Biographical Sketch in Tucker Papers.

55. Town Diary, Mar. 27, 1853; Magruder Diary, Apr. 11, 1846; Mar. 3, 1856; Bethell Diary, Dec. 3, 1856; Dec. 9, 1857; Greenlee Diary, Dec. 31, 1848; May 11, 1856; Dec. 3, 1863 (fast); E. G. Baker Diary, Dec. 30, 1855; Aug. 8, 1858; Sept. 4, 1859.

56. Herriot, quoted in George C. Rogers, Jr., *The History of Georgetown County, South Carolina* (Columbia, S.C., 1970), 375; *Life of William Grimes, the Runaway Slave. Written by Himself* (New York, 1825), 7–8, quote at 8; see also John Benwell, *An Englishman's Travels in America: His Observations of Life in the Free and Slave States* (London, 1857), 193–194; Ophelia Settle Egypt et al., eds., *Unwritten History of Slavery: Autobiographical Accounts of Negro Slaves* (Washington, D.C., 1968), 134.

57. [Edgar Allan Poe], "Critical Notices," *SLM*, 2 (1836), 337–339; [John Reuben Thompson], "Notices of New Works," *SLM*, 14 (1848), 62–63; Mrs. G. P. Coleman, ed., *Virginia Silhouettes: Contemporary Letters Concerning Negro Slavery in the State of Virginia* (Richmond, Va., 1934), 57–58. An old family slave, entering the room of his deceased master, sobbed that he had lost his best friend: Mrs. Y. B. Stewart to H. C. Nixon, n. d., probably 1912 or 1913, in Nixon Collection.

58. Cocke quoted in Carly Johnston, *Stewards of History: The Covenant of Generations in a Southern Family* (Internet ed., 1999), 72; JHTW, 4:433.

59. Hammond Diary, Nov. 2, 1841, in Bleser, ed., *Secret and Sacred*, 78; Egypt et al., eds., *Unwritten History of Slavery*, 3; Michel Mollat, *The Poor in the Middle Ages: An Essay in Social History*, trans. Arthur Goldhammer (New Haven, Conn., 1986), 263–264.

60. John Palfrey to Edward Palfrey, Sept. 8, 1816; Mita Lenoir to Julia Pickens, Dec. 14, 1829, in Cashin, ed., *Our Common Affairs*, 180; Forman Diary, Feb. 16, 1820; May 12, 1841, in W. Emerson Wilson, ed., *Plantation Life at Rose Hill: The Diaries of Martha Ogle Forman, 1814–1845* (Wilmington, Del., 1976), 97–98, 421–422; John C. Inscoe, *Mountain Masters: Slavery, and the Sectional Crisis in Western North Carolina* (Knoxville, Tenn., 1989), 94, 96 (Swain); also, Thomas Jackson Arnold, *Early Life and Letters of General Thomas J. ("Stonewall") Jackson* (Richmond, Va., 1957 [1916]), 162.

61. In Myers, ed., *Children of Pride*, see 763: C. C. Jones to Mary S. Mallard, March 16, 1861; Eliza G. Roberts to C. C. and Mary Jones, May 20, 1861; Eliza G.

Roberts to Mary Jones, May 31, 1861; C. C. Jones, Jr., to C. C. Jones, Oct. 7, 1861.

62. Rachel O'Connor to Mary Moore, Jan. 23, 1826; Nov. 28, 1840, in A. B. W. Webb, ed., *Mistress of Evergreen Plantation: Rachel O'Connor's Legacy of Letters, 1823–1845* (Albany, N.Y., 1983), 13, 228; Avery O. Craven, *Rachel of Old Louisiana* (Baton Rouge, La., 1975), 20, 28, 31, 34–35, 60, 79, 81; Maria Harford Bryan to Julia Ann Bryan Cumming, Apr. 15, 1833 (cow); April 15, 1837 (Patty); Jan. 12, Oct. 20, 1839, in Carol Bleser, ed., *Tokens of Affection: The Letters of a Planter's Daughter in the Old South* (Athens, Ga., 1996), 150–151, 193, 231, 270.

63. David Gavin Diary, Sept. 13, 1856.

64. Leak Diaries, 1848–52; Bond Diary, Feb. 25, 1860, in Kimberly Harrison, ed., *A Maryland Bride in the Deep South: The Civil War Diary of Priscilla Bond* (Baton Rouge, La., 2006), 145; Malinda B. Ray Diary, June 10, 1861; Leland and Hentz in Stephen Stowe, "Christian Faith and Mortal Crisis." Franklin L. Riley, ed., "Diary of a Mississippi Planter," in *Publications of the Mississippi Historical Society*, 10 (1909): Sept. 23, 1840 (334); July 10, 1853 (444); Sept. 23, 1855 (450); Apr. 3, 1859 (462); Aug. 8, 1860 (469).

65. G. deB. Hooper to Caroline M. Hooper, May 13, 1853; David Campbell Private Journal, July 7, 28, 1843; Greenlee Diary, April 14, 1850; Oct. 23, 1854.

66. Judith Page Rives to Alfred L. Rives, Dec. 5, 1856; Clitherall Autobiography (ms.), Dec. 19, 1852; Aug. 20, 1856; also, Hume Diary, May 24, 1860; Elizabeth W. Allston Pringle, *Chronicles of Chicora Wood* (New York, 1976), 64–65.

67. Troutman, ed., *Heavens are Weeping*, Feb. 16, 1853 (62); Apr. 10, 1854 (77).

68. Ruth Ketring Nuermberger, *The Clays of Alabama: A Planter-Lawyer-Politician Family* (Lexington, Ky., 1958), 15; Elizabeth Silverthorne, *Plantation Life in Texas* (College Station, Tex., 1986), 49; also, R. R. Barrow Residence Journal, April 21, 1858; James W. Mellon to A. C. Britton, Feb. 11, 1863, in Britton Family Papers; Agnew Diary, Oct. 8, 25, 1860; Dec. 22, 23, 1862.

69. W. C. Harrison to William H. Taylor, Jan. 18, 1853, in Dromgoole and Robinson Papers; Manigault Plantation Book, 1854; Rachel Weeks O'Connor to Mary Weeks, Jan. 23, 1826; *Anderson*, ed. Brokenburn, 87; *Linton Stephens* to R. M. Johnson, Sept. 3, 1858, in Waddell, ed., Linton Stephens, 155; also, John Palfrey to William Palfrey, May 30, 1832. Also, Orville W. Taylor, *Negro Slavery in Arkansas* (Durham, N.C., 1958), 152.

70. Taylor Diary, notes for 1794–96; Bills Diary, Dec. 16, 1857; May 26, 1862; Hutchinson Journal, Nov. 25, 1826; R. L. Dabney, *Life and Campaigns of Lt. Gen T. J. (Stonewall) Jackson* (Harrisonburg, Va., 1983 [1865]), 95; James M. Clifton, ed., *Life and Labor on Argyle Island: Letters and Documents of a Savannah River Rice Plantation, 1833–1867* (Savannah, Ga., 1978), 59, 115, 149.

71. Washington Wills to Master Richard, Oct. 30, 1864, in Wills Papers.

72. In Myers, ed., *Children of Pride*: Eliza G. Roberts to Mary Jones, Nov. 10, 1856 (263), C. C. Jones, Jr., to Mary Jones, Nov. 22, 1856 (266). Valentine Diaries, Feb. 8, 1850; Barrow Diary, Oct. 7, 1837 (100); Jan. 15, 1843 (280), in Davis, ed., *Plantation Life in the Florida Parishes*.

73. Randall M. Miller, ed., *"Dear Master": Letters of a Slave Family* (Ithaca, N.Y., 1978), 220; W. H. Holcombe Diary, April 13, 1855; for Holcombe, see Elizabeth Fox-Genovese and Eugene D. Genovese, *Slavery in White and Black: Class and Race in the Southern Slaveholders' New World Order* (New York, 2008), 142–143, 221–222.

74. James E. Matthews to Hannah W. Campbell, July 21, 1858; Elizabeth Early to Virginia Brown, undated, 1847–50, in Cashin, ed., *Our Common Affairs*, 185. In T. B. King Papers see: Anna Matilda King Plantation record, Jan. 27, 1857, Anna Matilda King to Floyd King, Sept. 5, 1858, and record of deaths, 1856.

75. W. H. Robbins to J. H. Thornwell, Nov. 1, 1842, in Anderson-Thornwell Papers; Bethell Diary, Jan. 1845, June 6, 1860; E. G. Baker Journal, July 1, 1854, also July 2, 1860; Waldon N. Edwards to Thomas Ruffin, July 26, 1859, in TRP, 3:40; Eron Rowland, *Varina Howells: Wife of Jefferson Davis* (New York, 1927), 274–275; Antonia Quitman to John A. Quitman, Sept. 14, 1855; also, Edmund Ruffin, Jr., Plantation Diary, March 6, 1857; M. Roach Diary, May, 19, 1853, in Roach-Eggleston Papers; Webb Diary, ms. pp. 130, 227.

76. Olmsted, *Seaboard Slave States*, 407; *Planters' Banner*, 14 (July 19, 1849).

77. Charles Pettigrew, *Last Advice of the Rev. Charles Pettigrew to His Sons, 1797* (EE: 2001 [1797]), 8, 10–11; "Biography of James Patton," (EE: 1996), 25; Dusinberre, *Them Dark Days*, 210; *Select Letters of St. Jerome*, trans. F. A. Wright (LCL), Letter 42 (209), and see Malachi 1:6.

78. D. W. Mitchell, *Ten Years in the United States: Being an Englishman's Views of Men and Things in the North and South* (London, 1862), 93; *The Golden Ass of Apuleius*, trans. Robert Graves (New York, 1954), ch. 2; Samuel Johnson quoted in Stuart Gerry Brown, "Dr. Johnson and the Old Order," *Marxist Quarterly*, #1 (1937), 286; Trescot quoted by Chesnut, Mar. 26, 1861, in Woodward, ed., *Mary Chesnut's Civil War*, 36.

79. Henry Bibb to Albert G. Sibley, Oct. 7, 1852, in John W. Blassingame, ed., *Slave Testimony: Two Centuries of Letters, Speeches, Interviews, and Autobiographies* (Baton Rouge, La., 1977), 52.

80. Alan Gallay, *Jonathan Bryan and the Southern Colonial Frontier* (Athens, Ga., 2007), 393 (Bolzius); Flyer, Dec. 19, 1839, in Preston Papers.

81. Elizabeth Preston Allan, *The Life and Letters of Margaret Junkin Preston* (Boston, Mass., 1923), 42–43; Charles Colcock Jones, *Suggestions on the Religious Instruction of the Negroes in the Southern States* (Philadelphia, 1847), 13; Friedrich Nietzsche, "Beyond Good and Evil," *The Philosophy of Nietzsche* (New York: Modern Library ed.), 472; Albert Memmi, *Dominated Man: Notes Toward a Portrait* (New York, 1968), 5.

82. William Alexander MacCorkle, *The White Sulphur Springs* (New York, 1916), 110; Edward J. Thomas, *Memoirs of a Southerner* (EE: 1997 [1923]), 8, 29; Seabrook, *Before and After*, 69; Howard Melanchthon Hamill, *The Old South: A Monograph* (EE: 1998 [1904]), 38; Wise, *End of an Era*, 222. For a particularly starry-eyed account of master-slave relations from an end-of-century perspective, see Mary Polk Branch, *Memoirs of a Southern Woman "Within the Lines" and a Genealogical Record* (EE: 1998 [1901]).

5. The Blacks' Best and Most Faithful Friend

1. "First Annual Message to the State Legislature of Georgia" (1824), in Edward J. Hardin, *The Life of George M. Troup* (Savannah, Ga., 1859), 242.

2. Articles in southern agricultural journals circulated well beyond the small number of subscribers; see John Majewski, *Modernizing a Slave Economy: The Economic Vision of the Confederate Nation* (Chapel Hill, N.C., 2009), 56.

3. Tryphena Fox to Anna Rose Holder, June 29, 1856; Nov. 1, 1857, in Wilma King, ed., *A Northern Woman in the Plantation South: Letters of Tryphena Blanche*

Holder Fox, 1856–1876 (Columbia, S.C., 1993), 31, 65; Adelaide Stuart Dimitry, *War-Time Sketches, Historical and Otherwise* (EE: 1998 [1911]), 90–91; Marli F. Weiner, ed., *Heritage of Woe: The Civil War Diary of Grace Brown Elmore, 1861–1868* (Athens, Ga., 1997), March 24, 30, 1865 (107, quotes at 121–123); Letitia A. Burwell, *A Girl's Life in Virginia before the War*, 2nd ed. (New York, 1895), 208; Amy Dru Stanley, *From Bondage to Contract: Wage Labor, Marriage, and the Market in the Age of Slave Emancipation* (New York, 1998), 42.

4. In Richard C. Lounsbury, ed., *Louisa S. McCord: Poems, Drama, Biography, Letters* (Charlottesville, Va., 1996), see McCord to Henry Charles Carey, Jan. 18, 1854 (297), McCord to Langdon Cheves, Jr., Apr. 13, 1856 (324); Lounsbury, ed., *Louisa S. McCord: Political and Social Essays* (Charlottesville, Va., 1995), 182–184, 240, 323, 358–360, 453.

5. *Remarks on the Subject of the Ownership of Slaves, Delivered by R. R. Collier of Petersburg, in the Senate of Virginia* (EE: 2000 [1863]), 3, 5; M. M. Henkle, *The Life of Henry Bidleman Bascom* (Nashville, Tenn., 1857), quote at 219.

6. E. G., "Slavery in the Southern States," *SQR*, 8 (1845), 352, 355–356; *JCCP*, 25:65; Solon Robinson, "Negro Slavery at the South," *DBR*, 7 (1849), 206–225; William C. Buck, *The Slavery Question* (Louisville, Ky., 1849), 16; T. W. Hoit, *The Right of American Slavery* (St. Louis, Mo., 1860), 38; William H. Holcombe, *The Alternative: A Separate Nationality or the Africanization of the South* (New Orleans, La., 1860), 4, 5–6; George P. Elliott, *An Oration, Delivered before the Artillery Company at Beaufort, South Carolina* (Charleston, S.C., 1852), 11; [David J. McCord], "Africans at Home," *SQR*, 10 (1854), 70–96.

7. Nov. 16, 1855, in Anderson Papers; Whitemarsh B. Seabrook, "Causes of the General Unsuccessfulness of the Sea-Island Planters," *SA*, 7 (1834), 178; Samuel Cartwright, "Slavery in the Light of Ethnology," in E. N. Elliott, ed., *King Cotton Is King and Pro-Slavery Arguments* (New York, 1969 [1860]), 690–728; Cartwright, *Essays... in a Series of Letters to the Rev. William Winans* (Vidalia, Miss., 1843), 18–23; for Cartwright: Steven Stowe, *Doctoring the South: Southern Physicians and Everyday Medicine in the Mid-Nineteenth Century* (Chapel Hill, N.C., 2004), 215–218; Reginald Horsman, *Josiah Nott: Southerner, Physician, and Racial Theorist* (Baton Rouge, La., 1987), 158.

8. J. S. Wilson, "The Negro – His Diet, Clothing, Etc.," n. s. 3 (1859), 197; also, Tattler, "Management of Negroes," *SC*, 8 (1850); *Transactions of the Medical Society of the State of North Carolina*, May 1851 (Raleigh, N.C., 1852), 6; M. W. Philips, "Plantation Economy," *SCTA*, Aug. 13, 1846; Citizen of Mississippi, "The Negro," *DBR*, 3 (1847), 419–420; *Plantation Life: The Narratives of Mrs. Henry Schoolcraft* (New York, 1969 [1860]), 49; Merrill in James O. Breeden, ed., *Advice among Masters: The Ideal in Slave Management in the Old South* (Westport, Conn., 1980), 178–189; "Management of Slaves," *SCTA* (Oct. 1, 1846). Also: John S. Haller, Jr., "The Negro and the Southern Physician: A Study of Medical and Racial Attitudes, 1800–1860," *Medical History*, 16 (1972), 238–253. For slaves' manipulation of the idea of black incompetence, see Roger D. Abrahams, *Singing the Master: The Emergence of African American Culture in the Plantation South* (New York, 1992).

9. Ray Holder, *William Winans: Methodist Leader in Antebellum Mississippi* (Jackson, Miss., 1977), 150–151; Samuel Galloway, *Ergonomy; or, Industrial Science* (Princeton, N.J., and Athens, Ga., 1853), 201–202; A. J. McElveen to Z. B. Oakes, Aug. 10, 1853, in Edmund L. Drago, ed., *Broke by the War: Letters of a Slave Trader* (Columbia, S.C., 1991), 48.

10. Thomas Roderick Dew, *Digest of the Laws, Customs, Manners, and Institutions of the Ancient and Modern Nations* (New York, 1884 [1852]), 36–37; Stephen B. Mansfield, "Thomas Roderick Dew: Defender of the Faith" (Ph.D. diss., University of Virginia, 1968), 63–64; Waddy Thompson, *Recollections of Mexico* (New York, 1847), 239. In Aylett Family Papers, 1851–54: W. R. Aylett, speeches on "Our Pacific Possessions," "American Progress," "Liberty, Patriotism, and Virtue."

11. John S. Brisbane, "An Address Delivered before the St. Andrew's Ashley and Stono River Agricultural Association," *SA*, 4 (1844), 253–254; William A. Booth, "Reports from Louisiana," in E. D. Fenner, *Southern Medical Reports*, 2 vols. (New Orleans, 1850), 1:215; H. S. King, "An Address Delivered before the Agriculture Society of St. Paul's," *SA*, 6 (1846), 305–306; John S. Wilson, "The Negro – His Peculiarities as to Disease," *ACP*, n. 2, 3 (1859), 228–229; Willie Lee Rose, *Rehearsal for Reconstruction: The Port Royal Experiment* (New York, 1964), 96; James M. McPherson, *The Negro's Civil War: How American Blacks Felt and Acted in the War for the Union* (New York, 2003), 57–58.

12. Ariela J. Gross, *Double Character: Slavery and Mastery in the Antebellum Southern Courtroom* (Princeton, N.J., 2000), 5; Charles Manigault to Louis Manigault, Dec. 28, 1850, in James M. Clifton, ed., *Life and Labor on Argyle Island: Letters and Documents of a Savannah River Rice Plantation, 1833–1867* (Savannah, Ga., 1978), 267; C. C. Jones, Jr., to C. C. Jones, June 20, 1854, in Robert Manson Myers, ed., *The Children of Pride: A True Story of the Children of the Civil War* (New Haven, Conn., 1972), 48; "Slavery," *Southern Literary Journal*, 1 (1855), 189–192; Eliza Frances Andrews, *War-Time Journal of a Georgia Girl* (New York, 1907), 340; Amelia E. H. Barr, *All the Days of My Life: An Autobiography. The Red Leaves of a Human Heart* (New York, 1980 [1913]), 214.

13. Will of John Cooper, 1791, in Helen Tunnicliff Catterall, ed., *Judicial Cases Concerning Slavery and the Negro*, 4 vols. (Washington, D.C., 1919–37), 1:109; Rufus William Bailey, *The Issue: Presented in a Series of Letters on Slavery* (New York, 1837), 8–9; Magruder Diary, April 9, 1846; Hammond quoted in Introduction to Carol Bleser, *Secret and Sacred: The Diaries of James Henry Hammond, a Southern Slaveholder* (New York, 1988), 19; Barbara Leigh Smith Bodichon, *An American Diary, 1857–8*, ed. Joseph W. Reed, Jr. (London, 1972), Feb. 13, 1858 (102); Richard B. P. Lyons to Earl Russell, Dec. 18, 1860, in James J. Barnes and Patience P. Barnes, eds., *The American Civil War through British Eyes: Dispatches from British Diplomats*, 3 vols. (Kent, Oh., 2005), 1:12–13.

14. Edward T. Tayloe to B. O. Tayloe, Aug. 17, 1832; "The Negro. By a Citizen of Mississippi," *DBR*, 3 (May 1847), 420; for Dowler, see Stowe, *Doctoring the South*, 239–240. For similar views from Texas, see *Randolph B. Campbell, An Empire for Slavery: The Peculiar Institution in Texas, 1821–1865* (Baton Rouge, La., 1989), 212; *Letters of Nathaniel Macon to Charles O'Conor* (Montgomery, Ala., 1860), 1–3. In C. Peter Ripley et al., eds., *The Black Abolitionist Papers*, 5 vols. (Chapel Hill, N.C., 1985–91), see, e. g., Peter Gallego to Thomas Rolph, Nov. 1, 1841 (2:87–94); "Report on the Committee on Emigration of the Amherstburg Convention, Jan. 17, 1853 (2:270–271); James McCune Smith to Horace Greeley, Jan. 29, 1844 (3:430–441). See also Peter Randolph, *Sketches of Slave Life: Or, Illustrations of the "Peculiar Institution"* (EE: 2000 [1855]), 13.

15. "The Human Family," *SQR*, 11 (1855), 155–157; [J. L. Wilson], "Revival of the Slave Trade," *SPR*, 12 (1859), 510–512; also, [J. L. Wilson], "The People and Languages of Western Africa," *SPR*, 15 (1863), 349–371; "J. M. W." [Laurens

Hill, Ga.], "Labourers for the South," *ACP*, n. s. 3 (1859), 12; Marinda Branson Moore, *Geographic Reader for the Dixie Children* (EE: 1999 [1863]), 10; see also George A. Baxter, *An Essay on the Abolition of Slavery* (Richmond, Va., 1836), 17; E. J. Stearns, *Notes on Uncle Tom's Cabin: Being a Logical Answer to Its Allegations and Inferences Against Slavery as an Institution* (Philadelphia, 1853), 22–23; *SQR*, 13 (1848), 246–248; Christopher Luse, "The Offspring of Infidelity: Polygenesis and the Defense of Slavery" (Ph.D. diss., Emory University, 2008).

16. Berkeley quoted in H. Shelton Smith, *In His Image... But: Racism in Southern Religion* (Durham, N.C., 1972), 11, also 19, 157–161; H. Shelton Smith, *Changing Conceptions of Original Sin: A Study in American Theology since 1750* (New York, 1955), 35; Frederick Dalcho, *An Historical Account of the Protestant Episcopal Church in South Carolina* (Charleston, S.C., 1970 [1820]), 48–49; Frederick Law Olmsted, *A Journey in the Back Country* (New York, 1970 [1860]), 385; Douglas Ambrose, *Henry Hughes and Proslavery Thought in the Old South* (Baton Rouge, La., 1996), ch. 5, esp. 166–167; John Fletcher, *Studies on Slavery, in Easy Lessons* (Natchez, Miss., 1852), 208–210; T. C. Thornton, *An Inquiry into the History of Slavery* (Washington, D.C., 1841), 145–147; James Warley Miles, *Philosophic Theology: Or, Ultimate Grounds of All Religious Belief Based on Reason* (Charleston, S.C., 1849), 230–231; on Jeter see Eugene D. Genovese, *A Consuming Fire: The Fall of the Confederacy in the Mind of the White Christian South* (Athens, Ga., 1998), 93. On the spread of scientific racism, see Luse, "Offspring of Infidelity," and the literature cited therein. On miscegenation-as-sin, see Claude H. Nolen, *The Negro's Image in the South: The Anatomy of White Supremacy* (Lexington, Ky., 1968), ch. 3; also, Leander Ker, *Slavery Consistent with Christianity*, 3rd ed. (Weston, Mo., 1853), 9–16, 27–30.

17. In *Christian Examiner and Religious Miscellany*, 37 (1844), see the letters of W. B. Carpenter (139–144, esp. 141) and S. H. Dickson (427–432); also, Dickson, "Slavery in the French Colonies," *SLM*, 10 (1844), 268–275; Jean H. Baker, *Affairs of Party: The Political Culture of Northern Democrats in the Mid-Nineteenth Century* (Ithaca, N.Y., 1983), chs. 5–6; Lorman Ratner, *Powder Keg: Northern Opposition to the Antislavery Movement, 1831–1840* (New York, 1968), ch. 4; Richard B. P. Lyons to Earl Russell, Feb. 4, 1861, in Barnes and Barnes, eds., *American Civil War through British Eyes*, 1:27; Stephen Douglas, Aug. 21, 1858, in Harold Holzer, ed., *The Lincoln-Douglas Debates: The First Complete, Unexpurgated Text* (New York, 1994), 55.

18. Louis B. Wright, ed., *The Prose Works of William Byrd of Westover* (Cambridge, Mass., 1966), 221; Tipton R. Snavely, *George Tucker as a Political Economist* (Charlottesville, Va., 1964), 119; Robert C. McLean, *George Tucker: Moral Philosopher and Man of Letters* (Chapel Hill, N.C., 1961), 4, 186; Introduction to Robert L. Brunhouse, ed., "David Ramsay, 1794–1815: Selections from His Writings," *Transactions of the American Philosophical Society*, n. s., 55, pt. 4 (1965), 35; Fredrika Bremer, *Homes of the New World: Impressions of America*, 2 vols. (New York, 1853), 1:291–292 (Poinsett); James L. Crouthamel, "Tocqueville's South," *Journal of the Early Republic*, 2 (1982), 386–387.

19. William T. Hamilton, *"Friend of Moses," Or, A Defence of the Pentateuch as the Production of Moses and an Inspired Document against the Objections of Modern Skepticism* (New York, 1852), esp. xvii, 470–471; Horsman, *Josiah Nott*, 121–122; Matthew Estes to J. C. Calhoun, Aug. 30, 1845, in *JCCP*, 22:98–100; Matthew Estes, *A Defence of Negro Slavery, as It Exists in the United States*

(Montgomery, Ala., 1846); Fletcher, *Studies on Slavery*, 504–505; [E. J. Pringle], *Slavery in the Southern States, by a Carolinian* (Cambridge, Mass., 1852), 38–39, 43; William J. Grayson, *The Hireling and the Slave, Chicora, and Other Poems* (Charleston, S.C., 1856), 168; Tamara Miner Haygood, *Henry William Ravenel, 1814–1887: South Carolina Scientist in the Civil War Era* (Tuscaloosa, Ala., 1987), 98; *Complete Works of the Reverend Thomas Smyth, D. D.*, ed. J. William Flinn, 10 vols. (Columbia, S.C., 1908), 7:27–28, 149, and "Unity of the Human Races," 8:359–360; Calvin H. Wiley, "A Practical Treatise: On the Duties of Christians Owning Slaves," ch. 1: #3–4 (ms.), ch. 2: quote at 32–33.

20. Henry Pattillo, *The Plain Planter's Family Assistant; Containing an Address to Husbands and Wives, Children, and Servants* (Washington, N.C., 1787), 23; Brunhouse, ed., "David Ramsay: Selections from His Writings," 123; John Finch, *Travels in the United States of America and Canada* (London, 1833), 227–228; George Shortridge, "Mr. Jefferson – The Declaration of Independence and Freedom," *DBR*, 26 (1859), 551; Stephen Meats and Edwin T. Arnold, eds., *The Writings of Benjamin F. Perry*, 3 vols. (Spartanburg, S.C., 1980), 1:368; Fletcher, *Studies on Slavery*, "Speech, Dec. 11, 1850" (420).

21. Edmund Burke, *Conciliation with the Colonies*, ed. Cornelius Beach Bradley (Boston, 1894), 31; John Drayton, *A View of South Carolina, as Respects Her Natural and Civil Concerns* (Charleston, S.C., 1802), 145, 148; "Speech on the Oregon Bill," July 12, 1848, in *JDP*, 3:364; "A Model Southern Plantation," *SC*, 10 (1852), 88.

22. *Southern Review*, 1 (1828), 223–224; Whitemarsh B. Seabrook, *A Concise View of the Critical Situation and Future Prospects of the Slave-Holding States in Relation to Their Colored Population*, 2nd ed. (Charleston, S.C., 1825), 9. For voluntary enslavement of free blacks, see Ulrich B. Phillips, ed., *Plantation and Frontier, 1649–1863*, 2 vols. (New York, 1969 [1910]), 2:161–164; "Slave Life Preferred by Negroes," *DBR*, 28 (April 1860), 481; Charles Sydnor, "The Free Negro in Mississippi before the Civil War," *American Historical Review*, 32 (1927), 769–788; Campbell, *Empire for Slavery*, 113; Marina Wikramanayake, *A World in Shadow: The Free Black in Antebellum South Carolina* (Columbia, S.C., 1973), 172, 183–184; James Benson Sellers, *Slavery in Alabama* (University, Ala., 1964), 171; Chase C. Mooney found no petitions for enslavement: *Slavery in Tennessee* (Bloomington, Ind., 1957), 208, n. 77. On reaction to Nat Turner, see Daniel W. Crofts, *Old Southampton: Politics and Society in a Virginia County, 1834–1869* (Charlottesville, Va., 1992), 17; Patrick Breen, "Nat Turner's Revolt: Rebellion and Response in Southampton, Virginia" (Ph.D. diss., University of Georgia, 2005).

23. *DBR*, 4 (1847), 291, 14 (1853), 90; "A Severe, but Just Rebuke," *Natchez Semi-Weekly Courier*, Jan. 26, 1849; Carl David Arfwedson, *The United States and Canada in 1832, 1833, and 1834*, 2 vols. (London, 1834), 1:337; *Plantation Life: Schoolcraft Narratives*, 253–255, 509–510, and Appendix; William Lyon Mackenzie, *Sketches of Canada and the United States* (London, 1833), 19, 24; Joseph Sturge, *A Visit to the United States in 1841* (New York, 1969 [1842]), 51, 70–71; Clyde N. Wilson, *Carolina Cavalier: The Life and Mind of James Johnston Pettigrew* (Athens, Ga., 1990), 110–111.

24. For the quotations, see Kenneth S. Greenberg, *Masters and Statesmen: The Political Culture of American Slavery* (Baltimore, 1985), 9; J. P. C. to *SCTA*, Nov. 28, 1844; N. B. Tucker, "An Essay on the Moral and Political Effect of the Relation between the Caucasian Master and the African Slave," *SLM*, 10 (1844), 338–339; William

C. Buck, *The Slavery Question* (Louisville, Ky., 1849), 14; Nimrod Farrow to J. C. Calhoun, Jan. 7, 1823, in *JCCP*, 7:410; Harrison Berry, *Slavery and Abolition, as Viewed by a Georgia Slave* (EE: 2000 [1861]), 22; Hermann Bokum, *The Testimony of a Refugee from East Tennessee* (EE: 1998 [1863]), 21.

25. Margaret Johnson Erwin to Caroline Wilson, June 5, 1859, in John Seymour Erwin, *Like Some Green Laurel: Letters of Margaret Johnson Erwin, 1821–1863* (Baton Rouge, La., 1981), 97–98; William S. Forrest, *Historical and Descriptive Sketches of Norfolk and Vicinity* (Philadelphia, 1853), 418; J. S. Buckingham, *The Slave States of America* (New York, 1968 [1842]), 1:571; William Chambers, *Things As They Are in America* (London, 1854), 355; Mrs. [E. M.] Houstoun, *Texas and the Gulf of Mexico; or, Yachting in the Gulf of Mexico* (Austin, Tex., 1968 [1845]), 164; Lillian Foster, *Way-side Glimpses, North and South* (New York, 1860), 172; Ker, *Slavery Consistent with Christianity*, 32; Susan Dabney Smedes, *Memorials of a Southern Planter*, ed. Fletcher M. Green (New York, 1965 [1887]), 89–90; Burwell, *Girl's Life in Virginia*, 12; C. C. Jones, *The Religious Instruction of the Negroes in the United States* (Savannah, Ga., 1842), 110–111.

26. Garnett Andrews, "Address, 1851," in Southern Central Agricultural Society, *Transactions, 1850–1851*, 96; [James Warley Miles], *The Relation between the Races at the South* (Charleston, S.C., 1861), 7–9; George S. Sawyer, *Southern Institutes* (New York, 1967 [1858]), quote at 197; Belle Boyd, *In Camp and Prison*, 2 vols. (EE: 1998 [1865]), 1:45.

27. Anne K. Thomason, "The Future Vision of a 'Raceless' World: James Forten and the Tragedy of American Reform, 1766–1842" (B.A. honors thesis, Macalister University, 1993), 114; David E. Swift, *Black Prophets of Justice: Activist Clergy before the Civil War* (Baton Rouge, La., 1989); L. Minor Blackford, *Mine Eyes Have Seen the Glory: The Story of a Virginia Lady, Mary Berkeley Minor Blackford, 1802–1896, Who Taught Her Sons to Hate Slavery and to Love the Union* (Cambridge, Mass., 1954), 108–110; *Memoirs of Raphael Semmes: Service Afloat During the War Between the States* (Baltimore, 1869), 558; also, John M. Taylor, *Semmes: Rebel Raider* (Washington, D.C., 2004), 107; Daniel Lee in *SC*, 12 (1854), 117–118, and 15 (1857), 42–45; "Could They Take Care of Themselves?" *Anti-Slavery Record*, 2 (Aug. 1836), 1–3; for a proslavery retort, see "J" [J. D. F. Jamison], "The National Anniversary," *SQR*, n. s., 2 (1850), 183.

28. William Cheek and Aimee Lee Cheek, *John Mercer Langston and the Fight for Black Freedom, 1829–65* (Urbana, Ill., 1989), 37; *ERD*, Feb. 15, 1857 (1:35); E. B. Washburne, *Sketch of Edward Coles, Second Governor of Illinois, and the Slavery Struggle of 1823–1824* (Chicago, 1882), 49–52; George Cary Eggleston, *A Rebel's Recollections* (Baton Rouge, La., 1996 [1871]), 8.

29. Baxter, *Abolition of Slavery*, 6–7; John G. Jones, *A Complete History of Methodism as Connected with the Mississippi Conference of the Methodist Episcopal Church, South*, 2 vols. (Nashville, 1908), 1:106; G. W. Featherstonhaugh, *Excursion through the Slave States* (New York, 1968 [1844]), 38 (on Madison); Peyton Harrison Hoge, *Moses Drury Hoge: Life and Letters* (Richmond, Va., 1899), 136; Henry Alexander White, *Southern Presbyterian Leaders* (New York, 1911), 401–402, 430; Maria Edgeworth to Rachel Mordecai Lazarus, Apr. 15, 1836, in Edgar E. MacDonald, ed., *The Education of the Heart: The Correspondence of Rachel Mordecai Lazarus and Maria Edgeworth* (Chapel Hill, N.C., 1977), 279; Edna Greene Medford, "Beyond Mount Vernon: George Washington's Emancipated Laborers and Their Descendants," in Philip J. Schwarz, ed., *Slavery at the Home of*

George Washington (Mount Vernon, Va., 20001), 137–157, Curtis quoted at 137. Medford says that little is known about Washington's ex-slaves who remained in Fairfax County. According to Jean B. Lee, Washington freed his slaves because he did not know what to do with them and had grave doubts about their future: Lee, "Mount Vernon Plantation: A Model for the Republic," in Schwarz, ed., loc. cit., 38. On blacks settled in the North, see Philip J. Schwarz, *Migrants against Slavery* (Charlottesville, Va., 2001).

30. In William H. Holcombe Papers, see "Autobiography," 32; Diary, April 19, May 13, 1855; Diary Notes, dated Jan. 29, 1855 (quoted), but obviously written in 1861 or later. W. H. Holcombe, "The Alternative," *SLM*, 32 (1861), 83–84, quote at 83.

31. Donald G. Mathews, *Religion in the Old South* (Chicago, 1977), 138–139 (Capers); Robert E. Corlew, "Some Aspects of Slavery in Dickson County," *Tennessee Historical Quarterly*, 10 (1951), 224–248, 344–365, esp. 349; John R. McKivigan, "Douglass-Smith Friendship," in Eric J. Sundquist, ed., *Frederick Douglass: New Literary and Historical Essays* (New York 1990), 211; Richard Fuller and Francis Wayland, *Domestic Slavery, Considered as a Scriptural Institution in Correspondence*, 5th ed. (New York, 1847), 158, n; Richard Fuller, *Our Duty to the African Race* (Baltimore, 1851), 4–5; B. W. McDonnold, *History of the Cumberland Presbyterian Church* (Nashville, Tenn., 1899), 412 (McLean); for Thom, see Catherine Thom Bartlett, ed., *"My Dear Brother": A Confederate Chronicle* (Richmond, Va., 1952), 24–25; for the Tennesseans, see David T. Bailey, *Shadow on the Church: Southwestern Evangelical Religion and the Issue of Slavery, 1783–1860* (Ithaca, N.Y., 1985), 138; Caleb Perry Patterson, *The Negro in Tennessee, 1790–1865* (Austin, Tex., 1922), 132–133; "Letter to Hon. John Forsythe," in Sebastian G. Messmer, ed., *The Works of the Right Rev. John England, First Bishop of Charleston*, 7 vols. (Cleveland, Oh., 1908), 3:118; Edward L. Tucker, *Richard Henry Wilde: His Life and Selected Poems* (Athens, Ga., 1996), 75. For comment on Gerrit Smith's emancipation, see *State Gazette* (Austin, Tex.), Sept. 5, 12, 1857.

32. [M. R. H. Garnett], *The Union, Past and Future: How It Works, and How to Save It*, 4th ed. (Charleston, S.C., 1850), 5; Samuel Dunwoody, *A Sermon upon the Subject of Slavery* (Marietta, Ga., 1850), 7; Burwell, *Girl's Life in Virginia*, 62, 172–173; Leonard U. Hill, "John Randolph's Freed Slaves Settle in Western Ohio," *Bulletin of the Cincinnati Historical Society*, 23 (1965), 179–187; David A. Gerber, *Black Ohio and the Color Line, 1860–1915* (Urbana, Ill., 1976), 18–19; Meats and Arnold, eds., *Writings of Perry*, 3:239; William Cabell Bruce, *John Randolph of Roanoke, 1773–1833*, 2 vols. (New York, 1970 [1922]), 1:104–106, 2:60; Boyd Coyner, "John Hartwell Cocke: Southern Original," *Bulletin of the Fluvanna County Historical Society*, #6 (1968), 3–13; William Meade, *Sketches of Old Virginia Family Servants* (Philadelphia, 1847), 5; John MacGregor, *Our Brothers and Cousins: A Summer Tour in Canada and the States* (London, 1859), 124. Also, Melvin Patrick Ely, *Israel on the Appomattox: A Southern Experiment in Black Freedom from the 1790s through the Civil War* (New York, 2004); T. Stephen Whitman, *The Price of Freedom: Slavery and Manumission in Baltimore and Early National Maryland* (Lexington, Ky., 1997), esp. ch. 5.

33. William W. Freehling, *The Road to Disunion, Vol. 2: Secessionists Triumphant, 1854–1861* (New York, 2007), 2:111; H. B. Bascom, *Methodism and Slavery* (Frankfort, Ky., 1845), 58. For slaves who bought freedom see Herbert Aptheker, *To Be Free: Studies in American Negro History*, 2nd ed. (New York, 1948), 31–49.

34. Thomas D. Morris, *Southern Slavery and the Law, 1619–1860* (Chapel Hill, N.C., 1996), 32, 35–36; Herbert Anthony Kellar, ed., *Solon Robinson: Pioneer and Agriculturalist: Selected Writings*, 2 vols. (Indianapolis, Ind., 1936), 2:269–270; Solon Robinson, "Negro Slavery at the South," *DBR*, 7 (1849), 214–222; Samuel Seabury, *American Slavery Distinguished from the Slavery of English Theorists and Justified by the Law of Nature* (New York, 1861), 98–99, 156–160; David Brown, *Southern Outcast: Hinton Rowan Helper and the Impending Crisis of the South* (Baton Rouge, La., 2006), 50–51; George Fort Milton, *The Eve of Conflict: Stephen A. Douglas and the Needless War* (Cambridge, Mass., 1934), 34–35; Eric Burin, *Slavery and the Peculiar Solution: A History of the American Colonization* (Gainesville, Fla., 2005). In California a few ex-slaves returned to their old masters in Texas and Arkansas: see Eugene H. Berwanger, *The Frontier against Slavery: Western Anti-Negro Prejudice and the Slavery Controversy* (Urbana, Ill., 1967), 74–75.

35. On Flagg, see James C. Bonner, *Milledgeville: Georgia's Antebellum Capital* (Athens, Ga., 1978), 113; also, Bryan Tyson, *The Institution of Slavery in the Southern States, Religiously and Morally Considered* (Washington, D.C., 1863), 13.

36. Bailey, *The Issue*, 10, 20, 28, quotes at 10, 28; Boyd, *In Camp and Prison*, 1:45; John Richter Jones, *Slavery Sanctified by the Bible* (Philadelphia, 1861), 30; [Philip Schaff], "Impressions of England," *Mercersburg Review*, 9 (1857), 352.

37. [William Hobby], *Remarks upon Slavery, Occasioned by Attempts Made to Circulate Improper Publications in the Southern States. By a Citizen of Georgia*, 2nd ed. (Augusta, 1835), 19. For examples, see William S. Powell, *When the Past Refused to Die: A History of Carswell County, North Carolina, 1777–1977* (Durham, N.C., 1977), 533; Charles Carleton Coffin, *The Boys of '61; Or, Four Years of Fighting* (Boston, Mass., 1882), 415; Catherine Cooper Hopley, *Life in the South from the Commencement of the War*, 2 vols. (New York, 1971 [1863]), 1:151–152; Paul Finkelman, *An Imperfect Union: Slavery, Federalism, and Comity* (Chapel Hill, N.C., 1981), 120–122; Joseph Dorfman, *The Economic Mind in American Civilization*, 5 vols. (New York, 1966), 2:845 (Cooper); A. J. L. Fremantle, *Three Months in the Southern States: The 1863 Diary of an English Soldier, April–June 1863* (London, 1863), 20.

38. Charles A. Farley, *Slavery: A Discourse delivered in the Unitarian Church, Richmond, Va.* (Richmond, Va., 1835),16; Charles M. Taggart, *Slavery and Law, in the Light of Christianity* (Nashville, 1851), 8; "Senator Hammond's Speech – Black and White Slavery," *Charleston Mercury*, April 2, 1858; Adelaide Stuart Dimitry, *War-Time Sketches, Historical and Otherwise* (EE: 1998 [1911?]), 88; "Slave and Free States as Tested by the Census," *Weekly Mississippian*, Feb. 11, 1862; Seymour Drescher, *The Mighty Experiment: Free Labor versus Slavery in British Emancipation* (New York, 2002), ch. 4, quote at 94.

39. Christopher Phillips and Jason L. Pendleton, eds., *The Union on Trial: The Political Journals of Judge William Barclay Napton, 1829–1883* (Columbus, Mo., 2005), 93–94; Mrs. Houstoun, *Hesperos: Or, Travels in the West*, 2 vols. (London, 1850), 2:199–201, 206–208; W. W. Wright, "Free Negro Colonization Unveiled," *DBR*, 28 (1860), 554–555; [R. J. Breckenridge], "Hints on Slavery," *Spirit of the XIXth Century*, 1 (1842), 437; [Philip Schaff], "The Prospects of Christianity in Africa," *Mercersburg Review*, 12 (1860), 626–633. Also, Ben S. Elliott to William Elliot, Nov. 11, 1848, in Elliott-Gonzales Papers; Blassingame, ed., *Slave Testimony*,

110–112; A. K. Farrar to Benjamin C. Yancey, July 22, 1856 [?], July 26, 1861, in Yancey Papers; Michael O'Brien, *Conjectures of Order: Intellectual Life and the American South, 1810–1860*, 2 vols. (Chapel Hill, N.C., 2004), 1:181–186.

40. For sympathetic overviews, see Tom W. Shick, *Behold the Promised Land: A History of Afro-American Settler Society in Nineteenth-Century Liberia* (Baltimore, 1980); Richard L. Hall, Jr., *On Afric's Shore: A History of Maryland in Liberia, 1834–1857* (Baltimore, 2000). Naval officer quoted in Allan Nevins, *The Emergence of Lincoln*, 2 vols. (New York, 1950), 1:163, n. 52; W. H. Holcombe Diary, Feb. 26, 1855. For the report of the international commission, see *New York Herald Tribune*, Jan. 11, 1931.

41. Phillis Jennings to Mary Pettigrew, June 10, 1803, in Sarah McCulloh Lemmon, ed., *The Pettigrew Papers*, 2 vols. (Raleigh, N.C., 1971, 1988), 1:306–307. For letters from former slaves in Liberia, see Blassingame, ed., *Slave Testimony*, 65–82, 97–108, 110–112; Susan Caphart to John Kimberly, March 1, 1859, in Kimberly Papers; Bell I. Wiley, ed., *Slaves No More: Letters from Liberia, 1833–1869* (Lexington, Ky., 1980); Randall M. Miller, ed., *"Dear Master": Letters of a Slave Family* (Ithaca, N.Y., 1978); Penelope Campbell, *Maryland in Africa: The Maryland State Colonization Society, 1831–1857* (Urbana, Ill., 1971), 144–145, 186; Malinda Rix to Duncan Cameron, Nov. 5, 1839, in Mordecai Collection. For blacks who imbibed southern republicanism and became leaders in Liberia, see Carl Patrick Burrows, "Black Christian Republicanism: A Southern Ideology in Early Liberia, 1822 to 1847," *Journal of Negro History*, 86 (2001), 30–44.

42. *Marion Harland's Autobiography: The Story of a Life* (New York, 1910), 100; Mrs. Burton [Constance Cary] Harrison, *Recollections Grave and Gay* (London, 1912), 22; Moses Legans to McDonnell Reid, Oct. 20, 1843, in Reid Papers. In Wade Family Papers, see York Walker to Isaac Wade, April 21, 1852; Randall Kilby to John R. Kilby, Jan. 26, 1856; Granville Woodson to Mrs. C. E. Wade, Feb. 16, 1853. Bodichon, *An American Diary*, 102

43. "Liberian Literature," *SLM*, 2 (1836), 158–159; "Liberia," *Virginia Historical Register and Literary Advertiser*, 1 (1848), 44; Philip Slaughter, *The Virginian History of African Colonization* (Richmond, Va. 1855), 115–116; *ERD*, May 26, 1857 (Atkinson), 1:78. Colonizationists stressed progress in Liberia: e. g., *AR*, 27 (June, 1851), 189–190, 161–177. Also, Hampden C. DuBose, *Memoir of Rev. John Leighton Wilson, D.D., Missionary to Africa and Secretary of Foreign Missions* (Richmond, Va., 1895), 97–102; T. R. R. Cobb, *Educational Wants of Georgia: An Address Delivered before the Society of the Alumni of Franklin College* (Athens, Ga., 1857), 8–9; Cobb, *An Inquiry into the Law of Negro Slavery in the United States* (New York, 1968 [1858]), ccxii, ccxxiv–ccxxviii.

44. Virginia Writers Program, *The Negro in Virginia* (Winston-Salem, N.C., 1991), 53–54 (Hunt); Philip Barrett, *Gilbert Hunt, The City Blacksmith* (EE: 1999 [1859]); and *ERD*, Aug. 22–23, 1859 (1:332–334); Peter Randolph, *Sketches of Slave Life: Or, Illustrations of the "Peculiar Institution"* (EE: 2000 [1855]), 25; *A Narrative of Thomas Smallwood (Coloured Man)* (EE: 2001 [1851]), 44.

45. Benjamin Drew, *A North-Side View of Slavery: The Refugee, or, the Narrative of Fugitive Slaves in Canada* (New York, 1968 [1857]), 113 (Jenkins), 271–273 (Siddles); Samuel Ringgold Ward, *Autobiography of a Fugitive Slave in the United States, Canada, and England* (Chicago, 1970 [1855]), 95–108. On white Canadians, see Collison, *Shadrach Minkins: Slave, Fugitive, Canadian* (Cambridge, Mass.,

1996), esp. ch. 12. Also, Robin W. Winks, *The Blacks in Canada: A History* (New Haven, Conn., 1971), 20–21, 142, 248–251; Ripley et al., eds., *Black Abolitionist Papers*, 1:31–34, 2:306–307, 2:136–137; Jason H. Silverman, "The American Fugitive Slave in Canada: Myths and Realities," *Southern Studies*, 19 (1980), 215–227.

46. Charles Lyell, *Travels in North America, Canada, and Nova Scotia, with Geological Observations*, 2nd ed., 2 vols. (London, 1855), 1:191; J. C. Mitchell, *A Bible Defence of Slavery and the Unity of Mankind* (Mobile, Ala., 1861), 30–31; Wayne Gridley, *Slavery in the South: A Review of Hammond's and Fuller's Letters, and Chancellor Harper's Memoir* (Charleston, S.C., 1845), 22; Richard H. Colfax, *Evidence against the Views of the Abolitionists* (New York, 1833); Eliza Middleton Fisher to Mary Herring Middleton, Feb. 10, 1845, in Eliza Cope Harrison, ed., *Best Companions: Letters of Eliza Middleton Fisher and Her Mother, Mary Hering Middleton, from Charleston, Philadelphia, and Newport, 1839–1846* (Columbia, S.C., 2001), 427–428; *DBR*, 18 (1855), 448–454, esp. 452; Dargan, in William R. Smith, ed., *The History of the Convention and Debates of the People of Alabama* (Montgomery, Ala., 1861), 93–95; J. K. Paulding, *Slavery in the United States* (New York, 1836), ch. 7; Solon Robinson, "Negro Slavery at the South," *DBR*, 7 (1849), 216–217. Also, Howard C. Perkins, "The Defense of Slavery in the Northern Press on the Eve of the Civil War," *JSH*, 9 (1943), 503–512.

47. "Curtius" [W. J. Grayson], "Hireling Labor and Slave Labor," *Mississippian and State Gazette*, Sept. 12, 1851; "Speech on the War with Mexico" (Jan. 4, 1848), in *JCCP*, 25:118, 131; "Speech on the Proposed Occupation of Yucatan" (May 15, 1848), in [Clyde N. Wilson, ed.], *The Essential Calhoun: Selection from Writings, Speeches, and Letters* (New Brunswick, N.J., 1991), 146–148; Henry S. Foote, *Texas and the Texans; Or, The Advance of the Anglo-Americans to the Southwest*, 2 vols. (Austin, Tex., 1935 [1841]), 2:10, 26, 33, 36; Robert L. Dabney, *Systematic Theology* (Carlisle, Pa., 1985 [1878]), 135.

48. Theodore Clapp, *Slavery: A Sermon* (New Orleans, La., 1838), 25; Clapp, "Thanksgiving Sermon," *New Orleans Daily Picayune*, Dec. 22, 1850; Jones, *Religious Instruction of Negroes*, 64, 142–143; Joseph C. Stiles, *Modern Reform Examined* (Philadelphia, 1857), 19–20, 36; W. R. Aylett speech on free blacks, ca. 1851, in Aylett Family Papers; *Speech of the Hon. F. W. Pickens, Delivered before a Public Meeting, of the People of the District, Held at Edgefield, C.H., S.C.* (Edgefield, S.C., 1851), 17; David Henry Overy, "Robert Lewis Dabney: Apostle of the Old South" (unpubl. Ph.D. diss., University of Wisconsin, 1967), 48; Lyon Report in *SPR*, 16 (July 1863), 10. Indian removal and probable extinction alarmed blacks: Peter P. Hinks, *To Awaken My Afflicted Brethren: David Walker and the Problem of Slave Antebellum Resistance* (State University, Pa., 1996), 123–134.

49. Capers's text in Albert M. Shipp, *The History of Methodism in South Carolina* (Nashville, Tenn., 1883), 488; William Winans to D. DeVinne, Aug. 31, 1841, in Ray Holder, ed., "On Slavery: Selected Letters, of Parson Winans, 1820–1844," *Journal of Mississippi History*, 46 (1984), 323–354, quote at 348; [Augustus Baldwin Longstreet], *A Voice from the South* (Baltimore, 1847), 17; O. P. Fitzgerald, *Judge Longstreet. A Life Sketch* (Nashville, Tenn., 1891), 97–98; Stringfellow, "Bible Argument" and "Elder Galusha's Reply to Fuller," in Elliott, ed., *Cotton Is King*, 491, 520–521; "Social Aspects – Love of Money," *Western Journal and Civilian*, 13 (1855), 382; *AR*, 27 (1851), 305; Edmund Bellinger, Jr., *A Speech on the Subject of Slavery* (Charleston, S.C., 1835), 16–17, 24.

50. Otey quoted in William Mercer Green, *Memoir of the Rt. Rev. James Hervey Otey, D.D., LL.D, the First Bishop of Tennessee* (New York, 1885), 94; Hughes, quoted in Maria Genoino Caravaglios, *The American Catholic Church and the Negro Problem in the XVIII-XIX Centuries*, ed. Ernest L. Unterkoefler (Charleston, S.C., 1978), 165.

51. In *JCCP*, see Calhoun to Richard Pakenham, Apr. 18, 1844 (18:273–278); Robert Monroe to Harrison Calhoun, May 4, 1844 (18:349), 429–435; Lewis Henry Morgan to Calhoun, June 30, 1848 (25:556); Francis Wharton to Calhoun, Mar. 19, 1849 (26:352); FitzWilliam Byrdsall to Calhoun, July 23, 1849 (26:512); also, Calhoun to William R. King, Aug. 12, 1844; Dec. 13, 1845, in J. Franklin Jameson, ed., *Calhoun Correspondence* (Washington, D.C., 1900), 631–633. Marvin E. Gettleman, *The Dorr Rebellion: A Study in American Radicalism* (New York, 1973), 17–18, 43–49, 129–130, 145; Robert D. Sampson, *John O'Sullivan and His Times* (Kent, Oh., 2003), esp. 231; Charles Edward Leverett to Milton Leverett, June, 29, 1859, in Frances Wallace Taylor et al., eds., *The Leverett Letters: Correspondence of a South Carolina Family, 1851–1868* (Columbia, S.C., 2000), 85; James A. Dorr, *Justice to the South!* (Ithaca, N.Y., 2006 [1856]), 4. Some conditions for blacks in New York City deteriorated after emancipation: Shane White, *Somewhat More Independent: The End of Slavery in New York City, 1770–1810* (Athens, Ga., 1991), 88, 113, 207–209.

52. G. W. M. Simms, "The South," *Southern Repertory and College Review*, 13 (1854), 224; Alexander H. Stephens, *A Constitutional View of the Late War between the States*, 2 vols. (New York, 1970 [1868, 1870]), see esp. Toombs' speech, Appendix G (1:625–647); Robert Toombs, "Slavery: Its Constitutional Status, and Its Influence on Society and the Colored," *DBR*, 20 (1856), 596–597; *ERD*, 3:287; William C. Davis, *Jefferson Davis: The Man and His Hour* (New York, 1991), 495, 649; Tyson, *Institution of Slavery*, 36–38, 2. For southern women writers, see Sarah E. Gardner, *Blood and Irony: Southern Women's Narratives on the Civil War, 1861–1937* (Chapel Hill, N.C., 2004).

53. Norma Lois Peterson, *The Presidencies of William Henry Harrison and John Tyler* (Lawrence, Kans., 1989), 191; John Johnson, "Utility, the Guide of Philanthropy," *VUM*, 3 (1858), 122–124; James P. Holcombe, "Is Slavery Consistent with Natural Law?," *SLM*, 27 (1858), 407–408; [Pringle], *Slavery in the Southern States*, 27, 47–48; Bledsoe, "Essay on Liberty and Slavery," in Elliott, ed., *Cotton Is King*, 403; Sawyer, *Southern Institutes*, 150–151; J. A. Turner, "Something More on Negroes and Slavery," *DBR*, 26 (Feb. 1859), 142–143; [A North Carolinian], *Southern Slavery Considered on General Principles, Or, A Grapple with Abstractionists* (New York, 1861), 19. Also, Samuel Davies Baldwin, *Dominion; Or, the Unity and Trinity of the Human Race* (Nashville, Tenn., 1858), 227, 378, 351; "Python" [John Tyler, Jr.],"The Issues of 1860," *DBR*, 28 (March 1860), 260–269.

54. Vernon Louis Parrington, *Main Currents in American Thought*, 3 vols. (New York, 1927), 2:38–39; Lester D. Stephens, *Science, Race, and Religion in the American South: John Bachman and the Charleston Naturalists, 1845–1895* (Chapel Hill, N.C., 2000), 167; Martin Crawford, ed., *William Howard Russell's Civil War: Private Diary and Letters, 1861–1862* (Athens, Ga., 1992), 104 (Aug. 18, 1861); Lumpkin in *Adams v. Bass* (1855), in Catterall, ed., *Judicial Cases*, 3:43; also, Lumpkin in *Seaborn C. Bryan vs. Hugh Walton*, in *Reports of Cases in Law and Equity Argued and Determined in the Supreme Court of the State of Georgia,*

14 (1854), 200, 205–206; Mason W. Stephenson and D. Grier Stephenson, Jr., "'To Protect and Defend': Judge Lumpkin, the Supreme Court of Georgia, and Slavery," *Emory Law Journal*, 25 (1976), 583–584; Frederick Grimke, *The Nature and Tendency of Free Institutions*, ed. John William Ward (Cambridge, Mass., 1968 [1848, 1856]), 435; John Henry Hopkins, *A Scriptural, Ecclesiastical, and Historical View of Slavery from the Days of the Patriarch Abraham to the Nineteenth Century* (New York, 1864), 34–35. For the Virginia clergy, see Patricia Hickin, "Situation Ethics and Antislavery Attitudes in the Virginia Churches," in John B. Boles, ed., *America: The Middle Period. Essays in Honor of Bernard Mayo* (Charlottesville, Va., 1973), 190–191, 198–199.

55. Baxter, *Abolition of Slavery*, 6–7; Brevard Diary, Oct. 1860–Jan. 1861; *Lieutenant General Jubal Anderson Early: Autobiographical Sketch and Narrative of the War Between the States* (EE: 1999 [1912]), x; B. F. Stringfellow, *Negro-Slavery, No Evil* (St. Louis, Mo., 1854), 11; [Benjamin F. Whitner], *A System of Prospective Emancipation, Advocated in Kentucky, by Robert J. Breckenridge, D.D.* (Charleston. S.C., 1850), 21; Lynette Boney Wrenn, ed., *A Bachelor's Life in Antebellum Mississippi: The Diary of Dr. Elijah Millington Walker, 1849–1852* (Knoxville, Tenn., 2004), Aug. 20, 1850 (75–76); [William Elliott], "A Trip to Cuba," *RM*, 2 (1857), 120; on alleged cannibalism, see Hampden C. DuBose, *Memoir of Rev. John Leighton Wilson, D.D., Missionary to Africa and Secretary of Foreign Missions* (Richmond, Va., 1895), 87–88, 111–112. See also the semifictional *Captain Canot, or Twenty Years of an African Slavery by Brantz Mayer of the Maryland Historical Society*; James Martin, *DBR*, 24 (1858), 358; Cunningham quoted in Gunja SenGupta, *For God and Mammon: Evangelicals and Entrepreneurs, Masters and Slaves in Territorial Kansas, 1854–1860* (Athens, Ga., 1996), 19; Frances Fearn, *Diary of a Refugee*, ed. Rosalie Urquart (New York, 1910), 12–14.

56. Alexander Gregg, *A Sermon: Preached in St. David's Church, Austin, on Sunday, July 20, 1862* (Austin, Tex., 1862), 11; *Marion Harlan's Autobiography*, 192–193; *Letter of Hon. Francis W. Pickens... Written to a Gentleman in New Orleans* (Baltimore, 1866), 15–16; *Speech of the Hon. F. W. Pickens at Edgefield, C. H.*, 13.

57. Frank Alexander Montgomery, *Reminiscences of a Mississippian in Peace and War* (EE: 1999 [1901]), 21, quote at 280; Thomas Hughes, *A Boy's Experience in the Civil War, 1860–1865* (EE: 1998 [1904]), 51–55; Myrta Lockett Avary, *Dixie after the War* (New York, 1918 [1906]), 181–182; Sam Aleckson, *Before the War and after the Union: An Autobiography* (EE: 2000 [1929]), 16.

6. Guardians of a Helpless Race

1. E. A Pollard, *Southern History of the War*, 2 vols. in 1 (n. p., 1977 [1866]), 202.

2. Solomon Northup, *Twelve Years a Slave* (New York, 1970 [1854]), 146; Charles L. Perdue, Jr., et al., eds., *Weevils in the Wheat: Interviews with Virginia Ex-Slaves* (Charlottesville, Va., 1976), 15; John C. Butler, *Historical Record of Macon and Central Georgia* (Macon, Ga., 1969 [1879]), 217. For slaves' reliance on masters against patrols and poor white violence, see Sally E. Hadden, *Slave Patrols: Law and Violence in Virginia and the Carolinas* (Cambridge, UK, 2001), 130–131, 182.

3. Gary Philip Zola, *Isaac Harby of Charleston, 1788–1828: Jewish Reformer and Intellectual* (Tuscaloosa, Ala., 1994), 97, 9; *Southern Review*, 1 (1828), 223; Charles A. Farley, *Slavery; A Discourse Delivered in the Unitarian Church,*

Richmond, Va. (Richmond, Va., 1835), 15, 18; Robert Y. Hayne, Jan. 25, 1830 (46); John Rowan, Feb. 4, 1830 (260–261); William Smith, Feb. 25, 1830 (324), in Herman Belz, ed., *The Webster-Hayne Debate on the Nature of the Union: Selected Documents* (Indianapolis, Ind., 2000); Weld to Lewis Tappan, Feb. 22, 1836, in Gilbert H. Barnes and Dwight L. Dumond, eds., *Letters of Theodore Dwight Weld, Angelina Grimké and Sarah Grimké*, 2 vols. (Gloucester, Mass., 1965), 1:263; B. F. Stringfellow, *Negro-Slavery, No Evil; or the North and the South* (St. Louis, Mo., 1854), 13.

4. David E. Swift, *Black Prophets of Justice: Activist Clergy before the Civil War* (Baton Rouge, La., 1989), 95 (Cornish), 151, 157, ch. 5; Albert S. Foley, *Bishop Healy, Beloved Outcast: The Story of a Great Man Whose Life Has Become a Legend* (New York, 1954), 17–18, ch. 2.

5. Anne Baker, "Geography, Pedagogy, and Race: Schoolbooks and Ideology in the Antebellum United States," *Proceedings of the American Antiquarian Society*, 113 (2005), 163–190.

6. [Gabriel Capers], *Bondage a Moral Institution, Sanctioned by the Scriptures of the Old and New Testaments, and the Preaching and Practice of the Saviour and His Apostles. By a Southern Farmer* (Macon, Ga., 1837), 41; June 11, 1835; Apr. 27, 1859, in *The American Diaries of Richard Cobden*, ed. Elizabeth Hoon Cawley (Princeton, N.J., 1952), 92, 176; Andrew Bell [pseudonym, A. Thomason], *Men and Things in America: Being the Experience of a Year's Residence in the United States, in a Series of Letters to a Friend* (London, 1838), Letter 12; Robert L. Paquette, *Sugar Is Made with Blood: The Conspiracy of La Escalera and the Conflict between Empires over Slavery in Cuba* (Middletown, Conn., 1988), 62–63, 110, 140 (Madden); Charles Lyell, *A Second Visit to the United States of North America*, 2 vols. (London, 1855), 2:82; Lynette Boney Wrenn, ed., *A Bachelor's Life in Antebellum Mississippi: The Diary of Dr. Elijah Millington Walker, 1849–1852* (Knoxville, Tenn., 2004), Dec. 10, 1851 (173).

7. "South Carolinian," in Carter G. Woodson, ed., *The Mind of the Negro as Reflected in Letters Written During the Crisis, 1800–1860* (New York, 1969), 10–12, 276–280, 332–333; Austin Steward in *Twenty-Two Years a Slave and Forty Years a Freeman* (Reading, Mass., 1969 [1857]), ch. 19; Samuel Ringgold Ward, *Autobiography of a Fugitive Slave in the United States, Canada, and England* (Chicago, 1970 [1855]), ch. 4; Hosea Easton, "Treatise on the Intellectual Character," repr. in Dorothy Porter, ed., *Negro Protest Pamphlets: A Compendium* (New York, 1969), 41–42; James M'Cune Smith, "On the Fourteenth Query of Thomas Jefferson's Notes on Virginia," *Anglo-African Magazine*, 1 (1859), 226. See Peter P. Hinks, *To Awaken My Afflicted Brethren: David Walker and the Problem of Antebellum Slave Resistance* (State University, Pa., 1996), 82; Arthur Zilversmit, *The First Emancipation: The Abolition of Slavery in the North* (Chicago, 1967), 222–223, 46–47, 53, 227; T. Stephen Whitman, *The Price of Freedom: Slavery and Manumission in Baltimore and Early National Maryland* (Lexington, Ky., 1997), ch. 1. Also, Irving H. Bartlett, *From Slave to Citizen: The Story of the Negro in Rhode Island* (Providence, R.I., 1954), ch. 3. For exploitation of black child labor, see Leslie M. Harris, *In the Shadow of Slavery: African Americans in New York City, 1616–1863* (Chicago, 2003), ch. 4.

8. Eugene Alvarez, *Travel on Southern Antebellum Railroads, 1828–1860* (University, Ala., 1974), esp. 128–130, 134–137; Arthur Charles Cole, *The Era of the Civil War, 1848–1870* (Urbana, Ill., 1987), 225, 227–229.

9. Mann Butler, "Review: Cotton Is King," *Western Journal and Civilian*, 14 (1855), 169–174, 250–256, quote at 169. In *SLM*, see J. A. W., "De Servitude," 20 (1854), 424; B., "The New Social Propositions," 20 (1854), 296; S., "Liberty and Slavery," 22 (1856), 387; "Horace Greeley and His Lost Book," 31 (1860), 219. In *DBR*, see "Southern Slavery and Its Assailants," 15 (1853), 491–492; 10 (1851), 520; 23 (1857), 561–570. William S. Forrest, *Historical and Descriptive Sketches of Norfolk and Vicinity* (Philadelphia, 1853), 417–429; T. R. R. Cobb, *An Inquiry into the Law of Negro Slavery in the United States* (New York, 1968 [1858]), cci–ccv.

10. Margaret Johnson Erwin to Samuel Sloan, Apr. 1, 1860, in John Seymour Erwin, *Like Some Green Laurel: Letters of Margaret Johnson Erwin, 1821–1863* (Baton Rouge, La., 1981), 102; Sally McDowell to John Miller, Apr. 1, 1856, in Thomas E. Buckley, S.J., ed. *"If You Love That Lady Don't Marry Her": The Courtship Letters of Sally McDowell and John Miller, 1854–56* (Columbia, Mo., 2000), 539; John Wood Sweet, *Bodies Politic: Negotiating Race in the American North, 1730–1830* (Baltimore, 2003), 11; Alexis de Tocqueville, *Democracy in America*, 2 vols., tr. Henry Reeve (Boston, 1873), 1:359–360; Lorenzo J. Green, *The Negro in Colonial New England* (New York, 1968); John Saillant, *Black Puritan, Black Republican: The Life and Thought of Lemuel Haynes, 1753–1833* (New York, 2003), 122; Jane H. Pease and William H. Pease, *They Who Would Be Free: Blacks' Search for Freedom, 1830–1861* (New York, 1974), 18–19.

11. C. Gray, *Slavery: Or, Oppression at the North as well as the South!* (Ithaca, N.Y., 2006 [1862]), 7–9; Sean Wilentz, *The Rise of American Democracy: Jefferson and Jackson* (New York, 2005), 192–195; V. Jacque Voegeli, *Free but Not Equal: The Midwest and the Negro during the Civil War* (Chicago, 1967), 9, 35, 88–89; Leonard P. Curry, *The Free Black in Urban America, 1800–1850: The Shadow of the Dream* (Chicago, 1981), chs. 2, 5, 6, 10. For northern antiblack riots, see Paul A. Gilje, *Rioting in America* (Bloomington, Ind., 1996), 87–91.

12. Eugene H. Berwanger, *The Frontier against Slavery: Western Anti-Negro Prejudice and the Slavery Controversy* (Urbana, Ill., 1967), 3, 124, 129–141, and ch. 2; Robert R. Dykstra, *Bright Radical Star: Black Freedom and White Supremacy in the Hawkeye Frontier* (Cambridge, Mass., 1993), chs. 1, 2, 5; David A. Gerber, *Black Ohio and the Color Line, 1860–1915* (Urbana, Ill., 1976), ch. 1.

13. Lane quoted in Edward E. Leslie, *The Devil Knows How to Ride: The True Story of William Clarke Quantrill and His Confederate Raiders* (New York, 1996), 11; George W. Julian, *Speeches on Political Questions* (New York, 1872), 127; Emma Lou Thornbrough, *The Negro in Indiana before 1900: A Study of a Minority*, 2nd ed. (Bloomington, Ind., 1993), esp. chs. 3, 5; Gunja SenGupta, *For God and Mammon: Evangelicals and Entrepreneurs, Masters and Slaves in Territorial Kansas, 1854–1860* (Athens, Ga., 1996), ch. 5; William Stuart to Earl Russell, Sept. 1, 1862, in James J. Barnes and Patience P. Barnes, eds., *The American Civil War through British Eyes: Dispatches from British Diplomats*, 3 vols. (Kent, Oh., 2005), 2:198–200; Robert Trimble, *The Negro, North and South: The Status of the Coloured Population in the Northern and Southern States of America Compared* (London, 1863), 2, 20–21; Harvey Levenstein, *Seductive Journey: American Tourists in France from Jefferson to the Jazz Age* (Chicago, 1998), 229.

14. James Madison, *Notes of the Debates in the Federal Convention of 1787* (Athens, Oh., 1966), 275; *Mississippian and State Gazette*, March 18, 1853; Joanne Pope Melish, *Disowning Slavery: Gradual Emancipation and "Race" in New England,*

1780–1860 (Ithaca, N.Y., 1998), 2–3, 82–83, 161, 163; F. F. Steel to Anna Steel, Dec. 15, 1860; Leon Litwack, *North of Slavery: The Negro in the Free States, 1790–1860* (Chicago, 1961); *AR*, 27 (1851), 150, 208–209, 316, 366–379; Benning and Brown, in William W. Freehling and Craig M. Simpson, eds., *Secession Debated: Georgia's Showdown in 1860* (New York, 1992), 120, 150–152. Also, William C. Wright, *The Secession Movement in the Middle Atlantic States* (Rutherford, N.J., 1973), 170–171.

15. John S. C. Abbott, *South and North; or, Impressions Received during a Trip to Cuba and the South* (New York, 1969 [1860]), 75; D. W. Mitchell, *Ten Years in the United States: Being an Englishman's Views of Men and Things in the North and South* (London, 1862), 17; Louis Filler, *The Crusade against Slavery, 1830–1860* (New York, 1960), 224–225; Mary Stoughton Locke, *Anti-Slavery in America: From the Introduction of African Slaves to the Prohibition of the Slave Trade (1619–1808)* (Gloucester, Mass., 1965), 35–36; "Journal of Capt. Henry Massie," *Tyler's Quarterly Historical and Genealogical Magazine*, 4 (1922), 80–81; Charles H. Bohner, *John Pendleton Kennedy: Gentleman from Baltimore* (Baltimore, 1961), 48; William Shepard Pettigrew to Ebenezer Pettigrew, Sept. 5, 1838, in Lemmon, ed., *Pettigrew Papers*, 2:385.

16. "Address of Hon. A. H. H. Stuart before the Central Agricultural Society of Virginia," *Southern Planter*, 20 (1860), 327–329, 338; *Speech of Col. Curtis M. Jacobs on the Free Colored Population of Maryland* (Annapolis, Md., 1860), 7; William A. Hall, *Historic Significance of the Southern Revolution* (Petersburg, Va., 1864), 20; "Table Talk," in Lindsley Papers, Dec. 9, 1860; Dec. 29, 1861; May 8, 1862; Norton quoted in Melish, *Disowning Slavery*, xiv; *The Backwoods Preacher: Being the Autobiography of Peter Cartwright* (London, 1870), 186.

17. On immediatist flexibility, see Gilbert Barnes and Dwight Dumond, eds., *Weld-Grimké Letters*, Introduction, esp. 9; Irem W. Smith, *American Slavery; A Prayer for Its Removal* (Middletown, Conn., 1860), 6–7; Robert H. Abzug, *Passionate Liberator: Theodore Dwight Weld and the Dilemmas of Reform* (New York, 1980), 93–95; Voegeli, *Free but Not Equal*, ch. 9; K. Alan Snyder, *Defining Noah Webster: Mind and Morals in the Early Republic* (Latham, N.Y., 1990), 131–134; Victor B. Howard, *Conscience and Slavery: The Evangelistic Calvinist Domestic Missions, 1837–1861* (Kent, Oh., 1990), 22. For black criticisms of the antislavery movement, see C. Peter Ripley et al., eds., *The Black Abolitionist Papers*, 5 vols. (Chapel Hill, N.C., 1985–91), 1:34, 300n.10; 3:221–222, 265, 375–377; 4:189–191, 274–275.

18. Morgan J. Rhees, *Letters on Liberty and Slavery: In Answer to a Pamphlet, Entitled "Negro-Slavery Defended by the Word of God,"* 2nd ed. (New York, 1798), 8; Charles Elliott, *Sinfulness of American Slavery: Proved from Its Evil Sources,* 2 vols. (New York, 1968 [1850]), passim in both volumes; W. G. Brownlow and A. Pryne, *Ought American Slavery to Be Perpetuated? A Debate* (Miami, Fla., 1969 [1858]), 239; Alexander H. Everett, *America, or a General Survey of the Political Situation of the Several Powers of the Western Continent, with Conjectures on Their Future Prospects* (New York, 1970 [1827]), 214–221, quote at 221. The abolitionist record on racial equality is extolled in Paul Goodman, *Abolitionism and the Origins of Racial Equality* (Berkeley, Calif., 1998); for a well-balanced examination, see John Stauffer, *The Black Hearts of Men: Radical Abolitionism and the Transformation of Race* (Cambridge, Mass., 2002).

19. Hugh Honour, *The Image of the Black in Western Art*, 4 vols. (Cambridge, Mass., 1983), 4: Part One, 18–21, 23.

20. John Barnwell, *Love of Order: South Carolina's First Secession Crisis* (Chapel Hill, N.C., 1982), 132, citing the *Federal Union*, Dec. 3, 1850; [Anon.], "An Englishman in South Carolina," in Eugene L. Schwaab and Jacqueline Bull, eds., *Travels in the Old South: Selected from Periodicals of the Time*, 2 vols. (Lexington, Ky., 1973), 2:572; for Claiborne, see Ervin L. Jordan, Jr., *Black Confederates and Afro-Yankees in Civil War Virginia* (Charlottesville, Va., 1995), 153; for Richards see Franklin M. Garrett, *Atlanta and Environs: A Chronicle of Its People and Events* (Athens, Ga., 1954), 1:557.

21. Frederick Law Olmsted, *A Journey in the Seaboard Slave States* (New York, 1968 [1856]), 58–59; Charles E. Beveridge et al., eds., *The Papers of Frederick Law Olmsted*, 2 vols. (Baltimore, 1977, 1981), 2:264. On "slavery in the abstract," see Elizabeth Fox-Genovese and Eugene D. Genovese, *Slavery in White and Black: Class and Race in the Southern Slaveholders' New World Order* (New York, 2008).

22. Amelia M. Murray, *Letters from the United States, Cuba, and Canada*, 2 vols. in 1 (New York, 1968 [1856]), 180; Richard H. Abbott, *Cotton and Capital: Boston Businessmen and Anti-Slavery Reform, 1854–1868* (Amherst, Mass., 1991), 9, chs. 4, 7; Stevens quoted in Robert Cruden, *The Negro in Reconstruction* (Englewood Cliffs, N.J., 1969), 35. See also "The Ethics of Secession," in Charles Francis Adams, *Studies, Military and Diplomatic, 1775–1865* (New York, 1911), and Willie Lee Rose, *Rehearsal for Reconstruction: The Port Royal Experiment* (New York, 1964), 65; for William Makepeace Thackeray's similar view, Joe Lockard, *Watching Slavery: Witness Texts and Travel Reports* (New York, 2008), 22. For the psychic and social consequences of the end of assimilation into white households, see Earl E. Thorpe, *Eros and Freedom in Southern Life and Thought* (Durham, N.C., 1967), 45.

23. L. M. Child to William P. Cutler, July 10, 1862, in Louis P. Masur, ed., *"The Real War Will Never Get in the Books": Selections from Writers during the Civil War* (New York, 1993), 48; Henry Hubbard, Mar. 7, 1835, *Congressional Globe*, Senate, 24th Cong., 1st Sess., 230. For Emerson's shifting attitude to blacks, see Len Gougeon and Joel Myerson, eds., *Emerson's Antislavery Writings* (New Haven, Conn., 1995), 35–36, 39–40; Merton M. Sealts, Jr., *Emerson on the Scholar* (Columbia, Mo., 1992), 185–187, and Lewis P. Simpson, *Mind and the American Civil War: A Meditation on Lost Causes* (Baton Rouge, La., 1989), 9, 54–55.

24. Jackson's sermon as a pamphlet and in the *New Orleans Daily Picayune* (see Carter Collection); Stephen Elliott, *God's Presence with the Confederate States* (Savannah, Ga., 1861), 21; *Address of the Rt. Rev. Stephen Elliott, D.D., to the Thirty-Ninth Annual Convention of the Protestant Episcopal Church of the Diocese of Georgia* (Savannah, Ga., 1861), 9–10; Stephen Elliott, *Sermon Preached in Christ Church, Savannah* (Savannah, Ga., 1862), 12–13; "Address," in *Journal of the Protestant Episcopal Church of Georgia, 1866* (Savannah, Ga., 1866), 24–29; Bishop Elliott's printed letter of Aug. 1, 1865, from Augusta (Andrews Papers); Richard H. Wilmer, *In Memoriam: A Sermon in Commemoration of the Life and Labors of the Rt. Rev. Stephen Elliott* (Mobile, Ala., 1967), 19; Edgar Legare Pennington, "Bishop Stephen Elliott and the Confederate Episcopal Church," *Georgia Review*, 4 (1950), 240.

25. George D. Armstrong, *The Christian Doctrine of Slavery* (New York, 1967 [1857]), 135, also 69, 136; Armstrong, *"The Good Hand of Our Lord Upon Us": A Thanksgiving Sermon* (Norfolk, Va., 1861), 10; on Lyon, see Ernest Trice Thompson, *Presbyterians in the South*, 3 vols. (Richmond, Va., 1963), 3:56, 61–62;

B. M. Palmer, *"The Rainbow Round the Throne"; or, Justice Tempered with Mercy* (Milledgeville, Ga., 1863), 38–39; Palmer, *A Discourse before the General Assembly of South Carolina on December 10, 1863* (Columbia, S.C., 1864), 16; H. M. White, ed., *Rev. William S. White, D.D., and His Times (1800–1873): An Autobiography* (Richmond, Va., 1891), 180–181; William Henry Elder, *Civil War Diary, 1862–1865)* (Natchez, Miss., n. d.), 56–57; on Elder, see James J. Pillar, *The Catholic Church in Mississippi, 1837–65* (New Orleans, La., 1964), 117–118; Bell I. Wiley, *The Life of Billy Yank: The Common Soldier of the Union* (Baton Rouge, La., 1978), 40–41, 44, and ch. 5.

26. Edmondston Diary, Aug. 23, 1863, in Beth G. Crabtree and James Welch Patton, eds., *"Journal of a Secesh Lady": The Diary of Catherine Devereux Edmondston, 1860–1866* (Raleigh, N.C., 1979), 455; J. W. McGuire, June 11, 1864, in Jean V. Berlin, *Diary of a Southern Refugee During the War, by a Lady of Virginia* (Lincoln, Neb., 1995 [1867]), 279; J. W. Booth, draft and "To the Editors of the *National Intelligencer*, April 14, 1863" in John Rhodehamel and Louise Taper, eds., *"Right or Wrong, God Judge Me": The Writings of John Wilkes Booth* (Urbana, Ill., 1997), 125, 147–148; Eliza Frances Andrews, *War-Time Journal of a Georgia Girl* (New York, 1907), June 27, July 1, 1865 (316, 340); on "corn women," see Davis Blake Carter, *The Story of Uncle Minyard Told: A Family's 200-Year Migration Across the South* (Spartanburg, S.C., 1994), 174–175; *Diary of William King, Cobb County, Georgia, 1864* (EE: 1999), 60, 73, 107–108; Warren Akin to Mary Frances Akin, July, 24, 1861, in Bell Irvin Wiley, ed., *Letters of Warren Akin, Confederate Congressman* (Athens, Ga., 1959), 21; Gordon A. Cotton, ed., *From the Pen of a She-Rebel: The Civil War Diary of Emilie Riley McKinley* (Columbia, S.C., 2001), May 20, 1863 (7); Robert T. Oliver, *A Faithful Heart: The Journals of Emmala Reed, 1865 and 1866* (Columbia, S.C., 2004), June 2, 1861 (104); Jan. 1, 1866 (133); *Autobiography of Col. Richard Malcolm Johnston* (EE: 1997 [1900]), 66–67.

27. Sarah Woolfolk Wiggins, ed., *The Journals of Josiah Gorgas, 1857–1878* (Tuscaloosa, Ala., 1995), xviii, 175, 205; *ERD*, Dec. 26, 1863; April 2, 1864; July 20, 1864 (3:287, 385–386, 505–507); Craft Diary, Feb. 8, 1864.; Carol Bleser, "Southern Planters' Wives and Slavery," in David R. Chesnutt and Clyde N. Wilson, eds., *The Meaning of South Carolina History: Essays in Honor of George C. Rogers, Jr.* (Columbia, S.C., 1991), 114.

28. John Richard Dennett, *The South as It Is, 1865–1866* (New York, 1965 [1867]), 6, 15, 102–103, 290; David Macrae, *The Americans at Home* (New York, 1952 [1870]), 132–133, 295; Agnew Diary, May 29, 1865; Bills Diary, Dec. 1, 1866, "Memoranda," Jan. 1, 1866.

29. T. W. MacMahon, *An Essay on the American Crisis* (EE: 1999 [1862]), 2–5, quote at 14; T. Harry Williams, *Beauregard: Napoleon in Gray* (Baton Rouge, La., 1955); *The Life and Times of Judge Junius Hillyer: From His Memoirs* (Tignall, Ga, 1989), 84–85; Edward King, *The Great South: A Record of Journeys*, 2 vols. (New York, 1969 [1875]), 1:33–34, 291; Hyman Rubin III, *South Carolina Scalawags* (Columbia, S.C., 2006), 10–13; E. Merton Coulter, *The South during Reconstruction, 1865–1877* (Baton Rouge, La., 1947), 38; Lee quoted in Capt. R. E. Lee, *Recollections and Letters of General Robert E. Lee, by His Son* (New York, 1904), 168.

30. Emma Christopher, *Slave Ship Sailors and Their Captive Cargoes, 1730–1807* (New York, 2006), 12, 99.

31. D. E. Huger Smith, *A Charlestonian's Recollections, 1846–1913* (Charleston, S.C., 1950), 29; Henry William Ravenel, "Recollections of Southern Plantation Life," ed. Marjorie Stratford Mendenhall, *Yale Review*, 25 (1936), 751–756; also, May 29, 1862, in Arney Robinson Childs, ed., *The Private Journal of Henry William Ravenel, 1859–1887* (Columbia, S.C., 1947), 143. For slaves' sales and earning, see, e.g., H. N. McTyeire, *Duties of Christian Masters*, ed. Thomas O. Summers (Nashville, Tenn., 1859), 102–103; Lynda J. Morgan, *Emancipation in Virginia's Tobacco Belt, 1850–1870* (Athens, Ga., 1992), 44–45; A. M. P. King Plantation Record; [Alabaman], *ACP*, n. s. 2 (1858) 21; R. W. Gibbes, in *DBR*, 24 (1858), 324; Loren Schweninger, *Black Property Owners in the South, 1790–1915* (Urbana, Ill., 1990), 31–37; Stephen Crawford in Robert William Fogel and Stanley L. Engerman, eds., *Without Consent or Contract: The Rise and Fall of American Slavery. Markets and Productions: Technical Papers*, 3 vols. (New York, 1989), 2:536–550, esp. 546.

32. Daniel R. Hundley, *Social Relations in Our Southern States* (Baton Rouge, La., 1979 [1860]), 356; George Rogers, *Memoranda of the Experience, Labors, and Travels of a Universalist Preacher, Written by Himself* (Cincinnati, Oh., 1845), 267. For cheats, see "Narrative of James Curry," in John W. Blassingame, ed., *Slave Testimony: Two Centuries of Letters, Speeches, Interviews, and Autobiographies* (Baton Rouge, La., 1977), 136–137.

33. Terry L. Seip, "Slaves and Free Negroes in Alexandria, 1850–1860," *Louisiana History*, 10 (1969), 147–165; Blassingame, ed., *Slave Testimony*, 274 275, 325–338, 427.

34. Wilson quoted by U. B. Phillips in *SBN*, 4:210; for the discussion in the agricultural journals, see the samples in James O. Breeden, ed., *Advice among Masters: The Ideal in Slave Management in the Old South* (Westport, Conn., 1980), ch. 17; Moses Liddell to St. John R. Liddell, Jan. 9, 1839; McLaughlin et al., eds., *Papers of Olmsted*, 2:186–187; James C. Bonner, *A History Georgia Agriculture, 1732–1860* (Athens, Ga., 1964), 200 (planter quoted); *Natchez Daily Courier*, Oct. and Dec. 1858. See also Ophelia Settle Egypt et al., eds., *Unwritten History of Slavery: Autobiographical Accounts of Ex-Slaves* (Washington, D.C., 1968), 5; Greenlee Diary, Feb. 12, 1849; Jan. 6 and Sept. 27, 1851; Bennett H. Wall, "The Founding of the Pettigrew Plantations," *NCHR*, 27 (Oct. 1950), 413–414. For slave sales of stolen goods to poor whites, see Bill Cecil-Fronsman, *Common Whites: Class and Culture in Antebellum North Carolina* (Lexington, Ky., 1992), 89.

35. Rosser H. Taylor, *Slaveholding in North Carolina: An Economic View* (Chapel Hill, N.C., 1926), 9, 12–13; Brown quoted in John Hebron Moore, *The Emergence of the Cotton Kingdom in the Old Southwest: Mississippi, 1770–1860* (Baton Rouge, La., 1988), 44; Craig Simpson, *A Good Southerner: The Life of Henry A. Wise of Virginia* (Chapel Hill, N.C., 1985); J. S. Buckingham, *The Slave States of America* (New York, 1968 [1842]), 1:210–212, and *EC*, 3:976.

36. On fishermen, see Harlan Greene and Harry S. Hutchins, Jr., with Brian E. Hutchins, *Slave Badges and the Slave-Hire System in Charleston, South Carolina, 1783–1865* (Jefferson, N.C., 2004), 22, 27. On wagoners, see Jean Bradley Anderson, *Piedmont Plantation: The Bennehan-Cameron Family and Lands in North Carolina* (Durham, N.C., 1985), 99–100. For rice planting: Peter A. Coclanis, *The Shadow of a Dream: Economic Life and Death in the South Carolina Low Country, 1670–1920* (New York, 1989); Coclanis, "Rice," in *EC*, 3:1327; also, James M. Clifton, ed., *Life and Labor on Argyle Island: Letters and Documents of a*

Savannah River Rice Plantation, 1833–1867 (Savannah, Ga., 1978), ix; Judith A. Carney, "From Hands to Tutors: African Expertise in the South Carolina Rice Economy," *Agricultural History*, 67 (1993), 1–30, and Carney, *Black Rice: The African Origins of Rice Cultivation in the Americas* (Cambridge, Mass., 2001). For technological contributions, see Charles H. Wesley, *Negro Labor in the United States, 1825–1925: A Study in American Economic History* (New York, 1927), 20–21; Richard Follett, *The Sugar Masters: Planters and Slaves in Louisiana's Cane Fields, 1820–1860* (Baton Rouge, La., 2005), 33–36. Also, Schweninger, *Black Property Owners*, 47–51; Bern Keating, *A History of Washington County, Mississippi* (Greenville, Miss., 1976), 30–31; Robert C. Black III, *The Railroads of the Confederacy* (Chapel Hill, N.C., 1952), ch. 3.

37. Janet Sharp Hermann, *Joseph E. Davis: Pioneer Patriarch* (Jackson, Miss., 1990), 157–158, chs. 3–4; James T. Currie, *Enclave: Vicksburg and Her Plantations, 1863–1870* (Jackson, Miss., 1980), ch. 4; Lyle Saxon et al., *Gumbo Ya-Ya: A Collection of Louisiana Folk Tales* (New York, 1945), 220; Durnford to McDonough, esp. for 1835, in Durnford Letters; *DNCB* (1979–94), 2:45–246 (Thomas Day), see also John McDonogh Papers on his projects; Marion B. Lucas, *A History of Blacks in Kentucky*, 2 vols. (Frankfort, Ky., 1992), 1:44.

38. Norma Lois Peterson, *Littleton Waller Tazewell* (Charlottesville, Va., 1983), 106; E. M. Coulter, *Thomas Spalding of Sapelo* (Baton Rouge, La., 1940), 85–86; G. E. Hunnicut, ed., *David Dickson and James M. Smith's Farming* (n. p., 1910), 23, 30; Henry Cleveland, *Alexander H. Stephens in Public and Private. With Letters and Speeches Before, During, and Since the War* (Philadelphia, 1866), 231; Weymouth T. Jordan, *Hugh Davis and His Alabama Plantation* (University, Ala., 1948), 63–65, 91; Barrow Residence Journal, Jan. 1, Apr. 29, 1857; *Father Henson's Story of His Own Life* (New York, 1962 [1858]), 41; William Edwards Clement, *Plantation Life on the Mississippi* (New Orleans, La., 1952), 179; Camilla Davis Trammell, *Seven Pines: Its Occupants and Their Letters, 1825–1872* (Houston, Tex., 1986), 65; Randolph B. Campbell, *An Empire for Slavery: The Peculiar Institution in Texas, 1821–1865* (Baton Rouge, La., 1989), 124. For black drivers as overseers, see Wilma A. Dunaway, *Slavery in the American Mountain South* (New York, 2003), 61.

39. Cuthbert, "On the General Management of Plantations," *SA*, 67; David F. Allmendinger, Jr., ed., *Incidents of My Life: Edmund Ruffin's Autobiographical Essays* (Charlottesville, Va., 1990), July 4, 1857 (91), and *ERD*, 1:86–87; D. E. Huger Smith, *A Charlestonian's Recollections, 1846–1913* (Charleston, S.C., 1950), 18, 23; Ashmore Plantation Journal, 72; William Dusinberre, *Them Dark Days: Slavery in the American Rice Swamps* (New York, 1996), esp. 107, 276–277. For overseer absenteeism, see Barrow Residence Journal, Jan. 1, 1857; Gould Diary, Jan. 2, 1855; Nevitt Papers for June 1827; "Pon Pon Plantation Book," April 12, 1840, in Elliott-Gonzalez Papers. For black achievement, see esp. Robert W. Fogel and Stanley L. Engerman, *Time on the Cross: The Economics of American Negro Slavery*, 2 vols. (New York, 1974), and Robert William Fogel, *Without Consent or Contract: The Rise and Fall of American Slavery* (New York, 1989), 73.

40. Olmsted, *Seaboard*, 206; Perdue et al., eds., *Weevils in the Wheat*, see A. F. Blakely, J. H. Winder, 31 (Mingo); Ophelia Settle Egypt et al., eds., *Unwritten History of Slavery: Autobiographical Accounts of Ex-Slaves* (Washington, D.C., 1968), 7. For the War, see Blassingame, ed., *Slave Testimony*, 535, 636, 658; for planters' sons and "bosses," see *TCWVQ*, 2:532, 3:1025, 5:2179.

41. Frederick Law Olmsted, *A Journey in the Back Country* (New York, 1970 [1860]), 143, 181, 265, 380–382; *DNCB*, 3:207 (Horton); Kemp P. Battle, *History of the University of North Carolina*, 2 vols. (Spartanburg, S.C., 1974 [1907]), 1:603–606; T. C. Thornton, *An Inquiry into the History of Slavery* (Washington, D.C., 1841), 102, 104–106; Lyell, *Second Visit*, 2:71–72; Walter B. Posey, *The Presbyterian Church in the Old Southwest, 1778–1838* (Richmond, Va., 1952), 87.

42. For African herbal medicine in relation, to religion see W. E. Abraham, *The Mind of Africa* (New York, 1962), 49; Geoffrey Parrinder, *African Traditional Religion* (London, 1974), 104–106. For the efficacy of herbal medicine, see Sharla M. Fett, *Working Cures: Healing, Health, and Power on Southern Slave Plantations* (Chapel Hill, N.C., 2002); Leslie Owens, *This Species of Property: Slave Life and Culture in the Old South* (New York, 1976), 34–35; Todd L. Savitt, *Medicine and Slavery: The Diseases and Health Care of Blacks in Antebellum Virginia* (Urbana, Ill., 1978), esp. 171–184; Mary Granger, ed., *Drums and Shadows* (Athens, Ga., 1941), 57. On black medical psychology, see Theosophus H. Smith, *Conjuring Culture: Biblical Formations of Black America* (New York, 1994), 31.

43. Frances Latham Harriss, ed., *Lawson's History of North Carolina* (Richmond, Va., 1941 [1709, 1741]), 15, 231; Wyndham B. Blanton, *Medicine in Virginia in the Eighteenth Century* (Richmond, Va., 1931), 212–213, 45 (dentists); John H. Russell, *The Free Negro in Virginia, 1619–1865* (Baltimore, 1913), 53; John Walker Diary, June 5, July 19, 1833; Frances Kemble, *Journal of a Residence on a Georgia Plantation in 1838–1839* (New York, 1863), 63; Richard Zuber, *Jonathan Worth: A Biography of a Southern Unionist* (Chapel Hill, N.C., 1965), 5.

44. John Hamilton to William Hamilton, Feb. 4, 1860, in the George Lester Collection; William Dosite Postell, *The Health of Slaves on Southern Plantations* (Gloucester, Mass., 1970), 58, 62, 64–66, 138; David John Mays, *Edmund Pendleton, 1721–1803: A Biography* (Cambridge, Mass., 1952), 1:42–44; Louis Morton, *Robert Carter of Nomini Hall: A Virginia Tobacco Planter of the Eighteenth Century* (Charlottesville, Va., 1969), 115–116; Franklin M. Garrett, *Atlanta and Environs: A Chronicle of Its People and Events* (Athens, Ga., 1954), 1:453; *DGB*, 1:46–47.

45. Mark A. Noll, *America's God: From Jonathan Edwards to Abraham Lincoln* (New York, 2002), 147–149; Parke Rouse, Jr., *Cows on the Campus: Williamsburg in By-Gone Days* (Richmond, Va., 1973), 8–9; Benjamin Quarles, *The Negro in the Making of America* (New York, 1964), 58; B. F. Riley, *A History of the Baptists in Southern States East of the Mississippi* (Philadelphia, 1898), 312–315. On Chavis, see Thompson, *Presbyterians in the South*, 1:207–208; *DHE*, 86–87; on Chavis's politics, see his letters to Mangum in Henry Thomas Shanks, ed., *The Papers of Willie P. Mangum*, 5 vols. (Raleigh, N.C., 1955–56), 1:563–569, 2:418–420; William M. Wightman, *Life of William Capers, D.D., One of the Bishops of the Methodist Episcopal Church, South, Including an Autobiography* (Nashville, Tenn., 1902), 124–128. For the eloquence of southern black preachers, see Abbott, *South and North*, 5–76.

46. Joseph Morrow, ed., "Tours into Kentucky and the Northwest Territory: Three Journals by the Rev. James Smith of Powhattan County, Va., 1783–1795–1797," *Ohio Archeological and Historical Quarterly*, 16 (1907), 384; Charles Lee Coon, ed., *The Beginnings of Public Education in North Carolina: A Documentary History*, 2 vols. (Raleigh, N.C., 1908), 2:536–537; *DNCB*, 2:239; Posey, *Presbyterian Church in the Old Southwest*, 87; Riley, *Baptists in Southern States*, 319–320; also, Caleb Perry Patterson, *The Negro in Tennessee, 1790–1865* (Austin, Tex.,

1922), 118; B. F. Riley, *History of the Baptists of Alabama from the Time of Their First Occupation of Alabama in 1808, until 1894* (Birmingham, Ala., 1895), 80, 186–187; John G. Jones, *A Complete History of Methodism as Connected with the Mississippi Conference of the Methodist Episcopal Church, South*, 2 vols. (Nashville, Tenn., 1908), 2:294; Timothy George, "'Faithful Shepherd, Beloved Minister': The Life and Legacy of Basil Manly, Sr.," *Alabama Baptist Historian*, 27 (1991), 15. See also *DBR*, 26 (1859), 173–183; 28 (1860), 352–353; Breeden, ed., *Advice among Masters*, 226, 230; R. Ingraham to Susan Fisher, Jan. 5, 1840, in Fisher Papers; Octavia Bryant to Winston Stephens, Jan. 29, Aug. 7, 1859 (41, 46, also 24), and Winston Stephens to Octavia Stephens, Feb. 11, Aug. 12, 1863, in Arch Fredric Blakely et al., eds., *Rose Cottage Chronicles: Civil War Letters of the Bryant-Stephens Families of North Florida* (Tallahassee, Fla., 1998), 200, 260.

47. "Stowe's Key to Uncle Tom's Cabin," *SQR*, 8 (1853), 222–224; Waddy Thompson, *Recollections of Mexico* (New York, 1847), 6; "On the Management of Slaves," *SA*, 6 (1833), 283.

48. Schweninger, *Black Property Owners*, supplemented by Larry Koger, *Black Slaveowners: Free Black Slave Masters in South Carolina, 1790–1860* (Columbia, S.C., 1995); Michael P. Johnson and James L. Roark, *Black Masters: A Free Family of Color in the Old South* (New York, 1984), and the family correspondence in Johnson and Roark, eds., *No Chariot Let Down: Charleston's Free People of Color on the Eve of the Civil War* (Chapel Hill, N.C., 1984); Fogel and Engerman, eds., *Without Consent or Contract: Technical Papers*, 606–613; Marianne Finch, *An Englishwoman's Experience in America* (New York, 1969 [1853]), 316; Slave Papers, #9, in Library of Congress. For Louisiana, see David O. Whitten, *Andrew Durnford: A Black Sugar Planter in Antebellum Louisiana* (Natchitoches, La., 1981); for Texas, *AS: Tex.*, 5 (pt. 4), 155–159; Lowry Ware, "Reuben Robertson of Turkey Creek: The Story of a Wealthy Black Slaveholder and His Family, White and Black," *SCH*, 91 (1990), 260–267; Eliza Ann Marsh Robertson, Dec. 13, 1855, in Joan E. Cashin, ed., *Our Common Affairs: Texts from Women in the Old South* (Baltimore, 1996), 201; Horace Cowles Atwater, *Incidents of a Southern Tour: or, The South as Seen with Northern Eyes* (Boston, 1857), ch. 11; Donald L. Shafer, *Anna Kingsley* (St. Augustine, Fla., 1994). For relations of colored and white elites in Charleston, see Marina Wikramanayake, *A World in Shadow: The Free Black in Antebellum South Carolina* (Columbia, S.C., 1973), 76–78.

49. David Galenson, *White Servitude in Colonial America: An Economic Analysis* (Cambridge, UK, 1981), 174; Russell, *Free Negro in Virginia*, 91–94, 151–155; Charles Campbell, *History of the Colony and Ancient Dominion of Virginia* (Spartanburg, S.C., 1965 [1860]), 145.

50. Joe Gray Taylor, *Negro Slavery in Louisiana* (Baton Rouge, La., 1963), 158; Joseph Karl Menn, *The Large Slaveholders of Louisiana, 1860* (New Orleans, 1964), 92–93; Sellers, *Slavery in Alabama*, 386–387; Johnson and Roark, *Black Masters*, and the Ellison family correspondence in Johnson and Roark, eds., *No Chariot Let Down*; also, Wikramanayake, *World in Shadow*, ch. 4.

51. Thomas Sergeant Perry, ed., *The Life and Letters of Francis Lieber* (Boston, 1882), Dec. 9, 1836 (114); Helen Tunncliff Catterall, ed., *Judicial Cases Concerning Slavery and the Negro*, 4 vols. (Washington, D.C., 1919–37), 1:210; John Hope Franklin, "James Boon, Free Negro Artisan," *Journal of Negro History*, 30 (1945), 156; Abdy, *Journal of Residence*, 1:191 (Savannah); *AS: Ala.*, 6 (pt. 1), 135–136; Feb. 9, 1834 n., in Mercer Papers; Whitman, *Price of Freedom*, ch. 5.

52. Schweninger, *Black Property Owners*, 24–25, 105; Frederick Law Olmsted, *A Journey through Texas. Or, a Saddle-Trip on the Southwestern Frontier* (Austin, Tex., 1978 [1857]), 400; for a proslavery view, see George S. Sawyer, *Southern Institutes* (New York, 1967 [1858]), 230. When Romaine Vidrine of Louisiana, son of a white slaveholder, became a planter, he forbade his family from fraternizing with the slaves: *AS: Tex.*, 5 (pt. 4), 155–159.

53. John Taylor, *Arator: Being a Series of Agricultural Essays, Practical and Political: In Sixty-Four Numbers* (Indianapolis, Ind., 1977 [1818]), 115, 117–118, 357, 358, quotes at 115, 117; "Free Negroes – A Plan to Get Rid of Them," *Weekly Raleigh Register and North Carolina Gazette*, Dec. 12, 1845 (from *North State Whig*); Dec. 11, 1850; Nov. 5, 1851; *Nashville Union*, Jan. 31, 1853; *Daily Morning News* (Savannah), Apr. 16, 1857 (from *Tallahassee Floridian*); *Mississippian and State Gazette* (Jackson), Mar. 17, May 26, 1858; George Fitzhugh, *Sociology for the South, or, The Failure of Free Society* (New York, 1965 [1852]), 259–271. For newspaper calls to expel or enslave free Negroes, see Wesley H. Wallace, "North Carolina's Agricultural Journals, 1838–1861: A Crusading Press," *NCHR*, 36 (1959), 299.

7. Devotion unto Death

1. T. R. R. Cobb, *An Inquiry into the Law of Negro Slavery in the United States* (New York, 1968 [1858]), ccxvii.

2. Donald S. Frazier, *Fire in the Cane Field: The Federal Invasion of Louisiana and Texas, January 1861–January 1863* (Buffalo Gap, Tex., 2009), 84; William Smith, Feb. 25, 1830, in Herman Belz, ed., *The Webster-Hayne Debate on the Nature of the Union: Selected Documents* (Indianapolis, Ind., 2000), 323; [William Drayton], *The South Vindicated from the Treason and Fanaticism of the Northern Abolitionists* (Philadelphia, 1836), 303–305; Mrs. [Matilda Charlotte] Houstoun, *Hesperos: Or, Travels in the West*, 2 vols. (London, 1850), 2:91–92.

3. Clarence L. Ver Steeg, *Origins of a Southern Mosaic: Studies of Early Carolina and Georgia* (Athens, Ga., 1975), 105–106; Jean Martin Flynn, *The Militia in Antebellum South Carolina Society* (Spartanburg, S.C., 1991), 33; Marty D. Matthews, *Forgotten Founder: The Life and Times of Charles Pinckney* (Columbia, S.C., 2004), 52; John Craig Hammond, "'They Are Very Much Interested in Obtaining an Unlimited Slavery': Rethinking the Expansion of Slavery in the Louisiana Purchase Territories, 1803–1805," *Journal of the Early Republic*, 23 (2003), 371–372; Juliet E. K. Walker, *Free Frank: A Black Pioneer on the Antebellum Frontier* (Lexington, Ky., 1995), 21; [Zephaniah Kingsley], *A Treatise on the Patriarchal or Co-Operative System of Society*, 2nd ed. (n. p., 1829), 6, 11; George Tucker, *Progress of the United States in Population and Wealth in Fifty Years* (New York, 1964 [1855]), 28; James Turner Morehead, *Address for the Dialectic Society* (EE: 2005 [1818]), 2.

4. Felix Huston, *The Military Strength of the Southern States and the Effects of Slavery Therein* (Nashville, Tenn., 1850), 2; Mrs. Chapman Coleman, ed., *The Life of John J. Crittenden: With Selections from His Correspondence and Speeches*, 2 vols. (New York, 1970 [1871]), 2:331; "Address in the House of Representatives of South Carolina, Dec. 11, 1850," in Stephen Meats and Edwin T. Arnold, eds., *The Writings of Benjamin F. Perry*, 3 vols. (Spartanburg, S.C., 1980), 1:355–356; J. G. deR. Hamilton, ed., *The Correspondence of Jonathan Worth*, 2 vols.

(Raleigh, N.C., 1909), 1:127, 142, 153; Drane quoted in *The Iron Furnace: or, Slavery and Secession. By Rev. John H. Aughey, a Refugee from Mississippi* (Philadelphia, 1863), 17–18; John S. C. Abbott, *South and North; or, Impressions Received during a Trip to Cuba and the South* (New York, 1969 [1860]), 345–346.

5. Hugh Legaré, "The Public Economy of Athens," *SR*, 8 (1832), 2:502ff.; Augustus Boeckh, *The Public Economy of Athens*, 2 vols. (Oxford, 1828), 1:343, 349; Robert E. Lee to Ethelbert Barksdale, Feb. 18, 1865, in James J. Barnes and Patience P. Barnes, eds., *The American Civil War through British Eyes: Dispatches from British Diplomats*, 3 vols. (Kent, Oh., 2005), 3:262; Cobb, *Inquiry into the Law of Negro Slavery*, xcvii–xcviii (Cato), xcii, lxxvii; lvii; also, Charles Minnigerode, *"He that Believeth Shall Not Make Haste"* (EE: 2001 [1866]), 10; "Masters and Slaves," in Seneca, *Epistles*, 3 vols., tr. Richard M. Gummere (Cambridge, Mass., 2002), 47.§§ 5, 10–11; George S. Sawyer, *Southern Institutes; Or, an Inquiry into the Origin and Early Prevalence of Slavery and the Slave Trade* (New York, 1967 [1858]), esp. 56–58, 97, 111. Southerners often alluded to Pedanius Secundus.

6. Peter Hunt, *Slavery, Warfare, and Ideology in the Greek Historians* (Cambridge, UK, 1998), 214–218; Elizabeth Rawson, *The Spartan Tradition in European Thought* (Oxford, 1991), 5; Paul Cartledge, "Rebels and Sambos in Classical Greece: A Comparative View," in P. A. Cartledge and F. D. Harvey, eds., *Crux: Essays in Greek History Presented to G. F. M. de St. Croix on His 75th Birthday* (London, 1985), 30; Victor Davis Hanson, *The Wars of the Ancient Greeks* (London, 2000), 75–77, 121–122; *Appian's Roman History*, 4 vols., tr. Horace White (LCL), 1:9.57; 3:1.1.9–10; 7.58, 60; 8.69, 75; 11.100; for a recent account of Tiberius Gracchus, see Adrian Goldsworthy, *The Punic Wars* (London, 2000), 361 and passim. In Moses Hadas, ed., *The Complete Works of Tacitus*, tr. Alfred John Church and William Jackson Broder (New York, 1942), see "Annals," Bk. 2:39–40 (Clemens) and "History," Bk. 4:50; Livy, *The War with Hannibal*, trans., Aubrey de Sélincourt (London, 1972), Bk. 22:57–59, Bk. 26:2; Plutarch, *The Lives of the Noble Grecians and Romans*, trans. Dryden; ed. and rev. by Arthur Hugh Clough, 2 vols. (New York, 1992), 2:309–310; Daniel L. Shafer, *Anna Kingsley* (St. Augustine, Fla., 1994), 1.

7. Hammond to Clarkson, Jan. 28, 1845 (129, 158), in [Clyde N. Wilson, ed.] *Selections from the Letters and Speeches of James H. Hammond* (Spartanburg, S.C., 1978), 32–33, 36–37; "Report and Resolutions of a Public Meeting at Pendleton," in *JCCP*, 12:549.

8. William Gilmore Simms, "The Morals of Slavery," in *The Pro-Slavery Argument, as Maintained by the Most Distinguished Writers of the Southern States* (Philadelphia, 1853); [Augustus Baldwin Longstreet], *A Voice from the South* (Baltimore, 1847); Robert R. Howison, *A History of Virginia from Its Discovery and Settlement by Europeans to the Present Time*, 2 vols. (Philadelphia, 1846), 2:113, 419, quote at 2:444; Samuel A. Cartwright, *Essays . . . in a Series of Letters to the Rev. William Winans* (Vidalia, La., 1843), 54–55, 59; Albert James Pickett, *History of Alabama and Incidentally of Georgia and Mississippi from the Earliest Period* (Sheffield, Ala., 1896 [1846]), 540; Patricia Bradley, *Slavery, Propaganda, and the American Revolution* (Jackson, Miss., 1998), 23. See also "Domestic Histories of the South," *SQR*, 5 (1852), 518–519.

On black Patriots in the Revolution and War of 1812, see John S. Pancake, *This Destructive War: The British Campaign in the Carolinas, 1780–1782* (Tuscaloosa, Ala., 1985), 47; John H. Russell, *The Free Negro in Virginia, 1619–1865*

(Baltimore, Md., 1913), 110–112; and Adam Rothman, *Slave Country: American Expansion and the Origins of the Deep South* (Cambridge, Mass., 2005), 139–162. For British exploitation of the black deserters, see Sylvia R. Frey, "Between Slavery and Freedom: Virginia Blacks in the American Revolution," *JSH*, 49 (1983), 375–398. For black military efforts in New England, see John Ward Sweet, *Bodies Politic: Negotiating Race in the American North, 1730–1830* (Baltimore, Md., 2003), ch. 5; for the Indian wars during and after 1835, see Randolph B. Campbell, *An Empire for Slavery: The Peculiar Institution in Texas, 1821–1865* (Baton Rouge, La., 1989), 59–63.

9. Calhoun to Austin, Dec. 28, 1837, in *JCCP*, 14:34; "Hall's Travels in North-America," in *HLW*, 2:293–294; Harper, "Slavery in the Light of Social Ethics," in *Pro-Slavery Argument*, 76; J. S. Wilson, "The Negro – His Mental and Moral Peculiarities," *ACP*, n. s., 3 (1859), 68; William Gilmore Simms, *The Partisan* (Richmond, Va., 1862).

10. Dew in *Pro-Slavery Argument*, 457–458; Nathaniel Beverley Tucker, *The Partisan Leader* (Richmond, Va., 1836), 55, 111; Livy, *The War with Hannibal*, trans. Aubrey de Sélincourt (London, 1972), 8:18. For slaves loyal to masters, see Patrick Breen, "Nat Turner's Revolt: Rebellion and Response in Southampton County, Virginia" (Ph.D. diss., University of Georgia, 2005).

11. E. A. Pollard, *Southern History of the War*, 2 vols. in 1 (n.p., 1977 [1866]), 1:363–364; Forrest G. Wood, *Black Scare: The Racist Response to Emancipation and Reconstruction* (Berkeley, Calif., 1968), 28–29; Robert Collins, "Essay on the Management of Slaves," *SC*, 12 (1854), 206; Breaux Diaries, Oct. 13, 1863; Plutarch, *Lives*, 2:528.

12. Simms in *Pro-Slavery Argument*, 221; Henry William Ravenel, "Recollections of Southern Plantation Life," ed. Marjorie Stratford Mendenhall, *Yale Review*, 25 (1936), 765; T. Michael Parrish, *Richard Taylor: Soldier Prince of Dixie* (Chapel Hill, N.C., 1992), 31–32. Helper called blacks cowards: Hugh C. Bailey, *Hinton Rowan Helper: Abolitionist-Racist* (University, Ala., 1965), 30; Beulah de Veriré Watts and Nancy Jane Lucas De Grummond, *Solitude: Life on a Louisiana Plantation, 1788–1968* (Baton Rouge, La., 1970), 11.

13. For an example of savage reaction to reports of insurrection, see, e. g., John Rozier, ed., *The Granite Farm Letters: The Civil War Correspondence of Edgeworth and Sallie Bird* (Athens, Ga., 1988), 155.

14. Lee quoted in M. E. Bradford, *Against the Barbarians: And Other Reflections on Familiar Themes* (Columbia, Mo., 1992), 122; on calls for reform of the slave codes, see David J. Libby, *Slavery and Frontier Mississippi, 1720–1835* (Jackson, Miss., 2004), 57–59. For slaves as "alien enemy," see William W. Fisher III, "Ideology and Imagery in the Law of Slavery," *Chicago-Kent Law Review*, 68 (1993), 1071. For armed free blacks, see Tommy L. Bogger, *Free Blacks in Norfolk, Virginia, 1790–1860: The Darker Side of Freedom* (Charlottesville, Va., 1997), 161–162. For the revolt of 1811, see esp. Robert L. Paquette, "'A Horde of Brigands'?: The Great Louisiana Slave Revolt of 1811 Reconsidered," *Historical Reflections*, 35 (2009), 72–96; Tommy R. Young II, "The United States Army and the Institution of Slavery in Louisiana, 1803–1815," *Louisiana Studies*, 13 (1974), 201–213.

15. Randolph, Dec. 10, 1811, *Annals of Congress*, 12th Cong., 1st Sess., Column 451; Preston, Jan. 7, 1835, *Congressional Globe*, Senate, 24th Cong., 1st Sess., 79; Josiah Quincy, *Address Illustrative of the Nature and Power of the Slave States and the Duties of the Free States* (Boston, 1856), 26; Moses Stuart, *Conscience*

and the Constitution (Boston, 1850), 93. On fire scares, see Frederic Trautmann, ed., "South Carolina through a German's Eyes: The Travels of Clara von Gerstner, 1839," *SCHM*, 85 (1984), 223.

16. Quoted in James Petigru Carson, *Life, Letters and Speeches of James Louis Petigru: The Union Man of South Carolina* (Washington, D.C., 1920), 66. In 1839, Charlestonians blamed blacks for the great fires of recent decades: William H. Thompson to Hannah L. Thompson, July 12, 1835, in Ruffin Thompson Papers; Gavin Diary, Oct. 29, 1860.

17. Thomas O. Summers, ed., *Autobiography of the Rev. Joseph Travis* (Nashville, Tenn., 1854), 149–150; Rachel Lazarus to George W. Mordecai, Oct. 6, 1831, in the Mordecai Collection; Freeman, in Benjamin Drew, *A North-Side View of Slavery: The Refugee, or, the Narrative of Fugitive Slaves in Canada* (New York, 1968 [1857]), 223; Sarah "Sallie" Conley Clayton, *Requiem for a Lost City: A Memoir of Civil War Atlanta and the Old South*, ed. Robert Scott Davis, Jr. (Macon, Ga., 1999), 33; James Oscar Farmer, Jr., *The Metaphysical Confederacy: James Henley Thornwell and the Synthesis of Southern Values* (Macon, Ga., 1986), 216–217.

18. Benjamin F. Allen to William Trousdale, Jan. 8, 1857, in Trousdale Papers; Conway, quoted in Harvey Wish, *George Fitzhugh: Propagandist of the Old South* (Gloucester, Mass., 1962), 63; Moncure D. Conway, *Addresses and Reprints, 1850–1907* (Boston, 1909), 93; M. D. Cooper to his father, Dec. 29, 1856. On spiked heads, see Joseph Howard Parks, *John Bell of Tennessee* (Baton Rouge, La., 1950), 313.

19. Gould Diary, Dec. 25, 1856; also, Morrison Journal, Dec. 31, 1856; Dr. McGuire Diary, Sept. 1837; William H. Thomson to Hannah L. Thomson, July 12, 1835, in Ruffin Thompson Papers; Rosannah P. Rogers to David L. Rogers, Oct. 29, 1831, in Renwick Papers; *Southern Watchman*, Jan. 1, 1857, in Ulrich B. Phillips, ed., *Plantation and Frontier: Documents, 1649–1863*, 2 vols. (New York, 1969 [1910]), 2:117; Charles E. Beveridge et al., eds., *The Papers of Frederick Law Olmsted*, 2 vols. (Baltimore, Md., 1977, 1981), 2:410–411, 414–415; M. Gillis to St. John R. Liddell, 1856, in Liddell Papers; Sherman to Thomas Ewing, Jr., 1859, in *DHE*, 4:248.

20. In *ERD*, Dec. 25, 28, 1856 (1:18–20); Sept. 5, 6, 1860 (2:456, 458); Jan. 4, 1862 (2:207–209); Dunbar Rowland, ed., *Mississippi: Comprising Sketches of Counties, Towns, Events, Institutions, and Persons*, 4 vols. (Spartanburg, S.C., 1976 [1907]), 2:683–684. For fires in the South, see, e. g., Thomas D. Morris, *Southern Slavery and the Law, 1619–1860* (Chapel Hill, N.C., 1996), 331–335; Dale Baum, *The Shattering of Texas Unionism: Politics in the Lone Star Sate during the Civil War Era* (Baton Rouge, La., 1998), 40.

21. Harvey Toliver Cook, *The Life Work of James Clement Furman* (Greenville, S.C., 1926), 199–201; Fitzgerald Ross, *Cities and Camps of the Confederate States* (Urbana, Ill., 1997), 84; Thomas Wentworth Higginson, *Army Life in a Black Regiment* (Boston, 1962), 10, also 32–34, 42–43, 52.

22. [Joseph Holt Ingraham], *The South-West. By a Yankee*, 2 vols. (n. p., 1966 [1835]), 2:260–262; Catherine Carson to W. S. Waller, Jan. 26, 1836, in Carson Family Papers (Small Collections).

23. John Herritage Bryan to Ebenezer Pettigrew, Sept. 20, 1840, in Pettigrew Papers; also, Sarah McCulloh Lemmon, ed., *The Pettigrew Papers*, 2 vols. (Raleigh, N.C.,

1971, 1988), 2:443; E. P. Guion to Thomas Ruffin, Aug. 28, 1831, in *TRP*, 2:45–46; William W. Freehling, *The Road to Disunion*, 2 vols. (New York, 1990, 2007), 1:181; Patrick H. Breen, ed., "The Female Antislavery Petition Campaign of 1831–1832," *Virginia Magazine of Biography and History*, 110 (2002), 377–398; Buchanan quoted in Roy Franklin Nichols, *The Disruption of American Democracy* (New York, 1948), 388.

24. Mary Jane Chester to Elizabeth Chester, Nov. 20, 1840, Elizabeth Chester to Mary Jane Chester, Nov. 1840; Emily P. Burke, *Reminiscences of Georgia* (Oberlin, Oh., 1850), 156–157; John Q. Anderson, ed., *Brokenburn: The Journal of Kate Stone, 1861–1868* (Baton Rouge, La., 1955), March 2, 1863 (171); Sept. 5, 1864 (298); Daniel E. Sutherland, *Seasons of War: The Ordeal of a Confederate Community, 1861–1865* (New York, 1995), 14 (trouble); Mary Own Sims Diary, Mar. 24, 1857, in Joan E. Cashin, ed., *Our Common Affairs: Texts from Women of the Old South* (Baltimore, Md., 1996), 206; Anita Dwyer Withers Diary, Sept. 3, Oct 1, 1863; Sept. 22, 1864; also, Thomas Goree to J. B. Johnson, April 30, 1861, in Yellowsley Papers. On women's fear of insurgents, see Patrick Breen, "In Terror of Their Slaves: White Women's Responses to Slave Insurrections and Scares," in Winfred B. Moore, Jr., Kyle S. Sinisi, and David H. White, Jr., eds., *Warm Ashes: Issues in Southern History at the Dawn of the Twenty-First Century* (Columbia, S.C., 2003), 69–84.

25. Jefferson Davis, remarks in the Senate, Apr. 20, 1848, in *JDP*, 3:315; *Speech of the Hon. Louis T. Wigfall, of Texas: In Reply to Mr. Douglas, and on Mr. Powell's Resolutions* (Washington, D. C., 1860), 12–13; John H. W. Underwood to Howell Cobb, Feb. 2, 1844, in Ulrich Bonnell Phillips, ed., *The Correspondence of Robert Toombs, Alexander H. Stephens, and Howell Cobb* (Washington, D.C., 1913), 55. For a more skeptical view, see Henry S. Foote, *Casket of Reminiscences* (New York, 1874), 247–263.

26. James R. Sparkman to Benjamin Allston, March 10, 1858, in J. H. Easterby, ed., *The South Carolina Rice Plantation, as Revealed in the Papers of Robert F. W. Allston* (Chicago, Ill., 1945), 345; Feb. 26, 1861, in *ERD*, 1:556–557; Steven V. Ash, *When the Yankees Came: Conflict and Chaos in the Occupied South, 1861–1865* (Chapel Hill, N.C., 1995), ch. 1; Davenport quoted in Winthrop D. Jordan, *Tumult and Silence at Second Creek: An Inquiry into a Civil War Slave Conspiracy*, rev. ed. (Baton Rouge, La., 1995), 14; Elliott Ashkenazi, ed., *The War Diary of Clara Solomon: Growing Up in New Orleans, La., 1861–1862* (Baton Rouge, La., 1995), May 8, 1862 (355).

27. Ervin L. Jordan, Jr., *Black Confederates and Afro-Yankees in Civil War Virginia* (Charlottesville, Va., 1995), 22; John Cimprich, *Slavery's End in Tennessee, 1861–1865* (Tuscaloosa, Ala., 1985), 13–14; Emma Holmes, Sept. 3, 1861; March 3, 1863, in John F. Marszalek, ed., *The Diary of Miss Emma Holmes, 1861–1866* (Baton Rouge, La., 1979), 86, 234; John K. Bettersworth, ed., *Mississippi in the Confederacy: As They Saw It* (Baton Rouge, La., 1961), 249, 294–296; A. M. Keiley, *In Vinculis; or, The Prisoner of War. Being the Experience of a Rebel in Two Federal Pens* (New York, 1866), 82–83.

28. Bond Diary, Dec. 31, 1861; *My Master: The Inside Story of Sam Houston and His Times, by His Former Slave Jeff Hamilton, as Told to Lenoir Hunt* (Austin, Tex., 1992), 127; also, Mrs. Irby Morgan, *How It Was; Four Years among the Rebels* (EE: 1999 [1863]), 90.

29. Cornish Diary, Nov. 8, 1860; Ernest McPherson Lander, Jr., *The Calhoun Family and Thomas Green Clemson: The Decline of a Southern Patriarchy* (Columbia, S.C., 1983), 201; Richard Hackley to J. A. Broadus, Nov. 5, 1860, in Archibald Thomas Robertson, *Life and Letters of John Albert Broadus* (Philadelphia, 1901), 177.

30. Natchez *Daily Courier*, May 14, 1861; W. E. Wight, "Churches in the Confederacy" (Ph.D. diss., Emory University, 1957), 53–54 (expulsions), 159–160; Jordan, *Tumult and Silence*, 171–172; Samuel Galloway, *Ergonomy; or, Industrial Science* (Princeton, N.J., 1853), 203; Frazier, *Fire in the Cane Field*, 195; Lindsley, "Table Talk," May 6, 1862.

31. F. Jay Taylor, ed., *Reluctant Rebel: The Secret Diary of Robert Patrick, 1861–1865* (Baton Rouge, La., 1959), April 8, 1864 (151–152); Bell Irvin Wiley, *The Life of Johnny Reb: The Common Soldier of the Confederacy* (Baton Rouge, La., 1978), 117, 327–328; Richard Taylor, *Destruction and Reconstruction* (New York, 1992 [1889]), 64–68; correspondence for 1861–62 in Guy R. Everson and Edward H. Simpson, eds., *"Far, Far from Home": The Wartime Letters of Dick and Tally Simpson, Third South Carolina Volunteers* (New York, 1994), 76, 123, 129–130, 147, 154.

32. T. V. Moore, *God Our Refuge and Strength in This War* (Richmond, Va., 1861), 18–19; for Smith and Davis, see *TCWVQ*, 5:1974. On body servants, see Jordan, *Black Confederates*, ch. 8; on blacks in arms for the Confederacy, see Dudley Taylor Cornish, *The Sable Arm: Black Troops in the Union Army, 1861–1865* (Lawrence, Kans., 1987), ch. 1; Charles Kelly Barrow et al., eds., *Forgotten Confederate: An Anthology about Black Southerners* (Atlanta, Ga., 1995), 4, 31, 37, 42, 94, 128; Edward E. Leslie, *The Devil Knows How to Ride: The True Story of William Clarke Quantrill and His Confederate Raiders* (New York, 1996), 86n; Noah Andrew Trudeau, *Like Men of War: Black Troops in the Civil War, 1862–1865* (Boston, 1998).

33. Edgeworth Bird to Sallie Bird, Jan. 10, July 9, 1862, in Rozier, ed., *Granite Farm Letters*, 51–52, 119; also, J. C. Dormon to Dear Parents, Dec. 5, 1863, in Chattahoochee Valley Historical Society, *War Was the Place: A Centennial Collection of Confederate Soldier Letters and Old Oakbowery, Chambers County, Alabama*, Bulletin #5 (1961), 94–95 (desertion). On resentment of body servants, see Armstead L. Robinson, *Bitter Fruits of Bondage: The Demise of Slavery and the Collapse of the Confederacy, 1861–1865* (Charlottesville, Va., 2005), 91–93; Hanson, *Wars of the Ancient Greeks*, 171.

34. W. Emerson Wilson, ed., *Plantation Life at Rose Hill: The Diaries of Martha Ogle Forman, 1814–1845* (Wilmington, Del., 1976), Sept. 20, 1816 (30); Charles H. Wesley, "The Employment of Negro Soldiers in the Confederate Army," *Journal of Negro History*, 4 (1919), 245–250; James M. McPherson, *The Negro's Civil War: How American Blacks Felt and Acted in the War for the Union* (New York, 2003), 241–245.

35. See the documents and interpretation in Robert F. Durden, *The Gray and the Black: The Confederate Debate on Emancipation* (Durham, N.C., 1972). Rivalries clouded the army debate. Cleburne opposed and Walker supported General Braxton Bragg. Russell K. Brown, *To the Manner Born: The Life of General William H. T. Walker* (Athens, Ga., 1994), ch. 13. In *ERD*, see June 12, 16, Aug. 6, 1863; March 3, April 22, Oct. 29–30, 1864 (3:9–10, 14–15, 100–101, 356, 403–404,

529–530, 628). For problems in the army, see J. Tracy Power, *Lee's Miserables: Life in the Army of Northern Virginia from the Wilderness to Appomattox* (Chapel Hill, N.C., 1998), 3–4, 250–263, 306–307.

36. Harriet Martineau, *Retrospect of Western Travel*, 2 vols. (London, 1838), 1:240; Marina Wikramanayake, *A World in Shadow: The Free Black in Antebellum South Carolina* (Columbia, S.C., 1973), 34, 38–39.

37. *Charleston Mercury*, Nov. 12, 1860; Joseph W. Cox, *Champion of Southern Federalism: Robert Goodloe Harper of South Carolina* (Port Washington, N.Y., 1972), 125–126; Joe Bassette Wilkins, Jr., "Window on Freedom: The South's Response to the Emancipation of the Slaves in the British West Indies, 1833–1861" (Ph.D. diss., University of South Carolina, 1977), 152, 158–160; John Saillant, *Black Puritan, Black Republican: The Life and Thought of Lemuel Haynes, 1753–1833* (Oxford, 2003), 141. For slaves as cowards, see, e.g., Quintilian, *Institutio Oratoria* (LCL), 1: Bk. III:31; William Fitzgerald, *Slavery and the Roman Literary Imagination* (Cambridge, UK, 2000), 40; Ruth Mazo Karras, *Slavery and Society in Medieval Scandinavia* (New Haven, Conn., 1988), 64–65. For black troops in the conquest and policing of the Americas, see Peter M. Voelz, *Slave and Soldier: The Military Impact of Blacks in the Colonial America* (New York, 1993). For African soldiers in European wars, see Hans Werner Debrunner, *Presence and Prestige: Africans in Europe. A History of Africans in Europe before 1918* (Basel, Switzerland, 1979), 123–138.

38. Harper in E. N. Elliott, ed., *Cotton Is King, and Pro-Slavery Arguments* (New York, 1969 [1860]), 613. Even the antislavery Harriet Martineau believed that rebellious slaves would throw down their arms at the command of whites, including white ladies. See Joe Lockard, *"Watching Slavery": Witness Texts and Travel Reports* (New York, 2008), 57.

39. Frederick A. Ross, *Slavery Ordained of God* (Philadelphia, 1857), 26; Cobb, *Law of Negro Slavery*, xliv, n. 4; Mrs. Bachman quoted in Lester D. Stephens, *Science, Race, and Religion in the American South: John Bachman and the Charleston Circle of Naturalists, 1815–1895* (Chapel Hill, N.C., 2000), 57; Ethel Trenholm Seabrook Nepveux, *Sarah Henry Bryce, 1825–1901: A Glimpse at a Remarkable Woman in the Turbulent Civil War Era* (Charleston, S.C., 1994), 26; Margaret Johnson Erwin to Caroline Wilson, Mar. 1, 1863, in John Seymour Erwin, *Like Some Green Laurel: Letters of Margaret Johnson Erwin, 1821–1863* (Baton Rouge, La., 1981), xiv–xv, quote at 129; "Miss Abby's Diary," Jan. 20, 1864, in Thomas G. Dyer, *Secret Yankees: The Union Circle in Confederate Atlanta* (Baltimore, 1999), 286. During and after the War, plantation women increasingly denigrated black men as "niggers," "ape-like," "gorilla," and "orang-outang."

40. Allen quoted in Vincent H. Cassidy and Amos E. Simpson, *Henry Watkins Allen of Louisiana* (Baton Rouge, La., 1964), 54; "Slavery in the Church Courts," *DQR*, 4 (1864), 546–547; Benjamin quoted in Robert Douthat Meade, *Judah P. Benjamin: Confederate Statesman* (New York, 1943), 361.

41. B. G. Reid, "Confederate Opponents of Arming the Slaves, 1861–1865," *Journal of Mississippi History*, 22 (1960), 252–253, 265, Cobb quoted at 267; on Miles, see Ralph Luker, *A Southern Tradition in Theology and Social Criticism: The Religious Liberalism and Social Conservatism of James Warley Miles, William Porcher DuBose and Edgar Gardner Murphy, 1830–1930* (New York, 1894), 152–153; Laura A. White, *Robert Barnwell Rhett: Father of Secession* (New York,

1931), 239 (Rhett quoted); Richmond *Examiner*, Nov. 10, Dec. 30, 1864, in Beth
G. Crabtree and James Welch Patton, eds., *"Journal of a Secesh Lady": The Diary
of Catherine Ann Devereux Edmondston, 1860–1866* (Raleigh, N.C., 1979), 651.

42. Walter Herron Taylor to Bettie Taylor, Feb. 16, 1865, in R. Lockwood Tower
with John S. Belmont, eds., *Lee's Adjutant: The Wartime Letters of Colonel Walter
Herron Taylor, 1862–1865* (Columbia, S.C., 1995), 224; [William Pitt Chambers],
Blood and Sacrifice: The Civil War Journal of a Confederate Soldier, ed. Richard
A. Baumgartner (Huntington, W. Va., 1994), 203–204 (Feb. 19, 1865).

43. Kate Stone, June 10, 1863, in Anderson, ed. *Brokenburn*, 219; Jane H. Pease and
William H. Pease, *They Who Would Be Free: Blacks' Search for Freedom, 1820–
1861* (New York, 1974), 246–249; Cornish, *Sable Arm*, esp. chs. 2, 6–7; Kenneth
W. Noe, ed., *A Southern Boy in Blue: The Memoirs of Marcus Woodcock, 9th
Kentucky Infantry (U.S.A.)* (Knoxville, Tenn., 1996), ch. 6; Roger S. Durham, *A
Confederate Yankee: The Journal of Edward William Drummond, a Confederate
Soldier from Maine* (Knoxville, Tenn., 2004), 63. On the shift in northern attitudes,
see, e. g., Randall C. Jimerson, *The Private Civil War: Popular Thought during the
Sectional Conflict* (Baton Rouge, La., 1988), ch. 4; V. Jacque Voegeli, *Free but
Not Equal: The Midwest and the Negro during the Civil War* (Chicago, 1967),
ch. 7; Gerald Schwartz, *A Woman Doctor's Civil War: Esther Hill Hawks Diary*
(Columbia, S.C., 1984), Oct. 1, 1862 (40–41); Feb. 20, 1864 (63).

44. Mrs. James M. Loughborough, *My Cave Life in Vicksburg, with Letters of Trial
and Travel* (Spartanburg, S.C., 1988 [1864, 1882]), 64; Maxwell Bloomfield, *American Lawyers in a Changing Society, 1776–1876* (Cambridge, Mass., 1976), 281;
William H. Nulty, *Confederate Florida: The Road to Olustee* (Tuscaloosa, Fla.,
1990), 55–57.

45. Wesley, "Employment of Negro Soldiers," 241; Janet Sharp Hermann, *Joseph E.
Davis: Pioneer Patriarch* (Jackson, Miss., 1990), 64, 126–127.

46. Thomas W. Cutrer, ed., *Our Trust Is in the God of Battles: The Civil War Letters
of Robert Franklin Bunting, Chaplain, Terry's Texas Rangers, C.S.A.* (Knoxville,
Tenn., 2006), 308–309, quote at 308; also, James G. Hollandsworth, Jr., *The
Louisiana Native Guards: The Black Military Experience during the Civil War*
(Baton Rouge, La., 1995), esp. 6–8.

47. Lewis Clarke, "Leaves from a Slave's Journal of Life," in John W. Blassingame,
ed., *Slave Testimony: Two Centuries of Letters, Speeches, Interviews, and Autobiographies* (Baton Rouge, La., 1977), 153.

Index